Building the Urban Environment

In the series *Urban Life, Landscape, and Policy,* edited by Zane L. Miller, David Stradling, and Larry Bennett

Also in this series:

Building the Urban Environment

Visions of the Organic City in the United States,
Europe, and Latin America

Harold L. Platt

TEMPLE UNIVERSITY PRESS
Philadelphia • *Rome* • *Tokyo*

TEMPLE UNIVERSITY PRESS
Philadelphia, Pennsylvania 19122
www.temple.edu/tempress

Library of Congress Cataloging-in-Publication Data

Platt, Harold L.
  Building the urban environment : visions of the organic city in the
United States, Europe, and Latin America / Harold L. Platt.
     pages cm. — (Urban life, landscape, and policy)
  Includes bibliographical references and index.
  ISBN 978-1-4399-1236-2 (cloth : alk. paper) — ISBN 978-1-4399-1237-9
(pbk. : alk. paper) — ISBN 978-1-4399-1238-6 (e-book)   1. City
planning—United States.   2. City planning—Europe.   3. City
planning—Latin America.   I. Title.
  HT166.P5455 2015
  307.1′216—dc23

                                                        2014050014

♾ The paper used in this publication meets the requirements of the
American National Standard for Information Sciences—Permanence
of Paper for Printed Library Materials, ANSI Z39.48-1992

Printed in the United States of America

9 8 7 6 5 4 3 2 1

In memory of my brother

BENJAMIN PLATT

Contents

Building the Urban Environment

I

Constructing Modernism

Introduction

Planners, Policy Makers, and the Grass Roots

T he architect and planner Teddy Cruz was sitting in his San Diego studio in 2006 when he looked out the window and saw an entire house being moved down the block on a flatbed truck. The Guatemalan-born American-trained architect followed this castoff of a consumer society as it crept across the U.S. border into Mexico and through the hilly streets of Tijuana on the other side. It eventually made its way into a huge, Levittown-like subdivision that looked like cornrows of two-car garages. He watched as a crane lifted the house onto a frame that had been jerry-built above and between two of these closely packed, tiny tract homes.[1]

Cruz found himself standing in the midst of a jungle of "guerrilla architecture."[2] The residents had appropriated and transformed their space with do-it-yourself ingenuity. They had built additions that filled the yards and converted their munchkin-sized dwellings into shops serving their neighbors' basic needs. "These tract [houses]," Cruz realized, "are perceived as open systems, their inherent uniformity giving way to occupants' collective desire for functionality and flexibility, for the freedom to activate improvisational, higher-density, and mixed uses—the very DNA of urbanism itself."[3]

This book is about the hybrid spaces like this barrio that grew out of processes of contestation among planners, policy makers, and the grass roots. In this case, the developers of the subdivision planned to maximize their profits by constructing as many minimum-sized houses as they could pack on their patch of real estate. Somehow conforming to the zoning and building codes, they were permitted to cover the land with houses, setting none aside for either public spaces, such as schools and parks, or commercial services, such as grocery stores and Laundromats. In response, the new homeowners rebuilt their environment, turning it from a sheet of cookie-cutter spaces into their own unique place of community, self-support, and urban life.

By including the guerrilla architects of the grass roots, this book is not about urban planning in the narrow, academic sense of formal architecture and design. In contrast to this kind of study of the ideas of great men flowing from the top down, the history of urban change after World War II requires inclusion of the conflicting visions of all three: planners, policy makers, and the grass roots. Or as the British scholar Alison Ravetz explains, "Once the focus is shifted from conscious [formal] planning to the urban environment, it is necessary and inevitable to consider technology, property, people, and mechanisms of control, as well as ideas."[4]

Consequently, this is a book about seeing all these agents of change interacting in the building of the urban environment. It is about seeing the city as both material space and symbolic place in peoples' imaginations. It is about "seeing like a state," looking down from architectural studios, planning offices, city halls, and other centers of power. But it is also about seeing from the bottom up, looking out at the city from bedroom windows, neighborhood street corners, and downtown plazas. Urban space is not just a neutral container—a physical thing. It is also a non-Euclidean place of human activity. Looking at the Tijuana neighborhood, Cruz could visualize the social relationships embedded in the physical alteration of this subdivision into a community.[5]

Giving agency to the grass roots requires an inclusive view of civil society. Marshall Berman supplies just this kind of perspective in *All That Is Solid Melts into Air*. In this seminal work in cultural studies, he examines the historical movement called modernism. Arising out of the industrial city, it was a revolt against tradition that blurred the lines between actor and spectator, fact and fiction. Berman proposes that modernism is "any attempt by modern men and women to become subjects as well as objects of modernization, to get a grip on the modern world and make themselves at home in it."[6]

From this point of view, the migrants who moved from farm to factory and self-built their houses and shops on illegal plots of land were also modernists. Their informal planning of shantytowns was literally an attempt to "make themselves at home" in the city of the present moment. In sheer scale alone, their efforts represent a major part of the transformation of the urban environment in the postwar era.[7]

The product of this kind of city building process is what I call "hybrid space," one of several terms employed in this book that need unpacking because they have several layers of meaning. Drawing on my own observations, contestation over Chicago's neighborhood parks exposes how the elasticity of this concept in terms of scale and symbolism is a useful way to describe the multifaceted complexity of the urban environment. One block from my home is Warren Park, a ninety-acre green space. A private golf club from 1896 until 1968, it was redesigned by the Chicago Park District to include a more diverse range of recreational activities. Besides retaining a nine-hole golf course, the park planners added a field house, tennis courts, sledding hill, and several baseball diamonds. Only a little room was left along the borders for picnicking, social gatherings, and other more leisurely pursuits.

Despite lots of community input and political wrangling over the fate of the park for over a decade, the plan was a complete mismatch of design and use. By the time work finally got under way in the late seventies, immigrants from South Asia and Latin America had become the dominant groups living around the park. Most of them do not play baseball, tennis, or golf; they are devoted to soccer and an occasional cricket match.

As I walk through the park, I see baseball fields transformed into soccer pitches with markers ranging from official-looking iridescent cones along the sidelines to makeshift goalposts built out of backpacks and jackets. And while the tennis courts stand empty, families and other groups crowd the fringe areas with their barbeques, turning them into picnic grounds. As with the Tijuana subdivision, the contestation between the planners and the grass roots over the recreational use of Warren Park has produced a patch of hybrid space.[8]

In another way, Warren Park is an exemplar of the interaction of two or more different, even paradoxical environments coming together to create an unplanned mixed-use space. In this case, gaggles of geese have turned the golf course into a place of urban nature during the off-season. With humans barred by a chain-link fence circling the course, its fairways and ponds have become the winter quarters for large flocks of them, numbering in the hundreds. Other birds and wild animals have found a safe haven there too, including raccoons and possums that forage for food on my back porch during the midnight hours.

The creation of hybrid space can result from contestation or adaptation, as in the examples above, or from conscious planning. While the geese have turned a golf course into a blend of the human made and the natural, landscape architects have also composed formal designs of urban nature. Consider "starchitect" Jeanne Gang's proposal to devolve Northerly Island—a former airstrip on the lakefront in the city center—back to its natural topography as a marshy sand dune. She wants to restore a presettlement landscape to turn it into a refuge for birds migrating along the shoreline of Lake Michigan. She believes a wetland thriving with wildlife will attract people and promote a greater appreciation of the civic value of greening the city. In broader perspective, the American Dream of homeownership in a suburban nature harkens back to deep-seated, cultural imaginaries of utopia as a pastoral landscape.[9]

The examples of hybrid space in Chicago parks highlight the importance of putting this complex, multidimensional term within a specific context of an actual place. In addition to the spatial dimensions of contestation over the urban environment, crosscurrents of people and culture contribute to its transformation from a physical shape on the ground into a place alive with the "DNA of urbanism." Cruz, for instance, was struck by the stark contrast between the skylines of his American city and its Mexican neighbor just across an increasingly militarized border.[10]

"Two completely different urbanisms," he observes, "expressing two different attitudes toward the city have grown up in reaction to the phenomenon of the border. If San Diego is emblematic of the segregation and control epitomized by the master-planned communities that define its sprawl, Tijuana's urbanism evolved [organically] as a collection of informal, nomadic settlements or barrios that encroach on San Diego's periphery. . . . Unavoidably, both cities seem to contain something of one another: In every 'first world' city, a 'third world' city exists, and every third world city replicates the first."[11]

Transnational urbanism moves back and forth across the United States–Mexican border, part of the globalization of the local, and the other way around. This book is about that globalization, but equally important here is not losing sight of the nation-state as a powerful filter, or lens, mediating between the global and the local. An ecological perspective on the environment can add another vital spectrum of views on the city as a hybrid space. At one end of the scale, it supplies microscopic images of disease organisms in drinking water supplies. At the other are satellite pictures of the air pollution rising above sprawling metropolitan regions. And in between are the struggles over the design and use of public parks and open spaces among planners, policy makers, and the grass roots.[12]

Of course, people themselves as well as material culture began flowing around the world at an ever-faster pace after World War II. As a Guatemalan American, Cruz personifies the success story of immigrants, who take on multiple identities. He is a member of an elite, albeit swelling, corps of globetrotting professionals, technocrats, and managers. After 1945, they began climbing the rungs of the corporate ladder of success by moving around the world from one foreign subsidiary to the next. Indispensable to bringing about the interconnectivity of markets and information, these nomads could demand oases of safety as they trekked with their families in tow from one strange land to the next. As Cruz observes, his own transplanted hometown has become a fortified landscape of gated communities and spatial segregation by class and race/ethnicity.

In contrast, Guatemala City has become home for more than ten thousand gang members deported from Southern California. They are the antipodes of the globetrotting elite; they are no-where men, trapped in a transnational space-time trajectory without a place to call home, except prison. Almost all of them had come to the San Diego–Los Angeles area as small children with their parents, making them undocumented permanent residents, not illegal immigrants. Most of them grew up in Mexican American or Mexican "cities-within-the-city," and they joined their neighborhood street gangs.[13] They all began as young people in search of place-based identities and self-defense in a hostile environment of social disorder and police brutality.

But they ended up being deported. In 1996, the U.S. Congress changed their status from local residents to global exiles in the aptly named Immigration Reform and Personal Responsibility Act. Even those convicted of a nonviolent offense could be summarily expelled. Treated like pariahs in Guatemala, they were tattoo-covered strangers in a strange land. Nonetheless, their membership in a U.S. street gang followed them, transporting their place-based identities into their new neighborhoods in Guatemala City.[14]

Like the top-to-bottom contestation over different visions of the ideal city, the global migration of people also included a full range of society, from elite starchitects to outcast gangsters. They all became agents of change who contributed to the building of urban environments. In the case of Southern California and Latin America, this flow of people back and forth represents what Elana Zilberg calls a "politics of simultaneity." "In the North–South relations under consideration here," she posits, "deported immigrant gang youth oscillate between 'home' and 'abroad,' where both home and abroad are themselves unstable locations. At the same time, gang youth who have never been to the United States construct their identities around imagined urban geographies of cities like Los Angeles."[15]

From simultaneous different points of view, then, the city itself takes on multiple shapes and layers of meaning. All these visions need to be included because studies of formal plans and official policies provide only a partial picture of the remaking of the urban environment after World War II. In the capitalist countries under review here, the real estate industry and the city's inhabitants often acted independently of, if not in opposition to, official blueprints of the future. As Ravetz shows in her brilliant analysis of the rebuilding of Great Britain's cities, even the most enthusiastic embrace of comprehensive planning resulted in only patches of change in the much larger quilt of the urban fabric.[16]

Conscious planning also generated unintended consequences, constructing urban landscapes unlike anything originally envisioned. Policy makers saw roadbuilding programs in terms of the planners' promise to speed up traffic; they predicted neither the resulting smog and congestion nor the populist highway revolts that shut them down. In the subdivision observed by Teddy Cruz, the plan to provide no public spaces or basic services led its residents to jerry-build their own places of community life literally on top of and inside their houses. And in some cities, the official plan was having no plan at all. Consider that in two of the world's biggest, Mexico City and São Paulo, self-built shantytowns on illegally occupied land cover more than half their metropolitan areas.

Struggles over whose vision of the urban environment would prevail among planners, policy makers, and the grass roots became caught up in much broader questions of political power and social justice. Who has rights to the city, who owns it, and who rules? The makeover under way in the Tijuana subdivision and countless other patches of land represents a largely untold, albeit crucial, part of the history of the city in the postwar era. With a few exceptions, planning historians have turned a blind eye to the grass roots as agents of change in the city building process.[17]

One of the rebels is Leonie Sandercock, who was trained in the fine arts but now holds a distinguished academic position as an urban planning theorist. She advocates including "insurgent planning histories" from the bottom up to balance accounts of conscious, formal planning from the top down. "Stories of resistance to 'planning by the state,'" she contends, "are as important a part of the historical narrative as are the more familiar heroic stories of master plans and master planners, of planning legislation and state planning agencies. There is a tradition of community resistance . . . and of community planning, which needs to be incorporated as a counterpoint to the modernist narrative."[18] This book aims to heed her call for a fuller account of city building as a contested terrain of social conflict that results in patches of hybrid space.

I now introduce the three main groups of actors in the building of the urban environment. First come the policy makers, because cities have always needed some form of government to provide for the health, safety, and order of their inhabitants. With the growth of large urban centers in the ancient world, moreover, rulers were needed to organize the provision of essential infrastructure such as waterworks and flood control, roads and bridges, and markets and wharfs. This group plays a central role in both the decision-making process and its enforcement. The power of the policy makers can range from absolute rulers to hamstrung administrators, who can be constrained further by democratic mechanisms of control such as frequent elections and mandatory referendums.[19]

Similarly, the everyday lives of the people have always been an intrinsic part of the city building process. For our purposes, the "grass roots" are defined as city people engaged in collective acts of informal planning and resistance against public policy. In the cases of the Tijuana homeowners and Warren Park soccer players, autonomous individuals acted spontaneously to fulfill a shared vision of community life. In other places, local residents mobilized around place-based issues to become organizational forms such as neighborhood associations, faith-based groups, and protest movements. And in some cases, their acts of resistance empowered them to play a role in the official planning and development of patches of urban space. In the extreme, albeit all-to-common experience of the shantytowns, informal planning from the bottom up was the only means available to provide the essential necessities of group survival.[20] As we see in the insurgent planning histories in this book, they extended from staking out the boundaries of home lots and roadways to building schools and utility networks.

The planners come last because they entered the stage of urban history relatively late as a self-conscious group of professional experts. To be sure, visions of utopia as a kingdom of heaven are as old as pastoral images of a Garden of Eden. But only during the opening decades of the twentieth century were comprehensive plans drawn from a self-proclaimed, scientific point of view. Even the most revered figure of the nineteenth century in town-planning histories, Baron Georges-Eugène Haussmann, was actually a civil engineer. Although some of his public works projects to renew Paris were on an unprecedented scale in the modern world, he never proposed an all-inclusive vision or systematic plan of the city of the future. As we discover in Chapter 1, the emergence of planning as a separate field of theory and practice by trained experts took another generation of urban reformers, technological revolutions, and scientific discoveries.[21]

Our story begins with the architects, engineers, and utopians who called themselves Progressives and redefined themselves as scientists of urban life and space. Drawing on age-old metaphors of the city as a living thing, they reenvisioned it in contemporary, biological terms, what they called the "Organic City." Since each planner used this term in his or her own way, its meaning can become problematic. Adding to the shape-shifting nature of this term, its conceptual framework as a natural system evolved over time in step with paradigm shifts in the life sciences, especially the new field of ecology.

Nonetheless, an interrogation of the use of the Organic City metaphor by succeeding generations of planners is crucial in gaining an understanding of their call for a "clean sweep" of the existing built environment.[22] Each planner had a vision to replace the industrial city with a complete, finished blueprint of the modern city of tomorrow. For Frank Lloyd Wright, on the one hand, "organic architecture" meant nature-based designs like his ground-hugging, prairie-style houses. Le Corbusier (Charles-Édouard Jeanneret), on the other hand, used the same language to describe a Radiant City of soaring skyscrapers and zooming motorways.

Yet the reformers of the Progressive Era shared a much more important set of underlying normative assumptions about nature, society, and the city. At heart, they were all environmental determinists; they believed that changes in physical space could produce changes in social behavior. And nature, however defined, remained their environmental ideal. At the same time, the planners demanded total control. In exchange, they promised that a metamorphosis of urban space would bring about social harmony and a rising standard of living for all.[23]

Called modernists after World War I, they shared an optimistic faith in the ability of science and technology to underwrite a sustained economic expansion. Furthermore, they did not question the necessity to segregate land use into hierarchies of residential, commercial, and industrial zones connected by high-speed transport. Nor did they examine how an almost totally male membership injected patriarchal values into their designs of the Organic City. They took for granted that the nuclear middle-class family represented the ideal household, whether living in a high-rise flat in a city center or a one-family bungalow in a garden suburb. Another unspoken assumption about the urban environment among professional planners was that women should be restricted from public space as much as possible.[24]

What made the adoption of the Organic City metaphor so universal among them was its facility in enabling people to envision all the infinite complexities of urban life in simpler, holistic terms, as a self-sustaining system of interconnected parts. Analogous to human metabolism, the city could be pictured as an open system of energy flows: food or fuel supplies in and waste by-products out. The morphology of this imagined organism turned real estate markets and land development into something natural: urban growth and decay.

For the nascent profession, moreover, adopting theoretical models of biology with their critical practical applications for medicine and public health helped establish the authority of its practitioners as scientific experts. And given the Progressives' sense of the impending doom of the industrial city, they portrayed its problems as medical pathologies of life cycles, bodily cancers, and mental breakdowns. They cast themselves as the doctors of the city. Only they had the special training and insight to restore its health to a state of physical growth, social order, and moral uplift.

Despite the undeniable utility of metaphors of the city as a natural system, a main contention of this book is that their costs far outweigh their benefits. Over the course of the twentieth century, the planners' vision of the Organic City resulted in three unintended, dire consequences for urban life in Europe and the Americas. The fatal flaw undermining this model of urbanism was the illusion of the city having a life of its own, independent from human agency. On the contrary, nothing is natural about the urban environment. Although there is nature in the city, the urban environment requires constant human control to keep essential services working and maintain public order.

As a theory of urbanism, the Organic City also obscured the primary question of political life: Who rules? Like the economists' "invisible hand" of the marketplace, this model of urban life hid the official planners and the policy makers behind a false facade of a self-regulating, natural system of growth and decay. In part, the massive uprisings of the urban grass roots in Europe and the Americas represented a protest against the Organic City idea. They rebelled against its denial of democratic participation in the formation of plans for the future of the community.

In the post–World War II period, the insulation of the planners from the grass roots provided by the Organic City metaphor contributed to its third disastrous consequence for everyday life in the urban centers of the Western world. Shielded in central bureaucracies from seeing the neighborhoods from a street corner point of view, they suffered a self-delusion of false belief. Their academic training taught them that the scientific foundation of the model enabled them to make value-free decisions. In effect, their theory of urbanism kept them from taking seriously outside criticism of it while inhibiting internal debate over the implications of its underlying assumptions. Their blind faith in the Organic City left them unprepared to meet the challenge from the bottom up on grounds of environmental, political, and social injustice. The urban crisis of the sixties would result in the downfall of the planners in the formation of public policy and the implosion of their model of the urban environment. Like a house of cards, a faulty foundation at the base of this conceptual framework would suddenly bring it crashing down.

The scope and scale of these populist uprisings in European and American cities suggests that comparative perspectives will help expose the roots of these struggles over the production of urban space. This method of seeing the city, sorting out the unique from the common conditions of the urban experience, is perhaps the best way to define the specific context of each place. The need to contrast differences between cities became crucial after 1945, a period of increasing globalization. The resumption of international trade and economic interdependence was intensified by the bipolar competition of Cold War politics. Decolonialization also spurred the participation of the so-called third world in the ensuing race among nations for technological modernization.[25]

In the United States and Western Europe, moreover, ideological consensus behind the International Style of architecture and urban design promoted advocacy of a single model of an Organic City. An East–West transatlantic comparison of these highly industrialized and urbanized countries goes a long way in identifying how this universal utopian image was refracted through the lens of national political cultures and institutions to project different outcomes in city skylines.

At the same time, a North–South contrast between developed and developing nations is also required to illuminate all the various ways cities were built in the postwar period. The exporting and importing of the professional planners' vision of the city of tomorrow became one of the most visible signs of globalization itself. Today, cities everywhere continue to hire starchitects like Frank Gehery, Renzo Piano, and Santiago Caladrava to make iconic postmodernist symbols of their world-class status.[26]

For our purposes, seven case studies illuminate the ways national institutions and cultures played a configurative role in the creation of hybrid space during the postwar period. Each city highlights a different matrix of influence among planners, policy makers, and the grass roots in the contestation over the urban environment. While all the countries of Western Europe shared the dual task of restarting their war-torn economies and rebuilding their urban centers, each followed its unique political tradition to reach this goal. The United States faced a different set of urban problems ranging from the physical deterioration of neighborhoods at the center to the geographic sprawl of suburbia at the periphery. Latin American cities faced similar problems in addition to having to cope with exploding populations of rural migrants (see Figure 1).

For Europe, the Netherlands represents the nation with the strongest tradition of democratic cooperation among planners, policy makers, and the grass roots. And Rotterdam was the place where the professional experts

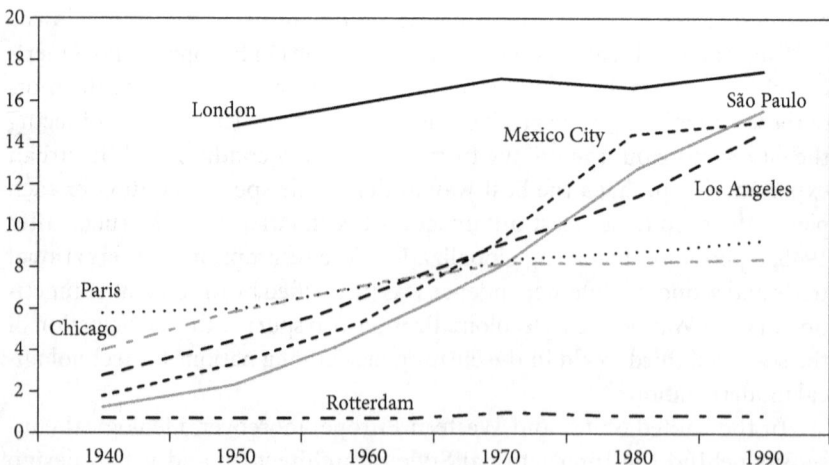

Figure 1 Population of Metropolitan Areas (in millions)

were given a virtual clean slate to rebuild a city center. It had been blanket bombed early in the war, giving its civic leaders plenty of time to draw blueprints of an Organic City that they could start erecting immediately after liberation. During the blitz of Great Britain, Parliament also kept the planners busy. And like the Dutch, British planners too envisioned comprehensive, clean-sweep plans for London's reconstruction on a regional scale.

Paris, in contrast, was spared from not only German bombs but also the modernist planners by local traditions of preservationism. Nevertheless, it would be swept up in national plans for breakneck economic modernization that would set loose unsettling "runaway technologies" and equally disruptive social movements against them. "Runaway technologies" Ravetz defines as "characterized not only by the magnitude of its possible disasters, but by the ultimate impossibility of locating responsibility and source of decisions, and so getting it back into control."[27]

For the United States, Los Angeles and Chicago offer a study of divergence, at least during the first twenty years following war's end. In Los Angeles, the focus of public attention was on growth and expansion at the periphery. In Chicago, civic discourse put a spotlight on problems of decay at the center, including the need to update the business district and to renew the surrounding ring of "blighted" African American neighborhoods. Although the same underlying forces of national policy and global integration were changing the two cities, they seemed to be headed in completely opposite directions on the surface of local politics and planning.

For Latin America, Brazil and Mexico were the two countries after 1945 with large enough populations to generate self-sustaining consumer, or Fordist, economies. Both countries, moreover, are blessed with rich natural resources. They enjoyed boom times during the war, kick-starting the growth of their industrial cities and a great internal migration of their rural populations in search of a better life. In São Paulo, on the one hand, an elitist and racist regime turned technocratic planning and international capital to advantage in making their city into the prime engine driving the national economy. In Mexico City, on the other hand, an inclusive, corporatist regime considered technical experts to be a threat to their complete hegemony of power. The politicians ignored the planners in the formation of public policy, which promoted the construction of illegal shantytowns to house the tsunami of newcomers pouring in from the countryside.

Taken together, these seven case studies provide a way to measure different visions of the postwar city against actual results in terms of the built environment. Telling their stories reveals the contestation among planners, policy makers, and the grass roots in the production of hybrid space. And contrasting how each city created unique places of urban life helps identify and separate out global agents of change from local ones.

The ultimate goals of this comparative approach are twofold. It seeks to gain a better understanding of how cities were built during the postwar era, and it hopes to shed light on the constellations of social and political relationships among the three groups that have the best prospects of creating hybrid spaces that are alive with "the very DNA of urbanism itself."

To achieve these goals, the book's chapters alternate between visionary theories of urbanism and actual practices of city building in the case studies. The chapters examining the history of ideas cover a broad spectrum of voices engaged in transnational discourse about the city, not just those of the planners and politicians. To be sure, the advocates of conscious, formal planning were far better at articulating their viewpoints than the mass of ordinary people. However, the case study chapters provide a counterweight by giving expression to their ideas in the form of material culture. Their guerrilla architecture and informal community planning tell their stories.

The shifting balance of power among planners, policy makers, and the grass roots divides the chronological order of the book into two parts. From 1945 to 1960, a consensus among planning experts behind a single vision of an Organic City helped them gain extraordinary influence in the formation of public policy. Chapter 1 looks back at the history of this model of the modern city from its origins in the 1890s to its widespread adoption after World War II. In large part, the shared class and cultural perspectives of the first generation of professional planners explains the emergence of the Organic City as a utopian ideal. This extraordinary unity not only established a powerful picture of the future but also led its advocates to dismiss alternative visions of the relationship between nature, place, and society. Further insulated from the grass roots after the war, the planners would lose sight of the point of view from the neighborhood street corner.

Chapters 2 and 3 trace the triumph of the planners' vision of the Organic City during the spread of the Cold War across the globe. The ensuing bipolar struggle between communist and capitalist blocs of countries marked a major turning point in the history of the city. Although the influence of the planners' urban ideal on policy makers and the general public had grown steadily before 1945, its consolidation into the International Style had been confined to an elite circle of intellectuals, led by Le Corbusier. After, the Cold War cast the city and the conditions of everyday life inside it into the larger race of technological modernization. Portraits of city skylines became a litmus test of which side was winning. In the Western bloc, policy makers gave the planners a remarkably free hand to turn their blueprints for comprehensive, clean-sweep reconstruction of the urban environment into actual shapes on the ground.

But beginning in the mid-1960s, cities around the world exploded in rebellion. Part II takes up the urban crisis with a pair of chapters on the critics of official visions of the Organic City. Both the political right and the left rose up in protest against conscious, formal planning by the state. The insurgency of people in the streets and in the voting booth grew into a global reform movement for political, social, and environmental justice.

Terrifying images on TV of people in Los Angeles crying, "Burn, baby, burn!" finally forced the planners and the policy makers to see what they had done from the point of view of those displaced by their runaway technologies of modernization. Their consensus behind a single vision of the Organic City collapsed just as quickly as the torched buildings going up in flames. Fractured and demoralized, the planning profession would become partisans in the ever more contested and crowded battleground over the future of the city.

During the next twenty-year period of the Cold War, the rising tide of insurgency from the grass roots against top-down planning would change not only the city's skyline but also the people's rights of citizenship to participate in decision making about the quality of their everyday lives. Chapters 6 and 7 survey the results from the shifting matrix of influence among planners, policy makers, and the grass roots. They explore both new visions of the Organic City and novel types of hybrid space.

Covering the time of the worldwide economic crisis following the oil embargo of 1973–1974, these chapters also look at the larger role of the globalization of markets and information in how cities were built. Coming on the heels of the urban crisis, the resulting global energy shortage and economic depression marked a second major watershed in the history of the city. As the implosion of urban theory had, the stagflation of the seventies undermined the academic foundations of postwar models of the economy. In the restructuring of capitalism that followed, the recovery produced rising levels of social inequality, led by the United States. After 1979, the growing significance of class would be expressed in spatial terms of increases in the segregation and the militarization of urban space. A psychological state of fear of violent crime in the urban jungle spread across the globe.

Like this infectious case of mass paranoia, the importing and exporting of ideas and people around the world continued to speed up the pace of urban change. Entire minicities of high-security gated communities were being stamped out everywhere at the same time as third world ghettos of exclusion were emerging in the urban centers of the first world. Postmodernist designs and building materials, worldwide webs and organizational networks, and national political realignments and global social movements helped inspire a new generation of urban theorists of the Organic City. Some would foresee the erection of computer-driven, cyborg cities of flows; others would envision a future of nature-designed eco-cities of citizens.

The conclusion, drawing from a half century of contestation among planners, policy makers, and the grass roots over the urban environment, suggests that we scrap organic metaphors of the city and use a multifaceted lens to envision it from many points of view. Literally like the Tijuana barrio observed by Teddy Cruz, patches of urban space are places of human activity that have several layers of meaning at the same time. Cruz has embedded this insight in plans for the development of patches of hybrid space in San Diego. As an architectural critic put it in 2006, Cruz recast the Mexican "shanty-town as a new suburban ideal."[28] The planner's project models reflected the shifts in the balance of power among the three groups. First, of course, he had to convince the city council to reform the zoning and building codes to permit higher densities and guerrilla architecture. He proposed to build a closely packed array of one-story concrete frames equipped with hookups for all the infrastructure systems of contemporary life. But the buyers are put in charge of turning these foundation platforms into homes, shops, offices, and ultimately, a community "alive with the DNA of urbanism."[29]

1

Growing the Organic City, 1890–1945

The Origins of the Organic City

The Birth of Modernism and the Planning Profession, 1890–1919

Starting the story of conscious, formal planning with an American, Frank Lloyd Wright, underscores the transatlantic context of the project to create the Organic City. The focus here will be on the beliefs of Wright and other urban visionaries about nature, science, and society. The ways that the Progressive Era generation of urban reformers like Wright understood the natural world through science—especially biology and sociology—played a major role in shaping those reformers' utopian plans for the built environment.

These reformers' ideas about the city as a natural system also provide a key to unlock their very different, even contradictory, uses of these organic metaphors. Wright, for example, gained his view of nature from real life experience growing up on a farm in the Midwest. In contrast, Europeans like Walter Gropius and Mies van der Rohe saw science through a philosophical lens as an abstract expression of universal laws. Nonetheless, they were typical in paying homage to the American as the first modernist.[1]

Wright served as a bridge that carried the Europeans from traditions of historicism in city building to something truly original, an "organic architecture." In 1909, the Chicagoan arrived in Berlin to promote a two-volume edition of his plans and drawings that had just been published in Germany and is known as the Wasmuth Portfolio. Work stopped when it arrived at the studio of Berlin's avant-garde Peter Behrens, where Mies and Gropius were apprentices. Another young aspiring architect from Switzerland, Le Corbusier, worked there too; he bought a copy. In Vienna, Richard Neutra was so inspired by it that he moved to Chicago to learn nature-based design directly from the master.[2]

The American was the proverbial right man at the right time and place to open the path from old to new for several reasons. Besides a supersized ego, he was able to bring the germinal ideas of his mentor, Louis Sullivan, to full bloom. Sullivan, Wright's *Lieber Meister*, was a transitional figure because his futuristic pronouncement that "form follows function" was offset by a backward-looking obsession with ornamentation.

In contrast, his student's simple cubist designs appealed to contemporary aesthetic values, while his homespun transcendentalism resonated with German idealism. Wright provided the vision to help the Europeans find their way across to the modernist shore, but they were not lacking in prior efforts to get there. The search for ways to counterbalance the harmful effects of industrialization on the city had been under way for at least a half century. For protomodernists, Wright's portfolio supplied what psychologists call an aha experience, an epiphany that suddenly snaps previously scattered pieces of a picture into focus.

Wright's architecture and urban designs were nature based because his immediate environmental surroundings served as the starting place. "I had an idea," he recalled, "that the planes parallel to the earth in buildings identify themselves with the ground. . . . I began to see a building primarily not as a cave but as broad shelter in the open, related to vista; *vista without and vista within*."[3]

Wright believed that he had integrated Sullivan's art nouveau style of naturalistic ornamentation into the structure of the building itself. "Here came a new sense of building on American soil," he exclaimed, "that could *grow* building forms not only true to function but expressive far beyond mere function in the realm of the human spirit."[4]

The result of this simplifying and synthesizing was what Wright meant by "organic architecture." "Conceive now," he imagined, "that an entire building might grow up out of conditions as a plant grows up out of soil and yet be free to be itself, to 'live its own life' according to Man's Nature. . . . I now propose an ideal for the architecture of the Machine Age, for the ideal American building. Let it grow up in that image. The tree."[5]

Wright appeared in Europe at the peak of a ferment of urban reform that had been brewing on both sides of the Atlantic. Percolating through this assault on the problems of the industrial city was a growing belief in environmental determinism; that is, changes in the physical world could cause changes in social behavior. Although this strategy spawned a broad spectrum of reform proposals for improving urban conditions, housing emerged as the one issue that attracted the most attention.

Perhaps the second great common cause of the Progressive reformers was urban sanitation and public health. Armed with a powerful new science, the champions of germ theories, like the advocates of cleaning up the slums, also believed that a humane and healthy city required a total reengineering of the built environment. The result was a radical shift in point of view from street-level accounts of the dangers of the mob to more distant, scientific studies of urban conditions.[6]

The reform strategies of the Progressives helped focus the attention of the nascent profession of planning on physical space and finished blueprints of idealized landscapes. The turn from the moral environmentalism of the Victorian era to the social environmental determinism at the turn of the century was one of several sources nourishing the birth of a modern form of urban planning. Architects and civil engineers were the closest established professions to be able to claim expert authority in these matters. Nevertheless, many would-be urban reformers drew on traditions of social utopianism for legitimacy.[7]

Chicago's Daniel Burnham is a good example of the metamorphosis of a skilled architect into a city planner. In 1891, he went from designing a world's fair to ever-larger urban renewal projects, culminating in the comprehensive Chicago Plan of 1909. In contrast, the creator of the Garden City idea, London's Ebenezer Howard, had no formal training. He was a court reporter by trade, but he was also a dedicated radical, who wanted to reconfigure nature to impose a socialism of cooperative behavior on its inhabitants.[8]

Another important fountainhead of the modernist movement at the end of the century sprang from the general uprising of the art world against the past. Like Sullivan's decorative motifs, art nouveau styles at the turn of the century represented a transitional phase in this shift in aesthetic values. Architectural manifestations cropped up everywhere, including Charles Rennie Mackintosh's Glasgow, Antoni Gaudí's Barcelona; Otto Wagner's Vienna, Victor Horta's Brussels, and Hector Guimard's Paris. And like Wright—the self-proclaimed rebel—a rising generation of architects followed up on Behrens's experiments in stripping off the ornamentation to give primary expression to the functionalism of a building's design. Neutra's first inspiration in Vienna, Adolf Loos, and Rotterdam's J.P.P. Oud would soon lead Europeans toward the new aesthetic, *de Stijl* (the Style), of cube-shaped forms made from glass, steel, and concrete.[9]

The crowning event in the formation of a modern vision of an Organic City was the 1910 Town Planning Conference and Exhibition. Organized by Raymond Unwin, England's foremost Garden City architect-planner, the London meeting brought together the leaders of urbanism throughout the

Atlantic world. According to planning historian Mervyn Miller, "Neither before nor since had town-planning enjoyed such prestige."[10] Wright was a no-show, but just about everyone else was there, including German Garden City designers, French traffic engineers, Daniel Burnham, and Patrick Geddes, Scotland's evolutionary biologist and regionalist.

Collectively, the ideas presented at the meeting helped institutionalize urban planning as a separate profession with a scientific point of view on people, place, and space. The various versions of the Organic City presented at the conference were founded on shared assumptions of environmental determinism. The final mastery of nature would allow planners to achieve a complete overhaul of the city into dispersed, human-scale communities of health, comfort, and beauty.[11]

By the outbreak of World War I in 1914, then, a new profession had taken shape around two different, albeit compatible, visions of the Organic City. The shared cultural perspectives of the international group attending the town-planning conference in 1910 far outweighed their differences over physical design. Adopting an identity as neutral experts, the first generation of urban planners believed that they could put science into the service of art to redraw the basic relationships between nature, the built environment, and society.[12]

The ultimate utility of this model of planning was its open-endedness, which gave expression to an incredibly broad spectrum of visionary cities of tomorrow. It could mean everything from Wright's inspirational portfolio images based on natural settings and materials to Le Corbusier's more abstract perceptions of a self-contained and self-regulating system that unfolds from within, a living cyborg. The all-encompassing quality of this planning model helped give its designers an attitude of total control. As Le Corbusier would soon command, "The plan must rule."[13]

The Great Fission of the Organic City

During the interwar years, urban planning professionals split into two camps with different albeit analogous imaginaries of the Organic City. Both of these visions of an ideal environment and society were deeply rooted in the transatlantic cultural values of the bourgeois classes. The Garden City model of Howard and Wright expressed a profound cultural bias against the city. Their plans for a better life emptied most inhabitants and factories from historic cores and relocated them in satellite settlements surrounded by greenbelts.

These modernists called for the containment of the city and the dispersal of its population and industry over vast metropolitan regions. American and British planners laid out Garden City designs composed of self-contained neighborhood units. They believed that a suburban environment would maximize family stability and natural health for the middle and working classes.[14]

The alternative Radiant City model of Le Corbusier expressed Europe's cosmopolitan culture of urbanism. This vision of modernism idealized the continent's great cities, which had created spatial and social hierarchies radiating from their historic centers. His designs for a new way of life concentrated the better-educated, middle classes downtown in tower block apartments, which he called "machines for living." Raising his skyscrapers on pillars (*pilotis*), they were surrounded by great open green spaces and speeding highways. Like their Garden City counterparts, modernists like Le Corbusier also envisioned greenbelt suburbs and industrial parks for the working classes. Home ownership and dispersed settlement were designed to maximize family and labor stability.[15]

For the Western world, World War I represented a definitive break between the old and the modern. Especially in shell-shocked Europe, the machine age arrived with a vengeance, as expressed by its Dada, surrealist, and expressionist artists. For its avant-garde architects, too, reaction to the war's devastation meant utter rejection of the past. They especially blamed aristocracy, hierarchy, nationalism, and paternalism for causing the catastrophe.

The modernists rejected the entire tradition of historical building styles and town-planning designs. Typical was Le Corbusier's denunciation of one of his most important prewar influences, Camillo Sitte. In the 1890s, the Vienna architect had been the first modern champion of looking at the city from the viewpoint of the pedestrian: one street and one plaza at a time. But following World War I, Le Corbusier condemned what he now saw as Sitte's "insidious pleas in the direction of the picturesque in town planning [because] they were based on the past, and in fact WERE the past." Now, he was determined to destroy the street and the anarchistic street life that Sitte idealized. In the machine age, in contrast, the speeding motorcar had to rule the road.[16]

During the interwar years, a neophyte profession of university-certified planners translated an increasingly unified version of the Organic City into formal zoning and building codes. On both sides of the Atlantic, private developers and financial institutions were in the vanguard of this kind of reform legislation to set minimum construction standards, institutionalize decision making on land-use regulations, and enforce restrictive real estate covenants of spatial segregation by class, race/ethnicity, or religion. Although the planners made large strides in gaining status and employment as professional experts, political and economic instability following the war meant that their influence remained extremely small, limited to pilot projects, temporary exhibitions, and individual residential commissions.[17]

Although the modernists' reconstruction of urban space was limited, their production of visions of the Organic City was prodigious. Despite their rejection of the past, they adopted long-standing traditions of looking at the city as a natural system. New were the interrelated use of science as authority for their urban designs and the comprehensive scope of their clean-sweep plans for social engineering the environment. Both were linked to fast-paced changes in biology and medicine, including the establishment of a separate branch of study in the 1930s called "ecosystems." As Sharon Kingsland, a historian of science, underscores, "The history of ecology is a history of changing criteria for imposing order on nature and resisting the alternative that all is really chaotic and contingent."[18]

These new ideas had significant effects on the planners' understanding of metaphors of the city as a living thing. The life sciences posited that the form and function of nature were far more complicated and interdependent than previously envisioned. Nonetheless, their paradigms were ultimately more reassuring than ever before of restoring the organic. Ecologists demonstrated their optimism by showing how sand dunes and forests had built-in mechanisms of self-regulation that inherently sought a state of equilibrium.

For the acolytes of modernism in both camps, the ecosystem approaches of the life sciences supplied a new model of total control of the built environment. Scientists displayed statistical models that promised to turn the chaos of nature or its human-made metaphor, the city, into the order of a mathematical formula. Echoing Frank Lloyd Wright, Mies van der Rohe stated in 1928, "We have to become master of the unbridled [natural] forces of our time and build them into a new order, an order that gives life free room to move (*Spielraum*) for its unfolding. . . . We do not need less but more technology."[19]

In the case of the Garden City form of modernism, Anglo-American cultural traditions preferred to envision nature as wild albeit picturesque landscapes. During the interwar period, European exports of plans for urban containment were consumed with enthusiasm by Americans. For example, Lewis Mumford and his fellow members of the Regional Planning Association of America (RPAA) promoted a suburban ideal of home and yard in a rustic neighborhood setting. Drawing heavily on Geddes, Mumford broadcast ideas about environmental determinism, social evolution, and regional ecology to much larger audiences. Although locked out of the centers of power, the association was able to design a few prototype communities, including Radburn, New Jersey, and the greenbelt towns erected during the New Deal. The U.S. government also sponsored an important experiment in regional planning, the Tennessee Valley Authority.[20]

In addition, the European export of ideas about urbanism helped the American reformer Clarence Perry give scientific precision to the "neighborhood unit." Perry was a social worker who advocated recreational activities as the antidote to the alienation and chaos of urban life. To promote mental and physical health, he became involved in programs to open schoolyards after school hours, build community centers, and lay out plans for recreational parks.

In the midtwenties, he joined the eminent urban planner and British émigré Tom Adams in drawing a comprehensive study, the *Regional Plan of New York and Its Environs*. Sponsored by his employer, the Russell Sage Foundation, the study allowed Perry to transform Raymond Unwin's work into an ideal garden suburb to save the American family. He envisioned a village-like community of homes, surrounded like an organism's living cell with a protective physical membrane and limited access to its inner arteries of residential streets. In the nucleus stood community centers such as schools and health clinics amid a green space of parks and playfields. An adjacent shopping mall added the final ingredient to this socially exclusive landscape of leisure, health, and consumption.

Perry's neighborhood unit became popular at home and abroad among planning experts. In large part, its growing status as the prototype of the suburban subdivision or estate derived from its amoeba-like flexibility. It could easily be plugged into larger metropolitan frameworks of residential development and highway construction.[21]

Moreover, the neighborhood unit's attraction stemmed from its ability to tap into antiurban fears as well as to offer solutions. In Perry's mind, for instance, the pathological environment of the slums at the city center conjured up a nightmare of "crimes, insanity, suicides!"[22] His designs would keep undesirables out with perimeter walls and security gates, while restrictive covenants would enforce social homogeneity within.

The work of Richard Neutra demonstrates that the modernists' holy grail of unity between the built and the natural environments could be achieved with Wright's approach to organic architecture. In 1928, the Austrian transplant to Los Angeles designed the first European-style modernist structure in the United States. Cut into a steep hillside, the Lovell House has a framework of exposed steel beams and cables that set it apart from the more textured, earthy facades of his mentor. "His philosophy of design," according to his biographer, "grew out of his interest in the biological sciences." Perhaps Neutra's new hometown in the land of sunshine and its Eden-like climate also influenced his designs, which seamlessly integrated inside and outside, high technology and the natural environment.[23]

Despite Neutra's exceptional success, nature-based ways of seeing were overshadowed by the ascendancy of the alternative design-based model of modernism. Respects were always paid to Wright, although he was now portrayed as a nearly forgotten founding father of the Organic City from the prewar era. Reduced to a has-been, Wright and most other nature-based planners were no match for what became known as the International Style.[24]

The previous year, 1927, the revolt of these modernists against the past reached a climax in Europe at the Weissenhofsiedlung Werkbund Exposition. Organized by an underemployed Mies, the architectural fair on the outskirts of Stuttgart, Germany, brought together leading apostles of modernism from all over the continent, including Le Corbusier, Oud, Gropius, Victor Bourgeois, and Otto and Max Taut. They built thirty-three residential buildings in a village-like setting. They were as committed as their Garden City counterparts to relocating people to healthy homes situated within open green spaces. Drawing about a half-million visitors, the exposition suggested a unity of aesthetic values in spite of the idiosyncratic fashions of each architect's work.

The following year, several of them founded the International Congresses of Modern Architecture (Congrès Internationaux d'Architecture Moderne, or CIAM) and appointed Sigfried Giedion to be its secretary-general. The Swiss historian of architecture helped them write a fiery declaration proclaiming that "works of architecture can spring only from the present time. . . . [A]rchitecture must be set free from the sterilizing grip of the academies that are concerned with preserving the formulas of the past."[25] Over the next few years, this proposition would become translated into a formal set of principles.

Written by Le Corbusier for the most part, the principles, known as the Athens Charter, would represent a manifesto of the International Style of design-based architecture and planning. It would also secure his reputation as the most influential architect-planner of the century. The charter originated in the fourth meeting of CIAM in 1933, on a ship cruise from Marseilles to Athens. The charter was first published ten years later. The old had to be plowed under, Le Corbusier charged, because "chaos has entered the cities."[26] Like the Progressives, he too saw bad housing as the primary problem. "Dwellings give families poor shelter," he complained, "corrupting their inner lives. . . . The evil is universal, expressed in the cities by an overcrowding that drives them into disorder."[27]

But against this basic need for human shelter, Le Corbusier put even greater emphasis on the scientific perfection of aesthetic design. He reiterated his belief that "architecture is the art above all others which achieves a state of platonic grandeur, mathematical order, speculation, the perception of harmony that lies in emotional relationships."[28]

In finding this purification of nature in scientific theory, the planning experts lost touch with the environmental settings and social circumstances of their projects. They lost sight of the social relationships that are an integral part of the production of urban space. The adherents of the International Style extended a mechanical model of physical space into the realm of human life. The modernists' scientific objectification of nature can be seen clearly in Radiant City layouts for the 85 percent of the land reserved for green space. The pure emptiness in Le Corbusier's original drawings ironically betrays an eerie urban landscape devoid of people.

From his God-like perspective above the city, he destroyed the street as he planned. His vision of the Organic City also had the unintended consequence of killing off the quintessential urban experience, the daily intercourse of people in the microworlds of the street corner newsstands and the shops in between. Pursuing a comprehensive, clean-sweep approach, he projected a utopian image of a self-regulating, cybernetic system. For him, the answer was reduced to a simple formula: "The city that achieves speed, achieves success."[29] While such a blinkered perspective can be useful, it comes at the price of screening out negative, unintended consequences.

Nonetheless, the modernists who shared Le Corbusier's perspectives believed they had achieved a scientifically objective view of the urban environment. The Stuttgart expo served to forge a united front among planners and a coherent vision of the Organic City to present to the outside world. Among the visitors to this seminal demonstration project were a British architectural writer, Henry-Russell Hitchcock, and a rich American art patron, Philip Johnson. In 1932, they would simultaneously coin the term "International Style." Johnson, moreover, would play a crucial role as an importer of European ideas to the United States when he mounted an exhibit on this architecture at the prestigious Museum of Modern Art in New York City.

Six years later, Johnson again promoted the International Style in a show devoted to German Bauhaus architecture and design. He also helped install two of its leaders, Gropius and Mies, in leading American schools of architecture. These European émigrés in turn would bring others; Gropius, for example, brought Giedion to Harvard, where his inaugural lectures would be published as the highly influential *Space, Time and Architecture.* Like their fellow architect-planners in the Garden City camp, the champions of the International Style made an extremely limited imprint on the urban fabric during the interwar years.[30]

Yet the crystallization of a shared consensus underlying the normative values of both versions of the Organic City would set the foundations for its rise like a phoenix after the war. Consider the scheme of Norway's preeminent architect-planner Eliel Saarinen. His "organic decentralization" makes a mockery of metaphors of the city as a natural system in the terminology of science. His visionary blueprints expose a mental decoupling of abstract ideals of physical space from actual places of human habitation. For example, Saarinen uses medical jargon to diagnose the city's dysfunctional metabolism. "The city-planner must realize," he implores, "that an inadequate street circulation affects the urban body as unfortunately as poor blood circulation affects the human body."[31]

However, the urban doctor's call for major surgery to carve up the patient into geometric segments separated by open spaces was just the opposite of biological metabolism. Furthermore, his proposal to put superhighways down the middle of the open spaces seems completely at odds with their intended purposes as greenbelts of fresh air, recreational activity, and spiritual renewal.[32] Echoing Le Corbusier, Saarinen recites his mantra of speed: "The decentralized city retains sufficient concentration of activity by increased velocity."[33]

Although professional planners had limited prospects of turning their sweeping urban designs into shapes on the ground during the interwar years, they became fully engaged in the never-ending debate over the future of the city. The following case studies take up this contestation among planners, policy makers, and the grass roots over the urban environment and the quality of life within it. After two decades of depression and instability, the postwar years would present the visionaries of the Organic City with an unprecedented opportunity to turn theory into practice.

Case Studies, 1929–1945

Rotterdam, Netherlands: The Reconstruction Plan of 1940

These studies present a succession of snapshots that attempt to capture the city within its national context. Primary attention focuses on relationships between planners and policy makers. Later chapters examine in greater detail the more complex interactions between them and the grass roots. Here I set the stage for the chapters that come next on the importance of the Cold War's race of technological modernization.

During the interwar years, the design-based architects and academic planners kept busy. They laid out the theoretical groundwork of their visions of the Organic City. They also planted the physical foundations of the International Style in both Europe and the Americas. Modernist demonstration models before 1939 of urban renewal projects, neighborhood units, and suburban shopping malls were ready made for ramping up to full-blown production after the war.

A fitting national tableau to raise the curtain is a picture of the Netherlands, the place where a social consensus in favor of comprehensive planning was the strongest. Here we see the planners' imaginary of a *Randstad* (Rim City). It has a central green zone ringed by four major cities: Amsterdam, Utrecht, Rotterdam, and The Hague. In rough order, the case studies then follow a declension from the positive embrace of urban planners by the

Dutch to their hostile rejection by Mexico's ruling group, the PRI (Partido Revolucionario Institucional [Institutional Revolutionary Party]).

Between the extremes, each country and locality wrestled with the ideological and political implications of expanding the scope of state-sponsored activities such as regulating land use and social housing projects at the expense of the vested rights of private property. These conflicts help account for the small footprint the International Style made on the ground before the postwar period. Nonetheless, the searing experience of the war would convince large electoral majorities throughout the Western world to put new confidence in the ability of their governments to engage in socially beneficial programs.[34]

The Dutch landscape also presents the clearest picture of the linkages among nature, the built environment, and society. Its watery topography defined a vision of the Organic City that resembled an inside-out version of Howard's Garden City (see Map 1). A soggy terrain not only defined local identities but also forced each place to look beyond them. The higher ground of hilly places along the rivers determined the location of major cities; low places between them were drained to become farmland. But water has no respect for human-made political borders.

The Dutch had to learn how to work together according to nature's hydrologic boundaries. Over time, they gained control of water flow and reclaimed the land. By the sixteenth century, they had constructed an urban network connected by canals. Large-scale public works and ongoing maintenance of them helped shape a political culture of cooperation and consensus building across municipal, regional, and national levels of government. The Dutch mastery of water even allowed them to be among the first in Europe to tear down their cities' medieval walls, opening up the suburbs. The threat of breaching the dikes and flooding the land effectively deterred invasion by foreign armies.

By the 1900s, broad social agreement behind state-sponsored activities involving urban design and environmental control were long-accepted parts of the Dutch political culture. The twentieth-century version of the planner was a highly respected professional, reflecting his or her all-embracing scope as an economic, social, educational, health, and housing expert, not just someone drawing visions of physical space.

CIAM founder and influential critic Sigfried Giedion singled out Amsterdam as an exemplar of urban planning ideals in the pre–World War II period. Its 1934 master plan made the city an archetype of the "planner's paradise."[35] The academic expert was elated by the work of a new generation of planners. They were leading the way in using sociospatial statistics that promised to achieve the holy grail of scientific certainty in predicting the future growth of the city.[36]

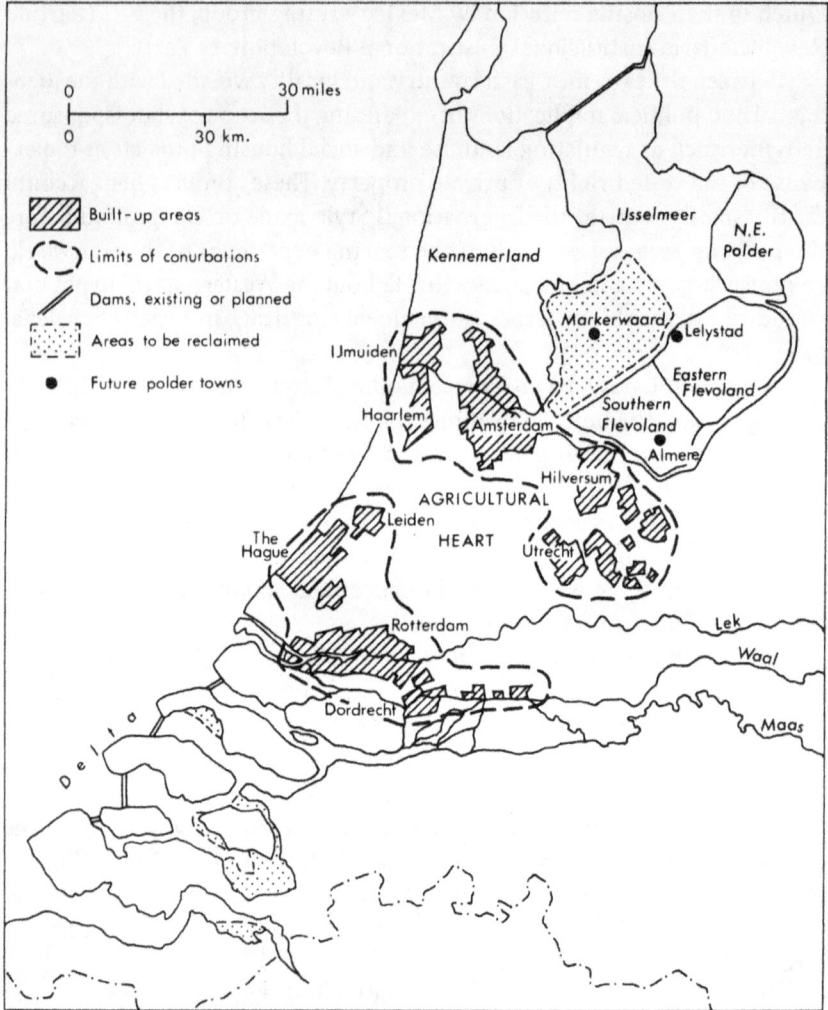

Map 1 Rotterdam: *Randstad/Groene Hart* (Rim City/Green Heart), circa 1930–1945 (Republished with permission of Peter Hall, *Urban and Regional Planning*, 3rd ed. [London: Routledge, 1992], fig. 4.1, p. 75)

About this same time, the country's planners embraced an even more fantastic prophecy of a regional-scale vision of the Organic City. Significantly, the original concept of a Rim City, or *Randstad*, came from a founder of the airline KLM as he was flying around looking for the best spot to build a national airport. That the two million people living there have never identified themselves as Randstaders made no difference to the new technocratic elite. On the contrary, the planners immediately claimed jurisdiction to decide where the people should live, work, and play in this 2,300-square-mile (6,000-square-kilometer) area.

Moreover, they declared the reclaimed wetlands in the middle to be the nation's *Groene Hart* (Green Heart). Like the priests of ancient times, the planners of modernism defined what was sacred space and appointed themselves the guardians of this holy land against the insidious social disease of suburban sprawl. Urban containment would be achieved through a combination of restrictions against building in the newly sanctified zone and incentives for moving to better housing elsewhere.

Depression, war, and occupation might have stymied implementation of these goals, but they hardly fazed the planners' pace of production. They kept busy pumping out drawings and reports on the networked metropolis of tomorrow. Paradoxically, the limitations imposed on their grand mission widened opportunities to realize small-scale models of individual visions.[37]

Of the four main cities, Rotterdam offers the best case study to observe the Dutch approach to planning. As Cordula Rooijendijk, a professor of planning, notes, "[Rotterdam] has been seen widely as emblematic of the modernist approach to planning that . . . define[d] postwar planning throughout the Netherlands and the West."[38] In part, the price of this enviable reputation was tragedy for the city's 600,000 inhabitants. On May 14, 1940, the Germans carpet bombed its business center and port facilities. By the time the fires were extinguished, 650 acres (260 hectares) had been leveled and 11,000 buildings destroyed; 1,900 persons were killed and another 78,000 were homeless. If Dutch planners had ever dreamed of a clean sweep of the old, they were now given their chance to rebuild on a blank page.[39]

Spurred by fears that the Germans would preempt its authority, the municipal council immediately abolished property rights and took possession of the bomb zone. The city architect, Willem G. Witteveen, also jumped into action, drawing a preliminary albeit comprehensive plan within three weeks. Virtually overnight, he was able to reconstruct images of this large and densely built-up area street by street and building by building. The amazing speed of the city architect's response revealed more than efficient record keeping.[40] It also reflected, more importantly, the social consensus in favor of conscious planning in Dutch political culture. Although Witteveen adhered to the historic preservation school of urban reconstruction, he was also a proponent of modernist principles of design-based architecture and urban planning. In 1924, he had moved to Rotterdam and had joined its planning department.

A student of avant-garde architect Hendrik P. Berlage, Witteveen sought to incorporate the latest technology in traditional, national styles. One of his first projects, for instance, was a bridge to link the historic city center to its burgeoning harbor and oil refinery complex on the other side of the Maas

River. The bridge was a sleek, double bascule design, but the four bridge houses had cone-shaped, copper-clad roofs that resembled the tops of wind-mills. In the years leading up to the war, moreover, he had drawn a series of large-scale yet flexible plans for suburban extensions of the city. The open-ness of his plans allowed room for free expression in designing a variety of both public and private buildings, attracting such influential architects as Oud, J. H. van den Broek, and Willem van Tijen to the city.

In fact, the vibrancy of its architect-planner community nurtured by Witteveen sparked a contentious debate over his reconstruction plan. Led by van den Broek, advocates of the CIAM school of urban renewal envisioned a high-technology model of the Organic City. They argued for an urban de-sign that would meet contemporary needs for skyscrapers, automobiles, and suburbs. By war's end, political support for the city architect's traditionalism would dissolve, and a new consensus would crystallize around the clean-sweep approach of the International Style.[41]

London, United Kingdom: The Greater London Plan of 1944

Between 1919 and 1945, both the possibilities and the limitations of formal planning became most fully evident in England. On the one hand, it became institutionalized. It achieved mature form in professional training, academic theory, and public control over urban space. But on the other hand, planning failed to contain suburban sprawl, let alone uplift the masses to bourgeois standards of morality. The seeming impotence of the profession undermined its social authority.

Even before the war began, the leading acolyte of formal planning, Raymond Unwin, had embodied the nation's antiurban ethos in a seminal handbook with the appropriate title *Nothing Gained by Overcrowding.*[42] The historian Helen Meller considers it "the most influential document on town planning up until the Second World War."[43] A greenbelt, or girdle, around the historic core of London, Unwin advised, was the only way to contain this ur-ban monster. Beyond, he proposed building garden suburbs and new towns. The only way to eliminate the twin evils of slums and sprawl in the future, he claimed, was to put complete control in the hands of the scientific experts.[44]

Like the Dutch, the English had long traditions of state activism that promised to empower planners with the tools they needed to achieve the unquestioned goal of the containment of London, if not its eventual dis-mantlement. The public policy initiatives of the Progressives in tearing down slums and putting up replacement housing at the city's edge was reinforced in 1909 by a landmark town-planning act. Many other official commissions, reports, and acts of Parliament would follow to expand the power of the central government over the metropolitan environment.

Moreover, in the wake of the tremendous sacrifices of the common people during the war, Prime Minister David Lloyd George pledged to mount a Homes for Heroes program on a massive scale. Death also struck the upper classes, breaking up their estates and bringing unprecedented amounts of land around London onto the market. Meller estimates that one-quarter of England's agricultural land changed hands after the war. Support for open space around London was widespread, including that of King George VI, who contributed Great Windsor Park to the greenbelt project.[45]

Unlike the Netherlands, however, England had a political culture of top-down paternalism that constrained public policy within boundaries set by the landed elites. In creating the girdle in the 1930s, for example, Parliament subsidized land purchases by local authorities. But it also allowed sellers to set restrictions on the future use of these plots. While some like King George were motivated by a sense of noblesse oblige, many others took advantage of the law to enhance the value of their adjacent properties. And, of course, landlords were free to work with private estate developers, cashing in on rising standards of living that translated into growing demands for suburban homes, at least while the prosperity lasted during the twenties.

The results were haphazard. Although over 68,000 acres (27,520 hectares) were added to the greenbelt during the interwar period, the project did little to stem sprawl. Ironically, the best way to convince the politicians of the indispensable need of urban planners turned out to be their promise to save the countryside. The first academic chair in town planning was held by Patrick Abercrombie at the University of Liverpool. He was a prominent spokesman for lobby groups such as the Council for the Preservation of Rural England and the Garden Cities and Town Planning Association.

Nonetheless, the accumulating force of a market-driven consumer culture overwhelmed the abilities of local planning authorities to respond to suburban visions of the Organic City. Whereas London's population increased by 20 percent, the amount of open space converted to urban use increased by 200 percent, or ten times as much. Formal plans for dismantling the central city achieved similar, mixed results. Escalating construction costs and waning political commitments to the veterans eroded ambitious wartime goals.[46]

For many of the displaced slum dwellers, the gains in improved physical surroundings were more than offset by emotional losses. A top-down political culture that maintained a rigid class structure was effectively deaf and blind to the views of the grass roots. "Because [the planners] were bound to an essentially physicalist conception of town planning," the scholar Nigel Taylor posits, "they tended to view towns and their problems only in physical (and aesthetic) terms. Because of this they simply *did not pay attention to social matters*; their theory of planning prevented them from really *seeing* social issues." Meller concurs that "the drive was to build houses, not to worry about the social consequences."[47]

As England entered World War II, then, the problematic nature of its planning vision for the containment of the urban monster was set. Built models of garden suburbs and new towns represented prototypes that the central government could duplicate with assembly-line efficiency. And like their Dutch counterparts, planning professionals looked at the extensive bombing of London as a golden opportunity for a clean-sweep approach to inner-city renewal.

The new warfare of air power also reinforced the prevailing, antiurban consensus by making the deconcentration of industry a priority of national defense. Several parliamentary commissions on postwar reconstruction translated the planners' grandiose theories into institutional terms. The center-piece was the creation of the Ministry of Town and Country Planning. Per-haps the most influential blueprint of the future, the Greater London Plan of 1944 was the work of Patrick Abercrombie. With his ideas for the dissolution of London enacted in the New Towns Acts at war's end, England set out on a clear, albeit myopic, path toward the Organic City (see Map 2).

Paris, France: The Defeat of Planning

Like England, France had strong traditions of central government power and even stronger practices of bureaucratic control over its localities. In sharp contrast to these traditions, its political culture also cherished a leg-acy of revolution that had enshrined individual liberty. Consider that most countries required mandatory smallpox inoculations during the nineteenth century; France did not. It rejected the requirement as an infringement on personal freedom. In a similar way, public health measures to clean up noto-rious slum dwellings filled with victims of tuberculosis were usually stymied by landlord protests in the courts.

In this long-standing contest between state and citizen, conscious plan-ning during the interwar years would be characterized by drift, default, and defeat. In the seminal work on the subject, Anthony Sutcliff calls it "the au-tumn of Paris." A more recent account by Colin Jones describes the period in similar muted tones as one of "faded dreams [and] lost illusions."[48]

If France's political culture was not enough to deny planners a modernist vision of Paris, then economic depression and political stalemate guaranteed that virtually nothing would get accomplished. Although Parisian officials had mapped the worst slum districts in 1906, little had changed by war's end. The buildup to the conflict and its aftermath left the nation with a deficit of resources to undertake urban renewal projects (see Map 3). Making matters worse, the city was caught in a vice between severe overcrowding and rent

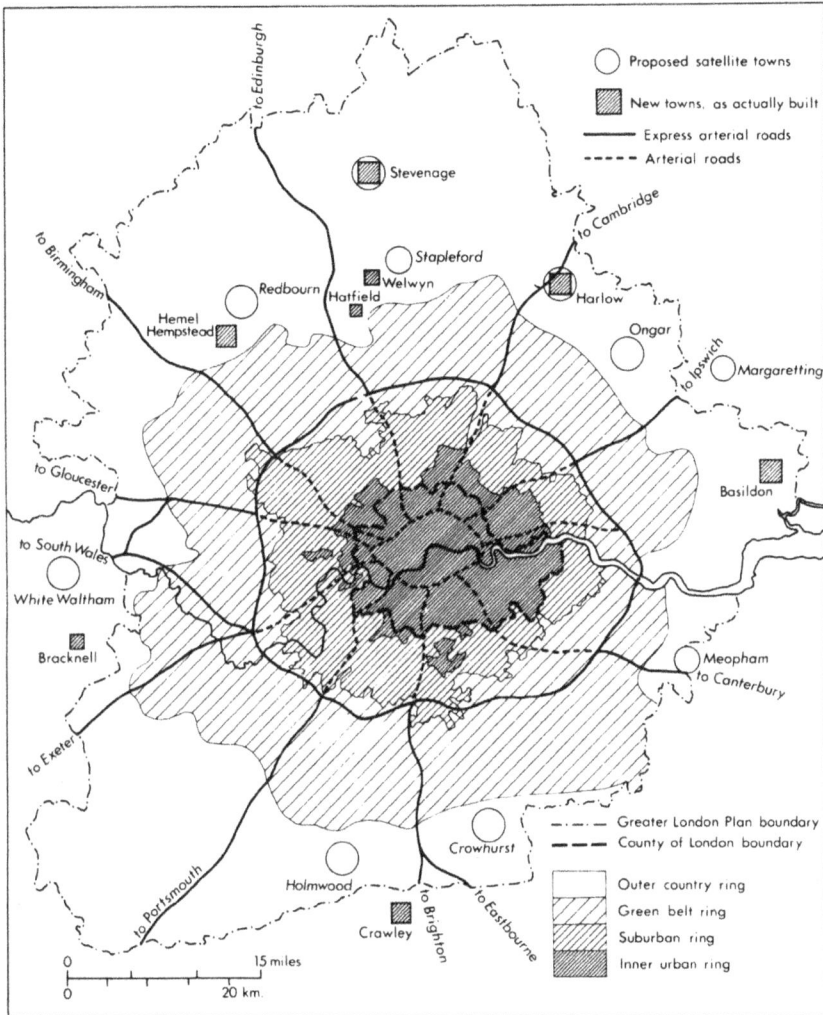

Map 2 London: Greater London Plan of 1944 (Republished with permission of Peter Hall, *Urban and Regional Planning*, 3rd ed. [London: Routledge, 1992], fig. 7.14, p. 198)

control. The resulting housing shortage effectively prevented the local government from tearing down people's homes that it could not replace.

Planners were also tied up in policy hammerlocks of their own. The wrestling for power among city, provincial, and national levels of government meant that by the time any plan gained all the necessary approvals, it was already obsolete. The 1932 plan for Paris, for example, took seven years to be enacted, just in time for the outbreak of World War II. Urban planning remained largely academic in France. Like their English counterparts,

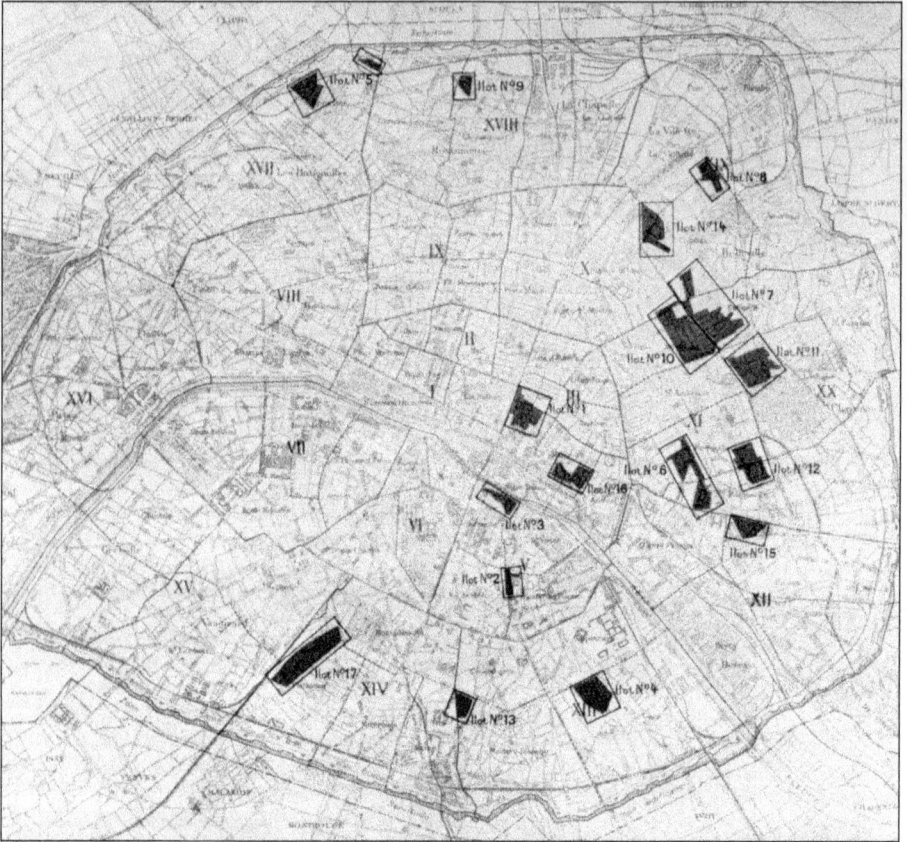

Map 3 Paris: *Îlots insalibres* (insanitary districts), 1919 (Republished with permission of Louis LaCroix, "Les îlots insalibres des Paris," *Urbanisme*, no. 6–7 [September–October 1932], p. 176; note that the original journal is now defunct)

French planners drew broad ideological links between physical design, nature, and social reform.

Weak land-use controls in France, as in England, led to suburban sprawl more than any other change in the urban environment. In the four decades leading up to World War II, the city's population increased 5 percent compared to a 50 percent increase in the suburbs, whose population reached two million people. These peripheral districts included not only bedroom communities for the well-to-do but also working-class zones of heavily polluting factories.[49]

Within the city, historic preservation came into vogue. Groups devoted to saving this old house or that decaying building sprang up throughout elite Parisian society, seemingly in lieu of any real construction activity. Perhaps this fever for preserving the monuments of the empire was fueled by their iconic representations of national glory, now fast slipping away. In any case, clean-sweep planners like Le Corbusier stood no chance against a society in serious embrace of nostalgia. In 1939, however, the rout of the French army by the Germans jarred the ruling classes into facing forward toward an inevitable future of technological catch-up and modernization of society.

Los Angeles, United States:
The Planning of Metropolitan Regions

In the United States, the influence of planners in policy formation underwent a sudden reversal of fortunes during the interwar years. Planners languished on the left-wing fringes during the Republican era, but their reputations were sent soaring during the following Democratic era of the New Deal. As in France, comprehensive clean-sweep planning in the United States remained largely theoretical during the postwar decade. But like their British counterparts, municipal engineers and planner practitioners created a professional infrastructure of academic programs, official positions, and national organizations. State highway and local planning commissions were established in hundreds of places, zoning laws were passed everywhere, and futuristic drawings of the Organic City Beautiful were presented to city councils and chambers of commerce across the American landscape.

But to an extent even greater than in England, a consumer-driven real estate market was the strongest force moving society toward a suburban vision of the American Dream of homeownership. Community builders, public highways, and private automobiles gave physical and social shape to the urban environment on a new, metropolitan scale. The neophyte city planners could, at best, barely keep up with the demand for permits to build and maps of roads, pipes, and sewers that were now prerequisites to opening up new subdivisions on the city's "crabgrass frontier."[50]

Planning historian Robert Fishman furnishes a good description of the exploded and fragmented topographies of the auto city. "Unlike the old cities," he explains, "these new cities had no recognizable centers or peripheries; within regions that covered thousands of square miles they included formerly urban, suburban and even rural elements; their only structure came from the patterns and intersections formed by the superhighway 'growth corridors' that created and sustained them."[51]

Los Angeles was perhaps most evocative in the 1920s of this kind of motorized city of the future. It was an idyllic Garden City: a hybrid space that combined high technology and mastery of a natural Shangri-La. Here was a boomtown paradise, thriving on Hollywood and seniors migrating from the frigid Midwest to the land of sunshine.

The urban economy was further boosted by the discovery of oil and gas, giving rise to heavy industries and manufacturing. Gasoline refineries and auto assembly plants belching smoke became new vistas on the urban landscape. From 1920 to 1940, the city of Los Angeles almost tripled in population, to 1.2 million people. More significant, the surrounding county grew at a faster rate, reaching 2.8 million in 1940 and 4.2 million just ten years later. By then, over half that number lived outside the city limits.[52]

Yet it would be a mistake to see this balloon-like expansion as completely unregulated or unplanned. Like Mexico City, Los Angeles has a drought-prone climate aboveground and an earthquake-prone geology below. Both settlements also endure a hydrological cycle of long dry spells followed by short bursts of torrential downpours. Since both sit at the bottom of steep hillsides, moreover, they have parallel histories of deadly flash floods and epidemics from water-borne diseases.

While every locality is at some risk of natural catastrophe, these two cities serve as case studies of planning for a disaster-prone environment. To overcome their droughts and deluges would require extending an urban infrastructure far beyond city borders into distant hinterlands. During the Progressive Era, reformers in both places initiated regional-scale plans to achieve these goals. They became modern exemplars of what can be called "hydroimperialism," building empires of power and control over vast territories. "Land is just land until it gets water on it," is the way Joseph Jensen, the chairman of the Metropolitan Water District of Southern California, put it at the turn of the century.[53]

At that time, Los Angeles was running out of water. A small river with wide banks had supplied the original source of water to the semiarid settlement. Usually little more than a pathetic stream, the Los Angeles River often burst its banks during the rainy season. As L.A. historian Marc Reisner quips, the perfect animal for this unlikely place would be a "camel with gills."[54]

Like the Dutch, American civil engineers knew that the hydrology of river basins, not political jurisdictions, defined the planning parameters of urban water systems. Moreover, Los Angeles's civic boosters understood that water would be a necessary pump primer to get a growth machine running on a desert landscape. At the same time, a flood-prone cityscape required equal attention to preventing storm runoff from overflowing the myriad channels coming down the hillsides and converging in the downtown area.

In the 1900s, Los Angeles would start planning to create an empire of water on a regional and interregional scale. The incredible success of Los Angeles's hydroimperialism would become the global prototype of urban growth strategies based on the capture and exploitation of water. Surpassing the gravity-fed aqueducts of ancient Rome, Los Angeles built a pipeline 233 miles (375 kilometers) across the desert to a mountain valley. This artificial river would empty a 100-square-mile (259-square-kilometer) lake, suck up its groundwater, and turn the Owens Valley into a moonscape (see Map 4).[55]

The aqueduct turned out to be just the beginning of the desert city's demand for more sources of water from great distances. While Los Angeles was turned into a Garden of Eden, the Owens Valley became a Sinai Desert. Starting with the building of the Hoover Dam on the "American Nile" (i.e., the Colorado River) in the 1930s, hydroimperialism would race around the world to outdo itself, reaching China's Three Gorges Dam by the end of the century. Los Angeles represents a case study in city building that strongly influenced national environmental policy.[56]

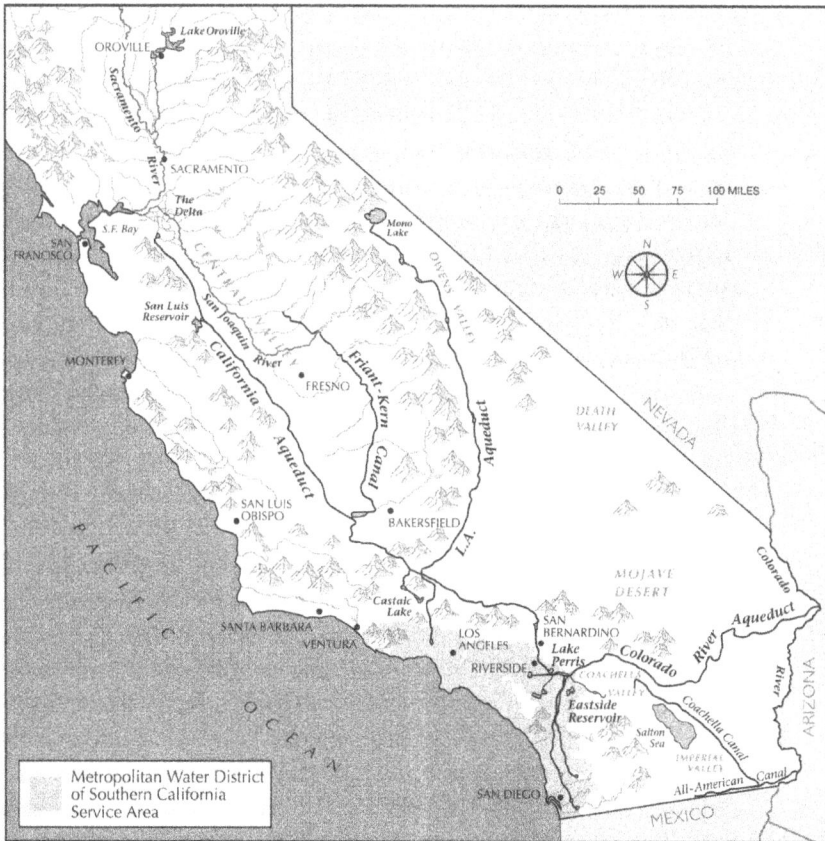

Map 4 Los Angeles: L.A. Metropolitan Water Delivery System (William B. Fulton, *The Reluctant Metropolis: The Politics of Urban Growth in Los Angeles* [Baltimore: Johns Hopkins University Press, 2001 (1997)])

Even before the Great Depression of the 1930s, the ambitions of the L.A. water pharaohs had permeated American government to the state and national levels. Their conservation experts agreed with the city's engineers that every unused drop of water in the West was a wasted drop that needed to be put to work serving useful ends. After years of contentious political battles over the water of the Colorado River, especially with Arizona, Los Angeles triumphed in the U.S. Congress and the Supreme Court.

In 1928, the national government approved the building of the world's largest hydroelectric generator, the Boulder (now Hoover) Dam. The policy makers, moreover, imposed a river-basin compact among seven states that favored California. Forming the Metropolitan Water District, Los Angeles united with its regional neighbors to gain the lion's share of Washington's largess of supercheap power for industry, heavily subsidized water for agribusiness, and abundant drinking supplies for a burgeoning urban population.[57]

Turning promises into progress, the Los Angeles Aqueduct reinforced national belief in the "technological sublime."[58] Under the New Deal, this ethos of conservation took command. The L.A. empire of water was adopted as an ideal strategy for regional planning. It became the environmental template for the creation of the Tennessee Valley Authority. In turn, this massive water and energy project became the prototype for the semiarid West. The hydroelectric generators at Hoover Dam spawned a thousand clones. What Reisner calls "cash register dams," the U.S. Bureau of Reclamation defined as irrigation projects within a holistic context of river-basin management.[59]

Contrary to the myth of Los Angeles as a nonplace of mindless suburban sprawl, then, it was an important seedbed of modernism, contributing to both urban planning and architecture. Beginning in 1913, according to the historian Mel Scott, a Progressive reformer, Gordon C. Whitnall, "almost single-handedly launched an area wide planning effort." He not only got a city planning commission inaugurated with himself as the director but after a decade of tireless work won approval for the creation of the first regional-scale authority, the L.A. County Regional Planning Commission.[60]

The successful collaboration between the city's planning experts and its civic, business, and media leaders brought a measure of control over the growth of this high-risk boomtown. The planners, led by the traffic engineers, created a concrete skeleton, a tree-and-branch framework of highways for orderly private real estate development. For the most part, the community builders followed the planners' prescriptions by adopting Perry's neighborhood unit to the garden suburb template. The very success of their visionary regional plans would help produce the sprawl, congestion, and smog of the postwar period.[61]

Chicago, United States: The Planning of Racial Containment

Chicago represents a second illustration of local initiatives in building the urban environment percolating up the system to become adopted as national policy during the New Deal. In this case study of residential housing, a political culture of racism and corruption combined with the sanctity of property rights to force a minority group of rural migrants into a ghetto. A white, mostly Catholic majority of the grass roots, policy makers, and planners conspired to make race the single most influential factor in determining the growth of Chicago into two separate and unequal urban environments. Discriminatory practices that barred African Americans from the American Dream of upward social mobility through homeownership were cemented into national housing policy for the next quarter century.[62]

Here, we need to take a step back in time to the Progressive Era before we can move forward into the interwar period. A ghetto had begun to take shape during the building boom set off by the Chicago World's Fair of 1893 on the South Side. Until then, the small number of African Americans—less than fifteen thousand in 1890—had lived in small, scattered enclaves near the central business district, or Loop. But they had begun to be excluded from neighborhoods enjoying rising property values and were forced to move to a strip of dilapidated housing running alongside the Rock Island railroad tracks.

As the pace of the Great Migration from the South picked up, the newcomers found themselves boxed in. Civic leaders had an elevated railway (the El) from the city center to the fairgrounds constructed down the middle of State Street to reinforce the color line. As the migrants' numbers soared from 44,000 to 109,000 during the decade of World War I, extralegal, collective violence was by far the white ethnics' most powerful weapon to enforce physical segregation. (see Map 5).

The first wave of African Americans from the South was greeted by a reign of terror, the great race riot of 1919. At the end of that hot July, Chicago itself became a war zone when a black youngster was stoned and drowned after his makeshift raft drifted on Lake Michigan's waters into an area of the beach near Twenty-Ninth Street reserved for whites. Mobs attacked the recent migrants all across the city, but for the first time, blacks fought back. Before the state militia could restore the peace, twenty-three blacks and fifteen whites were killed and over five hundred were injured, and there was property damage costing millions of dollars. Although the resistance of veterans and other "New Negroes" ended any further frontal assaults on the ghetto, this outburst of mob violence set the course of race relations for a generation.[63]

In Chicago, cultural values played an especially powerful causal role in the formation of the land policies that gave shape to its social geography of

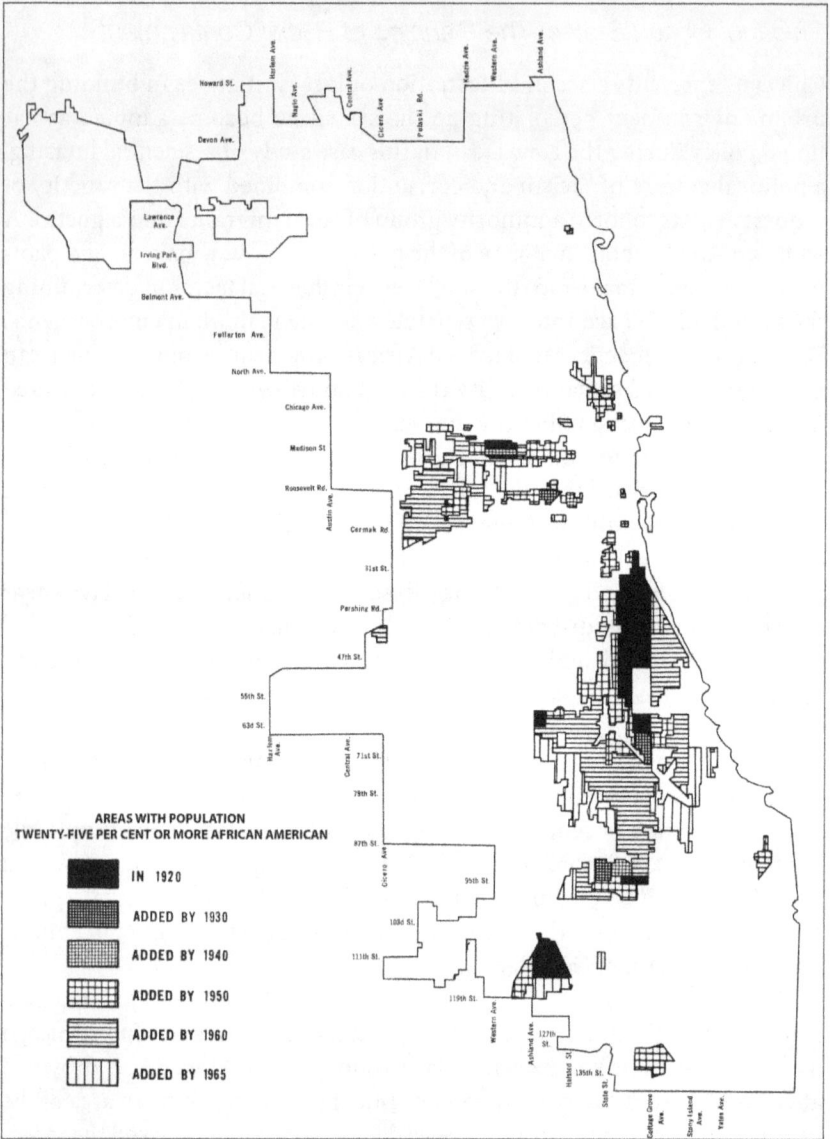

Map 5 Chicago: Expansion of the African American Ghetto in Chicago, 1920–1965 (Harold Mayer and Richard Wade, *Chicago: Growth of a Metropolis* [Chicago: University of Chicago Press, 1969], p. 411)

environmental inequality. Religious traditions of community among Catholics had led the city's bishops to permit each ethnic group to create its own national parishes. A home purchased within a parish became more than a commodity of exchange value; it became a sacred space consecrated by membership in the local congregation. There is no need to question that fears of financial loss from falling home prices drove many Catholics into the streets to repel perceived threats of an invasion of undesirables.

But recognizing additional emotional attachments to place is necessary to account for the resulting howling mobs. In this case, cultural values of religious community became embedded in the extralegal defense of parish boundaries. Immigrant Catholic culture also helped shape Chicago's political culture, giving it a self-perpetuating hierarchy of power devoted to maintaining the color line.[64]

The aftershocks of the street fighting in 1919 led to Bronzeville, the institutionalization of one of the first racial ghettos in Chicago, which became a leader in imposing restrictive zoning. In the early 1920s, the Chicago Real Estate Board created two interrelated systems composed of the city's first zoning ordinance and the organization of white neighborhoods to add restrictive covenants to their property titles barring their sale or lease to African Americans and other ethnic groups. Although the threat of mob action against invasion by a black family was always present after 1919, white homeowners resorted more often to property law to prevent integration. "Unlike other means," Wendy Plotkin underscores in her study of the subject, "covenants were state-sanctioned instruments of discrimination."[65] By 1939, housing expert Robert Taylor estimated, 80 percent of white homes within the city contained them. Both the public and private sectors were armed with an overwhelming force of law to evict "undesirables."[66]

White property owners and public officials not only exercised the law to lock African Americans out of the neighborhoods but also refused to enforce building and health ordinances inside the ghetto. With virtual immunity from prosecution, landlords within the tightly drawn boundaries of the Black Belt became slumlords. They cut down apartments into smaller and smaller units while jacking up rents to exorbitant levels. This open conspiracy of neglect encouraged landlords to make illegal conversions, ignore desperately needed repairs, and allow disease-breeding rats and bugs to run wild. Richard Wright's *Native Son* provides a vivid account of conditions in the slums of the South Side ghetto. The novel begins with a parable of his protagonist Bigger Thomas's confrontation/life with/as a rat being hunted down and sentenced to death.[67]

Driven by the same rage expressed by Wright, black Chicagoans had been fighting back since the 1919 race riot. They had organized under the Republican Party banner and formed civil rights organizations such as the

Urban League and the National Association for the Advancement of Colored Persons. But despite their grassroots campaigns for open-housing laws and equal public services, the residents of Chicago's Bronzeville watched their communities continue to deteriorate into landscapes of despair and misery.[68]

In other words, the period before the New Deal laid the groundwork for the rise of a biracial community, which was pitted against itself on the battlefield of the social geography of the city. What changed in 1933 was not this tug-of-war over the color line between the grassroots organizations of whites and blacks. Instead, the New Deal shifted the fulcrum of power over urban land-use planning from the private sector to city hall. There was a changing of the guard of the defenders of white privilege from the real estate agents and mortgage lenders to the politicians and bureaucrats. They now took charge of setting the ground rules of the housing market, and the making of a Democratic majority was forged out of this ongoing defense of race supremacy. During the twenties, party boss Anton Cermak had built a "house for all [white] people" that brought the previously fragmented and antagonistic groups of European immigrants under a roof of racial solidarity. The Democrats would exploit this new American identity of whiteness to tighten their hold on city hall into a virtual monopoly of power during the years of depression and war. Working closely with the real estate industry, the Democrats under Mayor Edward Kelly fulfilled the Chicago plan of racial containment for a generation.[69]

The most obvious result was packing too many people into the existing housing stock, much of which dated back to the nineteenth century. In the most comprehensive study of the ghetto, Otis and Beverly Duncan called this process "piling up . . . an increase in Negro population without a corresponding increase in living space." Perhaps the worst widespread practice was using cardboard as walls to convert previously spacious apartments into a number of tiny so-called kitchenettes.[70]

The New Deal during depression and war demonstrated the ability of the central government to plan the city of the future. Its policy makers had embraced the planners' ideas for engineering the environment. They were attracted to the "technological sublime" of big systems like hydroelectric dams, highway networks, and new towns. They projected a vision of an Organic City fueled by cheap energy that would produce an exploded metropolis on a regional scale. The New Deal housing acts also set the institutional foundations in the real estate market for residential segregation with blacks in the center and whites in the suburbs.[71]

São Paulo, Brazil: The Planning of the Center and the Periphery

Like Paris, São Paulo represents a Radiant City model of modernism. Taking European ideals of urbanism to an extreme, its civic elites built an environment of stark contrast between the center and the periphery, the haves and the have-nots. As in Los Angeles, what first might appear to be random patterns of rapid urban expansion were in fact carefully drawn plans of class and racial segregation. In this case, they reflected a political culture of extreme hierarchy called "patrimonialism." "The patrimonial order," Roberto P. Guimaraes explains, "is usually referred to by its concrete practices of social control, such as clientelism, patronage, or co-optation, which combine elements of paternalism, repression, hierarchy, and the power to rule and stand above social classes."[72]

After the belated abolition of racial slavery in 1889, São Paulo's planners and policy makers built one of the world's most powerful engines of urban growth. Cementing their patrimonial order in physical space, they would use technology to draw a sharp division between a high security zone of modernity at the center and a surrounding periphery of lawless shantytowns. As the city's population approached a million in 1930, they were forced to redraw their plans on a metropolitan scale. This year marked a critical transition in the growth of São Paulo in several ways in addition to the start of suburbanization. Most important was the creation of Brazil as a modern nation-state under the populist dictatorship of Getúlio Vargas (1930–1945). Before his consolidation of power, the federal government exerted little authority over the states like São Paulo, which had strong local elites. In many respects, their model of urban growth through government-business cooperation became the template for Vargas's project of nation building to transform Brazil into the *Estado Novo* (New State).

Like the success of Los Angeles, the success of São Paulo is based on a plan of hydroimperalism. Both combined cheap labor and cheap energy symbiotically to form the foundation for the rise of great industrial cities. But unlike Los Angeles and Mexico City, São Paulo had a felicitous location on a hilly plateau free of droughts, floods, earthquakes, or other natural disasters, thanks to the Jesuits who founded the city (see Map 6). Establishing their village on the banks of the Tietê River in 1554, the missionaries lived in a humid, subtropical climate blessed with ample soil, rain, and sun. Until the abolition of slavery, it remained a provincial center of the banana and coffee trade. While the subsequent flood of immigrants from Italy, Spain, and Japan fostered a cosmopolitan culture of ethnic neighborhoods, the body politic was kept small and homogeneous. Denied access to a basic education, the nonliterate masses were excluded from the most basic right of citizenship, the vote.[73]

During the interwar years, the commercial center of the coffee trade continued its metamorphosis into an industrial metropolis. Its immigrants came with craft skills or factory discipline to supply a budding manufacturing sector of textiles, food processing, and construction materials. The city

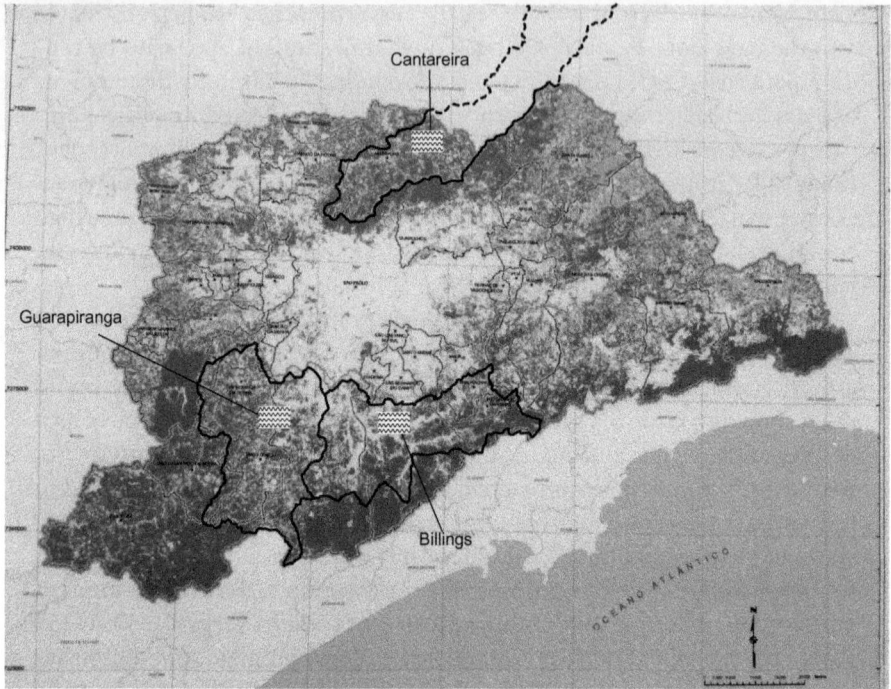

Map 6 São Paulo: View of the Metropolitan Area (EMPLASA [Empresa Paulista de Planeja-mento Metropolitano S/A State of São Paulo Department of Metropolitan Planning], State of São Paulo Government, Brazil)

had also attracted foreign investors during the Progressive Era. Consortiums of British and Canadians, for example, found this urban center an ideal loca-tion to install and operate a complete electrical system.

In the early 1900s, their international agents secured long-term monopo-lies over the region's water resources and the city's utility services. Then, their engineers erected a hydroelectric dam on the Guarapiranga River, and their business managers started the São Paulo Tramway, Light, and Power Company (SPTLPC). Strictly a profit-making venture without a civilizing mission, the private enterprise reinforced a socially constructed topography of exclusion.

The SPTLPC extended services to only the most affluent neighborhoods. The technological modernization of the city's transit, water, communica-tions, and energy systems in these exclusive enclaves significantly increased the gap in the quality of daily life between the haves and the have-nots. The company's handsome dividends spurred the investors to send their team of experts next to Mexico City to put in a hydroelectric network.[74]

Nonetheless, rich and poor Paulistas lived near each other before the 1930s and the advent of highways and motorbuses. São Paulo remained a relatively compact, albeit segregated, walking city. Geographic patterns of social exclusion had deep roots in a colonial society built on racial slavery. The rich lived in privately owned houses, while the poor rented space in communal tenements called *cortiços* (*vecindades* in Mexico City), where families had to cram into tiny, bare apartments and use the courtyard for cooking, washing, and sanitation. Stigmatized as low class, *cortiços* surrounded the factories, which peppered the central district.

The natural topography of São Paulo reinforced the policing of social and spatial distance between the classes. Buildings tended to be sited on the ridges of the rolling hills stretching out from the Tietê River, creating open spaces in the valleys between them. Even before the coming of the electrical revolution, the upper classes were importing the ideas of Progressive reformers about germ theories of disease and public health. They began moving to modern houses in streetcar suburbs with telling names such as *Higienopolis* (Hygiene City). They also brought in the British architect Barry Parker, who had been Raymond Unwin's collaborator in building the world's first garden suburb.[75]

But as this multiracial and multiethnic population approached a million people, policing the walls of segregation in public spaces became increasingly difficult. Moreover, the city's stark division between haves and have-nots had forced its most desperate inhabitants to occupy the areas at greatest risk of environmental disaster from flash floods and contaminated water. They had erected their *construçãos* (self-built homes) along the riverbanks and railroad tracks and at the bottoms of the rolling hills. Piped water and sewerage had been denied to their favelas, and the squatters' wastes polluted the Tietê River, the city's traditional drinking water source. Combined with swelling amounts of industrial effluents, it had become by default, the city's ultimate sink.

In response, the business and technocratic elite set into motion a new plan that would redraw the lines of spatial segregation between a highly ordered center and an anarchistic periphery. The planners and policy makers used zoning laws and building codes to remap the social geography into the city and the borderlands. Within the heavily policed central district, exclusive status was enforced by minimum housing standards. They were carefully calculated to cost more than the lower classes could possibly pay. The planners also began bulldozing highways and providing buses to force them to move out of the old neighborhoods and into cheap illegal subdivisions and free public land outside the swelling security zone.

Local leaders also installed a new generation of technology that not only restructured the urban economy but also reconstructed the spatial walls of segregation between the rich and the poor. The SPTLPC provided an alternative source of piped water for the upper classes by tapping into its Guarapiranga Reservoir. To offset the loss of hydroelectricity, its Canadian owners also invested in the construction of a second power plant, the Billings Dam. Its giant turbines stood poised to provide cheap energy to the industrial suburbs that were beginning to take root outside the protected central zone.

Inside the central zone, the planners and policy makers continued to tighten building codes and bulldoze highways through working-class neighborhoods that connected the downtown to the suburbs. In 1941, moreover, they effectively ended private investment in the traditional *cortiços* when they imposed a rent freeze as a temporary wartime measure. It would last for the next quarter century. Speculators in suburban real estate took advantage of the instant shortage of affordable housing by operating bus lines with low fares to lure potential buyers out to their (illegal) subdivisions.

At the dawn of Brazil's economic miracle during 1930s, São Paulo was already undergoing a metamorphosis into a city of homeowners divided into two completely different ecologies of everyday life.[76] Planners and policy makers used the highway and the autobus to begin a new phase of deconstructing a claustrophobic city of ethnic neighborhoods into a fragmented city of physical walls. São Paulo's civic elites had become increasingly insecure living in such proximity to worker districts after immigrant radicals led a series of labor strikes and political uprisings.

Factory owners responded by relocating their plants in distant suburbs. Their workers were forced to either move closer or endure long, two-to-three-hour bus rides each way commuting from the inner city. "Progress and modernity ended where the bus line began," São Paulo experts Nabil G. Bonduki and Lúcio Kowarick relate, "[and] from there it was a long wait, an overcrowded bus ride, a walk home from the bus stop through the mud, candlelight [at home], and contaminated water from the well in the backyard."[77]

National policies also promoted the resettlement of São Paulo's working classes to the suburbs. During the 1930–1940s, the Vargas regime turned the federal government into a growth machine by greatly enlarging its involvement in new industrial ventures. Applying import substitution policies, it squeezed profits out of agricultural and mineral exports to pay for the machines and experts to build a domestic consumer economy.

Despite their loss of political power, Paulistas were the major economic beneficiaries of the regime's policies. The public production of an industrial infrastructure leveraged private investment in manufacturing and urban development. The central government's technobureaucrats also promised to supply these mostly foreign-owned enterprises an army of surplus labor. A by-product of the squeeze on farm incomes was an internal migration to the city. The army and police promised to guarantee the social peace. At war's end, São Paulo's elites positioned their city to become the center of this national plan of modernization.[78]

Mexico City, Mexico: The Formal Plans of Informal Planning

During the interwar period, Mexico experienced a political revolution rather than an economic transformation like Brazil's. Overthrowing the dictator Porfirio Díaz in 1910, Mexicans paid a heavy price for the ensuing twenty years of civil war. A recent assessment calls this upheaval a "demographic catastrophe," costing the nation over two million lives. Arising out of the conflict was a political party run by army generals that took the reins of power. In 1929, the PNR (Partido Nacional Revolucionario [Institutional Revolutionary Party], later the PRI) was formed by President Plutarco Elias Calles to clamp a monopoly on electoral access to national office. In a client-patron, or godfather, system of personal relationships, party leaders would keep their hands on the levers of government power for the next seventy years.[79]

By gaining a handle on the national government, the PNR also took charge of Mexico City, which in 1920 had become a special federal district. As the national capital, Mexico City had long been privileged over other urban centers. For over six hundred years, it was truly an organic city in the sense of the evolutionary pace of change of its urban environment. Unlike most modern cities in the Western Hemisphere, it is old. In 1325, the Mexica, or Aztecs, had planted a city on an island in a lakebed that sat at the bottom of a closed crater-like valley more than a mile up in the mountains. They developed ingenious technologies and sophisticated aquacultures to take advantage of the basin's closed hydrologic cycle.[80]

However, the coming of the Conquistadors from the arid middle of Spain in the early 1500s changed all that. They were horsemen, and they immediately began filling in the drainage canals to get across them. For the next three hundred years, the inhabitants would suffer from too much water. Mexico City gained the dubious reputation of the unhealthiest national capital in Latin America. From July to September, the city suffered more or less flooding and contamination of drinking supplies with sewage, causing epidemics. Outside the historic center, or *El Centro*, the Spanish rulers took the highest ground and gained control of the most pure natural springs, which were located in the Chapultepec area on the west side. They also imposed spatial segregation by ethnicity/race, herding the native population into the low-lying Tepito district on the north side.[81]

From the start of European settlement, then, environmental inequalities of water set Mexico City's patterns of land use. In the absence of an official plan, the city developed residential suburbs for the upper classes in

the American style of private subdivisions on the relatively hygienic west
and south sides. The indigenous population and other poor people were
crowded into *vecindades* in the most hazardous zones on the north and east
sides. Each generation of city engineers attempted to control the seasonal
inundations and each generation failed, with flooding and public health
emergencies becoming more frequent and widespread with the outward
growth of new suburbs.[82]

Finally, during the Progressive Era, technological modernization took
command of the urban environment. Throwing hydroimperialism into reverse, Mexico City exported its wastewater to distant hinterlands. Under
the long dictatorship of Porfirio Díaz (1884–1911), the engineers were given
enough funds to fulfill their recurring dream of cutting a hole through
the mountains to get rid of the city's sewage (see Map 7). They bulldozed
a thirty-mile ditch with an ironic title, the Gran Canal de Desagüe (Grand
Drainage Canal), through working-class districts and built a six-mile tunnel that channeled the wastewater under the northeast rim of the valley and
down the Tula River Basin toward the Gulf of Mexico.

"The project," the scholar Emily Wakild remarks, "took on symbolic
political meaning. It provided Díaz and his advisors with the possibility of
controlling nature, saving the city from disaster, and guaranteeing the future
of the capital as a safe, healthy, and beautiful place."[83] During this period,
known as the Porfiriato, technological modernization also took the form of
a piped-water supply for downtown businesses and affluent homes.

Water drawn from shallow wells in courtyards was a traditional source
of drinking supplies. In a privilege also dating back to the Aztecs, the elite
had access to the coveted fresh springs most conveniently located in the foothills on the west side. These supplies were purified by a natural process of
recycling through the waterlogged subsoils under the original lakebed.

But in the 1880s, the engineers began tapping deeper fossil pools of water
with powerful steam-powered pumps to keep pace with growing demands
for more water. Within twenty years, the springs and wells dried up as the
water table began dropping at rates faster than the shallow aquifers were
being recharged with rainwater. Consequently, an alternative method of
supply was required for Mexico City's half-million inhabitants and budding
industrial sector. In 1905, four years after the opening of the Gran Canal,
Porfirio Díaz inaugurated piped-water service to the neighborhoods of the
upper classes.[84]

Unfortunately, his grand designs for reengineering the hydraulic environment quickly proved shortsighted. A mere four months after the opening
of the main drain, the hubris of the planners became painfully evident when
flooding overwhelmed their greatest achievement. Only two months later,

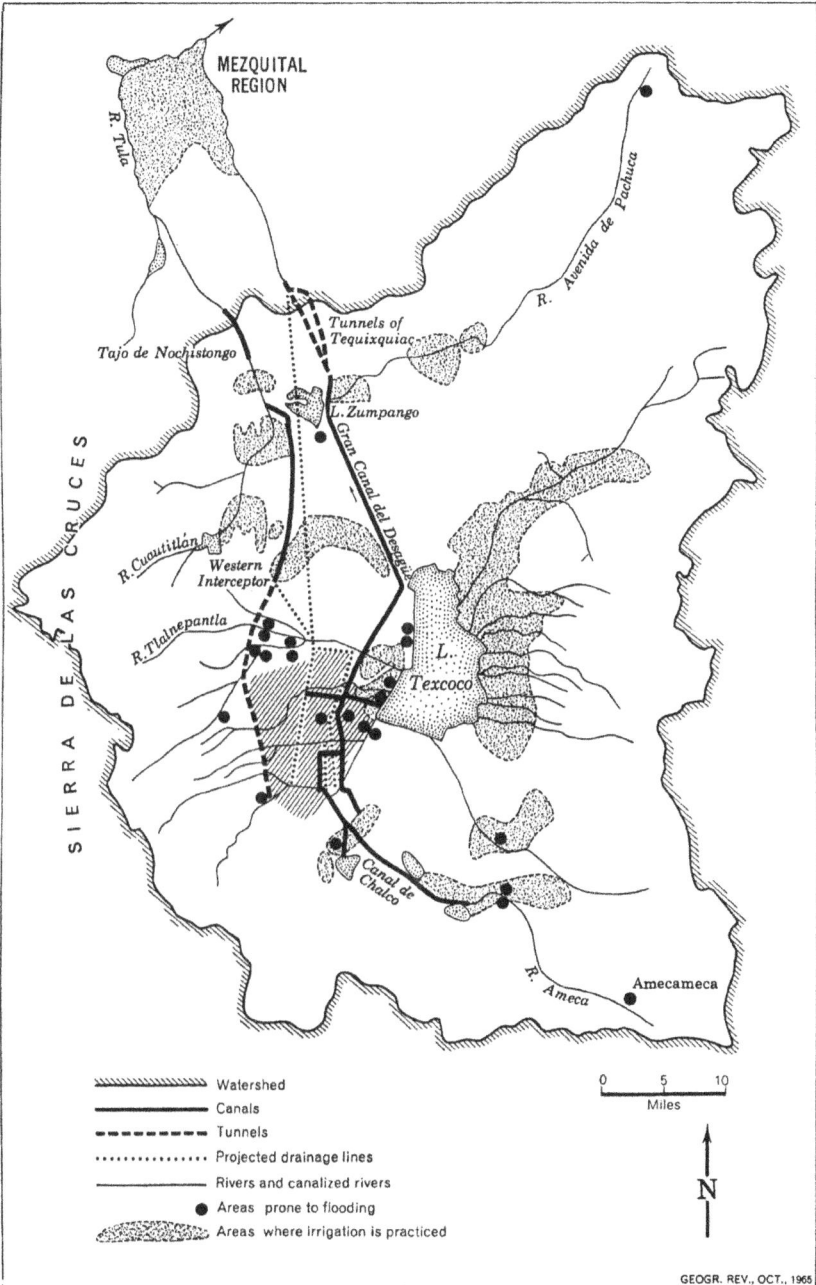

Map 7 Mexico City: Drainage System of the Basin of Mexico (David J. Fox, "Man-Water Relationships in Metropolitan Mexico," *Geographical Review* 55 [1965], fig. 414, p. 542)

another deluge again proved too much for it, causing streetcar platforms to disappear under the *aguas negras* (black waters) and disease rates to soar.

For the next half century, flash floods would return each rainy season to shower misery, sickness, and death on the lower classes living in the central city. Those forced by severe poverty to live near the always stinking, leaking, and often overflowing Gran Canal suffered the most. The canal's infamy in the annals of environmental injustice would eventually become a global scandal. *Newsweek* renamed it "the Canal from Hell."[85]

During the Porfiriato, the reengineering of the valley's hydrologic system had even greater perverse consequences, turning a hazardous environment into a full-fledged landscape of catastrophe. As a hydrologic scientist describes it, "The subsidence of Mexico City is one of the most remarkable cases in all the world." Exporting large quantities of water from the basin while withdrawing irreplaceable amounts from the deep fossil pools caused the city to sink at disastrous rates. Ground zero, *El Centro*, dropped twenty-nine feet (almost nine meters) in just a century.

The subsidence had begun long ago but was so gradual that it went unnoticed until the end of the nineteenth century. In the mid-1920s, a sewer construction engineer, Robert Gayo, blamed the cause of the subsidence on the Gran Canal for draining the aquifers' natural sources of recharge. In 1948, a geologist shifted the blame for the underground compaction to the city's pumps. They had increased their rate of extraction eighteenfold since Díaz had turned on the tap.[86]

Even less visible than subsidence was the slowly sinking city's biological links to the past in the form of the original peoples living just beyond the central square in the Tepito district. They trace their bloodlines back to 1521, when Hernán Cortez conquered the Aztecs and forced their ancestors to live in this area of *El Centro*, segregated from the Spanish. From 1900 to 1940, Mexico City experienced a threefold increase in population, to 1,650,000 inhabitants. Then the city overflowed with newcomers during the boom times of the forties to 3,250,000 people.[87] Nonetheless, Tepito remained a residential district of working-class dwellings. And its residents (*colonos*) were still engaged in service trades, street vending, outdoor markets, small shops, and handicraft trades near the Zócalo.[88]

Despite this urban explosion, formal planning had less influence on Mexico City than any of the other six case-study cities. Here the real estate market ruled without any constraint from the public sector until the 1920s. To be sure, there were monumental public works like the Haussmann-inspired Paso de Reforma of the mid-nineteenth century, but this grand boulevard merely reinforced the traditional separation of the city's rich and poor districts.

During the Díaz dictatorship, moreover, the technological modernization of *El Centro* further hardened the spatial gap between the social classes.

"If anything," the historian Diane Davis observes, "the *Zócalo* and the monumental state buildings that graced the area served to reinforce the social divisions that had long characterized the city."[89] After the establishment of the federal district in 1920, professional planners finally got a foothold in local government. But they accomplished very little over the next decade beyond setting up a planning commission and enacting basic zoning laws and building codes that helped stabilize the real estate market.[90]

The PRI's political culture of clientelism kept the technocrats out of the inner circles of power. Public policy was not a party goal, as opposed to fulfilling its promises of government benefits on a personal basis. Until the late 1970s, its leaders would portray planning experts as dangerous competitors threatening to undermine the party's political authority.

Davis puts their influence in the formation of policy in reverse proportion to increases in their training and standards. "In fact," she points out, "one might go so far as to say that the more formalized and powerful planning as a profession became, the more neglected were downtown areas of the city." They would come through the first half century with a lone modernist skyscraper. *El Centro* would retain a Baroque, if decaying, facade of colonial splendor.[91]

In effect, conscious formal planning for the overall benefit of the city ran counter to the party's number-one goal of self-perpetuation. The PRI kept control of the government by doling out public favors on a personal basis to its loyal legions. Planning as deal making between individual clients and party fixers meant that the plan for Mexico City was to have no comprehensive plan at all. Its metropolitan environment would continue to evolve under the piecemeal accretion of the subdivisions being built to meet the insatiable demand for more places to live.

Conclusions

The nation-state played a pivotal role in mediating between the global and the local. In each of the seven case-study cities, the national government acted as a prism that filtered international forces through a lens of political culture and institutional structures. The world began to shrink rapidly at the end of the nineteenth century, creating a more interdependent stage of human activity. Its scale and scope were demonstrated in not only the destructive power of two world wars and a Great Depression but also the constructive achievement of building megacities.

The national timing of industrialization played a large role in dictating the corresponding pace of the great global migration from farm to factory. London, Paris, and Rotterdam were already big cities with an imperial reach by the mid-1800s, with Chicago following over the next half century.

From 1900 to 1950, Los Angeles, São Paulo, and Mexico City entered the first stages of mushroomlike growth. But more important, these cities and many more around the world were all moving in the same direction. They were all becoming increasingly integrated in transnational webs of economic and political power.

Of course, the active role of these very cities in turning a world of nations into a global village represents the flip side of the story. From this point of view, concentrations of wealth, information, and transportation in central places allow decision makers to extend their reach at great distances across the globe over the lives of vast numbers of people. The origins of modern urban planning is a good example of an international movement arising out of an intellectual and cultural milieu among city-based social reformers and critics. The consolidation of a consensus behind an International Style of architecture and design during the interwar years provides further illustrative proof of the crucial role of the cities in the process of weaving the world into a single global society.[92]

While each city in the case studies had its own reasons for pursuing a policy of technological modernization, they would all jump on the bandwagon of the International Style after the war. "At its center," James C. Scott sums up, "was a supreme self-confidence about continued linear progress, the development of scientific and technical knowledge, the expansion of production, the rational design of social order, the growing satisfaction of human needs, and not least, an increasing control over nature (including human nature) commensurate with scientific understanding of natural laws."[93]

Every nation wanted to showcase its revitalized downtown and new superhighways leading to high-tech industrial parks and satellite suburbs. In the pell-mell after 1945 to get to the promised land of a better life, national governments would give design-based planners an extraordinary opportunity to influence the formation of public policy on building the urban environment. As we have seen, they thought they were well prepared to take on this task of translating academic theories into practical programs.

Their hands-on experiences in wartime operations research to improve supply logistics further inflated their insular sense of scientific certainty. They were eager to take on the job, which in their minds required the total reconstruction of nature, society, and the built environment. They had convinced themselves that only they had the expertise needed to envision the future metropolis.

After decades of disappointment, they proclaimed anew that the Organic City was just over the horizon. One such visionary was Frank Lloyd Wright. As the war was winding down in 1945, he published *When Democracy Builds*.[94] It was his blueprint for utopia: "Broadacre City." To be historically correct, it was an updated version of his 1924 book *The Disappearing City*. In his long career, these two decades might be considered the lost years, compared to his notoriety and commissions before and after the interwar period.

Wright was angry because trend-setting Americans had passed him over for the Europeans and their design-based versions of modernism. Undaunted, he was as self-assured as ever that he alone could clearly see the roadmap of environmental determinism leading to a "Free City of Democracy." "Our share in all the Americas," he asserted, "cannot longer afford to be without that [prophetic] interpreter of humanity—the Architect."[95] Such an authoritarian proclamation did not seem to bother the would-be master builder of the ideal, free society of the future.

For Wright, the future pointed toward the complete dismantling of the megacity. For him, its twin evils were skyscrapers and suburban sprawl. Echoing Raymond Unwin's *Nothing Gained by Overcrowding*, the architect tied the two evils together as the cause of insufferable highway congestion. Wright deserves credit for foreseeing a coming nightmare of gridlock. "If gridiron congestion is already crucifixion," he asked rhetorically, "what will the 'gridiron' be like in a few years as time multiplies Machine Age success?"[96]

But Wright was no Luddite. On the contrary, he had long embraced high technology: electric power, motorcars, and mass production. These were the essential tools the modern architect-planner needed to renew a healthy relationship between the land and the people. In Broadacre City, town and country, farm and factory, shopping mall and civic center would all be seamlessly integrated on an endless highway from coast to coast. Returning to his favorite metaphorical symbol, Wright expressed ultimate confidence that he had seen the master plan. "With Organic Architecture," he prophesized, "Man is a noble feature of his own ground, integral as trees."[97]

2

Running the Modernization Race, 1945–1960

Introduction: The Cold War and the Modernization Race

The year 1945—the end of World War II and the start of the Cold War—is remarkable also because it represents the urban planners' special moment. They saw the final defeat of the Axis powers as the dawn of a new day of hope. Frank Lloyd Wright was not alone in seeing visions of the Organic City in the morning light of peace. The promise of realizing dreams deferred for a quarter century stirred war-weary societies around the world to rally behind planners' models of the city of the future.

The postwar generation also looked to their national governments to lead them to prosperity as they had to victory. Policy makers applied current Keynesian theories to create Fordist production and mass consumption. Two of their most powerful tools were underwriting the cost of new housing and public works such as highway construction and slum clearance. Across Europe and the Americas, planners were put in charge of a massive project to reconstruct and renew the cities.

They drew ultramodern pictures of an Organic City in the International Style of design-based architecture and planning. While its leaders disagreed on many questions of aesthetic values, they shared a much more important mind-set of assumptions about society, the built environment, and nature. This collective vision gave them tremendous self-confidence in themselves and their finished blueprints of the future metropolis.[1]

For the next twenty years, this imaginary of high modernism became a template for imposing Le Corbusier–like makeovers: tower blocks, industrial parks, and garden suburbs strung together by high-speed motorways. Whether bulldozing old neighborhoods in the center or raising new towns at the edge, policy makers everywhere echoed the Frenchman's pronouncement: "The plan must rule." For the profession's leaders such as Le Corbusier, Eliel Saarinen, Mies van der Rohe, and Walter Gropius, of course, these were heady years of vindication and media-star status. What needs to be explained is why policy makers across the Atlantic world suddenly decided in 1945 to hand over so much power to such a relatively small, inbred group of academics.[2]

The simple answer is Cold War politics. The cities became pawns in a high-stakes game, a race of technological modernization. As bipolar tensions heated up between 1945 and 1950, high modernism in the Western bloc of nations was turned into a weapon in the propaganda war against the Eastern bloc. The planners' vision of the Organic City became an icon of technological progress and economic success. As with the arms race and the space race, urban environments rebuilt into places of soaring skyscrapers and zooming highways became potent symbols in the psychological gamesmanship being waged between capitalism and communism. Each escalation in ideological tensions brought a corresponding rise in the stakes of what I call the "modernization race."[3]

Unfortunately, building the urban environment is more complicated. The West's grand strategy of containment in the Cold War abroad was mirrored at home in the efforts of planners and policy makers to confine women to the domestic sphere of life. Reflecting male perspectives, they assumed that women would be happy to give up their wartime jobs and refocus their lives on the family. Spawning a baby boom, the postwar generation of parents blurred the boundaries between political ideology and family values. But containing women to the private realm paradoxically empowered them to become the legitimate representatives of children in the public realm.

Michelle Nickerson demonstrates that the mobilization of the middle-class suburbs in patriotic defense against communism abroad and at home put white, conservative women in the vanguard of community organizers.[4] The Beach Boys' "little old ladies from Pasadena" were anything but homeward bound in the no-passing lanes of contemporary civic life. Furthermore, their grassroots activism shows that Betty Friedan misrepresents them in her 1962 exposé *The Feminine Mystique* as contained within the domestic realm and isolated from each other.[5] A more accurate group portrait is a motion picture of "housewife populism" that rose up to resist getting run over by the city's growth machine.

Tracing their activism back to working-class ethnic neighborhoods during the interwar period, Nickerson links their maternal, communal, and antielitist attitudes to the Mothers' Movement, as it became known during the Cold War. To protect their homes and families, conservative suburban women believed they now had to move up to the frontlines as the moral guardians of the community. Rather than a backlash, their insurgency was driven by fear of invasion from the outside world. "Although they would be considered 'reactionary' or 'paranoid' by many . . . ," the historian underscores, "they believed that subversion flourished because of apathy and naiveté and that Communism appealed to people's passions and discontents, rather than to reason."[6]

In the process, they created "a vigorous female political culture." They took positive steps to warn their neighbors about the menace of the international communist conspiracy and the equally threatening imposition of a socialist-type collectivism by the national government. Working to organize their communities, these women were ready to take the offensive when these godless forces of subversion threatened their communities. Their grassroots activism would play a central role in the mobilization of place-based movements from the bottom up. In many stories of insurgent planning history, they would form the spearhead of reform. Women would get involved in public education, community health programs, library reading lists, and recreational activities.[7]

In contrast, the bipolar struggle of the Cold War kept pushing the male-centric world of the planners closer to the pinnacles of international power and money. It also boosted the prestige of two closely related academic disciplines that further solidified the planners' credibility among policy makers. These two branches of systems theory divide the artificial and the natural into cybernetics and ecology. During World War II, military leaders had learned that better computers and their underlying mathematical algorithms were not needed to run just the modern machines of war. They had become essential to national defense, especially in the new age of the atomic bomb.[8]

The fighting might have stopped on the battlefield in 1945, but the United States, the USSR, and other countries continued to shower money on academic experts in such previously obscure fields of study as communications, information systems, and games theory, in addition to operations research, virtual simulations, and robotics. In the life sciences, similar programs of enriched support for ecosystems research and population studies also brought rapid advances in analogous mathematical and computer models. Furthermore, the career officers of the military and the civil service were themselves coming increasingly from the ranks of these academic disciplines. Government bureaucracy became a technocracy, setting in motion a self-reinforcing point of view.[9]

Gains in systems thinking bolstered the professional planners' claims of scientific neutrality for their ever more comprehensive clean-sweep designs of metropolitan regions. Just as biologists could conduct experiments with increasing precision on open systems like ponds and forests, urban planners presumed that they too were getting better at manipulating physical space and the behavior of its inhabitants. In the boom times of the postwar period, they never paused to question the social assumptions and ethical values that formed the underpinnings of their environmental determinism. From their Olympian perspectives, the proponents of high modernism all drew the same roadmap of technological modernization as the only way to get to the Organic City.[10]

The International Style became a complicated exchange of ideas across the Atlantic about urbanism. Ironies of Cold War politics abound in this transnational discourse. Consider how Bauhaus émigrés Gropius and Mies were German exports to the United States during the 1930s, but their architectural values became American imports when they helped remake postwar West Berlin into a showcase of capitalism. Or consider the transatlantic influence of Brazilians Lúcio Costa and Oscar Niemeyer. They not only planned Brasília, the world's most complete Le Corbusier–like city, for their native country but also designed several significant buildings in Europe. Niemeyer's French Communist Party Headquarters in Paris, for example, became an instant icon of the most avant-garde aesthetics of modernist design.[11]

The onset of the Cold War in 1945 would usher in the golden age of planning. Images of the urban environment became one of the most important markers of which side was winning, capitalism or communism. Forced onto the ideological battlefield, the social and physical conditions of the city became propaganda weapons. While each side bragged about its tallest skyscrapers and fastest highways, it also broadcast exposés about the other's slums and ghettos. Thrust into the midst of this bipolar contest, planning experts would be given extraordinary influence in the formation of public policy. For a generation, the International Style of modernism would rule as the cities of Europe and the Americas experienced explosive physical expansion, economic development, and social change.

The contestation among the grass roots, planners, and policy makers over the production of urban space became part of the Cold War debate over the future of the world. For over a decade, the critics of technological modernization had been sharpening their attacks from general assaults on capitalism to focused advocacy of specific city plans and environmental policies. Consider the engagement of the most corrosive cynic of high modernism, Jane Jacobs. She got involved in the midfifties, when New York's all-powerful planner Robert Moses proposed bulldozing an expressway through her beloved Greenwich Village neighborhood.

But these voices of dissent would fall on deaf ears within the planning profession and mass media until the frightening cry, "Burn, baby, burn," pierced the comforting white noise of construction cranes and cement mixers. In August 1965, the planners would suffer a stunning fall from grace that equaled the rapidity of their rise to power twenty years earlier. The long-standing weight of the critics finally broke through the insular walls of the academic elites, isolated like Renaissance princes in the safety of their ivory towers. Their downfall came, according to one historian, "when urban civil disorder and advocacy planning blew the old methods of value-neutral planning to pieces." Taking its place would be a new "pluralist era."[12]

By taking a careful look at the pivotal year of 1945 and the twenty years that followed, we can begin to sort out the successes from the ultimate failure of the International Style of urban planning during the Cold War era. In the so-called first world nations such as Britain, France, the Netherlands, and the United States, urban renewal and housing construction became powerful instruments of national economic planning. Policy makers declared that a standard of living based on the mass production of high-tech consumer goods proved the superiority of capitalism over communism. In the so-called third world countries such as Mexico and Brazil, policy makers adopted modernism in planning and architecture for different, but no less important, political purposes as tangible symbols of national progress and postcolonial independence.[13]

Transnational Discourses:
The Cold War and the Atomic Bomb

The Triumph of Modernism

At the end of 1944, when Frank Lloyd Wright was imagining the Organic City of the postwar era in his studio in Wisconsin, Le Corbusier was doing the same thing in France. With the liberation of Paris in October, he was able to close the books on his disgraceful and humiliating relationship with the fascist Vichy regime and return to the apartment he had built twenty years earlier. When he arrived, British journalists sought out his predictions about the reconstruction of Europe's cities, and Le Corbusier spent the next several months answering their questions. When the journalists' project to publish the predictions failed, Le Corbusier looked for a French publisher. A few years later, he had his book with his answers about the future of Europe's cities translated into English as a short book, *Concerning Town Planning*.[14]

Le Corbusier proclaimed "the dawn of the neo-technic era." What he meant by this is worth unpacking because it helps explain why so many people subscribed to his vision of the Organic City. Borrowing the term from Patrick Geddes, the visionary projected a fantastic dream of modern technology bringing harmony between society and nature. Like Lewis Mumford, he believed that advanced transportation, energy, and communications networks would integrate the three functional zones of each region: farmlands, suburban "linear industrial" strips, and "radio-centric cities of exchange."[15]

"Man has made mockery of the provisions of nature," Le Corbusier railed. "The conditions of nature," he argued, "must be re-established in men's lives for the health of the body and the spirit." Decades of depression and war, rejection, and perseverance had mellowed the iconoclast. Now he proposed bulldozing only the slums while preserving the historic fabric of the urban cores.[16]

Le Corbusier's vision of utopia—the Organic City of technological automation—was bigger than Burnham's and Wright's. From his earliest futuristic images of "a contemporary city of three million" in the 1920s, he had implored his cousin and lifelong collaborator, Pierre Jeanneret, "We've got to do these drawings carefully, old man, we've got to go all the way."[17] Burnham in his 1909 plan of Chicago had indeed made "no little plans."[18] The plan's power was in the very detail of the graphic images of Chicago that dressed his ideas in the mantle of neoclassicism and science. Wright's Wasmuth Portfolio had also presented a big idea by breaking through stylistic conventions of historicism to create a truly novel organic architecture: prairie houses with strong horizontals, ribbon glass, and open interiors.[19]

Yet Le Corbusier emerged as the master illusionist of the twentieth-century city. He captured the popular imagination, cutting across several generations and international cultural barriers. He was a perpetually optimistic Pied Piper of the technological fix. "Perhaps no other architect of the modern movement so consistently exemplified its motivating spirit," the historian Norma Evenson comments. "Above all, the movement embodied a mood of hope, a genuine belief in progress and in a new efflorescence of human vitality."[20]

His drawings of superhighways and steel-and-glass skyscrapers became emblems of the International Style. While these once-futuristic images of the 1920s became everyday realities in the postwar era, the enduring success of Le Corbusier's ideas about urbanism stem in large part from their systemic qualities of flexible design and functionality. "Space is treated as an undifferentiated whole to be structured," Paul and Percival Goodman explain, "[and] the profile against the sky is the chief ordering of space and the prime determinant of feeling."[21]

More than anyone else, Le Corbusier helped others envision this skyline, this future of technological automation. He took an Olympian perspective on the city as a cybernetic machine in perpetual motion.[22] From such a distance, he could project appealing silhouettes of his "city of flows" but leave all the details out.[23] "The peculiar genius of the Modernist city plan lies in its 'empty vessel' quality," the architecture expert Michael Dear contends; "anyone can pour identity or signification into it."[24]

In the hands of Le Corbusier's best disciples like Mies van der Rohe, the apartment high-rise became molded into a pure expression of the "empty vessel." Mies, a German émigré, settled into Chicago's Armour Institute, which became the Illinois Institute of Technology, on the near South Side during the war years and set up a private architecture firm. Severe housing shortages soon translated at war's end into a building boom and commissions for his firm.

Mies's twin-tower apartment buildings at 860 North Lake Shore Drive became the master template of high modernism. They are the prototypes of the exposed I-beam and smoked-glass skyscrapers that have since become ubiquitous in the global megacity. In principle, they are based on Le Corbusier's original 1915 idea of the Dom-ino house that "less is more." The genius of this design turns out to be relatively low-cost construction and a high percentage of open floor space. It has load-bearing exterior beams that hold up concrete floors unobstructed by other posts or beams.

Expressing the ideal of mass production, Mies insisted on identical cladding for the duplicate, twenty-six-story towers, and he left the insides of the apartments completely bare. Since the walls separating the interior spaces were not load bearing, floor plans become infinitely flexible.[25]

But unlike Wright's idea of it, organic architecture for European-trained modernists meant the internally holistic. And like Le Corbusier's conception, the science of spatial proportion was Mies's sacred mediator of harmony between society and nature. To them, according to the scholar William Jordy, "'organic' [meant] design is utterly integral with structure and each part clearly articulated and defined in its working relation to all other parts within a harmonic order."[26]

His signature Lake Shore Drive Apartments provide an illustration of a man who was obsessed with overseeing every detail of building design but blind to the environmental setting. Mies demanded total control. He created the furniture for the public areas and ordered that all the window curtains be exactly alike in the private spaces. He went as far as installing clever curtain rods that allowed only three positions: open, half-open, and closed.

At the same time, he was oblivious to the buildings' privileged site on Lake Michigan. They are perfectly symmetrical and have no balconies or windows that open widely to take advantage of a beachfront location. As far as Mies was concerned, they could have been put anywhere, because they were organisms complete unto themselves. The scholar Detlef Mertins agrees that "they are at once pure technical forms, based in the structural logic of steel, and pure forms of Euclidean geometry, harmonically proportioned and ordered. They are autonomous organisms in both the technological and artistic sense."[27]

Yet this very blindness to natural site, when combined with mass production ubiquity, is what gave this type of skyscraper its generic appeal as a safe bet for investors. It was relatively cheap and easy to build using unskilled workers. Moreover, the skyscraper's skeleton on the inside of reinforced concrete or steel I-beams offers developers a wide range of options to make fashion statements on its outside, non-load-bearing skin.

On the larger scale of the metropolis, Le Corbusier's postwar version of the Organic City incorporated ideas about urbanism from both sides of the Iron Curtain. He borrowed from not only Geddes's technological eras of history and regional scale of geography but also Wright's linear vision of suburbia, Broadacre City. In addition, he had absorbed Russian Constructionists' ideas about a more industrially oriented complex of factories and worker housing stretching along a parkway of motor and rail lines. His concentrated Radiant City evolved into a sprawling space of endless movement among three functional zones: the city center, suburban periphery, and rural farmland.[28]

But still scorning the Anglo-American garden suburb, he continued to concentrate residential living in clusters of high-rise apartments. The cities would serve as the centers of information, commerce, culture, and tourism. Their location, the iconoclast turned preservationist conceded, was largely fixed by history. "Future cities are in general also ancient cities," he allowed.[29]

Le Corbusier's perennial success as the chief apostle of high modernism is completely at odds with his chronic failure as an architect and city planner. In the postwar period, this gap between theory and practice remained as large as ever. Although he mostly received rejection slips, he won a commission that should have been the capstone of his career. In 1947, the partition of India left the state of Punjab without an administrative center. The leaders of the new third world nation seized the opportunity to make a statement proclaiming their postcolonial independence and their aspirations to first world status. They asked him to build a capital city from the ground up.

Hiring a world-renowned Frenchman represented an important step toward making a complete break with India's past. Le Corbusier was told to erect an international showcase of high technology. Up rose Chandigarh, a modernist city on a desert plain in the shadow of the Himalayas. Rarely visiting the building site, he honored one of his core principles: he was oblivious to India's social and natural environments. In a culture dominated by pedestrians and street markets, for example, Le Corbusier designed a highway system for a motor traffic density equivalent to that of Los Angeles.

By remaining disengaged, he ended up erecting a time-bound monument to the International Style rather than a liberating "machine-for-living" for the one million inhabitants of the city.[30] He failed to follow his own prime directive to place top priority on the small individual dwelling and the big metropolitan plan. The family home and the overall transportation system, he had always maintained, were the key physical components in achieving the architect's ultimate goal of human scale. Strangely, he left these crucial tasks to Pierre Jeanneret and others.[31]

Instead, Le Corbusier concentrated on what he had previously judged least important, the city's monuments. He composed an ensemble of giant-scale landmarks. This complex of government buildings dwarfed pedestrians, who were baked by the sun as they crossed huge empty spaces to get from one office to another. Moreover, the Baroque-like capital zone hovered over the rest of the low-rise city, which also suffered from too much open space.[32]

For contemporaries, nonetheless, Le Corbusier drew the most convincing roadmap to the Organic City for all the true believers in the holy grail of technological modernization. Despite his tiresome diatribes against the chaos of auto congestion, he was secretly the man behind the wheel. This point of view, of the driver commanding a powerful machine traveling at high speed, was perhaps the decisive source of his appeal to the twentieth century. In the mid-1920s—Marshall Berman has dug out of the archives—Le Corbusier was transformed by the personal experience of driving a car. "The perspective of the new man in the car," Berman found, "will generate the paradigms of twentieth-century Modernist urban planning and design. The streets belong to traffic; he gets rid of the pedestrians and the streets [become] 'machines for traffic.'"[33]

Le Corbusier became the ruling visionary for a mass culture that had fallen in love with the automobile and the highway. Consider that within just a decade following the war, Americans more than doubled the number of cars on the road, to 54,000,000 vehicles.[34] His still images of the city in motion captured the spirit of the age: the freedom of the open road. In the twentieth century, the car became the "individual adventure machine," according to the historian Gris Mom, an "adventure of technology." The force of his vision of a cybernetic "city of flows" overcame his weakness as an architect and urban planner.[35]

Le Corbusier had to leave it to others like Mies, Gropius, and Saarinen to translate his ideas into silhouettes on the skyline. In the post-1945 era of the Cold War, these European émigrés to the United States had far more opportunities to gain commissions than their counterparts back home for several reasons. Of first importance was the simple equation in the private sector between wealth accumulation and pent-up demand for new residential and commercial space, including a massive exodus of the white middle class to the suburbs. Lots of Americans flush with cash from wartime profits could not wait to pour their money into downtown skyscrapers and suburban subdivisions and shopping malls.

Equally important was the determination of Harry Truman's administration (1949–1953) to turn the real estate market into a peacetime engine of economic growth. Vastly expanded New Deal housing programs, the GI Bill, and other legislation ramped up coverage of home mortgages by Federal Housing Administration (FHA) underwriters. Congress also approved additional funding for public housing construction and beefed-up powers for local authorities to clear slums and form urban renewal partnerships with private developers.

The Cold War added momentum to the race to modernize American cities with the latest technologies. In the name of national defense, the Dwight Eisenhower administration (1953–1961) turned New Deal roadbuilding projects into the most ambitious public works plan in history. The interstate highway network not only linked all the big cities without a stoplight but also paved the way for white flight to FHA-subsidized homes in the suburbs.[36]

At the same time, the propaganda eyesore of the shame of the ghettos in the North's industrial centers meant bipartisan support in Congress to rehouse African Americans displaced by the urban renewal bulldozer. Civil rights activists took advantage of the Cold War struggle for the third world by bring the conditions of the slums to the attention of the media. The swelling momentum of this grassroots insurgency added political pressure for urban reform.

Denunciations of urban renewal as a disguised form of ethnic cleansing, or "Negro removal," by leaders of urban popular movements further leveraged the global contest between the United States and the USSR to local advantage. Money began pouring into city planning and housing departments from the national capital. They were charged with building as many dwelling units as fast as possible and putting them wherever they could.[37]

The Cold War even engaged the high-brow world of art and architecture in the bipolar struggle for the hearts and minds of the third world. In the United States, New York City presumed that the international capital of the avant-garde had moved from Paris to Manhattan. As we have seen, the Bauhaus émigrés had already arrived to the acclaim of New York's cultural elites. Many other architects and artists would follow in the postwar era. Those in favor were then given international promotion by the Central Intelligence Agency and other propaganda arms of the national government.[38]

Perhaps no one had done more to promote the fortunes of these transplanted architects and designers in the United States than Philip Johnson. In 1947, he mounted an important exhibition, a tribute to Mies, at New York's

Museum of Modern Art. The architectural critic turned practitioner said thirty years later, "I thought of it as hagiography, exegesis, propaganda—I just wanted to show that Mies was the greatest architect in the world." He had to work hard because there were precious few examples of built projects to display before the real triumph of the Lake Shore Drive Apartments.

Nonetheless, Johnson's stamp of high-brow approval helped steer clients worldwide seeking a recognized architect for signature buildings toward Mies and his fellow academic apostles of the International Style. Within Western bloc nations, policy makers and planners embraced high modernism and its promise to bring technological harmony between society and nature. Exchanging ideas between Europe and the Americas allowed Le Corbusier, Mies, Niemeyer, and other leaders of the International Style to create a single vision of the Organic City.

For Mies, the success of the twin apartment towers fed on itself. In 1950, he began work on a nearly identical pair of tower blocks for the adjacent property to the north of his signature Lake Shore Drive apartments. Three years later, he would receive the culture capital's official seal of approval with the commission for the Seagram Building, the office-tower equivalent of the residential skyscrapers in Chicago. Furthermore, his Illinois Institute of Technology graduates found jobs in the Chicago-based architectural firm of Skidmore, Owings, and Merrill, which would have an increasing global reach in designing very tall buildings. If the disciples of Le Corbusier dominated architecture and city planning after World War II, it was because his images of a cybernetic city of flows resonated so deeply within so many people across generational, cultural, and national boundaries.

The Critics of Runaway Technology

The champions of the International Style of modernism prevailed during the Cold War despite their critics, who tended to cluster in two camps: the Jeremiahs of a Malthusian "plundered planet," and the prophets of a technological apocalypse of computers run amok.[39] Until the urban crisis of the midsixties, however, their common message of concern about mindless consumerism and runaway technology was heard only within relatively small circles of intellectuals. After, their voices of dissent became the springboard of an eco-populist uprising among young people that resounded worldwide in the city's streets from Watts to Chicago, Paris, São Paulo, and Mexico City.[40]

Both camps' assault on high modernism was nurtured in the new frontiers of thought about technology and culture that opened up during the interwar years at Germany's University of Frankfurt Institute of Social Research. Its scholars had used Marx and Freud to discover a fresh method of seeing, a "critical theory" to take on both modern corporate capitalism and orthodox Stalinist communism.[41] But their political affiliations caught the attention of the Nazi censors, forcing them to flee to the United States as had their fellow socialists (and Jews) in the Bauhaus School. During the war, two of the Frankfurt School's leaders in exile, Max Horkheimer and Theodor W. Adorno, wrote a seminal book about the unintended consequences of Western civilization's drive to gain control over nature.[42]

Dialectic of Enlightenment shed new light on how technology and society create each other. Like all the others mentioned below, these two German-Jewish critics were deeply disturbed by the suicidal tendencies of Hitler's grassroots movement and the irrationality of the masses that led to the Holocaust. In their grief and isolation, they asked, Why did modern civilization contain the seeds of its own destruction? How could a nation built on the Enlightenment's rule of reason end up marching under the Nazi banner?[43]

Their answers rested on a historical narrative that puts technology in the center of the drive to replace myth and magic with a single, unified scientific point of view. While it proved a powerful way of gaining mastery over the environment, it also led to an increasingly closed-minded technological society. "What men want to learn from nature," they argued, "is how to use it in order wholly to dominate it and other men. That is its only aim. Ruthlessly, in spite of itself, the Enlightenment has extinguished any trace of its own self-consciousness."[44]

The technological construction of society, in other words, comes at a price. In simple terms, they believed the "Enlightenment is totalitarian." The scientific method required an increasingly narrow definition of reality to fit nature within a single system. "To the Enlightenment," Horkheimer and Adorno asserted, "that which does not reduce to numbers, and ultimately to the one, becomes illusion."[45] Society had become spiritually uncoupled from all the other qualities of nature.

This disconnect erodes the authority of the scientific method as just another belief system. The two scholars attempted to explain contemporary society's one-dimensional understanding of nature and the environment. In the wake of the rapid advances in weapons of mass destruction during the war, it should come as no surprise whom the naysayers of technological modernization blamed for a world on the brink of nuclear annihilation. They pointed the finger at the scientists in charge of this macabre work: the biochemists, high physicists with their theories of everything, and systems theorists.[46]

In one camp were the forecasters of a biological catastrophe on a global scale. The science of ecology generated new perspectives in sociology, philosophy, and ethics. "[While] the Newtonian view encouraged hierarchy and rigidity, standardization and uniformity," the historian Stephen Toulmin states, "an ecological perspective emphasizes, rather, differentiation and diversity, equity and adaptability."⁴⁷ The pioneers in these new ways of seeing attempted to draw out the logical implications of nature's self-regulating and interdependent systems of balance and change.

Two of the early postwar frontiersmen of environmentalism were science-trained practitioners turned writers. Fairfield Osborn, the author of *Our Plundered Planet* (1948), worked for the New York Zoological Society. He updated Thomas Malthus's equations showing that geometric increases in the human population were rapidly depleting the soil's fertility. Like his early nineteenth-century predecessor, Osborn painted a picture of hell on earth from mass starvation, biblical plagues, gruesome epidemics, and genocidal wars of forced migration.

But the zoologist also presented a more reasoned approach to the relationship between society and the environment. Ecology had taught him that "all the component parts in the machinery of nature are dependent one upon the other. . . . This is a primary fact and there is no other comparable to it in importance."⁴⁸ The lesson Osborn learned from science was the inescapable need for humans to work in harmony with the environment rather than engage in its current "silent world-wide war" against it.⁴⁹

Aldo Leopold is considered the patron saint of the modern environmental movement in the United States. The author of the movement's bible—*A Sand County Almanac* (1949)—was a Yale-trained naturalist who worked for the Forest Service as a wildlife ranger in the West. In the 1920s, Leopold had traded in his rifle for a typewriter after shooting a wolf and watching the spark of life drain out of it. His epiphany led him to see predators as essential parts of the wilderness. Moving to a farm in Sauk County, Wisconsin, he began to search for ways to demote the human race to a more humble position in the planet's community of life.

What he found he called the "land ethic." Following in the literary footsteps of Henry David Thoreau, Leopold used such deceptively plain language as to almost obscure the profound meaning of the words. Like Osborn, Leopold had learned the "primary fact" of ecology: the interdependence of all living things. He included the earth's entire biosphere in the simple term "the land." "In short," Leopold wrote, "a land ethic changes the role of *Homo sapiens* from conqueror of the land-community to plain member and citizen of it."⁵⁰

In this role, people had to assume the educational task of reimagining the natural world from a utilitarian concept of economic commodities to something deserving respect in its own right. Neither Osborn nor Leopold were optimistic for the future. Yet both put their hopes in teaching the lessons of the life sciences in order to change social attitudes toward the proper balance between the built and natural environments.

In the other camp were the Chicken Little alarmists of an impending takeover by machines gone berserk. In the new age of atomic annihilation, the Goodmans reminded readers of what they already knew, "the future is gloomy." Their 1947 book *Communitas* raised questions about whether a society that placed blind faith in technology to fix its problems could see the unintended consequences of its well-meaning projects to gain control over nature.[51]

To forestall the coming of a latter-day Frankenstein, they sought ways to demote technology and technocrats to more humble positions in the process of social reform. The Goodmans had little faith in the experts' ability to handle modern technology without doing more harm than good. To them, these self-styled social engineers had bloated opinions of their power to change behavior by manipulating the environment. "Most physical planners vastly overrate the importance of their subject," they protested; "in social change, it is not a primary motive. When people are personally happy it is astonishing how they make do with improbable means."[52]

Although the academic prophets of doom hardly made a ripple in the mainstream media, widespread fear of runaway technology found popular expression in the tremendous commercial success of Hollywood's science-fiction films of the fifties. The ideas expressed by the critics of the modernization race tapped into a broad undercurrent of social anxiety about the Cold War. A whole genre of B-grade movies played on widespread apprehensions that the atomic bomb tests might accidentally unleash forces of evil beyond the control of their creators. The tests, of course, served as a tame surrogate for the real nightmare of an atomic war between the United States and the USSR.

The first of these Hollywood fantasies, *The Beast from 20,000 Fathoms*, became a classic. It would spin off a whole new genre: the giant-monster horror film. In the original gem, an atomic test in the Arctic Circle inadvertently unleashes a gargantuan dinosaur by releasing it from the ice. Like all the Godzilla-like monsters to follow in its path, the beast knows instinctively to immediately head to a large urban center.

The film-noir mood underlying all these sci-fi fantasies was a feeling of insecurity that mirrored the dark realities of the midfifties, the peak of Cold War paranoia. Both the arms race and the race of technological modernization fed underlying social anxieties about machines run amok. In the movies at least, great harm was the inescapable result whether they were set loose by accident or design. Each movie played out the unspeakable scenario of the need to prepare the public for martial law and military occupation of the cities in case of an alien—read Russian—attack.

Horkheimer and Adorno had anticipated that fear of runaway technologies would be one of the main by-products of postwar modernism. "The noontide panic . . ." they write, "in which men suddenly became aware of nature as totality has found its like in the panic which nowadays is ready to break out at every moment: men expect that the world . . . will be set on fire by a totality over which they themselves have no control."[53] In the sci-fi flicks, the Dr. Frankenstein stand-ins for evil usually came cast in parts played by the current celebrities of progress, the scientists. In contrast, urban planners avoided being portrayed by Hollywood in the role of madmen out to blow up the world.

But they could not escape entirely from being painted in slightly less damning hues by the critics of the modernization race. They began to see planners and policy makers as like-minded technocrats bent headlong on a similar misguided course of destruction in the name of progress. In 1957, William H. Whyte Jr. put together in a special issue of *Fortune* magazine one of the most perceptive early collections of critiques of the postwar city. As with the release of the sci-fi movies about the same time, reactions to the massive changes at home took about a decade to crystallize into a coherent response. Among the contributors was Jane Jacobs, who would draw national attention for her counterattack on city planners titled "Downtown Is for People."[54]

Whyte called the issue "The Exploding Metropolis." Echoing the Goodmans, he issued a warning against the planning experts, labeling them "anti-city" suburbanites. Their large-scale redevelopments of row upon row of Mies-like apartment towers, he charged, were "sterile and lifeless," alienating the very people who loved the city.[55] "Today it is the standard design for every kind of big housing project, for rich or poor—the wrong design in the wrong place at the wrong time."[56]

Whyte asserted that the postwar boom presented an opportune time for the renewal of city life, but planners and policy makers were producing just the opposite effect. "Large-scale action is necessary, to be sure," Whyte offered, "but little plans, lots of them, are just what are needed." He appealed to elite businessmen to become more involved as both private investors and civic leaders in reorienting the perspectives of city planning from the skyline to the street corner.[57]

In contrast, Jane Jacobs called on ordinary citizens to stop planners from wrecking the city. She was a freelance writer who had become an editor of *Architectural Forum*, contributing pieces on New York City. She too was appalled by the new developments. "These projects will not revitalize downtown; they will deaden it. For they work at cross-purposes to the city. They banish the street."[58] To fix the problem, she implored, "you've got to get out and walk. Walk, and you will see that many of the assumptions on which the projects depend are visibly wrong."[59] At the street-level view of the pedestrian, the life of downtown sprang from its chaotic diversity and unpredictable encounters.

According to Jacobs, the God's-eye viewpoint of the planning experts was rooted in reductionist impulses to unify urban space. To draw their clean-sweep blueprints of the Organic City, they consolidated the streets into superblocks. But in the process they created a self-contained, virtual reality that turned good intentions inside out. "Believing their block maps instead of their eyes," she stated, "developers think of downtown streets as dividers of areas, not as the unifiers they are."[60] More sinister, she predicted, was the totalitarian processes of policy making by which the planners' false reality became the real thing. "The image was built into the machinery," Jacobs observed, "[and] now the machinery reproduces the image."[61]

In her opinion, moreover, Whyte was turning in the wrong direction for help in changing the course of public policy. Rather than looking to the top strata of society, any hopes of saving the city rested at the bottom, neighborhood level of grassroots activism. Ironically, her appeal appeared in a magazine aimed at an elite audience of corporate and financial managers. To be sure, the articles in *Fortune* reached a wider and more influential readership than the more academic books of their fellow critics of modernism. But during the height of the Cold War, neither group of critics could shake the confidence of planners and policy makers in the power of technology to fix the urban environment and secure the national defense.

The Ascendancy of Systems Thinking

For two decades following 1945, the voices of dissent against the modernization race were swallowed up by the tsunami of media attention given to technological advances, scientific breakthroughs, and organizational revolutions. Spectacular results began splashing across new color TV screens by the midfifties, beginning literally with a big bang, the successful test of a hydrogen bomb. A stream of equally impressive, albeit less explosive, reports about the steady march of progress became a regular part of the evening news. Remarking on each step with which the West moved ahead of its communist rivals, the media pumped out stories about computers, robots, nuclear power, miracle plastics, communications networks, pharmaceuticals, management techniques, and even modern architecture. In May 1961, for example, Le Corbusier appeared as "Corbu" on the cover of the popular American newsmagazine *Time*. Riding this tidal wave of public opinion in favor of technocracy, urban planners enjoyed unprecedented influence in the formation of public policy.[62]

Equally important in their rise to power was their close association with the ascendency of fields of science, which were leading the way in systems theory. The spigot of defense dollars that boosted research in these academic disciplines during the conflict was opened wider during the Cold War. The Allies' funding of the modernization race that had helped defeat the Axis powers was not only vastly expanded but also extended to the life sciences of ecology.[63]

What tied urban planners to the system theorists and the eco-scientists of the Cold War was their conflating of the natural and built environments into organic metaphors. They perpetuated the age-old body-machine analogy rather than looking at the city as a hybrid space and a site of social life. The human body has often been depicted in mechanical terms, while machines and cities have an equally long history of metaphorical tropes as living things with their own metabolisms and morphologies. During the Cold War, systems theorists and eco-scientists reversed the body-machine analogy, ushering in a truly new information age. Rather than tailoring mechanical devices to mimic human bodies, they began reducing the natural environment to a circuit board of electric switches.[64]

In a similar conflation, the postwar planners presented models with built-in feedback mechanisms that appeared to naturalize the human made into an autonomous "city of flows." By offering to "make the visible invisible," they handed policy makers a potent means of social control without political accountability.[65] The planners assured policy makers that they could not only predict the shape of the coming city but also shape the behavior of its inhabitants. It did not take a rocket scientist in the postwar culture of the modernization race to see the close parallels between urban planning and systems theory. "Systems theory, above all," the critic Andrew Ross comments, "provides the most extended basis for comparing a biotic to an urban environment. It provides a language which casts the 'metabolism' of the urban system as subject to control mechanisms."[66]

Brief biographies of two mathematical geniuses will help us get a handle on the novelty of this way of looking at the real world as bubble diagrams and energy flows. In each case, these scientists hoped their work would help integrate society and nature into a state of equilibrium. They believed that technology and science could open the way for the rise of a new type of Organic City. They envisioned an eco-city, a human community in self-sustaining balance with the environment.[67]

The first story is fittingly about the inventor of the term "cybernetics," Norbert Wiener. Born in 1894, he was the son of a Harvard professor. A child prodigy, he graduated college at age fourteen with a degree in mathematics and then earned a doctorate in philosophy. After World War I, he took a position teaching mathematics at the Massachusetts Institute of Technology.

After the outbreak of World War II, the War Department asked him to build a computer that could aim and fire an antiaircraft gun. Modern bombers flew so fast and so high that humans were no longer able to calculate where to shoot. To create a robot to replace the gunner, Wiener worked the body-machine analogy back and forth, using the nervous system as a design model. Focusing attention on the feedback mechanisms that coordinate the eye, brain, and hand, he realized that control and communications were inseparable.

In 1948, he announced the opening of a new way of seeing. "We have decided to call the entire field of control and communications theory, whether in the machine, or in the animal," he proclaimed, "by the name cybernetics, which we form from the Greek [for] *steersmen*."[68] With the technological breakthrough of the electronic vacuum tube replacing the mechanical switch, his colleagues at MIT could begin building superfast thinking machines. As Cold War tensions mounted, the work continued to make them smarter and smarter. Each generation of computers was needed to design the circuitry of the next.[69]

Wiener, however, felt that cybernetic research put him and his fellow scientists in a "not very comfortable" moral position. Were they extending the power of the brain, he wondered, or giving birth to a Frankenstein of automation that would degrade the value of life for most people? He underscored the revolutionary potential of the "automatic factory" and computer-centered office to devalue work.[70] In the case of the antiaircraft gun, for instance, the gunner's role was degraded from that of a heroic warrior-hunter to a mere tender of the weapon's radar and reloading equipment.

Society would have to make a choice. His greatest worry was about the propaganda campaigns of the modernization race being mounted by the cold warriors. He feared they would drown out alternatives to marketplace solutions. "The answer of course," he concluded, "is to have a society based on human values other than buying or selling."[71]

The subject of the second biography is representative of the systems thinkers who transformed ecology after 1945 into a mathematical science of statistics. The scholar Sharon Kingsland shows how the Cold War sharply changed the direction of research in this field of study. "Not only were ecologists becoming versed in quantitative and statistical biology," she explains, "but in collaboration with mathematicians they were turning also to more esoteric branches of mathematics which were growing quickly during and after the war years. These included systems theory, information theory, mathematical programming, and game theory." Born during the war, this new branch of science sought "to establish cybernetic 'system' representations of whole ecosystems," according to her colleague Chunglin Kwa.[72]

These metaphors of self-contained organic machines appealed to policy makers, who drew their own analogies to the total control of society and the environment. No one was more fervent in advocacy of the new turn of science than Robert H. MacArthur. Like Wiener, he was an academic brat, the son of a geneticist. Born in 1930, he was too young for the war, growing up with a "love for the natural world, birds, and science, in that order," according to a good friend.[73] Pursuing these passions, he earned a doctorate in math at Yale University in 1957, took a year of additional fieldwork in ornithology at Oxford University, and then joined the faculty at the University of Pennsylvania. During his year in England, he published "On the Relative Abundance of Bird Species," an article that would instantly establish his reputation as the leader in the mathematical modeling of nature. "He had the kind of 'superbrain' charisma commonly enjoyed by celebrities in physics," according to the environmental historian Donald Worster.[74]

MacArthur made two related contributions to the creation of a cybernetic model of nature that reversed the organic-machine analogy. First was the theoretical tour de force of reducing entire ecosystems to a few equations. As Worster puts it, "Nature would appear as a machine, and true science, [MacArthur] argued, is always 'machinery oriented.'"[75] The second was throwing the scientific method into reverse by presenting the speculative hypothesis first and promising as an afterthought that empirical research would prove its statistical predictions.

For MacArthur, discovering patterns was the key task; it meant seeing each individual historical event or actor blurry eyed in order to see only enough of it to create a repeatable model. It was exactly this kind of systems analysis of complex social populations that the technocrats in the Defense Department loved to nurture with support grants during the Cold War. What sold them was the thought of gaining control over global ecologies and national societies.[76]

Linking ecosystem science and ideas about urbanism was the University of Chicago's human ecology school of sociology and one of its students, Homer Hoyt. He would create the intellectual bridge between modernist visions of the Organic City and practical policy making in the postwar era. He would make the visible hand of human agency over real estate markets into the invisible, an autonomous city of (capital) flows.

In and out of government from the early 1930s until his death in 1969, Hoyt would become the single most influential proponent of an organic theory of the life cycle of urban neighborhoods. Joining the Home Owners Loan Corporation and FHA in 1933, the land-use expert had directed the project that created the secret "Residential Security Maps," with their infamous redlining of "hazardous" investment zones. During the war, Hoyt returned home to apply his "sector analysis" to a new complete survey of land values for the Chicago Plan Commission. It, in turn, became the basis for new land-use and building codes. Hoyt designated fourteen thousand acres (5,666 hectares) of the South Side ghetto, which housed almost a million people, a "cancerous blight" and zoned the entire area for clean-sweep demolition and "renewal." He continued to influence the city's development patterns through a long-running series of newsletters for the First Federal Savings and Loan Association of Chicago.[77]

Moreover, Hoyt's ecological theories played a major role in defining the 1949 and 1954 national housing acts. His systems approach to urban development represents a case study in the influence of the local on the national and the global. It was within a cultural context of post-race-riot Chicago that Hoyt went back to school when he lost his fortune in real estate after the 1929 crash of Wall Street. Retooling from practicing attorney to land economist, he was well prepared to reenvision the businessmen's and the planners' now conventional visions of the Organic City in terms of the social scientists' novel models of human ecosystems. His teacher, Ernest Burgess, in his 1928 paper on residential segregation, had called for further investigation of the ways racial succession affected land prices and rents. In Hoyt, he found the perfect researcher.

What the economics student believed he found in the sociologists' models of the life cycle of neighborhoods was a scientific way to predict future land values. Analyzing a century of them in Chicago, he adopted his teachers' representations of the city as an open-ended ecosystem. "Stemming from a strong Darwinist tradition and basing its model on a comparison of urban development and plant biology," Calvin Bradford posits, "the human ecology model suggested that just as certain pieces of land are best suited for a particular type of plant, so urban areas and neighborhoods are inhabited by persons most suited to those areas. When one plant takes over land previously occupied by another species, the 'invading' plant, as it was called, drives out the original inhabitants because the invaders are better suited to that environment."[78]

Hoyt's contribution was a way of seeing the city that applied a systematic method of not only evaluating the current value of each city lot but also predicting its future mortgage risk. This way of envisioning the city in organic metaphors as a living thing would soon become one of the foundation stones of the New Deal's revolution in national housing policy. Of course, efforts to impose order on the urban land market's anarchistic "weave of small patterns" long predate the University of Chicago's school of sociology.[79] In 1899, for example, Adna Ferrin Weber's *The Growth of Cities in the Nineteenth Century* put historic and geographic demography on a new level of statistical sophistication.[80]

During the period leading up to World War I, moreover, the Progressives' debate on the future of the city crossing back and forth across the Atlantic was filled with ring and radial plans of expansive development. At the street level too, city people had their own mental maps of class, racial, and ethnic boundaries that helped them navigate the city. Perhaps Jane Addams's door-to-door, block-by-block maps of her near West Side neighborhood best captured some of this street-level perspective at the turn of the century.[81]

Building on the work of real estate appraiser and fellow Chicagoan Richard Babcock, Hoyt studied the history of the city's cycles of boom and bust. His analysis boiled down a long list of physical conditions of a property to its average monthly rent, which was ultimately a measure of class. He also incorporated Burgess's concentric rings of urban growth into the land appraiser's model. To account for the sociologist's radials of racial/ethnic expansion, Hoyt sliced through the rings with his sector analysis of racial/ethnic succession.

Reflecting the cultural viewpoint embedded in the real estate industry of Chicago's strategies of racial containment, Hoyt's ecological system portrayed the life cycle of neighborhoods in terms of Herbert Spencer's social Darwinism, not Darwin's evolutionary biology. While the culture-and-personality school of racial/ethnic difference might have been gaining the ascendancy in intellectual circles during the 1920s and 1930s, older ideas of a hierarchical Chain of Being coexisted in the popular imagination, including real estate underwriters.

Reverse engineering Chicago's Residential Security map, the historian Jennifer Light shows that race/ethnicity was the single most important factor in rating the neighborhoods into good and bad investment risks.[82] Using a survey of the real estate men's views of neighborhood succession, Hoyt constructed a hierarchy of racial/ethnic groups ranging from those having the least to those having "the most detrimental effect" on land values. Tied for first place were English, Germans, Scotch, Irish, and Scandinavians, with Negroes in ninth place, below southern Italians but above the very worst possible next-door neighbors, Mexicans.[83]

Hoyt's views of urban society in terms of a struggle for survival trumped his beliefs in scientific models of human ecology as the causal agent of neighborhood succession and decline. Drawing on what Paul Boyer calls "moral environmentalism," he blamed the slums of the transition zones on the failings of its residents. Consistent with a worldview straight out of a Dickens novel, Hoyt put the life cycle of neighborhoods on a teleological path of entropy. In sharp contrast, Burgess had put neighborhood succession in the nonjudgmental, neutral language of plant ecology. Racial/ethnic change from one group to another would lead to the reestablishment of a "climax" stage, which represented "the achievement of a new equilibrium of communal stability."[84]

Although Hoyt blamed the poor for their moral failings, he did not condone racial/ethnic prejudice. At the same time, he made a reasonable, street-smart argument that it had to be factored into any realistic model of future investment risk. "Part of the attitude reflected in lower land values is due entirely to racial prejudice," he believed, "which may have no reasonable basis. Nevertheless, if the entrance of a colored family into a white neighborhood causes a general exodus of the white people, such dislikes are reflected in property values."[85]

After six years at the national level of government, Hoyt's model of the life cycle of neighborhoods reduced mapmaking to simply color coding four categories using his racial/ethnic hierarchy of "detrimental effects" on land values. The Standard Technique of calculating future mortgage risk adopted by the FHA and the Home Owners Loan Corporation made the groups at the bottom of his list the primary causal agents of an irreversible ecological process of urban decline.

All areas and their residents were aging, Hoyt conceded. "These internal changes due to depreciation and obsolescence in themselves cause shifts in the locations of neighborhoods. When, in addition," he stated, "there is poured into the center of the urban organism a stream of immigrants or members of other racial groups, these [inharmonious] forces also cause dislocations in the existing neighborhood pattern."[86] Moreover, his radials of penetration of these invasions of nonwhites sharpened into a hard line of spatial segregation. "In wholly white areas," he now pronounced, "the gradual filtration of other than white races tends slowly to change the character of neighborhoods. The presence of even one nonwhite person in a block otherwise populated by whites may initiate a period of transition."[87]

Using extreme reductionism, Hoyt constructed a map that condensed all the different values a piece of land has to city dwellers to a mathematical calculation of their household incomes. Color coding by measuring monthly rents, he covered his racial/ethnic maps of "inharmonious forces" with a politically correct overlay of market-driven forces. Nonwhite or immigrant status was filtered out by colored shades of class. "The proportionate concentration of nonwhite persons in each block," the FHA's mapmaker warned, "is therefore significant in any study of rent gradations."[88]

In contrast, if his method had been based on the industry standard of rental price per square foot, then the worst, most crowded apartment buildings in the Black Belt would have scored highest in the marketplace. As their slumlord owners knew, they were goldmines because racial zoning had forced a piling up within the ghetto. Inside its walls, the density of the people living there was two to three times greater than the rest of the city. Richer households spent more per month for much larger, modern apartments but at a much lower cost per square foot than their domestic servants were paying for their rat-infested hovels. Richard Wright's novel *Native Son* and Lorraine Hansberry's play *A Raisin in the Sun* are painful representations of black Chicago's point of view on this stark dichotomy of material and social inequalities.[89]

Hoyt was cooking the books to turn discrimination against minority groups into individual measures of success on the economic ladder to middle-class homeownership. Hoyt's Standard Technique rated neighborhoods primarily by the racial/ethnic composition of their residents, determined partly by a 1938 copy of Chicago's map of mortgage risk districts. "In both the overarching risk index and the analyses of the estimation of individual risk classes," one study of his quantitative methods finds, "the presence of specific populations frequently received more weight than other factors that these maps tracked." Whites and racial/ethnic minorities received "differential treatment" from the administrators of the government's housing programs.[90]

For the leaders of the Cold War, the planner's vision of an Organic City of technological modernization, social harmony, and environmental equilibrium proved to be irresistible. In the United States, Holt's system of redlining created a sociospatial order of white privilege. Under the Truman and Eisenhower administrations, public and private planners like Hoyt would be given the resources to construct a new skyline. Almost ten million single-family homes would be built outside the city centers compared to four million inside them. A new suburban landscape of greenbelt communities, shopping malls, and industrial parks arose. But screening out race/ethnicity (and gender) from the planners' vision of the Organic City came at a heavy social cost of inequality and conflict.[91]

Global Movements: The Cold War and the Population Bomb

Unfortunately, the explosive growth of the world's population overwhelmed even the best-laid plans of the technocrats in charge of driving the engines of progress. As Horkheimer and Adorno had pondered, modernism seemed to contain the seeds of its own destruction. Beginning in the twentieth century, steady advances in raising agricultural productivity and lowering infant mortality were boosting rates of population increase across the globe. Moreover, comparable improvements in transportation technology meant that more people had more options to migrate from rural to urban areas and from poorer to richer countries.

The sheer number of people arriving in the cities overran the abilities of the planners and policy makers to keep up in most places. From 1950 to 2000 alone, the earth's population soared to almost six billion people, a historic increase of 137 percent. In the preceding century, the rate was about 30 percent during each fifty-year period. In other words, it took 123 years until 1927 to double the population to two billion but less than fifty years more to double it again.

Since 1945, about two-thirds of the increase in population has been absorbed in the cities. The pace of this urbanization of humanity is hard to grasp. One way is to compare the city population of 3.5 billion people today with an equal number of people on the whole planet only forty years ago. Or consider that the urban workforce doubled during the last twenty years of the twentieth century. The United Nations calculates that we have reached the point when, for the first time in history, more people are living in urban rather than rural areas. About half the urban dwellers, or 25 percent of the total population, live in large cities of over 750,000 inhabitants.[92]

Although the biblical catastrophes predicted by the postwar Malthusian Jeremiahs failed to strike during the Jeremaihs' lifetimes, the cities experienced some of their consequences. A growing proportion of city dwellers—perhaps one out of three—lived in substandard, unhealthy housing on land that they did not own. The crush of people moving from farm to factory outpaced the construction of decent housing and essential urban services in most places. Even the building of a brand-new metropolis of high modernism in the middle of nowhere, Brasília, fell behind, giving rise to illegal Freetowns all around it.

Makeshift, informal shantytowns became a regular, albeit contested, part of the process of modernization during the postwar period. The intermixing of planned and illegal land-use patterns was not the only way that planning from the bottom up contributed to the urban condition. In addition, the webs of the formal and informal economies became ever more inextricably intertwined, to say nothing of popular culture production coming out of the people's direct experiences of life in these communities of *necesidad* (survival).[93]

The very success of the postwar economic boom in the Western nations seemed paradoxically to be shackling their cities with the unbearable deadweight of the slums. To account for this drag on the modernization race, discourse within highbrow society demonized them. They were portrayed as breeding grounds of a criminalized and self-perpetuating "culture of poverty."[94]

Politicians, the mass media, and academic experts alike pointed a finger of blame at the *colonias populares* (shantytowns) and favelas for causing every ill afflicting modern society. The lower classes wanted to remain wallowing in squalor, living shameless lives of sin and dependency in "eternal slums," according to academic apologists like Oscar Lewis. His sociological theories provided a comforting moral blinder that allowed those profiting from economic development to put the poor out of sight and out of mind.

In countries like Mexico and Brazil with political cultures of paternalism and clientelism, the governments treated the rural migrants in condescending ways as marginalized, childlike losers and their illegal shantytowns as the inevitable result. Policy makers wavered between extending the hand of

charity down into the muck of poverty to pull out a deserving few and send-
ing the demolition and death squads out to surgically remove these "cancers"
threatening public order.[95]

In the late 1950s, however, new voices added a dissent to this policy debate, arguing that informal planning represented a good thing. According
to these critics, the new communities were melting pots of diverse peoples
who shared a common goal of improving their conditions. Over time, the
dissenters predicted, the illegal settlements would become woven into the
urban fabric.

In Latin American cities, Catholic priests and nuns espousing liberation
theology often became the inspirational organizers of popular movements.
Their message of community empowerment and the rights of citizenship
raised troubling questions about environmental justice. This mobilization
of the grass roots would eventually force planners and policy makers to confront conditions from the perspective of the neighborhood street corner.
But it would take civil unrest from Watts to Paris and back to Mexico City
to pull off their blinders of denial and open their eyes to the possibility that
the people of the slums represented part of the solution, not the problem.[96]

3

Case Studies, 1945–1960

I n the wake of war, the optimistic idealism of the planners and policy makers prevailed. Believing they could reconstruct the landscape into a modern Organic City, they brought many of their clean-sweep designs to fruition in their enthusiasm to rebuild the urban environment.

In this chapter I measure the goals of the planners and policy makers against the practical limitations they faced in building a new skyline. Although a consensus behind the International Style prevailed, the shifting gears of popular politics and financial markets acted as a powerful brake on the pace of urban renewal. Especially during the first decade of postwar recovery, Europe suffered shortages of material and capital. New housing and other urban projects had to take a back seat to national goals of repairing roads, ports, and other physical prerequisites of a functioning economy.

As this basic infrastructure was repaired, a rising tide of prosperity shifted the political momentum in favor of city planning departments. They went to work implementing Haussmann-like slum clearance and long-deferred social agendas. They sought to fulfill their goals of upgrading housing standards and uplifting community life. These are top-down stories of male-centric professions: the planners, engineers, and policy makers put in charge of rebuilding the world.

London, United Kingdom:
The Making of the Green Belt Plan

The unbroken path of planning history in England makes it the logical place to begin our examination of the postwar city. Ebenezer Howard's enduring legacy of urban containment fed directly onto the Cold War highway of technological modernization. The instant formation of what historian Peter Hall calls the British "planning machine" during some of the darkest days of the London bombing reflected the continuity of influence exercised by policy insiders.[1] Patrick Abercrombie and the Town and County Association remained at the center of the debate over the best way to build the urban environment.[2]

The Blitz of September 1940 taught the lesson that the reconstruction of the cities would require conscious, formal planning. Over the next four years, the experts did more than dream about rebuilding London into a New Jerusalem. They worked it all out in a series of official reports, which Parliament translated into law. Together, the planners and policy makers tapped a cultural consensus that shared a vision of picturesque Arts and Crafts villages surrounded by greenery. "The state's primary role in determining where people would live, in what social mix, and in what sort of houses (rented from public authorities) was not seriously questioned," according to the planning historian Gordon Cherry.[3]

In the case of England, the ebb and flow of power between the two political parties floated on a rising tide of economic prosperity, the great European miracle. About every five to six years, the English shifted political gears. "[For example,] housing policy remained a political football," according to Cherry.[4] These convenient chunks of time in the back and forth of housing policy furnish us a way to mark the changes wrought in London's skyline during the regime of the "planning machine."

The Labour Party began in 1945 with an impossibly ambitious program to revolutionize the nation's land values. But just six years later, the Conservatives won a majority in Parliament and repealed the program before it could get under way. In 1957, a party scandal made Housing Minister Harold Macmillan the leader of the Tories. His promotion came as the reward for fulfilling his promise to ramp up the total number of public and private housing starts to over three hundred thousand units a year. He led the government until the voters shifted alignment in 1962 back to the opposition Labour Party.

Taking advantage of the good times, the new prime minister provided further private incentives and public funding to spark a building boom. The race of technological modernization was on among the big cities' teams of planners, bureaucrats, architects, and builders to condemn entire neighborhoods by official dictate as slums. In their place, the technocrats of the planning machine united in starry-eyed thrall of the International Style. "Under the impetus of massive redevelopment," the urban historian Helen Meller laments, "more of the fabric of British towns and cities was destroyed in the 1960s than had been destroyed by the bombing in the whole of the Second World War."[5]

But standing in the midst of the rubble of London in 1945, of course, the view was completely different. At that moment brave planners laid out a roadmap of modernization for a battered nation. Much of what the planning experts had seen during the 1930s they did not like. They especially deplored the chaotic sprawl of private housing estates that had eaten up an average of 65,000 acres (26,300 hectares) of open space a year.

To be sure, Abercrombie and his antiurban lobby had helped save a green girdle, or belt, around London. But the suburbs had simply leapfrogged over it, creating a new outer ring of communities filled with middle-class commuters. Worse, more and more of them were abandoning public transportation for private automobiles. The planners were determined to contain this urban growth within a well-ordered template of the Organic City.[6]

Abercrombie's Greater London Plan of 1944 stands out as one of the greatest regional plans of the twentieth century. Like other influential visionaries, he painted an easy-to-understand geography of three concentric circles around an inner city core. Each suburban, greenbelt, and outer-county ring was about ten miles from inner to outer edge. On the basis of London's prewar demographics of a suburban trend of a static population, he saw the task at hand as essentially one of orderly resettlement to equalize densities. His plan called for moving what was termed "overspill population" from the center to new satellite cities and dying rural villages beyond the greenbelt.[7]

As soon as the war was over, Abercrombie's plan for new towns got a head start in the construction queue, including eight in the London area. And still embracing wartime ideals of a more equalitarian society, he built a mix of housing types and rental costs in these Garden Cities that blurred class boundaries. In retrospect, this small piece of social engineering might have been the most radical reform wrought at the hands of the planners. The new towns gave working-class families housing previously restricted to the middle class. Building them supplied Londoners a tangible sign of a New Jerusalem arising like a phoenix in a garden.[8]

Except for building the new towns, however, the central planners remained shackled to the starting blocks during six years of Labour Party rule. The country was not only broken but broke. Over 350,000 homes in London alone needed repair before they could again be inhabited. The London County Council (LCC) faced the practical job of finding shelter for as many of the homeless as it could as quickly as possible. They shifted power over housing policy from Abercrombie's main collaborator, the city architect J. H. Forshaw, to the city valuer, or tax assessor.[9]

The city valuer marshaled what very limited materials and labor he had to greatest effect, sacrificing modern standards of quality for quantity. He mostly fixed bomb-damaged homes and constructed some cheap cottages and low-rise flats by recycling plans from the interwar years. A public exhibition of the LCC's utilitarian "return to reason" strategy brought condemnation by the profession and the mass media alike. In the face of this withering criticism, the LCC restored the city architect in 1951 as the planner in charge of housing policy.[10]

Riding a swelling wave of consumer affluence, ordinary Londoners joined the chorus of elite critics demanding a great leap forward in the modernization race. They were swept away by what one best-selling novelist called "Neophilia," or an obsession with newness.[11] Within a cultural context of the Garden City ideal, this ethos supported the coming-of-age generation of urban planners and their visions of the future. They too were mesmerized by the twin icons of high technology: highways and high-rises. Postwar plans to conserve historic inner-city districts were rejected out of hand. They were bulldozed to make way for American-style shopping malls, downtown traffic corridors, and multistory carparks.[12]

Helping to lift the Conservatives into power in 1951, this popular impulse for all things new found political expression in reforms that shifted emphasis of housing policy from the public to the private sector. The government reduced the pace of its construction programs while reviving private markets in land development and homeownership. These steps increased the rate of new starts of modestly priced suburban houses by 50 percent.

As with other war-weary societies, a return to normalcy, if not reason, meant for the British a retreat to the privacy of family life. Housebuilders supplied prospective buyers with comforting, rustic-style facades. Inside, these dwellings were filled with all the modern conveniences and up-to-date appliances. In contrast, council housing continued to bear stigmas of poverty and criminality. Local authorities also imposed humiliating rules that treated residents more as prisoners than rent-paying tenants.[13]

As the suburban trend picked up speed in the early 1950s, however, Abercrombie's plan of urban containment appeared to be threatened, overwhelmed by its very success. In 1956–1957, the Conservatives pulled out all the stops to throw the private-sector development of London into high gear. By lifting height restrictions on office towers, Macmillan not only set off a building boom but also a hiring bonanza for white-collar professionals. The London plan contained factory employment, but it did not foresee the mushroomlike growth of service-sector jobs.

The increasing pressure on land and housing costs in the central areas was compounded by even-faster-growing congestion in the streets. New drivers coming from and going to the suburbs and the new towns clogged downtown London. In 1945, one in ten Brits owned a car; by 1980, three out of five would. During the fifties, one measure of the Tories' housing policy was the eight hundred thousand people added to the outer ring beyond the greenbelt. "Above all," Peter Hall remarks, "it was the rise of mass car owner- ship that perhaps took planners most by surprise."[14]

To catch up with and harness this groundswell of economic prosperity, the central planners reset the government's fiscal throttle wide open to speed up the modernization race. With the real estate boom filling its tax coffers, they embarked on two massive public works projects copied right out of Le Corbusier's Radiant City portfolio. They began constructing a system of na- tional motorways and metropolitan ring roads to support an emerging car culture of an affluent society.

But the centerpiece of the British planning machine was large-scale ur- ban renewal projects, complete communities of high-rise living. It oversaw slum clearance projects that replaced old neighborhoods with megastruc- tures and tower blocks. Over the next two decades, local authorities would demolish 1,165,000 housing units while erecting 440,000 high-rise apart- ments. "Tower blocks became a cultural expression of Modernism," accord- ing to the historians Keith Jacobs and Tony Manzi, "a national symbol of progress."[15]

When national economic indicators headed downward in the early six- ties, so did the political fortunes of the Conservative Party. Returning to power in 1962, the Labour Party tilted urban policy initiatives toward the public sector but without squeezing the private property markets. If any- thing, the incoming administration used housing policy to ratchet up the pace of the modernization race for the remainder of this go-go decade.

For example, Parliament authorized a second round of new towns. In contrast to Abercrombie's compact Garden City designs for fifty thousand to sixty thousand inhabitants, the development of Milton Keynes was planned along the lines of an American-style suburb. A quarter million people would live in single-family houses with attached two-car garages. And unlike Aber- crombie's equalitarian blueprints, the new housing designs re-embedded old class distinctions in a spatial hierarchy from center to periphery.[16]

In the town centers, the British planning machine's slum clearance pro- gram became a self-perpetuating growth machine in its own right. By the midfifties, the LCC had cleared the backlog of families left homeless by the war. Instead, households living in the path of the urban renewal bulldozer replaced them on the waiting list. Tearing down existing dwellings generated the names that, in turn, required the LCC to supply more slum land to build more apartments.

The skyrocketing cost of property in London forced the planners to demolish entire neighborhoods to assemble large enough plots to realize the community-building ideals of Clarence Perry's neighborhood unit. Unlike private housing estates, public housing projects included schools, clinics, shopping precincts, and open green space. This left little room for replacement housing, justifying the planners' preference for tower blocks.[17]

Only by amassing the dwelling units could the planners hire one of a handful of giant construction companies to build these projects with mass production methods. These politically connected firms promised to save money and time by applying assembly-line methods of building from start to finish. They precast concrete slabs in factories and then hauled them to the site. Traveling cranes pieced them together into apartments. As though attaching doors and windshields to a car frame, the cranes stacked them up inside the reinforced-concrete skeletons of the high-rises.

Quality continued to be sacrificed for quantity as stark images of gray megastructures in the mass media gave currency to their being dubbed "British Brutalism." The result was modern but inferior spaces to live in, places still carrying the stigma of a culture of poverty. Systems approaches, in Meller's judgment, provided "a second-class environment for second-class citizens and put into bricks and mortar an unbridgeable social divide."[18]

If the postwar rebuilding of London changed its physical skyline more than its social geography, the planning machine could nonetheless take pride in running a successful modernization race. As Cherry trumpets, "This period [from 1945 to 1965] was a high-watermark for town planning achievement and for its reputation world-wide."[19] The planners had shrunk the city core, down from 8.2 million to 7.6 million. In addition, most of the overspill had been resettled in the outer-county ring. Yet they had not anticipated the explosive growth of London's financial firms and other service sector jobs.

Nonetheless, the planners took good advantage of this growth machine of real estate development to fuel the money machine of the government's housing and motorway programs. From 1951 to 1971, the population of the London region increased from 15.2 million to 17.3 million people. New housing grew like mushrooms in the suburbs, overwhelming the planners' expectations. A ring of communities thirty to fifty miles from the center took form from the addition of 50 percent more inhabitants.[20]

England was well on its way to reaching an important milestone of planning history. By 1971, half its households would own their dwellings and another third would live in public housing. In effect, the planners had erased the shame of Dickens's Coke Towns and replaced them with Cold War symbols of nationalism.

A generation of "neophiliacs" engendered a political consensus behind their Le Corbusier–inspired visions of high modernism. Measured by their own metric of quantity of physical change, the British planning machine had accomplished its primary goal of urban renewal. An analysis of the social costs of this massive makeover of the built environment must await the following chapters. I simply observe here, along with the housing expert Patrick Dunleavy, that "on the whole, these costs were considered so trivial that they were not measured."[21]

Paris, France: The Making of *les Grands Ensembles*

France ran the modernization race so fast that a social process normally spread over a long period became a single event crammed into a decade. In the midst of this cultural revolution, one pop sociologist defined it as "future shock."[22] The sheer amount of new technology introduced into everyday life produced a collective reaction. "In the space of just ten years," the historian Kristin Ross observes, "a rural woman might live [through] the acquisition of electricity, running water, a stove, a refrigerator, a washing machine, a sense of interior space as distinct from exterior space, a car, a television, and the various liberations and oppressions associated with each."[23]

Ross's account of France's embrace of "fast cars, clean bodies" helps navigate the dizzy pace of change during the two decades of postwar reconstruction and renewal. Ross's rural migrant was not alone; every segment of French society was affected by the mostly American-inspired technological revolution of everyday life. From the farmers streaming into Paris to its avant-garde utopians, the temptations of consumer culture proved to be irresistible.

For many, new housing built in new styles with new methods of production became the litmus test of national progress. Urban planning became pivotal in achieving national success in the global competition of the Cold War. The rebuilding of the cities also became the political test of social justice: the right of every citizen to a decent place to live.

In 1968, Paris would explode in revolt against all that had been lost in this headlong rush to catch up with the world's superpowers. The protesters hated the makeover of Paris with apartment blocks in the suburbs and office towers in the center. City planners emerged as public enemy number one. They served symbolically as a class-bridging bond of solidarity between striking factory workers and university intellectuals. As their protest spread across the nation, a future-shocked society came to a standstill.

In the beginning, in contrast, a shell-shocked society welcomed anyone offering to catapult a defeated empire back into a leadership role on the world stage. The first priority of the nation was to build a new industrial base along

Fordist lines of production for the masses. The 1947 (Jean) Monnet Plan was the first in a series of five-year programs of economic development that used public policies to harness private enterprise.

Housing for the cities, however, was not included. Despite severe shortages from the war's destruction of old buildings and the post-1945 waves of newcomers from the countryside and the colonies, priority was given to the industrial infrastructure. The plan provided only minimal temporary shelters for hundreds of thousands of displaced persons. In the meantime, the urban rubble was cleared away and the national economy was restored.[24]

Escalating Cold War tensions between the superpowers steered the race of technological modernization in France in the direction of an American suburban ideal. In 1947, the United States enacted the Marshall Plan, providing financial and technical assistance to help revive the crippled economies of its Western allies. In France, for example, it jump-started the auto industry by erecting new factories for Renault. The factories implanted more than a novel mode of production, Ross remarks, and "the car marked the advent of modernization; it provided both the illustration and the motor of what came to be known as the society of consumption."[25]

The success of economic planning allowed the government to address mounting political demands for better housing. In Paris, conditions had deteriorated to a point that could no longer be ignored. The most marginalized social groups, North Africans and Asians, were being forced into inner-suburban shantytowns ringing the city center. They were called *bidonvilles*, after the oil drums they scavenged and pounded out to make shelters. Perhaps forty thousand of these mostly illegal immigrants, known as the clandestines, were living in these jerry-built camps of squalor.[26]

Like the automobile, urban housing became both a national economic motor and global cultural symbol of modernization. In September 1948, the central planners added home building to their list of key industries. One of its leaders, Eugène Claudius-Petit, was appointed minister of Reconstruction and Urbanism. He announced a bold goal of starting twenty thousand new housing units a month.

But the nation's chief planner faced shortages that had been accumulating for almost a century. The war alone had destroyed 450,000 homes and made an almost equal number uninhabitable. A survey of Paris in 1954 revealed that four out of five of its dwellings were built before World War I, only half had toilets, and only one in five had a bathtub or shower. The slum districts, *ilots insalubres*, of the Progressive Era stood virtually unchanged, except for a half century of additional decay.[27]

What French cities needed most was new construction. Claudius-Petit was determined to find industrial methods of construction equivalent to those used for Renault's new factories. The Ministry of Reconstruction and

Urbanism sponsored a series of competitions to design apartment projects of two hundred to eight hundred units that could be built efficiently on an assembly line. The jury-determined contests attracted the country's biggest contractors and most prominent architects, including Le Corbusier.[28]

The competitions reconfirmed a broad consensus in favor of his vision of the Organic City. The juries put his proposals on hold while they awaited the results of his experiment in Marseilles, l'Unité d'habitation. But almost all the contestants followed his lead in proposing standardized concrete panels that could be erected with a crane to create either taller, thicker towers or longer, thinner slabs. Open land sites on the urban periphery allowed a variety of parklike settings, with the buildings arranged either in simple geometric patterns in the midst of gardens or around the edges like walls sitting on *pilotis* (pillars).

Moreover, there was equal agreement among the planners, designers, politicians, and businessmen on the juries that the apartment buildings had to conform to the International Style of architecture. In the early 1950s, the winning entries in these contests would become the prototypes of gigantic projects in the suburbs called *les grands ensembles*. And as we have seen, Great Britain's planners would import these industrial building techniques a few years later to remake central London.[29]

Urban planning also became pivotal in the revival of the nation's regional centers. The goal of rebalancing France by containing the growth of Paris became integrated into the larger economic plan. Yet a no-growth strategy for the capital city did not exclude an attack on its problems of overcrowded and substandard housing. In 1954, the first of several *grands ensembles* began rising in the Paris suburb of Sarcelles. The project contributed to the 240,000 new housing starts of that year, which allowed Claudius-Petit to retire with the satisfaction of fulfilling his objective.[30]

But embedded within his plans of technological modernization were deep-seated traditions of class and ethnic/racial and religious prejudice. Without questioning his social justice ideals, the minister of reconstruction singled out the working classes, especially immigrants from the colonies. As France fought losing wars abroad against Vietnam (1945–1954) and Algeria (1954–1962), the clandestines became surrogate enemies in a more winnable war at home. They became the scapegoats of the unmodern: they could not be assimilated because they were lazy, dirty, and dangerous criminals who dragged against the nation's drive to get to the future.[31]

The planners perpetuated and reinforced Baron Georges-Eugène Haussmann's Janus-faced division of Paris into a showcase of civilization in the center for the rich and a wasteland of exclusion in the periphery for the poor. In the 1870s, Haussmann's urban renewal bulldozer had displaced an estimated 350,000 mostly poor people and added momentum to rents rising faster than wages could keep up with the cost of living. "It would appear," the scholars Daniel Noin and Paul White contend, "that for some people [like Claudius-Petit] the future vision of the residential map of the City of Paris would have little space for various unwanted groups."[32]

In what the city's biographer Norma Evenson terms the "reconquest of Paris," postwar planners and policy makers not only threw the urban growth machine back into gear after it had sat in idle for eighty years but also slammed the gas pedal to the floor.[33] Throwing the modernization race into overdrive, they tore down 60,000 old housing units, displacing 550,000 residents. At the same time, they put up 269,000 new ones, reinforcing a division of urban space between the rich and the poor.

By the time the oil embargo of 1974 brought the miracle of the growth machine to a screeching halt, the postwar city builders had outdone Haussmann. Their reconquest swelled the numbers of the upper classes (*cadres superieurs*) in Paris by 51 percent, while the working-class population plunged by 44 percent. By then, a million of them were housed in the great suburban projects, *les grands ensembles*.[34]

More than a decade earlier, Parisians were already beginning to show signs of future shock, or at least experiencing a collective sense of vertigo from the full-throttle pace of technological modernization. While it took fifteen years to double the number of cars in Paris to a million in 1960, it would take only five years to double it again. In a similar way, the momentum of housing construction also was ramping up the pace of production and its effects on French society. New starts were pushing past the three-hundred-thousand-a-year mark.[35]

Sarcelles became a national symbol of everything that was wrong about the makeover of France into an American-style society of consumption. The giant housing projects spawned a whole new vocabulary of dystopia. *La Sarcellite* was used to describe a collective sense of spatial isolation and social exclusion. With a juvenile delinquency rate five times as high as those in equivalent working-class districts in the inner city, Sarcelles drew the attention of government social workers as well as popular commentators. What they found was rather surprising: 61 percent of the residents of *les grands ensembles* found their advantages outweighed the disadvantages of their previous housing conditions. Overall, a slight majority gave a favorable rating to their current status.

Yet the experts also determined that just building more and more high-rise apartments was causing both social and individual problems. The planners had failed to provide a job base anywhere nearby. They also had neglected to provide residents public transportation to the city-center. The projects lacked schools and recreational facilities for the young and shops and services for the adults. In response, the planners began to change the direction of the modernization race from the urban containment of Paris to a more comprehensive approach.[36]

Perhaps the pivotal event in the making of this major shift occurred in October 1961, when the Battle of Algiers became the Battle of Paris. After a decade of making Muslim clandestines the scapegoats for rejection of colonialism abroad, the national government imposed a curfew on Algerians in response to an increase in domestic acts of terrorism. It also gave a green light to police to conduct a reign of terror using indiscriminate ethnic profiling. The national government stood by while police attacked a protest march. Hundreds of marchers were killed, according to some estimates. Then the police threw bodies into the Seine to cover up their crime. Following this violent turning inward of the colonial wars, the national government passed a series of laws over the next five years to begin winding down the construction of the *grands ensembles*.[37]

In the run-up to the later revolt, in 1968, French planners felt confident that their midcourse corrections would solve the minor ill effects of *Sarcellitis*. Their faith remained steadfast in environmental determinism. They believed in the power of spatial design to shape human behavior in socially beneficial ways. They had broken the stalemate, moving Paris past its seasons of autumn and winter to a new spring of renewal.

The planners and policy makers had kick-started a technological revolution, setting in motion changes in everyday life. They had taken on ambitious goals of replacing the housing stock and repopulating the regions. Although they had not stopped the growth of Paris, a baby boom that paralleled the housing boom was achieving the goal of reviving the nation's provincial centers. Until the explosion in the streets took them by surprise, the planners and policy makers were convinced that France was catching up in the modernization race.[38]

Rotterdam, Netherlands:
The Making of the Basic Plan

As we might expect, the Dutch ran the smoothest race of technological progress during the postwar recovery. A political culture of "consensus democracy"[39] and a planning tradition of environmental engineering gave them a head start on the road to the Organic City. Also greasing the wheels of urban change in the Netherlands was the functional coordination of national, regional, and local policy among like-minded technocrats, who cherished modernist values.

Like the British, the Dutch started making plans as soon as the fires from the bombs were extinguished. And like the French, they had institutionalized government-business partnerships in economic development projects such as public works and housing construction. This cooperative spirit further improved the efficiency of a society united in the pursuit of reclaiming its cities at home and its colonial empire abroad.[40]

Rotterdam's location at the mouth of the Maas and the Rhine Rivers made the reconstruction of its seaport a top priority of not only national planners but also Cold War strategists. The survival of capitalism seemed to hinge on speeding up the flow of trade moving through its docks between the United States and Western Europe. With funding from the Marshall Plan, the Netherlands built a new ship harbor over the next five years. As in the French case, limited materials, equipment, and workers meant that the homeless had to wait in temporary shelters until the seaport was opened again for business.[41]

In the 1950s, the momentum of the resulting economic revival allowed the planners' vision of the city to rise like a phoenix from the ashes of war. The city formally adopted the alternative plan led by Johannes Hendrik van den Broek and C. Van Traa, supporters of the International Congresses of Modern Architecture (Congrès Internationaux d'Architecture Moderne, or CIAM). The "Basic Plan for the Reconstruction of the City of Rotterdam" laid out a straight path to the future. It turned the historic entrepôt into a modern city of traffic flows. To achieve Le Corbusier's holy grail of speed, Van Traa added a new grid of crosstown boulevards for motorized vehicles. Equally important, they were interwoven with larger streetcar, highway, rail, and shipping networks.[42]

The success of the Basic Plan, according to one scholar, sprang from "the determination of all Rotterdammers to remodel their city as an up-to-date functional machine." Van Traa's main contribution was adding a vertical, three-dimensional transportation system on a metropolitan scale. The plan defined the superstructure and the infrastructure of an urban space in minute detail, while leaving its contents an empty vessel. It retained the mixed land-use patterns of the old city, reflecting its tolerant spirit of inclusive diversity.[43]

The Dutch ethos of consensus democracy supplied the political grease to keep Rotterdam's growth machine running smoothly. The planning process had built-in mechanisms of communication to ensure that policy makers heard from every segment of society. "Politics in Rotterdam," according to Justin Beaumont and Maarten Loopmans, "combine[d] top-down corporatist elitism with a strong populist tradition stretching back into history."[44] Business and professional leaders channeled their opinions through their Club of Rotterdam. It had public and secret committees that acted as a shadow government to city hall's planning department.

At the other end of the social hierarchy, an advisory community council in each neighborhood supplied an open forum for the voice of the grass roots. Here, large working-class majorities and the Dutch Labor Party ruled. The party gradually gained power, controlling the city council by the 1960s, giving Rotterdam the moniker "Kremlin on the Maas." Nonetheless, a civic culture of inclusion not only gave the entire community a sense of empowerment in making decisions about the future of their city but also generated a sense of commitment to make the plan work.[45]

With the seaport opening in the early fifties, Rotterdam began filling in its land-use blobs. A sampling of these functional zones—shops, offices, and housing—reveals a comparatively pure form of the modernist vision of the Organic City. The most obvious exemplar is the Lijnbaan shopping center, designed by van den Broek and J. B. Bakema.

Breaking with Dutch urban traditions, sixty-five shops and offices were housed in two steel and precast concrete slabs of two stories that bordered a pedestrian mall. Although the depth of the buildings was fixed, their simple modular design provided the built-in flexibility of nonsupportive interior walls, which could be moved sideways to make larger or smaller spaces. To offset the minimalism of the exterior facades, the open-air promenade was highly decorated.[46]

Completed in 1953, the Lijnbaan became an instant success. The popularity of the shopping mall was a direct result of the city's ethos of cooperative planning. In filling in this zone, Van Traa had first organized the merchants into the Lijnbaan Shopping Promenade Association and then brought it together with the architects. Out of this collaboration came a diverse, albeit unified, streetscape that became an attraction in its own right. The merchants agreed to adorn their shops with awnings that were uniform in dimension and individual in decoration.[47]

An empty vessel approach to the shopping zone created additional opportunities for diversity in the spaces adjacent to the mall. For example, the owners of the Bijenkorf Department Store chose Bauhaus acolyte Marcel Breuer to design their building. They were impressed by his provocative drawings of a temple of commerce. Widely copied, "the Lijnbaan shopping centre," according to the city's historian, John McCarthy, "came to be seen as an international example of the city of the future."[48]

In many respects, housing followed in the wake of the first wave of shops and offices to provide their workers with a place nearby to live. In this case, the planners sought to balance traditions of city life on the basis of mixed use of space and modernist impulses to separate work, residence, and play. The compromise solution was placing high-rise apartments just behind the Lijnbaan in courtyard settings. The complex contained a combination of three- and twelve-story steel-and-concrete structures, some with shops and offices on the lower floors.

To complement this ensemble of towers in the park, the planners filled in a public space across from the Lijnbaan Flats with the multipurpose Concetgeouw (Concert Center) set on an open plaza, the Schouwburgplein. Private investors provided a movie theater on the opposite edge of the complex. Although the prewar population of the city center had been cut in half, the residents who remained created the critical mass needed to spark the spontaneous generation of an urban culture.

To house working- and middle-class families with jobs outside the inner zone, Rotterdam drew on a rich architectural heritage of modernist designs for the suburbs. Continuities between past and present are most clearly evident in this example because most of the best prewar models of low-rise slabs-in-a-park remained unscathed by the bombings. In several cases, the planners simply pulled out the old blueprints and added extensions to existing social estates. In similar ways, public and private builders alike drew on the past experiences of everyday life in the suburbs in laying out Dutch-style neighborhood units.

Closer in, too, Rotterdammers could find a spectrum of design archetypes reflecting CIAM's spirit of the future. More indigenous urban ideals were also apparent in their plans to restore an intimacy with nature by intermixing park and residential spaces. Whether in the center or on the periphery, then, a prevailing social consensus allowed the planners and policy makers to create a supercharged high modernist version of traditional city life. The city builders were able to find the right balance of work, residence, and play; privacy and community; and green and built spaces to fine-tune their functionalist machine.[49]

The same cultural roots of consensus and environmentalism guided regional planners in mapping out the future course of the *Randstad* (Rim City). In 1951, they renewed their vows to save the *Groene Hart* (Green Heart). The Commission for the Western Netherlands marshaled the nation's defenses to contain the invasion of this now-sacrosanct semirural area by suburban sprawl. It sought to bring city populations in harmony with the open space needed for their health and recreation. To counterbalance the success of Rotterdam and the other three rim cities, the planners and policy makers put top priority on diverting new jobs to slower-growing areas of the country.

Their imaginary of the *Randstad* created a divisive source of friction in an otherwise smooth-running engine of rebuilding the urban environment. Local governments proved weak defenders against popular demands for suburban homes now that new highways and affordable cars were opening access to green space at the periphery. During the 1950s, however, this drag on the plan seemed to cause only an occasional sputter in the Netherlands juggernaut of technological modernization.[50]

Mexico City, Mexico: The Making of Modernism

In Mexico, the legal insecurity of property largely determined settlement patterns in the world's most prominent Shock City of the second half of the twentieth century. Between 1940 and 1960, the Federal District of Mexico City (Distrito Federal; DF) added 3.5 million people, more than tripling its population to over 5 million inhabitants. The government converted the wartime boom into a plan of national economic development through import substitution strategies.

In the same way that Los Angeles transferred wealth and water from the countryside, Mexico moved money and people from farm to factory. Government experts carefully plotted the technological modernization of the nation, but equivalent blueprints for worker housing and urban expansion did not exist. Instead, the official plan was the nonenforcement of the land laws.[51]

For the migrants, low wages were the root cause of the housing shortage; they simply could not afford a decent place to live. The trade-off for living in substandard self-built housing was freedom from the landlord and the tax man. About three out of every five inhabitants would come to live in dwellings without legal title. In the first two postwar decades, most of the housing in these shantytowns (*colonias populares*) was built within the boundaries of the DF.

Unlike the survival communities forming at the periphery, these were ancient places with identities of place deeply rooted in the foundations of the city's popular culture. Clustered around the national sacred space, the central plaza, or Zócalo, were working-class neighborhoods known as Tipeto, Alameda, Morelos, Guerrero, Buenavista, Tabacalera/Reforma, and Doctores. "Many [residents]," the urban scholar Susan Eckstein remarks, "view their neighbourhood as authentic, representing the 'soul' of Mexico City."[52]

The residents of El Centro had not only solid identities of place but also a strong class consciousness. Their occupations tended to cluster around the city center. Long ago, the Zócalo became established as having a distinct locational advantage for civil servants, street vendors and storefront businesses, bus drivers, and female garment workers jammed in sweatshops near the big department stores.

In the post–World War II period, traditional identities of place were reinforced in a classic not-in-my-backyard defense of residential neighborhoods against the wrecking ball of clean-sweep urban renewal. The government plan called for their replacement with a complex of International Style office, shopping, and condo towers, as in other first world capital cities. Many influential economic interests also endorsed the makeover of the historic core.

But standing against this powerful phalanx of modernism stood an unlikely local hero, Ernesto P. Uruchurtu. He would build a political machine independent of the national political party and consisting of two of the center's main residential and occupational groups: the street vendors and the bus drivers. Known as the Regent of Iron, Uruchurtu was ruthless in forcing the vendors to join syndicate-like associations to gain access to public space.

At the same time, however, he gave these organized worker groups legitimacy, and hence power, to their godfather-like leaders. They represented fifty thousand dues-paying members, who were also members of the same neighborhood, community, and parish networks at the grassroots level. For the bus drivers, for example, stopping urban renewal would pay off in direct benefits for their lives and livelihoods. Saving their central residential locations meant less commuting time to their jobs in a city becoming choked with auto congestion. Their resistance probably saved their jobs as well because modernist visions of a high-rise downtown included a metro subway system for white-collar office workers. From 1952 until his ouster from office as the *regente* (regent, or head) of the Department of the Federal District fourteen years later, Uruchurtu held the forces of modernist urban planning at a standstill. El Centro remained rooted in traditional identities of place and working-class consciousness, a lively urban space of people-filled streets.[53]

For the upwardly mobile business and political classes, breaking with tradition meant wrapping themselves in modernism. They endorsed the latest international fashions in their private lives as well as in the public sphere. But as in France, this open-arm embrace of new urban technologies and suburban life styles came at a psychological cost of future shock, or what the Latin Americanist Ramón Gutiérrez calls "modernism without modernity."[54]

This tension between progressive and traditional values is a central theme of Mexican culture. The revolution of the early twentieth century was inseparably linked to folk art representations of anticolonialism. At the same time, it expressed a kinship with the international avant-garde. Two projects at the leading edge of modernism illuminate the frictions generated in everyday life between local culture and global Cold War.

The exclusive subdivision El Jardines del Pedregal (the Gardens of Lava), following the L.A. model, reinforces Kristin Ross's thesis that a too-rapid transformation to mass consumption of fast cars and clean bodies can explode into a cultural revolution. Nearby, the rise of Cuidad Universitaria (University City) supplies a second illustration of the uneasy fit between national cultural traditions and the International Style of architecture and design.[55]

Despite scientific verification that Mexico City had become an ecology of hydrocatastrophe, the political party the PRI cranked up the urban growth machine to full throttle after the war. For the next six years, PRI leader and future president of the country Miguel Alemán was one of the city's most successful real estate speculators. Housing for the affluent classes continued to spread southwest of the Bosque de Chapultepec and Las Lomas.

However, Alemán choose to redirect development to a barren patch south of the colonial towns of San Angel and Coyoacan. Now streetcar suburbs, they were home to bohemians like Diego Rivera and Frida Kahlo. Beyond lay an area leading to the foothills of Ajusco, which was not suitable for farming.

About nine miles (fifteen kilometers) from El Centro, this desolate landscape began to undergo urbanization after the government expropriated *ejidal* (native peoples' communal land) land for the new campus of the National Autonomous University of Mexico. Subdivision builders like the modernist architect Daniel Barragán also moved in, marketing expensive houses in gated communities on the basis of such environmental amenities as cleaner air, lower densities, and less congestion.

The land grab was on. The big-scale public and private projects created thousands of construction jobs. Corrupt *ejidal* leaders and local officials conspired in the illegal subdivision and sale of lots—sometimes several times over—to working-class would-be homeowners.[56]

There is no doubt that Barragán and his partners in the upscale El Jardines del Pedregal were true cosmopolitans. Consider that Barragán was not only widely traveled in Europe and the United States but also had personal friendships with the avant-garde on both continents. His social circle included Le Corbusier, Frank Lloyd Wright, Richard Neutra, Philip Johnson, Buckminster Fuller, Louis Kahn, Paul Strand, Aldous Huxley, and many others.

After the war, he introduced German émigrés like Max Cetto to the city's patrons of the arts. Cetto was a founder of CIAM. In 1938 he had moved to San Francisco, where he worked in Neutra's studio during the war years. Barragán and Cetto would collaborate to build two model homes in the project. Or consider that the landscape design of the 3,110-acre (1,260-hectare) site was the work of Carlos Contreras. He had been trained as a city planner at Columbia University. Diego Rivera also got into the act as both an investor and the author of a master plan for the subdivision. A much longer list could be compiled of the other partners in the real estate venture with comparable connections to transnational urban networks of power and influence.[57]

The product they came up with was distinctly modern in the sense of an American version of a garden suburb. Priced in the luxury range, the houses were designed with an American sense of the pastoral. El Jardines del

Pedregal was planned to restore a direct relationship between its residents and nature. Homeowners lived in relative isolation from each other, with only 7 people per acre (17 per hectare). Even in the nearby suburban community of San Angel, 70 people lived on each acre (174 per hectare). Barragán's subdivision looked like a frontier settlement built in a forbidding wilderness of rocks.

Embracing this landscape, his generation remained committed to the revolution by incorporating national symbols into their works of art and architecture. The ruins of ancient cities had given El Jardines a long history as a site of mystery and myth. Its lava outcroppings, cacti, snakes, *palos bobos* (crazy trees), and perhaps ghosts of the Aztecs added to its identity as a special Mexican place.

Barragán resolved the tension between these national traditions and the universalism of modernism by making the private garden the centerpiece of the design concept. He rejected Le Corbusier's and other northern European planners' focus on the public park, favoring instead Mediterranean ideals of enclosing nature within domestic space.

Tracing their origins back to the Roman *domus*, the project's model homes could also pass the test of the International Style of architecture. They integrated inside and outside using Wright's and Neutra's nature-based techniques of nestling modular units with sliding-glass doors, decks, and balconies into dramatic landscapes. Wright's Fallingwater House became one of the iconic images in the project's early advertisements.

But Barragán also followed tradition by putting the built structures, courtyard gardens, and natural landscapes behind tall walls bordering the street. The architect was successful in creating a spatial concept for El Jardines appropriate to the site's natural and national histories. Despite their unmistakable resemblance to the designs of his American heroes, the local press insisted on labeling them as original and unique: Mexican modern. The journal *Arquitectura Mexico* reported that the houses represented "an architecture eminently modern and Mexican . . . [one that] reflects the soul of Mexico."[58]

Although the critics praised Barragán's work, he failed to convince many prospective buyers to join his project to modernize Mexican society. The advertisements did not persuade them that the car-dependent, American style of life that came with the house represented a step in the direction of progress. Five years after lot sales began in 1947, only thirty-one houses had been built or were under construction, rather than the one thousand projected in the plan.

At first, life within the gated community was isolated and difficult without a companion American-style infrastructure of highways and shopping centers. Before the coming of the city's first car-culture suburb, Mexicans had always counted on neighborhood *mercados* (markets) and street vendors for daily fresh food. But the changes in domestic life imposed by the low densities of El Jardines del Pedregal meant homemakers needed not only cars but refrigerators to keep their families fed. In the first two years after the war, Mexico had to import almost fifty thousand refrigerators because its factories were not yet making this convenience of the modern age.

At the end of 1952, a dismal sales record and a change in government combined to put the real estate venture on an entirely new footing. Coming in with the new president of the nation, Adolfo Ruíz Cortines, was his handpicked *regente* of the DF, Ernesto Uruchurtu. In losing their political sponsors, Barragán and his business partners were also stripped of the secret cover-up that had kept their property zoned as tax-exempt farmland.

The subdivision's promoters had also benefited from a loophole that allowed comparatively cheap septic tanks in rural areas instead of the sewer hookups required in the city. Now they would have to start paying municipal rates as well as submit to heavy fines for illegally subdividing the land in plots smaller than the minimum two and a half acres (one hectare) required for septic tanks. The original partners sold out to a big financial institution, which in turn, brought in a new team of marketing experts to repackage the product.

The new team's publicity campaign consisted of creating an American-style TV show to sell American-style suburbia. It was the brainchild of Héctor Cervera, who had been trained by the New York advertising giant J. Walter Thompson and who acted as negotiator between the two cultures. The program was aimed at the nation's elites, who could afford television sets. Cutting the lots down to more affordable prices, connecting the subdivision to the street grid, and opening the university also helped boost sales and property values. By 1958, El Jardines del Pedregal was essentially sold out. Academics from the new campus and other members of the city's *profesionalista* (professional, white-collar class) had moved into its nine hundred houses.[59]

These commuters and their cars formed a direct link to the government's premier symbol of Mexican modernism, Cuidad Universitaria. In this case, however, the resolution of the contradiction between the universalism of modernism and the nationalism of the Revolution was far less successful than the El Jardines del Pedregal project. The collaborative effort of 150 professional experts, the master plan for the university was the brainchild of two architects, Mario Pani and Enrique del Moral.

The PRI leadership chose them because they were outspoken apostles of the International Style and CIAM's Athens Charter. Pani had risen to the top of his profession by building the city's first high-rise public housing project. The two insisted on European spatial ideals of a classical geometric layout for the college campus. They also oversaw the construction of a collection of low-rise look-alikes of Le Corbusier's vision of a Radiant City. The homage to Mexico's cultural traditions—mural art—seems pasted on the slab walls rather than being an integral part of the architecture.[60]

Two dazzling exceptions reinforce the critics' assessment that the university represents a lost opportunity to express Mexican modernism. The first is Juan O'Gorman's library. He was famous for his prewar, International Style design of home studios for Rivera and Kahlo. But coming under the influence of Wright's and Neutra's nature-based architecture, he used the flat walls of the prescribed cubic structure, according to the architectural historian Edward R. Burian, "to connect to a mythical past for political and racial purposes." That O'Gorman was not only an architect but also a painter, muralist, and landscape designer was critical to his success in creating a truly organic piece of functional art.[61]

The other remarkable achievement in blending the ancient and the visionary into an original Mexican modern is the Olympic Stadium. Like O'Gorman, its designers were inspired by Barragán's incorporation of the site's strange environment and national myths into his architecture. Moreover, they would have faced virtually insurmountable cost overruns and technical problems if they had followed the modernist model. It called for the erection of an immense aboveground structure made of reinforced concrete for 110,000 spectators.

Instead, they excavated the lava to dig a bowl-shaped hole. They used the black rocks to build a pyramid of terraced steps around it that gave access to the seats. "The volcanic stone connects the architecture to the geologic time of the Xitle [civilizations]," the architect and professor Alberto Kalach explains. "The power of the space dislocates time and creates a place where past and future are present."[62]

In postwar Mexico, the forces of tradition and modernism, the past and the future, and the workers and the elites contested the meaning of the "soul" of the nation. Yet the main battlefields of this struggle to shape the city's identities of place were the huge amounts of land lost to illegal subdivisions and shantytowns. Each month, an average of fourteen thousand to fifteen thousand additional migrants were arriving in the city and finding a place to live in these sprawling areas.

The insight of the historian Alison Ravetz on the limits of formal urban planning puts the patches of Mexican modernism in proper perspective. They were swallowed up in the spreading prairie fire of the informal *colonias populares*. From 1950 to 1960 alone, *colonias populares* doubled in population and size.

The clientele regime of the PRI was ill equipped to respond to the great migration from farm to factory that its import substitution plan had fostered.

The success of a party godfather like Uruchurtu in El Centro highlights the larger failure of the PRI in the self-built survival communities growing like mushrooms at the fringes of the DF. In communities with preexisting local attachments and identities of place, politicians like Uruchurtu could establish their patron-client relationships with identifiable neighborhood, worker, and religious leaders.

But in the socially disorganized zones of migrants from all over the country, the party had few points of contact at the grass roots. Moreover, the national economic plan to exclude these neighborhoods from getting public utilities and services severely limited the local party's patronage. With little to give these desperately poor people and less to gain from them except their gratitude, Mexico City's political elites would pretend the problem simply did not exist most of the time. For at least twenty years after the war, they enjoyed living "where the air is clear," largely oblivious to the plight of millions of people building their houses in an ecology of urban catastrophe.[63]

São Paulo, Brazil: The Making of Hydroindustrialization

In the case of Brazil, the modernization race was expressed on a monumental scale, the construction of a brand-new capital city, Brasília, in the middle of nowhere. Moving the government to the geographic center of the country was a long-unfulfilled dream until 1955, when Juscelino Kubitschek became president. He chose the country's most famous students of Le Corbusier—Lúcio Costa and Oscar Niemeyer—to create a dramatic symbol of a nation catapulting itself into the machine age.

Starting with highways to achieve speed, Costa's Pilot Plan embodied all the tenants of modernism, including a hierarchy of land uses to display political power and social class in formal geometric patterns. It represents the apogee of modernism because it came closest to realizing the Radiant City ideal of total environmental control. Costa believed "the capital city must be imposed [on] and command [the landscape]." He made provisions for neither working-class housing nor future expansion of the city. Here, the perfect plan of the Organic City did rule.[64]

São Paulo, in contrast, reached another kind of zenith in the Cold War race of technological modernization. It became the place with the most supercharged urban growth machine. The Paulistas' formula of cheap labor and cheap energy lured a huge proportion of foreign investment in Brazil during the postwar period. These international companies set up industrial parks to manufacture cars, consumer durables, and construction equipment and materials.

The sprawling site of these Fordist-style factories was southeast of São Paulo's center in a group of suburbs, which gained the identity of the ABCD Region, referring to the names of the four adjoining municipalities composing this industrial complex. It became, in turn, the home base of the autoworkers and their populist organizations. Brazil's ex-president Luiz Inácio Lula da Silva comes from one of them, São Bernardo do Campo. Growing up in a self-built dwelling, he would become a machinist before emerging as a union leader and a founder of the Workers' Party.[65]

In overtaking Los Angeles in population by the end of the twentieth century, however, São Paulo wreaked havoc on its environment. The runaway success of its growth machine had the unintended consequence of taxing the human and natural resources of the region beyond the breaking point. Demands for housing, transportation, sanitation, and other essential services overwhelmed abilities to meet them. The city befouled its own nest, creating a landscape of environmental disaster, spatial segregation, and violent crime. What's more, São Paulo's ecology of risk was and continues to be the direct result of a deep-seated cultural obsession with social and spatial exclusion.[66]

The plans that increased inequality in São Paulo were small-scale versions of national plans based on import substitution economics. Compared to Mexico, the technobureaucratic regime built during the dictatorship of Getúlio Vargas was far more efficient in squeezing both rural farmers and urban workers. By exporting the nation's agricultural and industrial products, Vargas opened a spigot of foreign capital that flowed into manufacturing companies and state investments in energy, transportation, mining, and heavy industry.[67]

The hell-bent pace of capital investment set at the top imposed a regime of hardship and homelessness at the bottom. São Paulo, for example, went through a postwar period of severe shortages of basic commodities, setting off food riots. The price of building materials also skyrocketed, leaving thousands of migrants without the means to make even the most primitive shelters.

An exploding city made the planners and policy makers in the driver's seat of the growth machine fear that it was spinning out of control. In the local context, security from crime for the social elites took first priority in planning the modernization of the built environment. In the period leading up to the military takeover in 1964, São Paulo became a tale of two cities: a fortified, well-equipped center for the privileged elites and a lawless, hazardous periphery for the deprived masses. As in Mexico City, the official plan was to have no plan for the borderlands.

But in sharp contrast to Mexico City, São Paulo had a detailed blueprint for the future of the downtown area. Under Vargas, São Paulo had begun implementing the 1930 Plan of the Avenues to modernize the city's transportation system. It was designed to replace the electric streetcars with private cars for the rich and public buses for the poor. If its urban aesthetic still reflected Haussmann's Paris, the postwar revision of the plan shifted the vision to New York City and its high-speed parkways to the suburbs.[68]

This is a story of the intersection of the global Cold War and the local built environment. In the late forties, São Paulo hired New York's master builder Robert Moses to superimpose a network of highways on the metropolitan area. According to the planning historian Maria Cristina da Silva Leme, "The new avenues were planned to be larger and built independent of the preexistent system, under or over it."[69]

The origins of the Moses plan trace back to Nelson Rockefeller. He was assistant secretary of state for Latin American Affairs (1944–1945), a dedicated cold warrior, Standard Oil heir, and major investor in South America. After the war, he set up the International Basic Economic Corporation (IBEC) to provide expert consultants to foreign clients and investment opportunities for Americans.

In Brazil, the IBEC was involved in several projects of technological modernization. It was helping the national government improve farm crops. The São Paulo Tramway, Light, and Power Company (SPTLPC) also hired it to transform the Pinheiros River into a concrete canal. Rockefeller's letters of introduction to President Gaspar Dutra and other members of the power elite would result in assignation of this project to Moses.[70]

The Canadians in control of the region's water resources were investing heavily in the infrastructure of the city's growth machine. The SPTLPC was expanding its hydroelectric infrastructure of upland reservoirs and developing the land along its right-of-way to the river, which snaked through the city. As in Los Angeles, channelization of the river promised greater flood control. Moreover, it would increase power capacity because a greater amount of runoff from the hydroelectric dams could be released downstream.

The construction of a non-navigable canal also created new opportunities to draw a land-use plan for the banks on each side of the artificial river. To shorten the story, Moses's plan became the SPTLPC's plan. In July 1950, it became the city's plan when Mayor Lineu Prestes signed a contract with the IBEC.

The Moses plan marked a significant shift in perspective on the urban environment, from the imaginative vision of the European-trained architect to the system thinking of the American public works commissioner. As Leme tells it, the artistic establishment howled in protest against the philistine outsider and his overlays of highways, sanitation plants, and garbage landfills that completely ignored the historical fabric of their city. But the very audacity of the New Yorker's plan fit right in with the city elite's own point of view: technological modernization at any cost.

Although Moses's proposals were formally rejected with a change in the governor's office, its legacy as the first comprehensive plan on a regional scale became embedded in the future building of the urban environment. It became the skeleton for the expansion of São Paulo into a two-faced skyline of center and periphery. Profits from real estate speculation were the rocket fuel driving the engine of this growth machine.

The city's political and business insiders took over where the Moses plan left off. Like urban renewal in New York, expressway construction served a dual purpose of speeding up inner-city slum clearance and suburban lot sales in illegal subdivisions. Linking the two was a public bus system, which allowed city hall to hand out franchises to real estate developers. They had to promise transportation for would-be home builders from distant locations to other bus stops that could eventually get them to their jobs and back again.[71]

For the poor, the only relatively secure places to call home were the open spaces and hillsides of private subdivisions and public lands at the city's edge. These remote suburbs became safe havens for building illegal homes known as *construções* (self-built homes). These dwellings were known as Sunday homes, because their builders had only one day off a week from their jobs to construct them. "A worker buys a piece of land," a local newspaper observed in 1946, "[and he] himself digs a well after-hours, buys bricks. . . . In a few Sundays he puts up his home . . . the ones that shake in the wind."[72] These home builders also had to accept the hardships and risks of daily life without the essential infrastructure of a modern urban environment. They started without piped water and sanitation services, paved roads and streetlights, hospitals, schools, or even reliable public transportation to their jobs. Lula da Silva's memories of childhood remind us that everyday life had no resemblance to romantic fantasies of Horatio Alger types rising from rags to riches. He recounts, "I lived in houses that were flooded by water. Sometimes I had to fight over space with rats and cockroaches, and [human] waste would come in when it flooded."[73]

Living outside the central zone, moreover, condemned the residents of the borderlands to a reign of violence by criminals and police, who used deadly force with impunity. The police were a part of the problem, not the solution to end São Paulo's cycle of violence. Dangerous criminals were everywhere in the metropolitan area, but their main victims were the most vulnerable, poor families living in suburban *construções*, who became so traumatized by the chronic epidemic of violence that they applauded the secret death squads of off-duty police officers.

Yet compared to the risks of unemployment, forced evictions by landlords, and homelessness, the home builders counted on a lack of land law enforcement by the police. To be sure, rent control did provide an important government subsidy for middle-class apartment renters and poorer tenement dwellers in the center. But it was undercut by a high risk of being displaced by the urban renewal bulldozer. And for the truly desperate, land invasions along the railroad tracks, riverbeds, and around the reservoirs would gradually fill in the urban environment and become full-grown favelas.[74]

During the boom years leading up to the military takeover in 1964, these adjustments seemed worthwhile for large numbers of the rich and the poor alike. As long as São Paulo's growth machine of hydroimperialism kept generating industrial jobs, everyone seemed to be riding on a tidal wave of hope in the race of technological modernization. Nevertheless, living within the protected bubble of the center came with its own price. Paulistas would pay more for personal bodyguards, private police, and armored cars than the big rich anywhere else in the world.

But the rise of good fortune was so rapid that the civic elite became delirious on its own uplifting slogans of boundless faith in technological progress. It broadcast to the world its mantra of optimism: "São Paulo must not be stopped." And it showed its disdain for the past by paving over the city's historical core of green courtyards and riverbanks with concrete skyscrapers and canals.[75]

If the growth machine was underwriting the building of a fortified "city of walls" in the center, it was also paying off for many homeowners in the periphery. Little by little, they eked out improvements in personal well-being and neighborhood improvements. One of the most universal indicators of the human condition is the infant mortality rate. In the city of São Paulo, that rate fell by two-thirds, from over 150 per 1,000 live births in 1930 to about 50 in 1960. This was only one tangible proof among many other more visible signs of material gain in some of the shantytowns.[76]

Belief that they were getting closer to reaching their dreams inspired the organization of place-based community groups. As networks of these grassroots movements gelled into an increasingly powerful voice in the city council, the technobureaucrats in charge of the growth machine in the state and national governments began reaching for the emergency brake of martial law. In contrast to labor unions, the emergence of grassroots political organizations in the postwar era grew out of tenant resistance to urban renewal projects. The landlords' illegal tactics of forcing families into the streets in the middle of the night brought neighbors together in self-defense.[77]

In similar ways, home builders in the outlands banded together around neighborhood efforts to obtain infrastructure improvements and social services. Unlike the modern American suburb, of course, the *construção* favelas of São Paulo were erected from scratch on farmland and hillsides barren of public infrastructure and modern conveniences. Neighbors had to join in a united political front to get the essential hardware of an urban environment.

They campaigned to turn dirt paths into paved roads, replace contaminated wells with piped water, and send their children to official, state-sponsored schools. Fierce competition among place-based groups for limited public resources stirred the city council into a political maelstrom.

In the early sixties, fears among the country's policy makers of a general democratic insurrection would prompt them to clamp a lid of martial law on all political activity. Under the command of the technobureaucrats, Brazil lurched both backward to dictatorship in 1964 and forward in an accelerated pace of economic development. In São Paulo, the suppression of the labor unions and other working-class organizations left only the depleted remnants of the neighborhood groups. Under the nurturing of Catholic priests and nuns espousing liberation theology, their identities of place would survive. Eventually, they revived to spearhead a new uprising of the grass roots.[78]

Conclusions: Brasília, Brazil— The Apogee of Modernism

In the years leading up to the military crackdown, the accumulating problems stemming from historic patterns of racial/ethnic and class inequalities could be glossed over by diverting attention to cultural symbols of postcolonial nationalism. The guardians of Brazil's postwar image projected a motion picture of a progressive society united by racial democracy, bossa nova, soccer, and pride in its shining new capital of Brasília. On an inaccessible site without a road or an airport, they would raise the ultimate monument to the International Style of architecture and urban design. And as with its counterpart in India, Le Corbusier's Chandigarh, an overblown inhuman scale would result in a similar dead zone of alienation.[79]

An empty space of 2,300 square miles (6,000 square kilometers) of jungle allowed Costa and Niemeyer to fulfill their master's obsession with complete control. They gained a popular reputation for having a democratic spirit by hanging out with the construction workers in their shantytowns. But more telling was that the planners had located the shantytowns on the bottom of an artificial lake to ensure that they would be literally erased from the face of the earth by the water rising behind the new dam.

In Brasília, the plan did rule in its purest form. The Radiant City idea was expressed in a design that reveals an unbridgeable gulf between its abstraction of nature and its inescapable consequences for the built environment. Costa stripped off a lush tropical ecosystem to impose a minimalist aesthetic of geometric shapes on the city's open spaces. These sunbaked barrens are environmental determinism with a vengeance since they remain pristine, forbidden territory. The unforgiving nature of these heat-stroke zones is legendary. Brasília's residents responded almost immediately by opening up alternative gathering places with shade trees and basic amenities.

A less explored line of inquiry is how the modernists' philosophy of science disconnected their plans of the city from its larger environmental context in the natural world. Certainly, the planners cannot be blamed for bad intentions. Typical is Costa's use of organic metaphors. He declared that Brasília "should be conceived of not as a simple organism capable of administering, satisfactorily and effortlessly, the vital functions of any modern city, not as an URBS, but as a CIVITAS, having the attributes inherent in a capital city."[80]

But focusing intensely on aesthetic ideals of urban space came at a cost of screening out its environmental setting. This failing is made even more glaring when consideration is given to the architects' outstanding landscaping of individual buildings and apartment projects. Niemeyer's Ministry of Justice, for instance, takes full advantage of tropical foliage, rainfall, and so on, to integrate the organic and the artificial into a harmonious whole. Or consider the dome of the Cathedral of Brasília with its transparent ceiling and ever-changing light show of blue sky and white clouds. Yet on a larger scale, the plan had to rule, creating a blistering landscape of soulless alienation on a monumental scale.[81]

The official inauguration of Brasília on April 21, 1960, might have been the high-water mark of the International Style. After World War II, the planners had been given extraordinary opportunities to refashion the physical tissue of urban society. They could account for only patches of modernism after twenty years of work, but these changes had permanently changed the scale and the skyline of the city. Despite good intentions for the most part, the professional experts were also responsible for greasing the wheels of growth machines that increased the spatial distances and social inequities between classes and racial/ethnic and religious groups.

While the building of the urban environment was driven by national economics and global politics, the planners drew a coherent, albeit tunnel, vision of the roadmap to the future. They became leading participants in the Cold War race of technological modernization. Seeing like a state, they helped obscure the widening gap between utopian illusions of the Organic City and the everyday lives of millions of people forced by low wages to endure substandard conditions of environmental risk and social disorder.[82]

II

Deconstructing
Modernism

4

Uprising against the Planners, 1960–1968

Introduction: The Many Afterlives of the Sixties

After running the modernization race for twenty years, government planners and private developers were changing the city skyline in the Western bloc of nations. Pieces of the modernist vision of the Organic City could be seen everywhere: high-rise towers, urban renewal zones, public housing projects, downtown expressways, greenbelt suburbs, shopping malls, industrial parks. However, this start-up period of turning plans into shapes on the ground was also showing unmistakable signs of inadvertent, even perverse, results. Patches of neighborhood deterioration and social disorder, street crime and gang violence, and racial/ethnic and class segregation were spreading inside the city. At the periphery, the environmental impacts of sprawl in suburbs and shantytowns alike were already out of control.

In August 1965, what started as a minor traffic arrest in the Watts section of Los Angeles, California, spiraled out of the control of the local police and shattered the consensus among the planners and policy makers underpinning their vision of the Organic City. Over the next three years, mass marches and violent uprisings in the streets of cities throughout the West challenged the legitimacy of central authorities to dictate the fate of local communities. Following Watts, incidents involving white police brutality in African American ghettos escalated into armed rebellions in virtually every major city in the United States.[1]

Cranked up to full speed by the early 1960s, the growth machines of the great metropolitan centers of Europe and the Americas had become runaway technologies on collision courses. Despite their good intentions, the planners and policy makers were steering them straight into a head-on collision with an urban crisis, a countermovement of grassroots protest against the planners and the results of their work. Asserting control of the street in many different ways, these local uprisings repeatedly intensified from peaceful marches into pitched battles against the state authorities. They, in turn, often retaliated with brutal repressions of the marchers' community and student and labor organizations.

The protests culminated in 1968, beginning in April, when insurrections swept through American cities in the wake of the assassination of Rev. Martin Luther King Jr. A month later, mass movements took control of the streets in cities across Europe following in the footsteps of two million Parisians. They organized a general strike to "stop the machine." In Europe, 1968 became a "magic year" of urban protests against the culture shock of Fordist-style production and mass consumption. A youth movement that transcended nationalism swept across the continent.[2]

America's civil rights and black power leaders made transatlantic connections to Europe's critics of capitalism by adopting their rhetorical tropes of anti-imperialism. The Europeans, in turn, adopted more direct-action tactics of protest to engender autonomous movement cultures of local self-determination and social transformation, if not political revolution. At the height of Cold War tensions, distinctions became blurred between occupations of subaltern peoples by armed forces in the colonies and at home.[3]

In Latin America, the insurgents demanded the democratization of civil society in Bolivia, Ecuador, Venezuela, Chile, Argentina, Brazil, Uruguay, and Mexico. Student and labor groups engaged in deadly street battles against authoritarian dictatorships. The single most horrific retaliation against the struggles of that year occurred in Mexico City. On October 2, the security forces of the national government ambushed university students near their housing complex of Tlatelolco and massacred three hundred to seven hundred of them. With the opening of the Olympic Games just days ahead, the politicians used all the forces at their command to preserve their image of Mexico City as a modernist icon of national progress.[4]

Everywhere in the West, the patches of urban space built by the postwar planners came under attack as symbolic but concrete manifestations of runaway technology. The urban crisis of 1965–1968 caused a breaking point in history; it was a momentous, fleeting moment when the West took stock of itself and changed direction. The protest marches and street battles created an alternative public space that challenged the fundamental tenants of postwar liberalism and its social welfare policies.

The critics of modernism gained public support because their explanations blended ideas about current events and technology into a powerful holistic account of capitalism and its environmental consequences. In contrast, the planners' standing among the power elite and their scientific model of the Organic City collapsed like a house of cards. A string of human-made unnatural catastrophes seemed to make permanent their reversal of fortunes. Sealing their fall from grace were the hammer blows of deadly smog, toxic land, polluted water, dead birds, oil spills, and radioactive fallout in the children's milk. Every step forward in reducing environmental risk from one runaway technology seemed to be offset by two new catastrophes, each more unimaginable than the last.[5]

The first bookend of this multivolume record of shameful environmental disasters was London's killer fog of December 1952, when "smoke ran like water." In just five days, the city's coal-fed air pollution left four thousand people dead and another hundred thousand sick with respiratory distress.[6] At the other bookend was the *Torrey Canyon* shipwreck of March 1967, when 120,000 tons of crude oil ran into the waters of the English Channel. Causing the first great oil spill, the breakup of the jerry-built supertanker contaminated 120 miles (190 kilometers) of the coastline of Cornwall and 50 miles (80 kilometers) on France's side.[7]

Although the planning profession weathered these unnatural disasters by declaring them acts of God, the explosion in the streets of Los Angeles caused an implosion of its postwar consensus. Triggering a crisis of theory and practice, the revolt of the cities split planners into hostile camps. Many sought to vindicate modernism by redoubling the search for value-neutral scientific methods of comprehensive physical planning.

The problem was not a God's-eye point of view, these reformers declared, but simply a blurred focus that incremental advances in systems theory would clarify. They asked the profession to strive harder to bring about this next stage of urban planning. Driven by the invisible hands of market forces and computer programs, the Cybernetic City, they believed, would bring a revival of the profession's fortunes.

Others took up the protesters' call to end the Cold War and to stop its headlong race of technological modernization. These reformers acknowledged a need for new paradigms of planning that incorporated ethical dimensions of social and environmental justice. Moreover, they believed the profession should make a related shift in roles from physical designers to community advocates.

The profession needed to reposition itself within a democratic structure of policy formation, the reform critics contended. Planners should act as facilitators between the place-based organizations at the grass roots and the policy makers at the top levels of government and business. Claiming that cultural and political values were inherently embedded in the production of urban space, the reformers sought to shift power over planning into the hands of local communities.[8]

This polarizing debate within the planning profession over the future of the city was emblematic of larger ideological positions being staked out in what contemporaries came to label the "New Right" and the "New Left." Both attacked the postwar consensus behind the expanded roles of their central governments but from opposite points of view. It would take another six years before the Middle East oil embargo would succeed where the urban uprisings of 1968 had failed in bringing the growth machines of the capitalist nations to a halt. Literally and figuratively running out of gas, they would sputter in a rudderless limbo of stagflation for almost a decade.

Within this larger picture of the coming of a true crisis of capitalism, the focus here is more narrowly concentrated on the attacks mounted against social welfare liberalism and its technocracy of urban planners. It is also limited to contemporary debates on the national and the global levels. Case studies that give meaning to each unique uprising follow in the next, companion chapter. However, we must not lose sight of the ideas linking the local, national, and the global because they played a prominent part within New Left discourse.

There have been "many afterlives" of 1968 because the voices of some participants were privileged over others.[9] The first generation of stories tended to come from male student leaders from affluent families, who went on over the next two decades to become successful professionals and businessmen. Looking back, they promulgated a highly scripted myth of a nonpolitical, coming-of-age block party for a baby-boomer generation of hippies and dropouts.

"In fact," cultural historian Kristin Ross retorts, "May '68 in France was the largest mass movement in French history, the biggest strike in the history of the French labor movement, and the only general insurrection the overdeveloped world has known since World War II." Despite at least seven deaths during the protests, the first accounts erased them from history. They recast a radical political movement of society as a self-indulgent, youth culture of narcissism.[10]

In the Mexican student revolts that summer, the privileging of the male activist leaders and their stories over those of the women foot soldiers led to the construction of a similar consensus behind a contorted point of view. In this case, widely shared traumatic experiences in prison among the male elites after the massacre shaped a single account of another, nonpolitical myth of individual heroism. But a completely different story line than Che Guevara machismo emerged when women activists were interviewed.

Their neglected memories relocate the space of 1968 from the meeting rooms of the leadership to the marketplaces of the people. There, women organized a popular base of support for the movement. They played a crucial class-bridging role in translating the dense, Marxist manifestos of the intellectuals at the top into a spoken language that could be understood by the masses at the grass roots.[11]

The examples of Paris and Mexico City alone caution against drawing any direct links between ideas about urbanism expressed in the media and subsequent activism in the city streets. The standard accounts of the sixties have reduced a complex series of events that accumulatively represented a rupture in history to a literary trope of self-defeating individualism. Cast into binaries, they not only have inverted the political and cultural, the social and individual, the top and bottom, and the male and female roles but also have thrown cause and effect into reverse.[12]

What brings the critics and the protesters together is the currency of the times, a common but by no means unified reaction against the changes under way in the city skyline. They shared alternative views that rejected the planners' and the policy makers' roadmap to the Organic City. They saw it as a runaway technology, a growth machine on a crash course of social conflict and environmental disaster.

Transnational Discourses:
The Urban Crisis of Runaway Technology

Critics of Systems Thinking

Within the larger context of the Cold War, two interwoven strands of this international discourse on capitalism had especially important bearings on ideas about city building: technological modernization and environmental preservation. Although expressions of opposition to the machine age were not novel, their audience grew exponentially with each shocking news flash of another human-made unnatural catastrophe. Jane Jacobs deserves credit for writing the single most influential critique of modernist planning, *The Death and Life of Great American Cities*.[13]

From the opening sentence, Jacobs declares war on its model of the Organic City and its theoretical underpinnings. In a brilliant inversion, the book's title challenges the core assumption of biological determinism derived from Patrick Geddes that cities and neighborhoods have life cycles like plants and animals. "Medical analogies, applied to social organisms, are apt to be far-fetched," she quipped, "and there is no point in mistaking mammalian chemistry for what occurs in a city."[14] So-called urban renewal projects were not surgically removing cancerous tumors; they were cutting out the heart and soul of the city. "This is not the rebuilding of cities," Jacobs charged. "This is the sacking of cities."[15]

Moreover, Jacobs implicitly attacked the influence of the sociologists from the University of Chicago who had recast Geddes's *Cities in Evolution* into a new science of ecology during the interwar years.[16] In doing so, they had proposed a Darwinian process in the rise and fall of residential districts in which, moving from center to periphery, "concentric zones" of land followed a preordained course from upward-bound new neighborhoods to deteriorating slums on the way down. Combing medical and ecological analogies, Homer Hoyt and his fellow social scientists, policy makers, and real estate developers had confused cause and effect, blaming "undesirable" racial and ethnic groups for urban decline.[17] As if invasive weeds, their infestation of homogeneous communities of good citizens upset the natural equilibrium and turned their neighborhoods into breeding grounds of disease, vice, and crime. To stop this pathological "blight" from spreading like cancer, the inescapable conclusion was clean-sweep demolition and dispersal of degenerate populations.[18]

The Chicago School grew out of local conditions but attained universal currency in the West because it reinforced the myth of biological determinism in the making of the modernist skyline. Hoyt's Standard Technique of mapmaking created a seemingly value-free scientific system that translated the natural laws of human ecology into the invisible hand of land values. His theory of neighborhood succession provided a platform of marketplace inevitability that the planners used to justify their paternalistic, Olympian point of view. Uprooting thousands of poor people and small businesses, thus generating social conflict and resentment, the economics of urban renewal was a "hoax . . . resting on vast, involuntary subsidies wrung out of helpless site victims."[19]

Jacobs saw the modernist vision of the Organic City as an antiurban "mirage," for which both Howard's Garden City and Le Corbusier's Radiant City were to blame.[20] Rather than studying how urban spaces actually work as social places, the profession had fallen under the thrall of these utopian prescriptions of how cities ought to be and how inhabitants ought to act. Following their own visions, the postwar city rebuilders were blind to the lived urban experience. "They take this [image] with such devotion," she protested, "that when contradictory reality intrudes, threatening to shatter their dearly won learning, they must shrug reality aside."[21]

Like Le Corbusier, they had become impatient motorists behind the wheel rather than the *flâneur* (wandering pedestrian). She challenged planners to walk the city, seeing how the spaces between the buildings were the sites of authentic and spontaneous human intercourse—"the very DNA of urbanism itself." Unable to see what made physical spaces work as social places, the planners and policy makers were causing more harm than good. They were creating the intolerable conditions of everyday life in the slums, ghettos, barrios, *bidonvilles, colonias populares*, and favelas of cities around the world. "The age of the buildings," she proclaimed, "is no index to the age of a community, which is formed by a continuity of people."[22]

Without this vital ingredient of a collective attachment to a place, slum spaces tended to become self-perpetuating "vicious circles." Successful residents keep moving away because of the absence of a sense of community. Lacking an identity of place, an anarchistic reign of terror now ruled the streets. But youth gangs and violent crime were coming to dominate life not only within the slums. A city's entire population, Jacobs noted, was held in a grip of fear, afraid of danger lurking in what had become in the popular imagination an "urban jungle."[23]

The dramatic increase in the scale of clean-sweep projects and redlining policies was a second reason why the plans of the "slum shifters" was so destructive.[24] Since the end of the war, the nation's financial institutions and housing laws had been based on backward equations of land economics. Inner-city decline and suburban sprawl were not the inevitable results of market forces. On the contrary, the design of this urban machinery was the creation of the New Deal's "high-minded social thinkers."[25] "Credit blacklisting maps, like slum clearance maps" Jacobs railed, "are accurate prophecies because they are self-fulfilling prophecies."[26]

Jacobs proposed that the planners and policy makers reverse course in their thinking, from neighborhood demolition to community conservation. Drawing on the same New Deal idealism, she pointed in the direction of the road not taken: unslumming the slums. Her research had shown that the spark of neighborhood revival was ignited by a core group of families and shopkeepers that stayed and nurtured a sense of community. It was a mistake to bulldoze these residents out to replace them with the middle class.

History showed that "cities grow the middle class,"[27] she believed. Jacobs threw a spotlight on several success stories of officially designated slums that had become attractive places to live, including her Greenwich Village, Chicago's Back-of-the-Yards, and Boston's North End. In each case, the persisters had worked to provide basic amenities and safe streets. These, in turn, kindled a collective sense of identity.

Jacobs urged the planners and policy makers to redirect their gaze from the suburbs to these upward bound, inner-city communities. Instead of redlining them, they should be green-lined for urban conservation. She argued that these places were the mostly likely patches of urban space to benefit from the postwar flood of investment capital pouring into the fuel tanks of the cities' growth machines.[28]

Silent Spring deserves equal credit for defining the discursive framework of the urban crisis.[29] Written in plain language by Rachel Carson, it became one of those rare books that change the course of history. Like Jacobs, Carson drew on traditions of the American conservation ethic. But the marine biologist's stories of nature under siege went beyond preserving patches of wilderness.

Carson taught the postwar generation the primary lesson of ecology: all living things are interconnected. She introduced a suburban nation to concepts of environmentalism similar to Aldo Leopold's land ethic. In a convincing case study of a runaway technology, she showed how disregard of the life sciences could have horrific consequences. Government programs to eradicate bugs by spraying massive amounts of pesticides like DDT were killing off the birds and fish that ate the bugs. And no one was held accountable.[30]

Carson took aim at suburban homeowners, striking a deep chord of anxiety about the environment. The missing sound of birds singing in backyards sparked a different kind of populist uprising against the city growth machines. Led to a large extent by middle-class women, volunteer organizations began sprouting up to defend local patches of open space. They appeared in hundreds of different forms, ranging from homeowner associations of tax rebels to tree-hugging monkey wrenchers.

Americans inspired by *Silent Spring* to take a stand to save nature were emblematic of the appearance during the sixties of grassroots protest against technological modernization throughout the Western bloc of nations. In 1968, the Catholic Bishops of Latin America would endorse a bottom-up liberation theology of place-based activism to demand citizenship rights to the city. Two years later, a worldwide celebration of Earth Day would announce the coming of age of the global reform movement.[31]

Carson's blockbuster put the government's agricultural planners on trial for the environmental consequences of a modernization race that had spun out of their control. Although overshadowed by *Silent Spring*, another book published in 1962, *Our Synthetic Environment*, put the planners under a social lens of critical analysis.[32] It was written by a dedicated radical, Murray Bookchin, who created a holistic concept of "social ecology," or human lifestyles within their environmental settings. He enlarged the notion of environmental risk from the individual to the community.

Ten years earlier, Bookchin, a labor organizer from New York City, had testified before Congress on the health hazards of food crops and animals containing cancer-causing chemicals approved for use on farms. Now he called for a social revolution to save the planet. "Modern man" was eating "highly processed foods that impair health," and, Bookchin charged, the planners and policy makers were subjecting people's mental health to unbearable stress. The present condition of "over-urbanization" was driving the middle-class "organization man" straight toward an emotional breakdown. "He is a nervous, excitable, and highly strained individual," Bookchin wrote, "who is burdened by continual personal anxieties and mounting social insecurity."[33]

Political conservatives too bemoaned an "eclipse of community" that had turned us into a "lonely crowd."[34] Casting a nostalgic look back, these commentators asked whether the machinery of urban development had become a runaway technology bulldozing a fast-vanishing past. In 1964, Jacques Ellul supplied an answer in an influential book that proposed that the West and the East alike had become a single-minded "technological society."[35] The French philosopher accused the Right and the Left of suffering from the same myopia. He argued that this shortsightedness resulted in plans that created two new problems for every one they attempted to solve. These unintended consequences would become increasingly catastrophic as long as modern society continued to have blind faith in a technological fix for all of its urban and environmental problems.

An invisible and self-perpetuating process that Ellul called "technique" was now the predominant force of cultural, economic, and political change. Society was being reorganized along a single line of maximum cost efficiency. "When technique enters into every area of life, including human, it . . . progressively absorbs him. In this respect, technique is radically different from the machine. This transformation, so obvious in modern society, is the result of the fact that technique has become autonomous."[36]

In the same year, Marshall McLuhan showed how television and other communications systems could be used to bring about such a totalitarian world of technological modernization. The ubiquity of these electronic networks, the Canadian literature professor made clear in *Understanding Media*, would turn the Stalinist Big Brother of the dystopian novel *1984* into an impotent, albeit comforting, Wizard of Oz. He imagined the Internet before it was built, predicting that an interactive, worldwide web of interconnectivity would transform the condition of humanity into a "global village." Looking into the future, McLuhan hoped for the dawning of an age of information, when access to the new electronic media would become universal. Yet he also warned that it could become a runaway technology and threaten to turn this virtual community of digital bytes into a genocidal cauldron of tribal, ethnic, religious, and racial conflict.

McLuhan aimed to make the invisible visible. His provocative thesis "the medium is the message," turned the analytical lens of communications theory upside down. The causal source of change was the relationship between humans and their technologies, not the content of these means of transmitting information. "In terms of the electronic age, [it] means that a totally new environment has been created," he explained. McLuhan urged us to open our eyes, to become aware of how electronic media was drawing us into a virtual all-encompassing reality.[37]

Herbert Marcuse came to similar conclusions about a narrowing of visions to a monolithic idea of progress as a modernization race. Part of the émigré group from the Frankfurt School of critical theory, the social philosopher explored the psychological affects of modern life. What he found was that everyone was becoming a systems thinker. Thinking like a technocrat, he claimed, "becomes a way of life . . . and as a good way of life, it mitigates against qualitative change. Thus emerges a pattern of *one-dimensional thought and behavior* in which ideas, aspirations, and objectives . . . are redefined by the rationality of the given system."[38]

Marcuse's critique of reductionist systems thinking comes full circle to Jacobs's charge that the primary cause of urban decline was rooted in the modernists' metaphor of the Organic City. Their utopian vision was fast becoming a self-fulfilling reality in the Western bloc of nations. Marcuse did not deny that modern technology offered economic well-being for unprecedented numbers of the masses. But he protested against the totalitarian ways it restricted the measurement of individual and social value only to things that could be reduced to a quantitative equation.

Marcuse aimed at the power elite in charge of the formation of government and business plans. Unlike Ellul and McLuhan, he took an openly political stand by putting faces on the autonomous, social, and cultural forces of change. True to the principles of the Frankfurt School, Marcuse blamed the capitalist overseers of the race of technological modernization.

These planners and policy makers, the critic concluded, were producing a middle-class level of material affluence but at too great a cost of social and environmental injustice. On the one hand, a "false consciousness" of managed choice was replacing an "inner freedom" of individual thought. On the other hand, the ultimate irrationality of systems thinking was replacing the natural world with a garbage dump of consumer waste. Marcuse called for an uprising against the modernists before it was too late.[39]

Implosion of the Planning Profession

The Watts uprising shifted the national spotlight from the success stories of white homeowners in the suburbs to the failed lives of black slum dwellers. In the immediate afterlife of the urban crisis in Los Angeles, public blame was placed on recent Southern migrants. President Lyndon Baines Johnson co-opted the official account by engineering the appointment of his former CIA chief, John McCone, to take over the investigation from state and local authorities.[40]

The former sharecroppers were perfect scapegoats because they were guilty of a "culture of poverty."[41] They lacked virtually everything needed to succeed in the city, from job and educational skills to personal hygiene and family cohesion. The McCone report's "riffraff theory" would be repeated in several variations to explain the volcanic eruptions of African Americans in the streets of urban America. More careful analysis later, however, would show that permanent residents, not newcomers, made up the vast majority of people participating in these civil disorders.[42]

Planners and policy makers could no longer bury the perverse social and environmental consequences of their model of the Organic City under a politics of denial. The shockwaves of Watts might have been contained within conventional narratives of race riots if the riots had remained an isolated incident, like the Zoot-Suit Riots during the war.[43] But the disturbances set in motion during the long, hot summer of 1965 continued to boil over in inner-city ghettos across the nation for the next three years. Other groundswells of protest added to the pressures that would burst the Cold War consensus behind the modernization race. Activists organized grassroots movements against environmental catastrophes like the *Torrey Canyon* wreck and human tragedies like the Vietnam War. By the late sixties, public discourse became dominated by a backlash politics of fear and rage.[44]

The combined momentum of the uprisings of the urban underclasses, suburban eco-protesters, and global anti-imperialists finally shattered the planning profession's insular image of itself and its mission. "The emergence of the view that town planning was a value-laden, political process therefore raised not so much the question of what the town planner's area of specialist expertise should be, but, more fundamentally, the question of whether town planning involved any such expertise at all," according to Nigel Taylor.[45] "There was a still stronger reason why the existence of the paradigm was not questioned," Alison Ravetz suggests, "for to do this would seem to challenge the very existence of official planning, and this . . . was regarded as not legitimate."[46]

Now suffering a loss of confidence, the profession fractured into warring camps. At the same time, all sides could agree on a need for more holistic approaches. The social and ecological dimensions of contemporary life had to be incorporated into the planning of physical space. Academia's planner elites could no longer ignore the timely challenge posed in mid-1965 by insider critics like Christopher Alexander that "a city is not a tree." Throwing down the gauntlet in *Architectural Forum*, he stated that the profession was "trapped in a tree."[47]

Alexander meant that a God's-eye point of view locked it within its own utopian models of biological determinism. Like Jacobs, he exposed the ways

organic metaphors of the city limited planners to a stripped-down, hierarchical perspective of trunk, branch, and stem. "For the human mind," he
scolded, "the tree is the easiest vehicle for complex thoughts. But the city is
not, cannot, and must not be a tree. The city is a receptacle for life."[48]

Eager to take on the critics' challenge, the defenders of the postwar regime of the International Style of modernism redoubled their efforts to put
a scientific foundation of mathematical precision under both the theory and
practice of official planning. Marching hand in hand with electronics engineers, they built much more ambitious computer simulations of a cybernetic
city of flows. Moreover, they promised that the shortcomings of previous
models would be corrected by broadening the geographic scale to regional
proportions.

Consideration of three of their most influential texts illustrates the response of the systems thinkers to the urban crisis. Four years after Alexander's critique, J. Brian McLoughlin published *Urban and Regional Planning:
A Systems Approach.* He translated the still images of the modernist vision
of the Organic City into motion pictures. "The physical environment is a system of spatially differentiated activities," he wrote, "which interact in various
ways through the flows of persons, goods, or information."[49]

In effect, McLoughlin replaced artistic designs of urban morphology
with dynamic simulations of functional metabolism. Like the mechanical
engineers in charge of electrical grids and water-supply networks, planners
too were experts. They were social engineers, the managers of movement
within metropolitan regions. Their professional role, McLoughlin asserted,
"[was] the deliberate control or regulation of this system so that the physical
environment shall yield the greater social benefit in relation to costs."[50] For
the next decade, his textbook dominated planning school education in the
English-speaking world.

In France, the stalwarts of the technological fix reacted to its critics
with renewed determination to speed up the race to the Cybernetic City. In
1958, Yona Friedman wrote *Mobile Architecture* and organized the *Groupe
d'études de architecture mobile.* He believed that modernism needed to replace the now-tired iconography of Le Corbusier's Radiant City with futuristic images of society running on high technology. To achieve his idol's
goal of liberating the individual within such a constructed space, Friedman
designed a "mobile architecture." A society of nomadic organization men
(and women) would carry standardized "pods" everywhere like backpacks
and plug them in anywhere in the global village.[51]

Running alongside the new functionalist theories of physical space, the
conservators of modernism laid out parallel systems approaches to planning
itself. They sought to turn the process of policy formation into a scientific
method. Called "rational process" and "decision theory," these models were

rooted in Geddes's original three-step formula: survey, analyze, plan. To meet the critics' protest against this tree-like structure, ecological and operational models were incorporated to create never-ending loops of modifying blueprints and updating goals. Planners became managers of a complicated process of monitoring feedback mechanisms and measuring progress.[52]

After Watts, the systems thinkers made sure to insert a community-input step somewhere in their flowcharts of decision making leading to the one best way to win the modernization race. Yet the cultural historian Larry Busbea exposes how they were dedicated to saving the modernist paradigm of the Organic City. His assessment of the French provides insight on this transatlantic group of planners. "We can recognize in their projects," he observes, "the persistence of a total faith in technology's ability to enhance the quality of life, the continued assertion of the necessity of a 'synthesis of the arts,' and a profound failure to establish a critical (or even ironic) relationship to the relatively newly defined phenomenon of mass or consumer culture."[53]

Painfully sensitive to this blind spot, the architect Robert Venturi cross-dressed the International Style in the fashions favored by its critics. In 1966, he declared that "complexity and contradiction" were intrinsic goods in the design of buildings and cities. To counter the tendency of these modernists toward concrete megastructures, Venturi issued an appeal for a return to historicism. Just as the artist Caravaggio had reacted against the Renaissance perspective, Venturi extolled examples of asymmetrical Mannerist styles that dissolved boundaries between interior and exterior spaces.[54]

One of the planning elite's most preeminent academics, Yale University's Vincent Scully, endorsed Venturi's strategy of beating the critics of modernism at their own game. In a defiant introduction to Venturi's textbook, the world-famous connoisseur of high-brow culture turned against his own generation of designers influenced by Le Corbusier and Bauhaus.[55] Outdoing Jacobs's rhetorical fireworks, he mocked that generation's "utter lack of irony, its spinsterish disdain for the popular culture but shaky grasp on any other, its incapacity to deal with monumental scale, its lip-service to technology, and its preoccupation with a rather prissily puristic aesthetic."[56] He and Venturi used ridicule to prod the profession into turning from its one-dimensional prewar aesthetics of "noble purism" to a new postmodernist era of humanistic diversity and consumer fantasy.[57]

To the critics of the official planning regime, however, the reforms of its elite defenders represented a mere course correction to get the profession through the crossroads of the urban crisis without making any major turns in new directions. On the contrary, improved systems approaches to spatial functions, inclusive theories of decision-making processes, and vernacular styles of architecture were all aimed at reinforcing the profession's ideological foundations with a fortified mantle of social science and computer wizardry.

After the Planners, Robert Goodman's 1972 memoir of an academic insider turned radical protester, provides an especially useful way to illuminate the response of the New Left faction within the profession.[58] He became one of its reformers, exploring alternative routes to a postmodernist future of local self-determination and environmental justice. In learning how to become a grassroots activist, Goodman more or less invented "advocacy planning" along the way.[59]

After getting a degree in architecture and in reaction to the uprisings of the sixties, he dropped out of the graduate program at MIT and moved into an officially designated slum in Boston. He started by helping the boosters and shopkeepers of the working-class neighborhood turn their visions of the community into formal proposals for public funding under various conservation programs. In 1966, he confronted the city planner about implementing the community's proposals but was told in emphatic terms that Boston already had a plan: his, the planner's, plan.

Goodman's experience led him to denounce the planning profession for becoming a technocracy of "outside experts." They were no longer capable of seeing everyday life. Although they were well intentioned, he conceded, they had become tools of a "repressive social structure, which is biased against the people their plans are supposed to serve."[60] Goodman condemned Venturi's book as a prime example of how the profession had become a servant of this regime of class and racial/ethnic inequality. Its language of aesthetic values and organic metaphors obscured the real political and economic forces behind the production of urban space. In a similar way, the official planners covered up their partisan roles in the regime. They had disguised themselves as benevolent "urban doctors," scientists healing society and the environment.[61]

By the conclusion of his reeducation, Goodman had learned not only how to become an advocate planner but also what the limits of community planning were. He had worked with other activists and professionals to formulate conservation plans that won the policy debate within the bureaucratic process of decision making. But they had proved to be Pyrrhic victories because Boston politicians vetoed funding for any plans other than those of the city planner.

Goodman still held out hope that a "guerrilla architecture" of vernacular styles would grow out of a democratic process of community empowerment.[62] He envisioned giving the building of cities a new direction and making them into "containers for human activity." Yet Goodman's experience left him doubtful about the possibility of turning the West from its headlong course of technological modernization.[63]

In the early 1970s, the enthusiasm of reformers like Goodman turned into disillusionment. Significantly, McLoughlin joined Goodman in questioning planning theory and the profession's role in a technological society. After applying his own textbook's lessons to Leicester, United Kingdom, according to a close collaborator, he "came to almost disown the book and certainly to reject many of its ideas." He came to understand, H.W.E. Davies recalls, that the "systems approach of the 1960s shared some of the same basic assumptions as those in the earlier paradigm that had underpinned planning in the 1940s. Both had their basis in assumptions that 'society rests fundamentally on consensus.'"[64]

But the uprisings of the sixties taught him that contemporary life in the city was a cauldron of multicultural diversity. Another colleague confirms that McLoughlin's experience led him to conclude that "the whole approach was good at maintaining the status quo and working with trends. It was much less effective at changing trends."[65] McLoughlin also came to share Goodman's point of view about the role of the profession. If the creation of a scientific, value-neutral model of urban functions was problematic, then its practitioners could not escape embedding their own biases in the production of urban space. The systems approach to planning theory, he decided in the end, "offered prizes for all: to bureaucratic empire builders, to academics wanting disciplinary distinctiveness and academic 'respectability,' to the modellers and the symbiotic computer salespersons."[66]

Caught in the crossfire of the warring factions among the elite theorists of the planning schools were the thousands of ordinary practitioners in cities across the Western world. For many of them, the urban crisis turned into a personal crisis of professional status and future income. They were already feeling under siege by the grass roots. Now the attacks on them from within by the systems thinkers for not being scientific enough and for being too "prissily puristic" in their aesthetic values came as especially heavy blows to their sense of confidence.

The most common reaction of planning practitioners was to shut the entire controversy out of their day-to-day work routines. The planning schools might have reformed their curricula to incorporate the social and environmental dimensions of the city; however, their graduates clung to the certainties of their roles as artistic urban designers of modernist patches of physical space. In fact, their inertia exerted a massive drag on changing directions in theory and practice.[67]

Yet the mobilization of dissent arising both from the grass roots and within the profession did cause a historic shift in urban planning to a postmodernist paradigm. Resistance to growth machines of technological modernization became permanent after the urban crisis of the 1960s, creating new discursive and institutional frameworks of urban planning. Community organizing around place-based issues itself became a career. Perfected by Saul Alinsky of Chicago's Back-of-the-Yards Neighborhood Council, its practitioners learned to apply his strategy of uniting local residents behind confrontational, albeit winnable, campaigns of local self-determination against the powers that be. In coming years, professional experts trained in the Alinsky method would be hired by every kind of special-interest group, ranging from white homeowner associations to black community councils.[68]

Citizen participation in the planning process, moreover, became mandated throughout the Western bloc of nations. Policy makers insisted on the inclusion of maximum community input in the formation of local plans. A year after the Watts riots, in 1966, for example, the U.S. Congress initiated a Model Cities program that gave legitimacy to grassroots organizations in the decision-making process for the first time.

This institutional shift in power was matched by changes in funding formulas that gave greater priority to saving neighborhoods rather than bulldozing them. The United Kingdom took urban conservation a step further the following year, when Parliament passed the Civil Amenities Act, creating a new category of special protected zones where higher standards of historic preservation would apply.[69]

Britain's lawmakers followed up by redrawing county borders and passing the Town and Country Planning Act of 1969. This structural reform broke the postwar regime in two, taking the power to decide the fate of local development projects away from the central planners. In a very British style of protest, local activists, including Patrick Abercrombie, had clogged up the courts with a virtually endless number of technical objections to the ministries' finished plans.[70]

Under the new two-tier system, town hall bureaucrats had to provide open forums for public input early in the process. This allowed the grass roots to present alternative plans while they could still be given serious consideration. Other European nations also installed various structural mechanisms that empowered communities to participate in the building of the urban environment.[71]

To be sure, this wave of reform legislation enacted by national policy makers in response to the urban crisis did not ensure compliance by local politicians and planners. They often greeted it with their own bureaucratic forms of resistance. Until the 1974 oil embargo, funds for urban renewal, highway, and other infrastructure projects kept flowing through their hands. Although these streams of public and private investment capital began drying up in the mid-1960s, there was still plenty in the pipeline to maintain the momentum of their growth machines in the same direction. "One of the ironies of planning's lip-service to 'community,'" Ravetz notes, "was that in the course of restructuring the city it destroyed the older working-class neighbourhoods that had in many ways the best claim to that title."[72]

And in a similar way, the general failure of systems theories when put into practice did not stop most of the planning schools from continuing to base their curricula on them. Authors such as Andreas Faludi persisted in their belief in environmental determinism. They continued to claim that their approaches were the only way to make the practice of planning into a value-free scientific process of decision making.[73]

In spite of these continuities, the urban uprisings of the sixties represent a historic crossroads of fundamental change in planning theory and practice. The institutionalization of resistance is one of the hallmarks of postmodernity. Irreparably shattered, the Cold War consensus within the profession was replaced by warring factions engaged in battles from different points of view about the coming city. Whether accepting or rejecting the new planning theories after Watts, the profession could no longer deny the emergence of a postmodern condition of transnationalism, multicultural diversity, and social fragmentation.

Global Movements: The Postmodern Condition of Popular Resistance

In the shambles of the modernist vision of the Organic City, unmistakable signs were arising of a new worldview, in which all sources of authority become contested terrain. The philosopher of science Stephen Toulmin, for one, sees Watts as the death knell of the Enlightenment. "The cultural changes that began around 1965," he reflected a quarter century later, "were . . . cutting into our traditions more deeply than was widely appreciated."[74]

In addition, a mass media smokescreen of "riffraff theories" dominated the immediate afterlife of Watts, making it difficult to get to the root causes of the civil disorders. For a while, this fog of misinformation and its scapegoat analogues in other countries helped cover up not only the depth of the cultural divide separating the eras but also the social, economic, and political dimensions of the urban uprisings that spread from the United States to Europe and Latin America. By the opening of the Olympics in Mexico City on October 12, 1968, this chain reaction of protest against the runaway technologies of the Cold War appeared to have run its own course to an inclusive endgame.

But a pair of raised black-gloved fists by two African Americans made an unforgettable gesture that resistance to the powers that be was the new order of the day. Only ten days after the massacre of the students near Tlatelolco and four days into the games, gold-medalist Tommie Smith and his bronze-medalist teammate John Carlos mounted the winners' podium dressed symbolically as members of a transnational movement. To protest against segregation and oppression at home and abroad, according to Smith, they wore, "the shoeless socks of racist poverty, the black scarf of Pan-African pride, and the clenched hand of black power."[75]

The whole world was watching as they stood joined together in unity with their free arms held high. Then they turned their heads away from the American flag during the playing of the national anthem. Although they were banned from the competition and ejected from the Olympic Village by the International Olympic Committee, the officials could take away neither their athletic achievements nor the dignity of their protest.[76]

Their act of defiance has been reinterpreted many times since 1968. From today's perspective, these kinds of "stories of resistance" from the sixties, as Leonie Sandercock calls them, have become incorporated in an "epistemology of multiplicity." An example would be the "insurgent planning histories" of Mexico City's female activists. Their stories have both enriched and complicated our understanding of what happened there.[77]

A vantage point of almost a half century has been equally important in putting the urban uprisings of the decade into historical frameworks that stretch back to the taproots of the Cold War era. Rather than narcissist spasms of self-destruction, they are now portrayed in this larger context as the breaking point in a long-term accumulation of modernist changes in the city's skyline and its patterns of everyday life.

Consider the case at hand of the massacre and the Olympics in Mexico City from these current perspectives. Michael Soldatenko writes, "Our thinking on contemporary México commences with our interpretation of México '68. . . . Our constant interpretation and reinterpretation of the student movement turns it into mythology, a form of social amnesia, and the experience of it is fading into oblivion. We forget the universe created by people's actions. Therefore we need to imagine how self-determination and participatory democracy created a new, though temporary political space."[78]

Putting the origins of the athletes' raised fists of resistance in larger historical context illustrates how a half century of retrospection also produces more multifaceted, provisional interpretations of the sixties. Scholars such as Peniel E. Joseph now trace it back to "the New Negro radicalism of the 1920s and the subsequent freedom surges of labor, civil rights, and grassroots activists around the nation."[79] In this case, the Olympic sprinters' gesture becomes contextualized within a continuing legacy of African American protest against racism in sports. During the twentieth century, resistance against racial stereotypes stretches from the boxer Jack Johnson in the 1920s to Joe Lewis and the transformation of Cassius Clay into Mohammad Ali in the early 1960s.[80]

The backstory of Smith's and Carlos's black power salute is grounded in their membership in the Olympic Project for Human Rights (OPHR). It, in turn, is based in the civil rights movement on college campuses across the country. The OPHR worked to gain more African American–oriented programs and personnel, including head coaches in the athletic departments. The OPHR also joined a worldwide movement to pressure the International Olympic Committee to exclude South Africa and Rhodesia from the games on account of their regimes of racial oppression.

After achieving this goal, its secondary objective was the removal of the committee's American chairman, Avery Brundage. An anti-Semitic sympathizer with Adolf Hitler during the 1936 Olympic Games as the leader of the U.S. delegation, he had risen in the world of sports to become its most conspicuous personification of racial/ethnic discrimination. Refusing to step down, Brundage was the intended target of the protest. He held on to his position, while Smith and Carlos paid a heavy personal price for their momentary, albeit enduring, act of defiance. After 1968, nonetheless, a clenched raised fist became the international symbol of resistance.[81]

In spite of the tendency of recent historical perspectives to melt the tree-like lines of the modernist narrative into a matrix of "complexity and contradiction," there is plenty of solid evidence that the urban uprisings of 1965–1968 opened a new age in the history of the West. Consider that 1968 marked the first time the Olympic Games were held in a Spanish-speaking and Latin American country. This gesture on behalf of multiculturalism signaled a departure from the past by inspiring new alternative imaginaries of the future.

In 1968, the sports world's recognition of the coming of age of the third world was made much more substantial at a meeting of Catholic bishops in Medellín, Colombia. Attendees professed a new liberation theology, marking a radical reversal of church authority from the pope to the poor as well as from holy scripture to daily practice. In that pivotal year, the Brazilian-born and American-educated Rubem Alves published *A Theology of Human Hope*.[82] He and other followers in the footsteps of earlier Catholic worker movements such as France's Paul Gauthier and Peru's Gustavo Gutiérrez took a stand of resistance against the conservative social agenda of the Second Vatican Council (1962–1965).

To implement its teachings, the Latin Americans at the meeting turned the hierarchical structure of the church upside down. They began seeing each layperson as a source of sacred authority. The reformers would build a grassroots movement of Christian-base communities on neighborhood issues of social and environmental injustice.[83]

Historians have been discovering more and more of these previously hidden markers of a sea change during the three years of insurrection against the planners. A broad spectrum of them has became visible, ranging from the everyday meetings of community organizations to the utopian ether of abstract imaginaries. If the inauguration of liberation theology is evidence of the path of the New Left, then the formation of the World Society for Ekistics (WSE) in 1965 illustrates the main course of change pursued by the New Right.

Founded by a Greek planner and businessman, Constantinos A. Doxiadis, the WSE created a platform to broadcast his visionary response to the urban crisis. He called his model of a good place "Entopia." Doxiadis would lead the way in recalibrating computer simulations of urban growth machines to global scale.[84]

His remarkable career exemplifies the metamorphosis of the modernist urban planner into a New Age global futurist. Trained as an engineer in Athens and Berlin, Doxiadis became the chief planner of the Greek capital city in the decade before World War II. Then, as a hero of the resistance, he became public planner of urban housing and reconstruction. In the early 1950s he also became the owner of a construction company, being awarded an extraordinary share of lucrative government contracts to build social housing. While serving in a government ministry, Doxiadis participated in creating the United Nations and conducting its first worldwide studies of the city. The trajectory of his public and private consulting work as an international planner of cities catapulted him into the highest echelons of the world's power elites.

Doxiadis made two major contributions toward reducing a planetary ecology to a mathematical algorithm. In 1961, he set up a company to build and operate a supercomputer on a par with those in the hands of the military and the universities. He also sponsored a number of forums on the future of the world, inviting such well-known experts as the American technologist R. Buckminster Fuller, French geographer Jean Gottmann, and Scottish architect-planner Sir Robert Matthew. At the third Delos Symposium, in 1965, they formed the WSE to plot a roadmap to their vision of a global network of a thousand villages. Doxiadis also published a related book that explained why a rational systems approach to the universal problem of human settlements would lead to a resolution of the urban crisis.[85]

Searching for a middle ground between dream and reality, the Greek planner started with an admission of guilt. He agreed with Jacobs's and Goodman's indictment of the profession. "We build bad places," Doxiadis confessed, "we build dystopias and we live in them!"[86] He also joined critics like Ellul and Marcuse who blamed the runaway technologies of the modernization race for the disorder of urban society. Furthermore, he took a stand with Bookchin and Carson on behalf of the environment. "Now man is forced to accept his cohabitation with the machine," he observed, "disputing the same space with it, breathing its exhausts."[87]

Given his background, Doxiadis envisioned the problem in terms of physical space and technology. For him, the geographic sprawl caused by the mindless production of cars and highways had destroyed the human scale of the city. But in complete contrast to the New Left's demand for local self-determination, Doxiadis called for tighter bonds of interdependence in a tree-like structure of command and control. "The solution . . . ," he declared, "is not de-centralization but new-centralization."[88]

And in opposition to the eco-protesters, he proposed a technological fix to building the urban environment. He envisioned binding a world of Jane Jacobs–sized communities into a McLuhan-like global village. "All types of much more developed networks are going to turn the whole Earth into one neighborhood," he predicted.[89] Entopia, he concluded, would need to depend on systems approaches. In the immediate afterlife of 1968, his WSE seemed to fade into the shadows. It was eclipsed by a new group of much more powerful world leaders and their Club of Rome, which soon achieved what Doxiadis had dreamed of seeing: the whole earth shrunk to the size of a computer screen.[90]

If the plans of this internationally renowned expert to build a cybernetic, global city appeared visionary, then the publication of Italo Calvino's *Invisible Cities* in 1972 dispelled any further doubt that the West had entered a new postmodern world. In this brilliant deconstruction of our image of the city, Calvino weaves memories and observations, symbols, and signs into a mind-bending trail of stories that Marco Polo tells to Kublai Khan. Bursting the boundaries between dream world and scientific knowledge, Calvino left readers no other conclusion: urban space is a different place in the eyes of each and every beholder.[91]

5

Case Studies, 1960–1968

Grassroots activism and protest against planners and policy makers arose in each city considered in this book. In exploring these events I respond to Leonie Sandercock's call for "insurgent planning histories" that act as counterweights to the official account.[1] As she predicted, these alternative interpretations of the city often feature women. Stretching back to the Progressive Era, their defense of home and family has been the most common impetus to take place-based opposition to public policies. In some cases, they became the spearheads of reform movements in much larger battlegrounds of state and national politics.

The activists in these stories of resistance take ideological positions from the extreme Right to the radical Left. What the protesters shared was a point of view that funneled global and national issues down to a local and personal perspective. Conversely, their uprising against the modernist city illuminates how grassroots movements percolated up hierarchies of power in the formation of public policy and political culture.[2]

Los Angeles, United States: The Politics of Racial Fear

In Los Angeles, commentator Mike Davis warns, shining a light on its insular communities of white privilege will reveal a "labyrinth of micro-history—a dark chronicle of the tractlands."[3] Their stories of resistance against racial integration of the public schools, however, require taking a preliminary step back before moving forward into the sixties. The city's legacy of attacking labor unions gave incendiary potency to a politics of fear during the formative period of the Cold War. After 1945, moreover, regional planning and national housing policies constructed a suburban landscape of racial/ethnic and class segregation. The accumulating inequalities resulting from white privilege and nonwhite exclusion go a long way in explaining the buildup of political tensions to explosive levels of social disorder.

In this context, it is useful to examine the story of South Gate, located on the other side of Alameda Street, where Watts begins (see Map 8). Its insurgent planning microhistory is a story of racial fear, a microhistory that started as a place-based defense of community but ended up transforming the personal, class, and party identities of its inhabitants. Like Watts, South Gate began as what Becky Nicolaides refers to as "my blue heaven," one of the many working-class suburbs that sprang up during the interwar years.[4] Its neighborhoods of single-family dwellings arose within a larger emerging landscape of a fragmented metropolis. A patch of the South Central area, it was built among industrial zones and transportation hubs about seven miles south of the downtown.[5]

But after the war, the second Great Migration split into two streams of Southerners, with whites moving into South Gate and blacks into Watts. Moreover, the increasing economic isolation and physical deterioration of the African American neighborhood could not have stood in greater contrast to the up-and-coming middle-class look of the community just across the color line on its eastern boundary. Residents of Watts remember Alameda Street as a "virtual Berlin Wall," dividing despair from hope.[6] In Watts, two out of five households fell below the poverty level after a decade of factory closings in the area. Despite a protest campaign, the electric street railway was shut down in 1961, making car ownership almost a prerequisite for a job.

On the other side, daily life in South Gate seemed to be on track toward the fulfillment of the American Dream. "Self-help, individualism, Americanism, homeowner rights, and a distaste for activist government persisted as core values," Nicolaides finds in her study of this community.[7] What changed for these families in the sixties was that their aspirations for upward mobility became dependent on their identities of place. To achieve the social status of middle class in Los Angeles had come to mean being rich enough to afford to live in an all-white school district. "In the new context of economic prosperity and racial encroachment," she notes, "they blended easily with the southern political style."[8]

She calls the toxic, racist cocktail of mass resistance that resulted "a new working class populism."[9] It grew out of fears of an invasion of enemies from the outside world that posed an ever-greater threat to destroy their way of

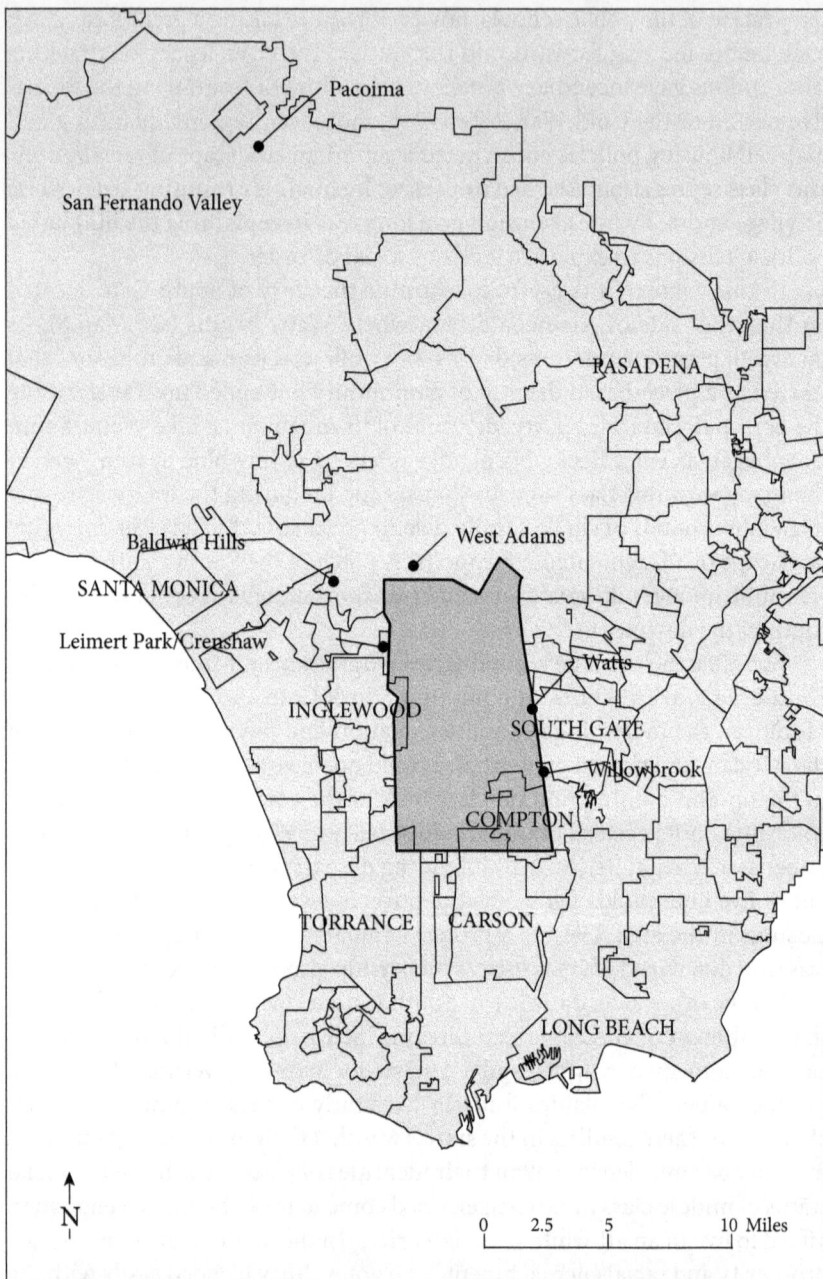

Map 8 Los Angeles: The South Central and the Greater Los Angeles Area (Republished with permission of Josh Sides, *L.A. City Limits: African American Los Angeles from the Great Depression to the Present* [Berkeley: University of California Press, 2003], map 1, p. 209)

life. In defending the community against school desegregation, South Gaters did not submerge their blue-collar identities under new self-images of whiteness. Nicolaides is careful to point out that, on the contrary, race and class remained "inextricably intertwined."[10]

In Los Angeles, the civil rights movement suffered defeat in its campaign to open up the suburbs. White grassroots activists trumped national and state fair housing laws with local land-use controls and restrictive zoning. The battle lines of racial privilege formed along the boundaries of the local school districts. White flight in Los Angeles was unusual because it was driven by not the integration of the city's schools but paranoia of anticipation. Affluent families with children began escaping beyond the city boundaries after the landmark *Brown v. Board of Education* Supreme Court decision in 1954, or more than a decade before the Watts uprising. It would take another ten years to achieve meaningful desegregation.[11]

Angelinos feared African American students would put their children in harm's way of interracial violence, lower academic standards, and higher crime rates. Their anxiety generated an unbearable sense of insecurity. Many moved out of the county altogether. Next door in Orange County, for example, they could move into established communities or new subdivisions with restrictions against sales to nonwhites. For the homeowners of South Gate left behind, identity of place meant mounting a defense to prevent kids from Watts from coming into their neighborhood to attend the public schools. Its virtually all-white South Gate High stood only a mile from the all-black Jordan High in Watts.[12]

In June 1963, Rev. Dr. Martin Luther King Jr. helped organize a grassroots movement by making these two schools the focus of the city's black freedom struggle. "In the process," according to an account of the Watts rebellion, "a new and durable pattern of political cleavage, based on race and ideology, began to dominate city politics."[13] The matchup of the two schools was the movement's response to the racial infamy of Alameda Street as the Line and the Wall in the mental landscape of Los Angelinos. Forming the United Civil Rights Council (UCRC), seventy-six groups joined in demanding the redistricting of school boundaries.

The UCRC employed the tactics of civil disobedience. At the beginning of the 1963 school year, in September, they organized a boycott of Jordan High to dramatize their renewed determination to integrate the L.A. Unified School District. The UCRC also filed a lawsuit on behalf of a Watts family to get state courts to force local officials to comply with desegregation rulings. In the fifties, the civil rights lawyers charged, overcrowding in Watts had led to half-day shifts, while there were many classrooms with empty desks east of Alameda Street in South Gate. In other words, the board of education was guilty of racial gerrymandering.[14]

In South Gate, the ensuing battle against school desegregation had the effect of transforming personal identities and giving birth to a New Right. "As whites mobilized in opposition to educational civil rights," Nicolaides writes, "they began formulating the ideological and organizational bases of a conservative countermovement."[15] The historian notes that as many men as women became activists, which kept working-class traditions of patriarchal gender roles in place. Forming the South Gate Education Committee, they worked together to enlist local support. Taking the offensive, these grass-roots activists collected 17,500 signatures on petitions against busing. They also filled the seats at meetings of the board of education and the city council with protesters. Furthermore, they expropriated the national discourse of the civil rights movement into a local defense of racial/ethnic inequality.[16]

Trying to preempt the courts, the board of education issued a report in November that backfired because it stiffened the resolve of the combatants on both sides of the color line. The policy makers maintained a steadfast denial of any responsibility for de facto segregation due to racial patterns of residential settlement. Defending the color line, the board refused to bus the children of Watts into South Gate. The city's civil rights movement had hit a solid wall of resistance, defeating its campaign to begin school integration.

But rather than jubilation, Los Angeles's suburban warriors felt betrayed by the policy makers. To avoid coming under the control of the courts, the board had inserted a legal loophole in its report. It held open the possibility of redrawing boundary lines in the future to reduce racial imbalances in the school district. Even this minor concession was alarming enough to frighten the working-class populists in South Gate and other white-only suburbs into a new frenzy of grassroots activism in the battle against change imposed by the outside world.[17]

The next two years leading up to the Watts uprising were pivotal in transforming collective and individual identities in the white tractlands of Los Angeles. Loyalty to the two major parties dissolved and was replaced by a self-image of the citizen homeowner under siege. South Gaters became what political commentator Garry Wills described in 1968 as those "who succeeded but felt somehow cheated, forgotten, un-respected, mocked."[18]

Fueling a politics of resentment, they adopted Homer Hoyt's market-place theories of land values to assert civil and political rights to local control over who lived in their neighborhoods.[19] No longer able to deny the Line, working-class populists repackaged the racism of white privilege into a positive movement to expand individual liberty by shrinking the public sector.

In the new language of rights talk, voicing opposition to racial/ethnic equality became advocacy in favor of freedom. It reinvented the right of association, the free market, and its self-help ethos of individual success. Like

Hoyt, its spokespersons used a color-blind lens of denial to view their "possessive investment in the privileges of whiteness."[20]

During this period of flux, their defense of segregation in the schools and the neighborhoods grew into an extralocal, insurgent political movement to strip the government of its powers of control over local communities. In June 1963, this counteroffensive of suburban secession found organizational expression in the formation of a nonpartisan statewide organization, the Taxpayers' Rebellion. Less money for the government would reduce its capacity to wage its war of forced integration on behalf of racial and ethnic minorities. Busing was at the top of the tax rebels' hit list of wasteful public spending.

For South Gaters, the state government confirmed their conspiracy theories of New Deal collectivism, if not an imminent communist takeover, when it enacted the Rumford Fair Housing Act. They were already feeling under siege by the school board and the county tax collectors. The new law banned discrimination in the sale or lease of private property. The state's real estate board immediately took charge of mobilizing a grassroots insurgency of homeowners to overturn the law. This defense of white privilege became a powerful movement, a Southern-style politics of racial fear.

Community activists in South Gate and other white-only communities campaigned for Proposition Fourteen, an initiative on the state ballot to reverse the "Rumsford 'forced' Housing Act" and deny the policy makers and planners authority to limit the rights of individuals to decide the fate of their property.[21] In the fall of 1963, a poll of South Gate residents revealed that 96 percent supported the initiative. In Los Angeles as a whole, the insurgent movement of conservatives recast the November 1964 contests for the governor's mansion and the White House in personal and place-based terms of upholding the rights of white privilege.[22]

In South Gate, racial fears dominated politics at every level of the federal government. Consider that President Lyndon Baines Johnson was persuaded to campaign there by state party leaders. They hoped he could staunch what they feared would be a wholesale defection of their base of support in the working-class suburbs to the Republicans.

At the same time, the local hero of white supremacy and anticommunism and mayor of Los Angeles, Sam Yorty, challenged Governor Pat Brown in the Democratic primary for signing the fair housing act into law. The challenger couched his racist appeals to the grass roots in the new language of rights talk. He became a champion of Proposition Fourteen. Yorty denounced Brown's decision as an act of betrayal to the citizen-homeowner. In addition, the seasoned Red baiter tapped into white Angelinos' racial fears and insecurities. Yorty was among the first to exploit white fears of personal violence at the hands of blacks, Latinos, and other minorities.

"Law and order functioned as a 'bridge,'" the historian Michael W. Flamm posits, "enabling the right to tap into existing streams of conservatism at the municipal level and divert them into national politics. The rhetoric constructed at the national level also mobilized grassroots conservatives, giving them a language of protest. . . . The symbiotic and symbolic qualities of law and order thus enhanced its political power and potency."[23]

In South Gate, the election returns reflected the pivotal nature of this period of political and ideological realignment. While Johnson held the loyalty of 57 percent of its voters, they elected a Republican by about an equal margin to represent them in Congress. More significant for the future, almost nine out of ten voted in favor of the initiative to put public controls over their private lives in a constitutional straightjacket.

But the statewide victory of Proposition Fourteen did little to reduce white homeowners' insecurities of social status and identity of place. In fact, the election results had the opposite effect, deepening their sense of being under siege from outside forces attacking their way of life. Paranoia mounted in anticipation of violent retribution from the black community in the wake of the repeal of the fair housing law. Mayor Yorty's reassurance that Police Chief William H. Parker had the situation under control was no match for a self-reinforcing culture of fear within a community of like-minded residents.[24]

For them, the uprising of Watts the following August was the tipping point in their political realignment from New Deal liberals to New Right conservatives. As they literally took up arms along Alameda Street in defense of white privilege, their metamorphosis into citizen-homeowners was complete. "The Watts Rebellion," Nicolaides concludes, "confirmed the righteousness of their stand against civil rights like nothing else could have."[25]

South Gate's men with guns stood their ground on the east side of Alameda Street because their individual identities of class had become "inextricably intertwined" with their collective identity of place.[26] "Taken together," the historian Kevin Kruse sums up, "these 'movements in defense of whites'' 'freedom of association' accelerated the earlier movement away from community and consideration of common interests and instead toward individuality, privatization, and the concern for self-interest above all else."[27]

In Watts, the election returns of November 1964 represented not only a major setback in the civil rights movement's assault on the outer walls of ghettoization. The voters' reinforcement of institutional racism in the schools and housing also became a green light for a significant escalation in the paramilitary occupation of the police inside the community. Mayor Yorty kept goading Chief Parker to step up the pace of his crackdown on street crime. For the grassroots activists of the black freedom struggle, the backlash of violence directed against the police came as no surprise.

Watts was different. "Unlike the earlier Detroit case [of 1943] but similar to other riots of the 1960s," a study of the urban crisis by Janet L. Abu-Lughod highlights, "Watts was not a battle between white and black residents but rather one between some members of the local community and the 'forces of law and order,' including the largely white police and fire services and even the National Guard."[28]

Calling the insurrection of Watts the first "drive-in riot," Abu-Lughod is careful to underscore that civil disorders on this scale create chaotic spaces of social and political crosscurrents.[29] They are full of actors moving in different directions: some became street fighters, while others became peacemakers. In the case of Watts, nonetheless, the residents shared a list of place-based grievances that played a part in causing the uprising. Feeling locked inside a ghetto, they listed the deficit of jobs and excess of consumer rip-offs, the bad streets and housing conditions, and the lack of physical facilities such as public transportation, good schools, shopping centers, and green spaces.[30]

A careful reading of the official account substantiates their complaints in spite of its candy-coated gloss.[31] Commission head John McCone, as a member of the city's inner elite, had to uphold the line that Los Angeles remained a heavenly land of sunshine for African Americans compared to the inner-city slums of Northern cities. His report's key recommendations for better schools, more adult training programs, and improved public transportation would have gone a long way toward reducing the single most important cause of urban deterioration in Watts, a lack of work. Sixty percent of its unemployed residents reported that their search for jobs outside the South Central area was futile because they could not afford to buy a car to get to them.[32]

But whatever sympathy the McCone Commission report might have engendered in the white tractlands for the plight of the "disadvantaged Negro[es]" was more than offset by turning them into scapegoats. McCone blamed their deficiencies for causing the riots.[33] Its residents were found guilty of a "spiral of failure." They had turned Watts into a pathological breeding ground of dysfunctional families, youth gangs, and psychological despair.[34]

Like Hoyt's theory of neighborhood succession, McCone's riffraff theory of the Southern migrant became a self-fulfilling prophecy by turning imaginary perceptions into concrete realities. After Watts, the stream of white flight from the L.A. school district swelled into a veritable flood. Holding out hope of producing just the opposite results, the commission report recommended a massive upgrading of the schools in "disadvantaged areas." These magnets of educational excellence could draw families back to the city. Yet the report back peddled away from its own key recommendations, limiting the outcome of integration to a distant "possibility."[35]

At the same time, the McCone Commission turned African American students into scapegoats, condemning them to a preordained path of academic failure. The school board was blameless of discrimination because African American parents irreparably damaged children before they even stepped foot in the classroom. Their "earliest childhood experiences" kept them from learning how to read, which had "the frequent direct consequences of . . . delinquency, welfare problems, unemployment, poverty, and political and social isolation."[36]

The report's reiteration of racial stereotypes of inferiority could have had only the boomerang effect of strengthening a politics of racial fear within the white tractlands. Escape from the L.A. school district seemed to be the only way to protect their children's immediate safety and long-term future. In the next four years alone, the district lost 80,000 white students while gaining only moderate numbers of African Americans and Latinos. By 1980, the white population in its schools had shrunk from 400,000 to 127,000 children; enrollment in private schools swelled to 200,000 students.[37]

In a similar way, what Mike Davis calls the "militarization of urban space" also became a part of a self-reinforcing downward spiral into a political culture of fear.[38] The great escape to the physical safety of Orange County to the south and the San Fernando Valley to the north tended to foster the opposite of their intended psychological effect of bringing peace of mind. Exclusionary zoning and gated communities only increased a sense of insecurity and victimization among white homeowners. In the wake of Watts, a suburban nation became a "gunfighter nation" living in fear of home invasion and random violence in the streets.[39]

Racial fear and its political repercussions became all pervasive. Whether in an inner-city South Gate or a more distant security zone community, a state-of-siege mentality percolated from the grass roots up through the federal system. Over the next three years of urban crisis, the conservative movement rode the insurgent wave of working-class populism from Los Angeles's tractlands to the California governor's mansion and the White House. After Yorty's and presidential contender Barry Goldwater's defeat in 1964, the Republican activists of Orange County turned to one of their own local spokesmen, Ronald Reagan. They mobilized conservatives behind his run for governor in the 1966 elections on a platform of restoring the social peace and the individual rights of the homeowner.

Reagan's victory encouraged another Californian, Richard Nixon, to re-enter politics as the law-and-order candidate for president against the Democratic candidate Hubert H. Humphrey. Nixon declared a war on crime on behalf of a silent majority of taxpaying citizen-homeowners. Nixon's identification with their sense of victimization, however, was no match for a true personification of Southern-style populism, Alabama governor George

Wallace, whose viable campaign on a third-party ticket was testimony itself to the crisis mentality of the nation.

In South Gate, the two conservatives, Nixon and Wallace, received the support of three out of five voters, while the Democrats fell into the minority. Four years later, the Republicans consolidated their gains with a 60 percent majority of the community in favor of President Nixon's reelection.[40] "The unraveling of liberalism," Michael Flamm proposes, "was therefore not simply the result of racism per se. It was, rather, due also to the widespread loss of popular faith in liberalism's ability to ensure personal safety."[41]

Chicago, United States:
The Politics of Racial Succession

Chicago's "insurgent planning histories" are stories of defeat for both white and black grassroots activists at the hands of its Boss, Richard J. Daley. Elected mayor in 1955, Daley brokered a deal with the civic-commercial elite to throw the city's growth machine into high gear. Together, they remade the downtown into a modernist showcase of the International Style. It helped keep the city competitive in an emerging global economy.

The new business-government partnership also erected a racial buffer zone around the downtown, a new-style color line of color-blind urban renewal projects. Following Homer Hoyt's plans, city hall smashed highways and redevelopment zones through the neighborhoods regardless of whether they were the sacred spaces of Catholic parishes or the conservation districts of well-organized communities. In control of both city hall and the local Democratic Party, Daley ruled with an iron fist, crushing all local groups protesting against his master plan of technological modernization.[42]

The only part of the plan that Boss Daley could not control was the movement of people. Thousands of households being uprooted by the urban renewal bulldozer had to find new places to live in the private sector of rental apartments and home ownership. In addition, Southern migrants and foreign immigrants continued to pour into Chicago, while its inhabitants kept streaming outward to new housing in the suburbs. Sprawl at the edge simultaneously opened up space in the center. The growing list of properties for sale in white neighborhoods undermined the institutional barriers of racial/ethnic segregation embedded in national housing and local school policies.[43]

The resulting contestation over racial succession also became the political battleground between the grass roots and Mayor Daley. Histories of these community-based resistance movements against his plans for rebuilding the urban environment must begin with the story of the Woodlawn Organization (TWO) on the South Side. Perhaps the first grassroots uprising during

Daley's administration to reach city hall, the Alinsky-created group certainly became the most celebrated in the many afterlives of the urban crisis. During the fifties, the Woodlawn neighborhood, a community of about sixty thousand, had undergone a complete change from almost all white to black.[44] In the midst of the ghetto uprisings, the national media held up TWO as a model of black self-determination that had created a "slum with hope."[45]

At the street level, however, repeated explosions of violent riots on the West Side between 1965 and 1968 illuminate a more accurate portrait of the inner city as a ghetto bursting with rage, resentment, and despair. Organizing to stem the buildup of racial tensions was a wide range of groups, including white liberal reform groups, black civil rights movements, neighborhood homeowners' associations, and a radical all-male group led by African American ex-convicts, the West Side Organization, which worked to find jobs and help welfare recipients on a one-by-one basis.

Yet none of these place-based movements could stop the accumulating effects of racial succession. Instead, a Watts-scale insurrection of burning, looting, and shooting at the police would erupt in the days following the assassination of Rev. King. Mayor Daley had to ask President Johnson to bring in the army to restore order.[46]

The backstory to the revolt against the policy makers and the planners is the rise of Richard J. Daley into the mayor's office. A decade after war's end in 1955, the impacts of national and local postwar planning were plain for all to see. The effects of slum clearance and redlining were turning the neighborhoods into battlegrounds of a guerrilla war among its racial/ethnic groups. A decade of urban renewal, moreover, was doing little to renew the central business district. The relatively modest forty-story Prudential Building was about the only visible sign in the downtown area of a changing skyline.

Feeling pressure from all sides, the ward bosses dumped the divisive incumbent, Martin J. Kennelly (1947–1955) and installed a rising powerbroker, party chief Richard J. Daley. He vowed to break the logjams holding the city back in the race of technological modernization, to make Chicago "the city that works." Within a year of his victory, the new mayor fulfilled his campaign pledge to kick-start the city's growth machine into overdrive. Over the course of the next decade, the mayor oversaw a remarkable transformation of the central business district.

But the benefits of the downtown renaissance came at a calculated cost of abandoning the outer rings. Redlined neighborhoods like Woodlawn and the Near West Side became prey of speculators and loan sharks. Given the limited resources of city government, Daley chose to give the downtown businesspeople everything they wanted at the expense of the material conditions of everyday life for most of the city's residents.[47]

As his biographers tell in the official story, Daley's success stemmed from several sources.[48] In part, it came from a charmed life of fortuitous political timing. He entered office just as new federal laws and money finally got major renewal, highway, and housing projects off the drawing boards and into the construction phase of development. He would also take credit for Kennelly's achievements at official ribbon cuttings for such projects as the West Side Highway and the Prudential Building. In large part, however, the city center owed its renaissance to Daley's consolidation of power over the formation of planning policy from the feuding ward bosses, professional experts, and business groups.[49]

A year into office, the new superboss of the Democratic Party and city hall took command of the makeover of the city skyline; his plan would rule. He downgraded the Chicago Plan Commission to an advisory group and shifted its functions to his own creation, a department of planning. He installed James Downs, one of the Chicago Real Estate Board's best and brightest, in charge of the new department's housing and redevelopment division. He, in turn, opened the door for his son, Anthony, into the inner sanctums of government and business. Daley locked out the plan commission's technocrats and buried their eye-opening report on the fate of the first wave of black Chicagoans forced to relocate by urban renewal in the city's dual housing market.[50]

While the mayor stiff-armed the critics, he embraced the brand-new organization of the civic elite, the Chicago Central Area Committee (CAC), formed in 1956 by Holman Pettibone of Chicago Title and Trust Company. The mayor anointed the CAC as the official voice of the business community and handed the private group control over public planning. The result was a new political partnership between the boss of the Democrats and the fat cats of the Republicans. In 1958, the planning department dutifully published the CAC roadmap to the future as the city's official plan.[51]

The mayor's first order of business was to deliver the passage of a new zoning code that had stalled in the city council during Kennelly's second term. A streamlined version would remove the safety features from previous designs of the city's growth machine. The key reform the CAC wanted was an ingenious imaginary called a "planned unit development," which is equivalent to a Monopoly Get out of Jail Free card. A designation awarded by the planning department, a planned unit development exempted private plans from the zoning ordinances.[52]

With Daley firmly in the driver's seat, private developers poured high-octane fuel into the tank of Chicago's souped-up growth machine. Under the mayor's clientele regime of deal making, the new government-business partnership erected a quartet of the world's tallest buildings. During his twenty-one-year reign, the city's Mies-inspired modernist architecture helped the city back into the global competition for investment capital. The First National Bank, John Hancock Insurance, Standard Oil, and Sears Buildings became iconic trademarks, advertising Chicago's economic diversity as the metropolis of the midcontinent.

Daley also made good on his promise to give the CAC the radials of high-speed transportation called for in its Central Area plan. They were intended to link the Loop to the white suburbs and global markets. In his first year in office, the mayor broke a six-year standoff between Kennelly and the airlines over sharing the costs of building the new O'Hare Field. Turning this stalemate into a win-win endgame, he persuaded his suburban counterparts to give a corridor of land to the city for a highway to the airport. After the historic 1956 Federal-Aid Highway Act kicked in, Daley had contractors working day and night leveling neighborhoods and pouring concrete to the north, northwest, southwest, and south.[53]

By the time of his reelection campaign in 1959, Daley could show off lots of world-class shrines of modernism changing the skyline. In the media, he boasted about the busiest airport and highways, the biggest water filtration and sewage treatment plants, and the single largest public housing project of tower blocks (under construction). In the white Bungalow Belt, he also bragged about greater police presence and more sanitation workers in the streets. In the black community, he held out the promise of equal opportunity to reach the American Dream in Chicago.

The voters rewarded Daley with a landslide victory. After winning big, he and his partners from the business elite felt more confident than ever that Chicago was well along the way to victory in the race of technological modernization. The following year, the mayor's critical help in getting the national Democratic candidate, John F. Kennedy, into the White House cemented his political power as the Boss.[54]

In Chicago, the one-man rule of Richard J. Daley cultivated a bunker mentality. He felt threatened by any community-based organization operating outside the control of the party's established hierarchy of power. TWO's insurgent planning history was just one story of the much larger history of the black freedom struggle for open housing, school desegregation, and the end of plantation politics.

During his second term, moreover, the mayor faced a growing insurgency of resistance to racial succession arising from the grass roots of his white base of support in the Bungalow Belt. From 1947 to 1961, Hoyt's master plan of clean-sweep renewal projects alone forced 180,000 people, or almost 50,000 households, to pile up in the ghetto or move into a white neighborhood.[55] As a result, according to the political scientist Barbara Ferman, "racial conflict and, to a lesser through increasing extent, ethnic divisions became the defining characteristics of the political system."[56]

The siting of the new campus of the University of Illinois on the Near West Side exposed Daley's conscious choice to favor the business center at the expense of the residential zones undergoing racial succession. Here, Daley sacrificed two white neighborhoods to satisfy the business elite. He turned a deaf ear to the voices of these working-class communities of white ethnics, Latinos, and African Americans. The politicians and the press stereotyped them as poverty-stricken, ignorant Southern migrants and foreign aliens.[57]

Bringing the state university to the site of his choice turned one of Daley's personal dreams into another great leap forward in the global race of urban modernization. It also illustrates his pivotal role as the supreme powerbroker between government and business in the remaking of Chicago. At the same time, the mayor's plan also granted the CAC's insistence on constructing the protective cordon sanitaire around the central business district envisioned in Hoyt's and Saarinen's designs of the Organic City.

Like a chess master playing several games at once, the mayor made one brilliant move after another to checkmate all his challengers in deciding the fate of the campus. His plan triumphed over alternatives put forward by non-elite and nonlocal business groups, upstart suburbs, blue-ribbon commissions, university trustees, and grassroots community-based organizations. He chose the Near West Side location of the Hull House–Little Italy area because the Hoyt plan had already earmarked federal land-clearance funds for a model residential conservation project. A rich racial/ethnic mix of people in the path of the bulldozer lost their homes and businesses. Between 1961 and 1965, Daley's plan forced the relocation of fourteen thousand people and over six hundred businesses. Daley got what he wanted, and the CAC got the buffer zone it wanted.[58]

There can be no doubt that a large number of households displaced by city hall's redevelopment plans contributed to the mounting problems on the West Side in the wake of racial succession. A third ghetto, according to Janet Abu-Lughod, had formed with the inevitability of a falling row of dominos along a one-mile-wide, two-mile-long stretch of neighborhoods. Holding three hundred thousand mostly poor people, this new Black Belt in redlined zones like Garfield Park, West Garfield Park, and Lawndale was in a distressed state of physical deterioration, overcrowding, and social disorder.[59]

The changing shapes on the ground resulting from fulfilling Mayor Daley's plans reinforced a self-perpetuating belief in the planners' theory of the life cycle of the neighborhoods.[60] In North Lawndale, for example, those forced to relocate from renewal sites were a part of the reason it had changed from 87 percent white to 90 percent black during the decade of the fifties. In the next decade, West Garfield Park would go from being all white to 84 percent African American.[61]

For good reason, then, the election map of Daley's third victory in 1963 bears a remarkable resemblance to the city's redevelopment maps. Falling from a 70 percent to a 55 percent majority, he lost the vote in the Bungalow Belt to its white knight, former Cook County state's attorney Benjamin Adamowski. This, combined with an election result a year earlier, in which voters rejected an urban renewal bond issue for the first time, contributed to Daley's decision to reverse course on his strategy of racial politics.[62]

This election marked the racial divide of the Daley machine from a "black machine" to a "white ethnic working- and middle-class machine."[63] In the years to come, Boss Daley would put all of the considerable clout at his command into play to hold the color lines of segregated schools and neighborhoods. The decisions made by Mayor Daley and his business partners, not the invisible hand of the market, were pivotal in putting Chicago's growth machine on a collision course with a massive uprising of violent social disorder.[64]

Political choices, not economic imperatives, account for the West Side becoming a tinderbox of simmering frustration, anger, and despair. Alarmed at his losses of white homeowners at the polls, Daley redoubled his commitment to shore up his administration's two main pillars of defense against integration, the schools and the police. Also alarmed at the gains of place-based civil rights groups like TWO, the mayor directed his chief of police, O. W. Wilson, to unleash his troops in an all-out assault on street gangs and oppositional community-based organizations. He formed an elite Gangs Intelligence Unit and declared, "The gangs must be crushed."[65]

The city's system of justice turned a blind eye on a reign of police terror on racial/ethnic minorities. How brutality and forced confessions in the jailhouse became routine are just now coming to light in the federal courts. Watching the West Side burn down five years after his reelection, in 1968, Daley would issue his infamous order for the police to "shoot to kill."[66] It would be the only breach in this master illusionist's color-blind screen of equal opportunity that gave a momentary peek at his grand strategy of racial containment.[67]

If the election returns of 1963 gave Daley cause for concern on the home front, he still projected an image of a city that works to the world. At the annual meeting of the National Association for the Advancement of Colored People (NAACP) in July, the mayor proudly pronounced that there are "no ghettos in Chicago."[68] He knew better, because he had had Anthony Downs and the city's planners secretly project demographic patterns of neighborhood change over the next decade. They predicted that in 1975 white flight and racial succession would make the city an 85 percent black majority. The mayor buried their report, but TWO's Nicholas von Hoffman got hold of a copy and exposed its findings in the *Chicago Daily News*. Downs recalled that the Boss "had a conniption. . . . This was the first time a city report mentioned race in the history of the city since Daley [became mayor]."[69]

In August 1965, Boss Daley's power to contain the racial succession of the neighborhoods reached the breaking point. In the shadow of the flames engulfing Watts, a riot of black teenagers in Lawndale took the city by surprise. That a traffic accident was the spark drawing three hundred young people into a running battle with the police for two nights reflected just how volatile city streets had become throughout postwar America. A fire engine of the all-white department had run over a black woman standing on a street corner. The following evening, a protest vigil at that spot turned into hand-to-hand combat with the police. The scorecard of this battle was sixty injuries and over one hundred arrests.[70]

After Watts and Lawndale in the summer of 1965, a public discourse on race and urban policy could no longer be imagined away by a politics of denial. More and more American cities became engulfed in flames of insurrection and anarchy. In the case of Chicago, Martin Luther King's arrival the following year refocused media attention on the local struggle for civil rights. In part, he chose Chicago for his first Northern campaign to heal the fractured and demoralized coalition of grassroots organizations, which had been utterly defeated by Mayor Daley in the battle of school integration.[71]

King mistakenly believed that he could cut a deal with Boss Daley. In the spring of 1966, he moved into an apartment building in the far West Side community of Lawndale. But in the midst of his campaign that summer to organize a Freedom Movement, a second, much larger insurrection erupted that would take the National Guard to suppress. Civil rights leaders had been forewarned just a few days beforehand when the black youth gangs attending a mass rally at Soldier's Field renounced nonviolence and staged a walkout.

A second case of spontaneous combustion, this explosion of rage was set off on the near West Side. Kids were getting relief from the scorching summer heat from fire hydrants, and police tried to restore water pressure in the pipes. A riot erupted. This time, the scorecard of the battle for the streets of Chicago racked up two deaths, eighty injuries, and over $2 million worth of property damage.[72]

After the so-called summit to end the marches of the Freedom Movement in August 1966, King learned that Daley was a double-crosser who never intended to make a deal on ending the city's dual housing market of racial containment. Returning a year after the mayor and the Chicago Real Estate Board had reneged on all their promises, a dejected King confessed defeat. But this time, he warned, the loss for the civil rights movement was also a setback for its nonviolent approach. His defeat gave victory to the advocates of armed resistance.[73]

About a year after this weary announcement of unconditional surrender, the death of King became the tragic, albeit ironic, spark that ignited the most ferocious of the insurrections on the West Side. The mayor should have declared a day of mourning. But he refused to break the grand illusion of a color-blind world and ordered the schools to remain open.

The rebellion started with a nonviolent walkout of high school students. It picked up steam as it became a protest march toward the Loop and burst into a raging mob that overwhelmed the police and fire departments. Mayor Daley had to ask President Johnson to send in the troops. As Johnson received several similar calls from other mayors across the country, he could look out the windows of the White House and see the flames of black rage all around him.[74]

For Chicago, the uprisings of the West Side represented the death knell for a color-blind lens of urban planning and policy making. After avoiding an orderly process of integration for twenty years following World War II and seeking containment, the strategy of government and business snapped. The disorders triggered white flight away from the city's public schools, mean streets, and gripping fear of violent crime.

For those left behind and the newcomers moving into neighborhoods on the West Side, the civil disorders brought a new regime of predatory homeowner loans. This round of antireform resulted in the death knell of the area's communities. They were sucked dry and left as wastelands populated by empty lots, crack houses, and liquor stores. On official planning maps, these neighborhood and many others throughout the city had reached of the end of Hoyt's life cycle.[75]

Mexico City, Mexico: The Politics of Patriarchy

In the third world of Latin America, the urban uprisings of the sixties were different from those of the first world of the United States and Western Europe. In both Mexico and Brazil, groundswells of worker unrest and student frustration provoked military reprisals and gave birth to new forms of grassroots democracy. After 1945, these two nations had become exemplars of import substitution economies. But over time, they became archetypes of what economists call "distorted development."[76]

Differences of national political cultures and institutions cast Mexico's insurgent planning histories in a completely different light from Brazil's and other countries' in the Americas. Like Brazil, Mexico was fully engaged in the modernization race, but its local protest movements reflected its unique postrevolutionary experience. Since the 1930s, the country had been drawn together under a banner of the patriarchal father that fused the identities of family, party, and the nation (see Map 9).

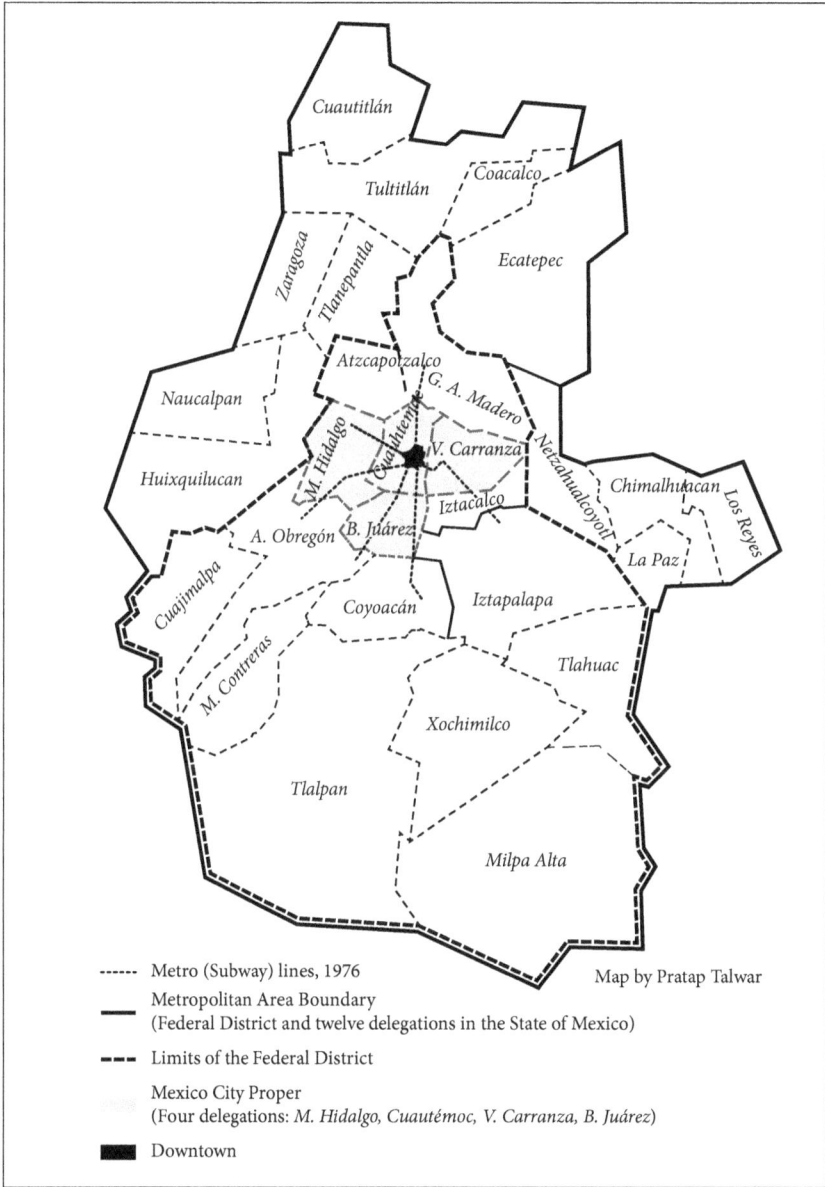

Map labels (within the map):
- Cuautitlán
- Coacalco
- Tultitlán
- Zaragoza
- Tlanepantla
- Ecatepec
- Atzcapotzalco
- Naucalpan
- G. A. Madero
- M. Hidalgo
- Cuauhtémoc
- V. Carranza
- Nezahualcoyotl
- Huixquilucan
- Chimalhuacan
- Los Reyes
- A. Obregón
- B. Juárez
- Iztacalco
- Cuajimalpa
- M. Contreras
- Coyoacán
- Iztapalapa
- La Paz
- Tlahuac
- Xochimilco
- Tlalpan
- Milpa Alta

Legend:
- - - - - - Metro (Subway) lines, 1976
────── Metropolitan Area Boundary
(Federal District and twelve delegations in the State of Mexico)
- - - Limits of the Federal District
Mexico City Proper
(Four delegations: *M. Hidalgo, Cuautémoc, V. Carranza, B. Juárez*)
■ Downtown

Map by Pratap Talwar

Map 9 Mexico City: Mexico City Metropolitan Area (Diane E. Davis, *Urban Leviathan: Mexico City in the Twentieth Century* [Philadelphia: Temple University Press, 1994], p. xiv)

The clientele regime of the Partido Revolucinario Institucional (PRI; Institutional Revolutionary Party) had formed bureaucratic links between the grass roots and the policy makers. Although these agencies of welfare capitalism were staffed from the top down by party leaders, they did serve as sounding boards for their members to make appeals back up the ladder of power. For over a quarter century, the combination of the PRI's godfather system and the constitution's six-year term limits had created an exceptionably stable nation of benevolent, albeit machismo, authoritarianism.

The roots of Mexico's uprising against the policy makers and the planners in 1968 lay in the very success of their goal to build a national consumer economy. From 1940 to 1960, this Fordist model of technological modernization had given the country a remarkable 6 percent annual rate of economic growth. The PRI's self-proclaimed "Mexican Miracle" had kept the social peace by greatly expanding the urban industrial and middle classes. But as in Brazil, this type of growth machine came at an accumulating cost of shrinking the real incomes of farmers and nonfactory service workers.

And like Brazil, Mexico reached the endgame of the import substitution strategy by the 1960s, creating unsustainable distortions in the nation's development. Farming had become so unrewarding that Mexico had to import food, adding to its soaring foreign debt. With only one-third of the population living above bare subsistence, the domestic economy was slowing down. The government found itself becoming increasingly dependent on foreign loans to pay its bills and on foreign capital to underwrite investment in the private sector.[77]

As pressure mounted on the party from more and more discontented groups to offset the resulting inflation in consumer prices, its primary goal became containment of all political expression within its institutionalized channels. In 1958–1959, when sixty thousand railroad workers went on strike, the Interior Ministry sent in the army and arrested three thousand protesters, including their populist leader, Demetrio Vallejo. The administration of President Adolfo López Mateos (1958–1964) sentenced him to sixteen years in jail. In Mexico City, the government took a similar hard line against public school teachers who broke with their official organization and joined the Revolutionary Teachers' Movement (El Movimiento Revolucionarios del Magisterio; MRM).[78]

These early signs of revolt against the patriarchy became increasing visible at every level of society, from the imaginary father of the nation to the real dads of the baby-boomer generation of the urban middle classes. Perhaps the greatest beneficiaries of Mexico's economic plan, this relatively affluent group of high school and college students burst the walls of the PRI's strategy of political containment. Eventually, they questioned the very legitimacy of its authoritarian reign of power.

In the mid-1950s, their protest began as social expressions of High Modernism and its consumer culture. Watching the government's violent repressions of the railroad workers and the teachers, these so-called *rebeldes sin causa* (rebels without a cause) would take a cynical view of the PRI. Its clientele regime was "insular, authoritarian, 'dead,'" according to the historian Eric Zolov.[79]

A decade later, their anarchistic counterculture of *rocanrol* morphed into a massive political mobilization that permanently tore asunder the patriarchal banner of family, party, and nation. The student movement of 1968 created a tear in history by splitting a nation's understanding of itself between those who "defended traditional models of post-revolutionary Mexico . . . [and those who] developed new approaches."[80]

Zolov's study of Mexico City's middle-class baby boomers illuminates how the transnational business of culture nourished a homegrown spirit of contesting authority. Beginning with Elvis Presley and Bill Haley in the midfifties, rock-and-roll music came to epitomize more than everyday life in Marshall McLuhan's global village. It also expressed a generational and gendered politics of resistance against patriarchy. In Mexico, the new music entered the city as a dance step played by "jazz bands" in pricy, adult nightclubs.[81]

Neither a class nor a racial/ethnic threat in this context, the first wave of rock and roll was portrayed in the public sphere as youthful, fashionable, and cosmopolitan. The PRI and the local music industry alike felt caught between their endorsement of modernism and condemnation of degenerate, foreign influences that broke the patriarchal bounds of *buenas costumbres* (proper family values). While the government levied a prohibitive tax on imported records, the media companies enforced a self-imposed policy of containment. They hoped to ward off any potential loss of profits from official censorship of their products.[82]

In 1964, however, the British invasion of the Beatles abruptly ended the golden era of the *Refritos* (Refried) Elvis, or Mexican and Mexican American imitators of global rock stars. In the new age of *La Onda* (the Wave), middle-class youth demanded authentic music and lyrics, which had to be sung in English. The Beatles label, Capitol Records, and other media transnationals responded by setting up subsidiaries to manufacture the records and promote them in affiliated radio, film, and TV outlets. Although domestic culture companies such as Orfeon also profited from *La Onda*, their economic, social, and political influence eroded under a rising tide of extralocal control of the marketplace.

The British cultural invasion was typical of the failure of Mexico's industrial sector to compete against superior imports. Two decades of government subsidies and party corruption in favor of its local businesses had unintended consequences. Its factories produced lower-quality goods and services.[83]

Incoming president Gustavo Díaz Ordaz (1964–1970) faced a future of challenges from abroad and at home. The nation was becoming increasing dependent on global capital to sustain economic development. At the same time, its youth was growing more independent from parental authority. Boys wearing long hair and girls dressing in jeans hardly make a revolution, but they did represent political acts of subversion in the Mexican context. Over the next four years leading up to the Olympics in October 1968, the counter-culture of the hippies became a topic of heated debate. It extended from the private realm of the family home to the boardrooms of the record companies and the public arena of the mass media.

As Zolov notes, "the line between rock as fashion and rock as social pro-test was becoming blurred."[84] In the three months immediately preceding the opening of the games, a cycle of student protest and government repression spiraled into the tragic massacre at Tlatelolco. As in Brazil, the first confronta-tions took place between college-bound high school students and the authori-ties. After charges of police brutality were levied, students from the National University and the National Polytechnic Institute met to discuss whether to call a sympathy strike of support of the high school students who were beaten by the police. They formulated a six-point petition, which became their po-litical manifesto throughout the ensuing mobilization of a mass movement.[85]

Perhaps fearing that bad publicity would ruin its global showcase of the Olympics, the policy makers overreacted. They sent in the army to take control of several student-occupied secondary schools. At the San Idelfonso Preparatory School, the soldiers used a bazooka to blast open its wooden doors, four-hundred-year-old artistic treasures. At least five students were wounded in the ensuing assault. Mass arrests dragged many more off to prison. Two days later, President Díaz Ordaz tried to save face in what be-came called the "extended hand" speech of reconciliation.[86]

Over the next two weeks, both teachers and students throughout the metropolitan area formed organizations to begin the promised negotiations with the president. The umbrella group of the students, the Comité Nacio-nal de Huelga (National Strike Committee), eventually represented over 230 schools. They also marched in the hundreds of thousands to pressure Diaz Ordaz to honor his pledge to engage in an open discussion of their six-point petition. His interior minister, Luis Echeverria, called for "a frank and peaceful dialog," but the administration refused to meet with the protesters' representatives in a public forum.[87]

The following month of stalemate became the most revolutionary pe-riod of student activism. Students formed brigades, took to the streets, and sought to explain their cause to the working people of the city. They distributed handbills, collected contributions on buses, painted slogans on public buildings, and staged lightning meetings in neighborhood markets to dodge beatings and arrests by the hated *granaderos* (riot police).

"Little by little, working-class people began to teach us how to talk like them," student leader Salvador Martinez de las Roca recalls. "And the way they applauded," he says, "showed us we understood each other. We began to learn about Mexico and its sad realities. This was an everyday experience in the brigades."[88]

In the process of making a movement culture, the students opened a temporary crack in history. It engendered what the historian Michael Soldatenko calls a "utopian moment. . . . Mexican student activism created democratic possibilities that erased the institutional imaginary. In less than a month the legitimacy of the PRI state and the Mexican government vanished. . . . A new world was on the horizon; one had only to grasp it."[89]

The climax of this revolutionary moment came on September 13, the day of the Great Silent Demonstration. The march was the students' answer to the PRI-orchestrated media blitz attacking their *desmadre* (disorder) as a communist plot. "To the People of Mexico," their handbill announced: "You can see that we're not vandals or rebels without a cause—the label that constantly has been pinned on us. Our silence proves it."[90] The successful demonstration of the students' power of organization and self-discipline made as deep an impression on its local participants as on its national audience. "New perspectives opened up," student activist Gilberto Guevara Niebla remembers; "that is what the Silent Demonstration accomplished."[91]

Unfortunately, these democratic vistas were exactly what the PRI feared most. These alternative visions of civic life uncoupled the legitimacy of the party from its imaginary identity with the authority of the nation and the patriarchy of the family. The power of the protest march to shatter the postrevolutionary myth not only reunited the students but also galvanized the government into action.

Unable to cut a deal with the National Strike Committee behind closed doors, President Díaz Ordaz crushed the movement before the international press arrived to cover the opening ceremonies of the Olympics. Resorting again to brute force, he ordered the army to invade Cuidad Universitaria (University City), the Polytechnic Institute, and Santo Thomás campus. Pitched battles erupted between the soldiers and students armed with Molotov cocktails. Several of these resistance fighters were killed or wounded; many other students and teachers were arrested and tortured in prison. The secret police began conducting a wide dragnet, rounding up everyone even remotely suspected of participating in the movement.

In hindsight, the battle of Santo Thomás on September 24 should have been ample warning that the government would use whatever violence it

thought necessary to restore the social peace. Rather than issue a final ul-
timatum, however, President Díaz Ordaz and Interior Minister Echeverria
set a trap. On October 1, the army ended its occupation of University City,
prompting the National Strike Committee to announce a meeting the following evening at the Plaza of the Three Cultures, next to the Tlatelolco
housing complex. Drawn into an ambush, no one was spared from the bul-
lets of the rooftop snipers or the salvos of gunfire coming from the battalions
of riflemen boxing them in.

In that moment of terror, the movement died. Faculty activist and an-
thropologist Mercedes Olivera de Vazquez speculates that the social housing
project was chosen because it was emblematic of the political links being
formed between the people and the students. Students had been helping its
residents organize an independent tenants' union. That is why Tlatelolco
became the bloody killing field where the government "stamp[ed] out the
movement once and for all."[92]

True to its machismo traditions of the "revolutionary family," the PRI
mixed harsh repression with benevolent reform. Its stabilizing development
plans as well as its clientele regime were in crisis. "By 1969," Diane Davis
observes, "many of Mexico's citizens blamed Díaz Ordaz . . . for skyrocketing
inflation, greater income polarization, visible inequality, and the growing
concentration of wealth in a few large, internationally and financially linked
industrial firms."[93]

His replacement, Luis "the Enforcer" Echeverria (1970–1976), instituted
a series of major changes in economic planning and political institutions.
To rehabilitate the party's bloodstained image, he made major concessions
to its constituent groups. But his plans to tax transnational subsidiaries
and banks and global agribusiness to pay for them were blocked, forcing
his administration to borrow even more than his predecessor's record-
breaking amount. Nonetheless, his free-spending policies underwrote a
revival of support for the PRI at the grass roots. In a similar way, he took
the political initiative in calling for a "democratic opening" in the public
sphere.[94]

As Davis points out, however, grassroots movements in Latin America
did not necessarily bring greater democracy to civil society. The case of Mexico, in particular, represents such a contrary outcome. Mexico City's uprising against the policy makers irreparably shattered the postrevolutionary
identity of the family, party, and nation under an authoritarian mantle of
patriarchy. Yet the student movement rose and fell without effecting fundamental changes in the country's political culture or its political institutions.
Instead, the PRI would take advantage of the urban crisis of the sixties to
solidify its hold on the reins of power.[95]

Conclusions: Paris, France—The Politics
of Postmodernism

While the residents of Watts were witnessing a living hell of arson, anarchy, and armies in the streets during the hot summer of 1965, the followers
of French *Nouvelle Vague* (New Wave) were safe inside cool movie theaters
watching a different imaginary dystopia. Filmmaker Jean-Luc Godard en-
capsulated all the anxieties of the middle classes that had been accumulating
since the start of the Cold War in a science-fiction parable, *Alphaville*. View-
ers' suspicions were confirmed that the modernization race was on a path
leading to a frightening future of a robot-like existence. An intergalactic po-
liceman, Lemmy Caution, is sent on a mission to assassinate the totalitarian
ruler of this cyborg world, a sentient computer named Alpha 60.

Despite being set in a distant future, all of *Alphaville*'s visual and historical references are set in the present, down to the detective's obligatory trench
coat. Godard used locations in the streets and interiors of Paris to frame his
cautionary tale of technological dictatorship. Entering a gated city of walls
in a Ford Galaxie, the secret agent from the Outlands has to pass through
several checkpoints on a long highway from the periphery to the center. In
the end, the all-seeing machine—the enemy of nature, especially human
nature—is slain by the emotional power of poetry.[96]

Three years later, the swelling malaise of the postwar era would burst
and spread into massive strikes and protests throughout France. In many
respects, the demonstrators, who marched on some of the same streets as
Lemmy Caution had, were on the same mission. They too sought to stop a
society in the grip of runaway technology. "With the largest strikes in French
history," the historian Kristin Ross posits, "May '68 would bring all the problems and dissatisfactions surrounding the French lurch into modernization
to the light of day. It was the event that marked the political end of the accelerated transition into Fordism."[97]

Too many "fast cars, clean bodies" too fast had created a future shock
that Godard visualized so perfectly by using a film noir style. *Alphaville*'s
on-location shots in modernist structures expressed a common revulsion
against the urban renewal plans under way in the city. For Parisians, Le
Corbusier–inspired architecture such as the monster Maine-Montparnasse
skyscraper in the center, the *grands ensembles* tower-block housing projects
in the suburbs, and the jammed highways in between had become the everyday signs of technology out of control (see Map 10).

One of these public housing sites, Sarcelles, had become a national symbol of the modernization race on a crash course. Dissolving the line between
science fiction and reality, its landscape of alienation gave birth to a new

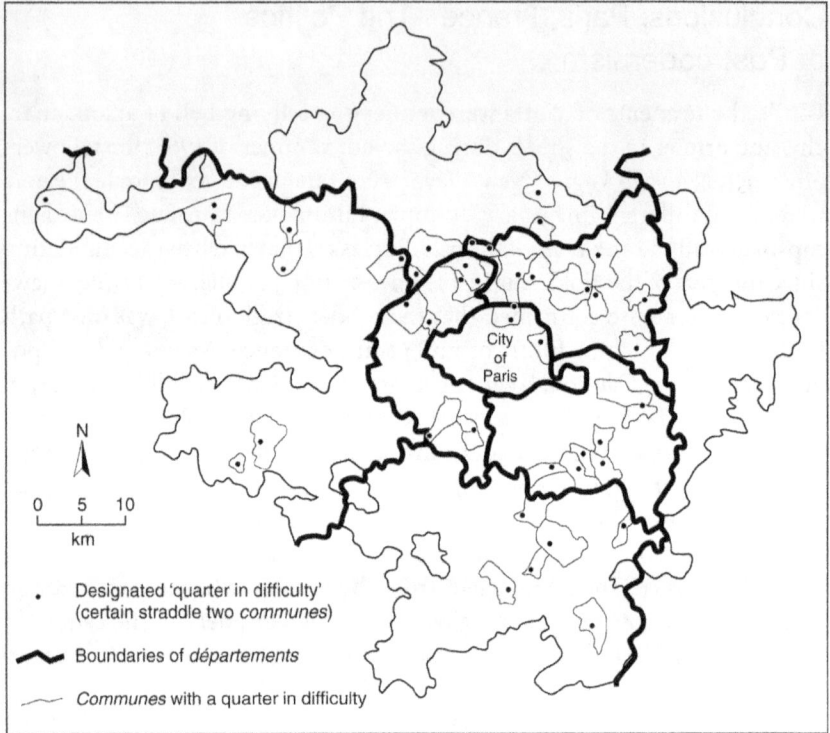

Map 10 Paris: Location of "Quarters in Difficulty," 1991 (Republished with permission of Daniel Noin and Paul White, *Paris* [New York: Wiley, 1997], p. 100)

social disease, *Sarcellitis*, which was "characterized by juvenile delinquency, bored housewives, nervous breakdowns, and a rocketing suicide rate," according to city biographer Colin Jones.[98] In 1961, Christiane Rochefort's prize-winning novel *Les petits enfants du siècle* (Little children of the century) captured the contemporary mood:

> You arrive in Sarcelles over a bridge and all of a sudden, a bit above you, you see the lot. Crickety! And I thought I lived in amongst blocks of flats! . . . For miles and miles and miles, flat, flats, flats. All the same. Lined up. White. Flats, flats, flats, flats, flats, flats, flats, flats, flats, flats. Flats. Flats.[99]

The shock of technological modernization led the intellectuals and the mass media alike to turn their attention to the crisis of everyday life. The French imagination, or at least its popular culture, became briefly obsessed with death by cars crashing at high speeds. Scholars like Fernand Braudel reconstructed the structures of daily life in the past in minute detail, while New Wave filmmakers like Godard took aim with their cameras to lampoon the postwar lifestyles of the middle classes.[100]

By turning urban space into the site for the "colonization of everyday life," the planners set off a backlash against their runaway race of technological modernization.[101] Compared to the other cities under study here, the planners' and policy makers' reconquest of Paris had been the most successful. Achieving a clean-sweep renewal of the city center, they had bulldozed a quarter of its land and dislodged over a half million people, or more than Baron Georges-Eugène Haussmann. Like him, they had relegated manufacturing industries and poor people to the suburbs. "The expulsions," the urbanist David Pinder found, "were centered along class and ethnic lines."[102]

In May 1968, millions of students, workers, and farmers contested the modernist vision of the planners and the policy makers. The uprising attempted to change the conditions of everyday life. They wanted to create new, alternative social spaces of equality in the universities and factories and, ultimately, the public sphere. Enough has already been said here on student protest movements and countercultures to focus attention on the massive workers' strike for *autogestion*, which translates imperfectly into English as "self-administration" or "self-determination."

Defying their company and union bosses, ten million to twelve million blue-collar workers staged spontaneous sit-ins. The workers' critical moment of utopian possibility started on May 13 as a union-sanctioned one-day general strike in symbolic support of the students. The next day, however, the rank and file in a government-owned airplane factory near Nantes sealed it off, took its manager hostage, and continued the work stoppage. Over the next forty-eight hours, the seizure of mass production sites like Renault's auto assembly plants spread as if wildfire across the country. What millions of French assembly-line workers wanted on the shop floor was democratic structures of decision making.[103]

What they got was a sellout by union officials. On the twenty-seventh, they agreed to a deal that gave the strikers a pay raise plus some official acknowledgement of worker rights for the first time. The rechanneling of their dissent within formal institutions of collective bargaining and electoral politics brought their momentary crack in history to an end. "Thus, the awakening of 1968 ended for many people," a scholar concludes, "as the shaping of alternative lifestyles and individualization of life's opportunities and risks, but also as political retreat into the private realm."[104]

If these stories of uprisings against the planners do anything, they confirm Jeremi Suri's thesis that "we can have no grand narratives of 1968."[105] Like other great "critical moments" in history, the urban crisis of the sixties has many afterlives. A comparative approach helps explain why these kinds of pivotal events or seismic shifts in history become contested terrains of evidence, memory, and interpretation.

The most outstanding feature of the insurgent planning histories told here is their sheer range and diversity. To be sure, common threads of the times hold them together, such as a transnational youth culture, an antimodernist, anti-imperialist critique, and the rise of ecological environmentalism. Yet the hallmark of the revolt against the modernist vision of the Organic City between Watts and Mexico City was different national and local conditions that engendered a unique story in each case.[106]

In a larger Cold War context, the revolt against the planners and the policy makers was just one of the most visible manifestations of a more general crisis of modernity itself. "The highly visible counter-culture of the 1960s," Stephen Toulmin surmises, "was not essentially a youth culture: the intellectual, psychological, and artistic material for the new movement had been there for fifty years, waiting for a generation to see the point and seize the day."[107]

At the risk of reductionism to a simple dichotomy, then, the resulting crisis of planning theory and practice can be seen as a choice between two divergent paths. On one side, the saviors of modernism retained an optimistic faith in technology to free the human spirit by constructing a safe, healthy, and uplifting environment for individual self-fulfillment. They drew roadmaps to a future Cybernetic City of flows.

On the other side, the prophets of postmodernism believed that these worthy goals could be achieved only by first dismantling just such a technological society. It had become an authoritarian hierarchy of power and wealth. They laid out plans to get to an alternative Eco-City of citizens.[108]

What the urban protesters had not anticipated was that grassroots activism cut both ways in giving rise to political power. Consider that Watts residents believed that their uprising would result in more white sympathy and public support. But their attack on established authority had just the opposite effect among a great majority of white suburban warriors, who mounted an effective counterattack behind a media star, Ronald Reagan. Becoming governor of California in 1967, he and other leaders of a New Right began galvanizing local conservative groups into electoral majorities.

In the devolution of planning authority that followed, power to decide the future development of urban space was decentralized to local levels of government and business. In the early 1970s, the advocates of accelerating the modernization race to reach the Cybernetic City completed their redefinition of the profession and its tasks within the rationalist paradigm. Replacing the discredited finished blueprints of land use were more flexible procedural approaches. Updated computer programs incorporated dynamic feedback loops to adjust to changes in real time. Moreover, the new systems view of planning, could even plug in equations to take account of political variables in sequential order of policy formation, plan production, implementation, and impact.

As Robert Venturi had predicted, "complexity and contradiction" superseded what appeared to be have been an oversimplified theory of urbanism.[109] The saviors of modernism replaced the iconic, static images of Burnham and Le Corbusier with interactive computer models of entire metropolitan regions. Failing to prevent suburban sprawl or renew more than a patchwork of the city, the guardians of official planning now complained that their designs had not been comprehensive enough.

Urban containment, they promised, could be achieved by rechanneling development to new towns and regional growth centers. And Le Corbusier's block tower of the 1920s could remain the default architecture of the International Style. In Paris, for example, the urban renewal bulldozer was still working around the clock at several sites. Prime Minister Georges Pompidou exclaimed, "There is no modern architecture without towers."[110]

6

Contesting the Organic City, 1968–1980

Global Movements: The Environmental Crisis of Runaway Technology

The Turning Point and Postmodern Visions of the Organic City

In the midst of the urban crisis, there were unmistakable, if largely symbolic, signs of the dawn of a new era of global movements. In 1966, lunar orbit photographs of Earth rising from behind the moon forever altered human perceptions of our world. Over the next three years leading up to the moon landing, these grainy black-and-white images were replaced by brilliant pictures of a green, white, and blue planet spinning in space.

They inspired many, including R. Buckminster Fuller, who mesmerized American audiences with his vision of an organic machine, Spaceship Earth. The seventy-year-old futurist became the "technocrat for the counterculture."[1] With his *Operating Manual for Spaceship Earth*, which appeared in 1969, the engineer-architect helped popularize the idea that planning on a global scale would become the new norm.[2] In his vision, experts like him would be put in charge of piloting our planetary capsule on a path of sustainable smart growth. But Fuller did not foresee that globalization was simultaneously generating a new kind of political activism on a local scale.[3]

Grassroots contestation against the planners and the policy makers also became a permanent, defining characteristic of the postmodern condition. Technological and economic forces of interdependence produced not only new forms of urban space but social relationships as well. The impacts of globalization on the patterns of everyday life in the city were becoming stronger. In other words, the nation-state was becoming less important as an active agent in building the urban environment. Instead, it began playing more of a configurative role as a conduit of interaction between the global and the local. Taking its place was a multidimensional, transnational social geography of centers and peripheries, rich and poor, citizens and aliens.[4]

The incremental growth of these global movements reached a turning point in 1973–1974, when an oil embargo triggered a worldwide recession. While the urban crisis of the sixties had opened up the debate over the ideal city of the future, the economic crisis of the seventies narrowed the outcome to the visions of the systems planners. By then, the modernization race of the Cold War had significantly increased both the speed and the volume of information, capital, and goods flowing around the world.

Two events that took place before the turning point of 1973–1974 indicate that the West had already come to the crossroads of a postmodern condition. They illustrate the simultaneous processes of the globalization of the local and its mirror image. On April 22, 1970, the first celebration of Earth Day represented the emergence of urban social movements of the grass roots woven in worldwide webs of information. In contrast, the formation of the Club of Rome by an elite group of international policy makers was emblematic of the ascendency of systems planning in government and business. Both movements had long roots stretching back generations in different directions, but both came to the same conclusion at the same time: an environmental crisis existed on a global scale.

The polygenesis of Earth Day gave this event distinctly postmodern characteristics. It was an evolutionary process of grassroots mobilization occurring autonomously and simultaneously. What began as teach-ins on the environment at college campuses in the United States spread in a polymorphous way into a worldwide movement. It had no beginning or end, top or bottom, leaders or followers. It transcended ideological and national boundaries.

The multiple origins of Earth Day at the grassroots and top levels of government created an inclusive movement with a nonhierarchical structure. One of its founding fathers, U.S. senator Gaylord Nelson, recalled, "Earth Day worked because of the spontaneous response at the grassroots level. We had neither the time nor the resources to organize 20 million demonstrators who participated from thousands of schools and local communities. That was the remarkable thing about Earth Day. It organized itself."[5]

Moreover, the incredible outpouring of popular support across the world that day marked a sea change in the history of environmentalism. Another important figure in organizing the first Earth Day was Barry Commoner, a

university biology professor. Like Rachael Carson, he could translate ecological science into layperson's terms, becoming an outspoken champion of
a global point of view. The universal appeal of Earth Day, he realized, "shows
that there *is* an environmental crisis."[6] After the event, Commoner noted, the
focus of public discourse shifted decisively to identifying causes and finding
remedies. Indeed, the seventies marked the heyday of legislative activism to
ameliorate the harmful side effects of the Cold War throughout the West.[7]

Crossing national borders, the Club of Rome was a second highly visible
manifestation of the emergence of a postmodern era of transnational urbanism. Like Earth Day, the dream of restoring Eden has long antecedents in
Western thought. Composed of self-declared "world citizens," the Club of
Rome commissioned systems planners to produce mathematical simulations
not only of complex regional environments but the entire planet. Professors
at the Massachusetts Institute of Technology built a supercomputer named
World 3.

The Club of Rome was fundamentally different from its predecessor
World Society for Ekistics of Constantinos A. Doxiadis. The club's membership comprised actual world leaders of government and business. They put
the planning experts of the Doxiadis group to work designing computer
simulations of the earth's natural resources, the benefits of their economic
development on a global scale, and the costs of the resulting environmental
impacts on the health and welfare of an exploding human population. In
1972, the Club of Rome issued its first report, *The Limits to Growth*. According to the organization's website, it has become the best selling book ever on
the environment.[8]

Responding to the "world problematique," *The Limits to Growth* fore-
cast a Malthusian future of doom. Sustaining standards of consumption
enjoyed by the first world would be possible only at the expense of denying
the masses of the third world the basic necessities of life. The report recommended that policy makers create a "world system" that would remove
barriers to the flow of trade as the one best way to allocate scarce natural
resources. Critics quickly picked apart World 3's brain and its forecasts of
doom, but its sponsors were not discouraged. The race was on—one that
continues today—to design a real "smart city" that perfectly mirrors the
computer's virtual simulation of city life.[9]

Conflating free markets and freedom, the Club of Rome laid out a roadmap for a systemic restructuring of capitalism. It called for the privatization of the government's role in economic development. Deregulation and
decentralization meant a diminishing role for official planning. At the same
time, the adaptation of systems approaches in the business models of large
multinational corporations was becoming an ever more integral part of their
decision-making processes.

Local governments also came to rely on these computer models to keep up in the modernization race. The public sector became increasingly dependent on partnerships with the business sector in the global competition to design and build the Organic City of the next postmodernist generation. "By the end of the 1980s," the historian Nigel Taylor contends, "planners increasingly saw themselves as partners working 'with' the market and private sector developers."[10] Only a year after the publication of *The Limits to Growth*, its predictions of apocalypse seemed to be coming true when cheap energy from the Middle East stopped flowing to the West.[11]

The oil/energy crisis threw the postwar growth machines of the capitalist nations into an uncontrollable spin. The dream-like miracle of affluence that had lasted an unprecedented quarter of a century suddenly turned into the nightmare of stagflation. Defying Keynesian theory, soaring inflation was occurring simultaneously with falling production.

During the deep recession that followed, public opinion shifted decidedly to the political right. Rejecting the cries of the urban uprisings for social and environmental justice, a grassroots backlash of fear and rage gained momentum. The triumph of the New Right was complete in 1980, when Ronald Reagan was elected president of the United States, joining like-minded conservatives Margaret Thatcher in Great Britain and Georges Pompidou in France.[12]

Promising to shut down the welfare state, they popularized neoliberal theories of global free trade and "enterprise culture."[13] In effect, they rebranded social Darwinism's survival of the fittest into the value-free terminology of the invisible hand of the market. At an extreme, albeit extremely influential, pole of this antistatism was the novelist-turned-political-activist Ayn Rand.[14]

Consider Alan Greenspan, one of the early converts to her philosophy of objectivism. An economics professor, Greenspan entered politics in 1968 as an advisor to Richard Nixon and became the chairman of the U.S. Federal Reserve in 1987 during the Reagan administration. Reappointed by the next three presidents, Greenspan would become the most powerful planner in the world, the chief architect of the restructuring of capitalism until his retirement in 2006.[15]

The postwar planning systems of the first world were not so much closed down as undermined. In Thatcher's England, for example, "Enterprise Zones" and "Urban Development Corporations" subverted the central authority.[16] These New Right projects forced the experts in local planning departments to form partnerships with the private sector in order to finance real estate development and technological modernization.

For the great majority of planning professionals, day-to-day practice remained rooted in the physical design of patches of urban space. They were far removed from the academic theories of rational systems and controls. But in the post-oil-embargo era of deep cuts in funding for urban public works, these planning bureaucrats became ever more dependent on private developers and investors and their systems approaches to building the urban environment.[17]

The New Right leaders of first world nations, moreover, used their leverage with international monetary funds to pressure indebted third world nations like Mexico and Brazil to restructure their economies. These nations were compelled to dismantle their protective systems of import barriers and government management of basic industries. Under a Cold War cloak of anticommunism, authoritarian regimes in these countries implemented programs to privatize their large manufacturing and public utility sectors.

The dismantling of import substitution models in Latin America had long-term impacts on the quality of daily life for the urban working classes. They suffered disproportionately from the uneven process of recovery that followed in the 1980s and 1990s. Those at the bottom experienced the greatest hardships. They had to cope with factory closings, blue-collar job losses, homeowner foreclosures, rising crime rates, and declining neighborhoods.

Similar repercussions from the global shockwaves of the oil embargo were felt in the inner cities of the first world. Global economic restructuring of mass production industries brought severe hardship to them, whether the Watts–South Gate district of Los Angeles, the Brixton neighborhood of London, or Alma Gare in Roubaix. "*Social polarization* was intensified," the scholar Brian D. Jacobs states, "by the stark contrast between the condition of the underclass and the prosperity of those who had benefited from the 'enterprise culture.'"[18]

Although the counterinsurgency of the New Right overwhelmed the revolt of the New Left, the protesters could at least declare a small victory in the modernist planners' fall from grace. The two political poles shared an antistatist perspective as well as a skepticism toward the authority of experts. While the conservatives renewed their faith in the enterprising spirit of free markets, the progressives reaffirmed their reliance on local communities to act as self-propelled, democratic engines of social and urban reform.[19]

At the crossroads of ideas about urbanism, the planning profession fractured into several antagonistic and mutually exclusive camps that continue to have fundamental disagreements about the best ways of seeing the city and its future. Practitioners chose a path of methodological perspectives of either physical planning or social reform as the starting point of analysis. The saviors of the rationalist paradigm of modernism retreated behind an academic curtain of theoretical abstraction. By entirely denying Jane Jacobs's questions about human values and the quality of everyday life, planning theory could be stripped down to a logical, step-by-step system of decision making. Their faith in the computer to predict the future like a fortune-teller's crystal ball became the new holy grail in the search for the ultimate technological fix.[20]

For the followers of Jacobs, the path to a postmodernist Organic City had to begin with the empowerment of the grass roots. An insurgency of citizens from the bottom up had to tear down the "pentagons of power" that had built a one-dimensional society of mindless materialism.[21] According to urban planners taking her point of view, these transnational hierarchies of class, ethnic/racial, and gender inequality bore primary responsible for the "world problematique."[22] Focusing on the local scale, they put their belief in place-based community groups to solve the interrelated urban and environmental crises.

The Spatial Turn and the Deconstruction of the Local

In the first afterlife of the sixties, social scientists began shining new light on the relationship between society and the production of urban space. As planning theory collapsed, the liberal arts also went through a crisis of epistemology. While some scholars drew on systems approaches to design computer-driven methods of quantitative analysis, others explored more hybrid approaches that mixed postmodernist theories and empirical research. A generation of urban ethnographers was born.

Looking back in 2006, the social geographer Manuel Castells recalled how the people in the streets of Paris in 1968 inspired him to ask, How does the resistance of grassroots movements to the official plans help shape the built environment? "The decisive contribution of social struggles to the actual forms and meaning of urban space . . . [had been] generally overlooked," he remembers. "Citizens were considered to be consumers of the city, not its producers."[23]

What became called the "spatial turn" of urban studies grew out of that question.[24] The Spanish-born Castells together with his Parisian colleague Henri Lefebvre and British-born American-transplant David Harvey changed our modes of inquiry to a postmodern way of seeing the city and envisioning its future. The three geographers built on the traditions of the Frankfurt school of critical theory. But instead of deconstructing the underlying meanings of literary texts, these scholars sought to expose how different societies encode their topographies of power and resistance in the architecture, design, and land use of the built environment. They began broadening the scope of their work from the classic dialectic of class conflict to a multidimensional analysis of settlement patterns.[25]

In a seminal paper delivered at the 1969 meeting of the American Society of Geographers, Harvey challenged the profession to find new ways to illuminate how these spatial systems act to distribute social justice in the city. He prodded it to take up the pressing issues of the times: "urbanization, environment, and economic development." He proposed that they were related and would require an "interdisciplinary approach" to sort out their interactions.[26]

He also believed that the uprisings of the sixties represented a revolutionary turning point in a transition to a postmodern society. A parallel paradigm shift in the social sciences was needed to gain an understanding of the unforeseen groundswell of urban social movements around the world. These uprisings had burst the current frameworks of analysis. Neither the reductive systems of quantitative methods nor the dialectical approaches of Marxist economics could account for them.[27]

The most philosophical of the three, Lefebvre laid the intellectual foundations for the resulting hybrid approach to urban studies, the spatial turn. In his first post-1968 book, *The Urban Revolution*, the scholar posed a new way of looking in opposition to the "blind field" of the system planner.[28] What James C. Scott would later term "seeing like a state," Lefebvre originally called "the urban illusion."[29] "As with any ideology," Lefebvre argues,

> it does not stop at being simply reductive. It systematically extrapolates and concludes, as if it held and manipulated all the elements of the question, as if it had resolved the urban problematic in and through a total theory, one that was immediately applicable. . . . This extrapolation becomes excessive when it tends towards a kind of medical ideology. The urbanist imagines himself caring for and healing a sick society, a pathological space. He perceives spatial diseases . . . , which must be taken care of, so [the city] can be returned to (moral) health. The urban illusion culminates in delirium.[30]

The geographers raised two related questions about the ongoing impacts of globalization on the spatial dimensions of social justice in the city. First, had the economic equations of international development been thrown into reverse, making urbanization the engine of industrialization? Since 1945, the greatest migration in history was entering its final stages in the movement of humanity from the country to the city. Were the world's urban growth machines—fueled by an exploding population—now the prime movers of economic development?[31]

Second, what role was played by local structures of power and resistance in the building of the urban environment? Was the fusion of global standardization triggering a fission of tribal subcultures in defensive reaction to what seemed like an outside invasion of alienating forces into daily life? And how was this new burst of local identities of place, in turn, being expressed in the "created spaces" of the city?[32] Like Italo Calvino's imaginary "invisible cities," the urban landscapes of postmodernism became contested terrains of meaning and interpretation.[33]

Was globalization transforming urban society's former class-based identities into hybrids that mixed community identities and universal rights? Coining the term the "post-industrial society" in 1971, Alain Touraine was among the first to shed new light on the formation of these hybrid identities in the contemporary global city. In his ambitious book, subtitled *Tomorrow's Social History*, Castells's mentor described current trends in order to project an image of an emerging society. He also called it "technocratic" and "programmed," his preferred term. "All domains of social life—education, consumption, information, etc.," the French sociologist asserted, "are being more and more integrated into what used to be called production factors."[34]

However, these global forces of economic development were shredding the social fabric of the urban community, and sapping the democratic spirit of its citizens. "Ours is a society of alienation," Touraine observed, "not because it reduces people to misery or because it imposes police restriction, but because it seduces, manipulates, and enforces conformism." He warned that control of information and mass communications by global elites was reducing citizenship to a powerless condition of "dependent participation."[35]

While Touraine sought to unravel the inner dynamics of "tomorrow's social history" of the city, Harvey's pursuit of the deconstruction of urban space led him to reexamine Homer Hoyt's theories of land use. Focusing on residential location, he found these models one dimensional. They were based, on the one hand, on the use or social value of the housing to its inhabitants or, on the other, on its exchange or economic value.

Harvey found a hybrid of both calculations operating simultaneously in the minds of a complex group of actors. For instance, house buyers were not only consumers of housing; they were also producers, because resales of their properties accounted for two out of three transactions in the residential real estate market. Other Janus-faced actors included owner-occupiers, realtors, landlords, developers, and mortgage brokers.

Harvey concluded that urban studies should be limited to contingent theories because of the sheer complexity of the social relationships giving form to the city's built environment. Although he was attracted to Hoyt's theories of rings and radials for their powers of locational analysis, he was appalled by their misuse in the United States to institutionalize racial/ethnic injustice. These models of land use contributed to the current urban problematic, Harvey charged, because they "are a mixture of *status quo* apologetics and counter-revolutionary obfuscation."[36]

In *Everything in Its Place*, Constance Perin followed up on Harvey's deconstruction of theory to excavate a cultural anthropology of contemporary land-use policy in the United States. She conducted an ethnography of home builders and buyers to expose how American society's underlying worldview, its "shared system of signs," played a role in creating spatial patterns of inequality. "The built landscape of metropolitan areas [is] still best described . . . as a white noose around the poor and the blacks of central cities."[37]

Using Houston and Philadelphia as laboratories, Perin found a striking disconnect between the producers and the consumers of housing. The former saw the street as a boundary line of residential blocks of development. In contrast, the latter looked out their windows at the houses facing them on the other side and saw the street as the middle of their neighborhood.

Homebuilders constructed structures according to their own ideas and then marketed them without knowing what their prospective inhabitants really wanted. For example, prospective buyers wanted bigger rooms, but builders would give them only the minimum sizes required by law. In their worldview, the demand for more interior space was dismissed out of hand because larger rooms would simply be "too big" for their customers.[38]

A second major contribution of Perin's ethnographic study was unearthing some of the forces driving suburbanization in spite of rapidly rising home prices across the country. In just three years, between 1971 and 1974, they had skyrocketed by one-third. Yet the suburbs were adamantly opposed to allowing the construction of more affordable townhouses and apartments. Drawing "maps of society," Perin created a "sociology of sprawl" by deconstructing the zoning laws and restrictive land use policies of the two cities.[39]

Perin showed that the spread of homeownership in the postwar period was the result not of the logic of capital but government subsidies and laws that favored the single-family detached house over other types of habitation. The economic and status divisions between owners and renters were socially constructed through manipulation of land, capital, and purchasing power. At the same time, her interviews gave her insight on the ways that the anti-urban, pastoral ethos of American culture also helped account for suburban sprawl. Like their British forebears, Americans had long conceptualized the city as monster, a place of danger, fear, and sin. Both societies tended to use distance and walls to prevent unwanted invasions of personal, private space by the "other." In the United States, physical isolation in supposedly homogeneous neighborhoods had become a self-reinforcing process.[40]

Another early explorer drawing "maps of society" was the urban design theorist and practitioner Charles Jencks. In *The Language of Post-modern Architecture*, the American-born Scottish transplant cast the skylines of the global city in a new light. Hailing the death of modernism, he celebrated the resulting liberation from its "virtual stranglehold on the profession and academies from the late 1930s to the 1970s."[41] Now the reigning orthodoxy was pluralism, which perfectly mirrored the paradoxical condition of contemporary society. "Most of the time in the huge megalopolis," he wrote, "we are all minorities."[42]

Jencks gave Jane Jacobs's devastating critique of modernism credit for setting off a revolution in planning theory. Its models now had to take account of the city's "organized complexity." "All the key Post-Modern sciences," he exclaimed, "are rooted in this new episteme: ecology, ethnology, biology, holography, the cognitive sciences, psycholinguistics, semiology, chaos theory, neural nets, and so on."[43]

Looking ahead, he called for a self-conscious architecture of architecture to express the new era of pluralism in public space. This mind-bending process of "double-coding" was intended to produce hybrids that would mix contradictions such as classical and high-tech styles, vernacular and commercial facades, and local and global fashions.[44]

Jencks, also a landscape architect, drew a sharp contrast between what he believed would be an eclectic burst of diversity and the orthodox purism of Le Corbusier's "univalent form." Echoing Jacobs, Jencks protested, "Buildings today are nasty, brutal and too big."[45] Coming in for particular scorn was Mies van der Rohe, whom Jencks blamed for creating a "universal language of confusion." All the buildings on Mies's Illinois Institute of Technology campus in Chicago, Jencks chided, looked alike because of an excess of minimalism that had reduced architecture to a single design, the glass box.[46]

The Spatial Turn and the Unification of the Global

Despite Jencks's enthusiasm for a flowering of architectural historicism, he set the profession's artistic liberation within the boundaries of free-market capitalism. He worried that it would demand the same kind of commercialized cliché that had led to the cookie-cutter sterility of the International Style. "Radical eclecticism," he admitted, could quickly descend into a crass "Disneyworld Postmodernism." Furthermore, he wondered what a more expressive language of urban architecture could say about the culturally bankrupt, consumer societies of the West that would be really novel.[47]

In *The City and the Country*, Raymond Williams asks the same question from a historical point of view. This work by the Welsh literary scholar and New Left social critic is important here because it opened new perspectives on the ways that societies react during periods of explosive urban growth. His study of England from the early modern period, the sixteenth and seventeenth centuries, examined the West's first case of massive rural migration and the rise of London as a megalopolis with a million inhabitants at the dawn of the Age of Industry.

Deconstructing the antiurban ethos of the nation's fiction writers, Williams exposed a story of class exploitation hidden under their portrayal of the city as monster. Blaming the city as a living organism for social injustice, he found, "can shift our attention from the real history and become an element of that very powerful myth of modern England in which the transition from a rural to an industrial society is seen as a kind of fall, the true cause and origin of our social suffering and disorder."[48]

In England's transition from a rural to an urban nation, its literary works gradually shifted the causes of social injustice from moral choice to environmental determinism. Early novels cast London as a lively rich setting overwhelmed by the chaotic disorder of strangers moving through the streets. Beginning with novels about the exploding industrial centers of Manchester and Birmingham, in contrast, Elizabeth Gaskell, Charles Dickens, and other writers gave city people a greater sense of purpose and meaning. They recast the built environment as a degrading place of squalor and gloom.

Reformers kept a focus on urban density as the primary cause of social pathology. "The evident fear of crowds," Williams reasons, "with the persistence of an imagery of the inhumane and the monstrous, connects with and continues that response to the mob which had been evident for so many centuries and which the vast development of the city so acutely sharpened."[49] Ever since the Progressive Era, this deep-seated bias against the city had motivated generations of planners and policy makers to empty it out, relocating its people in suburban enclaves, garden cities, new towns, and regional growth centers.[50]

Immanuel Wallerstein reframed England's migration from field to factory in a global context that spanned five hundred years of economic development. In *The Modern World-System*, the "father" of the study of globalization proposed that the spread of capitalism since the sixteenth century had integrated the world's labor force. Beginning with the exploitation of natives and unfree labor in agriculture and extractive enterprises, the colonial empires of Europe were joined by the United States (and Japan) during the twentieth century in outsourcing industrial jobs to countries with cheap labor.[51]

Over the centuries, this pool of urban workers has remained virtually bottomless, fed by the population growth and the restructuring of traditional farming into agribusiness. While more than half the inhabitants of the planet live in urban areas for the first time in history, most of the other 3.5 billion still live in rural areas of poverty and deprivation. The "reserve army" of those ready to work for less continues to widen the gap between the rich and the poor, as well as between the core countries and those at the periphery.[52]

Throughout the seventies, Wallerstein, Lefebvre, and other social scientists debated whether a new postmodern era had begun, when globalization takes command. On the one hand, Wallerstein and his defenders argued that the oil/energy crisis was just another round in the *longue du-rée* of capitalism. On the other hand, Lefebvre and his supporters argued that an accumulating array of global forces was creating something new. The quantitative effect of this long buildup of capitalist development had transcended national boundaries to produce a qualitative difference, post-modernism. To William Robinson, "The twenty-first century is witness to emergent forms of transnational hegemony by social groups operating through multiple states, through intra- and supranational organizations, states and other institutions."[53]

For the most part, this debate over the current status of the world re-mained literally academic during a decade of stagflation that seemed to defy everybody's models of economic development. Under these circumstances, David Harvey's appeal for modest contingent theories made good sense. While he agreed with Lefebvre's predictions of long-range trends, he was more circumspect about the present moment. Harvey was willing to give it only a tentative label as a period of "transition." Whether "industrializa-tion, once the producer of urbanism, is now being produced by it," remained problematic during the first afterlife of the sixties.[54]

Transnational Discourses:
The Crossroads of Postmodernism

Dreaming the Eco-City of Citizens

In the crossroads of the post-1968 decade, contestation among planners, pol-icy makers, and the grass roots over the urban environment became not only permanent but also more complicated. The postmodern condition blurred their roles, morphing into new forms of hybrid identities and social rela-tionships. Grassroots leaders became planners, self-proclaimed "advocate planners" acted as though politicians, and elite policy makers rebranded themselves as populists.

Taking on characteristics of each other, the struggle among the three groups melted the boundaries between the abstract theory and the actual practice of city building. After the planners' fall from grace, their splinter-ing into antagonistic factions pursuing different visions of the Organic City was not much different from other professional groups undergoing the same epistemological transition to postmodern ways of seeing and knowing. Like the social scientists, some planners sought to use computer simulations to unify the local into a single global system. Others wanted to deconstruct transnational topographies of power into multiple-sized, overlapping com-munities of self-governing citizens.

Followers of the English social scientist E. F. Schumacher's mantra "Small is beautiful" come first in the transnational discourses that follow below because they represent the undercurrent of contemporary thought about urbanism during the seventies and eighties. Calling for the re-empowerment of the individual, their influence cannot be measured in terms of buildings built or highways stopped. Yet these academic theorists laid out a course of action to build their utopians visions of an Eco-City of citizens.[55]

In 1972, the Norwegian philosopher Arne Naess supplied a platform for a "deep ecology movement" of individual morality in everyday life. His "ecosophy" translated Aldo Leopold's land ethic into a code of personal conduct and political action. Naess drew interconnections between "ecology, community, and lifestyle." Saving an overpopulated planet from a culture of consumption imposed a moral obligation on everyone. Each person had to act to change this unsustainable condition into "an appreciation of *life quality* . . . rather than adhering to a high standard of living. There will be a profound awareness of the difference between big and great."[56]

The following year, Schumacher's book reinforced the proposition that a change in individual lifestyles from materialism to humanism was the starting point of urban and environmental reform. He rejected the New Right's free market approaches. He argued that their global restructuring of capitalism was accelerating the concentration of power and wealth in the hands of an emerging transnational urban elite.

Following in the anarchist footsteps of Peter Kropotkin and Mahatma Gandhi, Schumacher laid out an alternative approach, "Buddhist Economics." It called for the disassembly of large-scale organizations and their replacement with patterns of local production from local resources for local needs. "From the Buddhist point of view," he observed, "economists themselves, like most specialists, normally suffer from a kind of metaphysical blindness, assuming that theirs is a science of absolute and invariable truths, without any presuppositions."[57]

To Schumacher, the free marketers were looking upside down at the means and ends of economics: work and production. Rather than pursuing ever-higher levels of production, Schumacher pointed to ancient wisdoms about the value of work for self-fulfillment, social solidarity, and community survival. "The aim [of any 'economics as if people mattered']," he stated, "should be to obtain the maximum of well-being with the minimum of consumption." Schumacher laid out a path to a world of permanence, beauty, and health. "Two million villages" would be engaged in Arts and Crafts methods of production that had roots in the antimodernism of William Morris and Frank Lloyd Wright.[58]

Like the professional planners, the academic prophets of postmodernist visions of the Organic City debated whether social reform or physical design would be the engine driving the dismantling of urban space into these communities of self-determination. Murray Bookchin gave primary agency to the grass roots. In *The Limits of the City*, he took another step in his intellectual journey toward the formulation of a full-blown philosophy of social ecology.[59]

An inspirational speaker on radical anarchism, Bookchin called for a new Athens of insurgent citizenship. "The Hellenic mind," he imagined, "concerned itself little with a design that is meant to please a cosmic supra-human deity that views man's works from the skies, or for that matter, an Olympian architect who places geometric symmetry above the mundane experiences of everyday life."[60] Bookchin reenvisioned the organic architecture of Wright in social rather than aesthetic and artistic terms.[61]

But like Lewis Mumford, he projected a romanticized picture of the disorders of everyday life in the cities of the preindustrial era. Bookchin turned the historic, albeit chaotic, growth of Athens into a virtue of democratic self-determination. The crowning achievement of this insurgent citizenship was the Acropolis. It represented a symbolic expression of Athenian society's good sense that their political empowerment far outweighed the physical hardships of living in slum-like conditions.[62]

Taking an opposite approach of community building through the physical design of urban space was the advocate planner Oscar Newman. In his influential report on the public housing projects of New York City, *Defensible Space*, he demonstrated that "[the] crime rate has been found to increase almost proportionately with building height."[63] Newman's study recorded a three-to-one differential in crime between a tower block project and an adjacent one with an equal population density but built in the New Deal style of townhouses grouped around courtyards.

He argued that the physical design of the low-rise homes allowed the residents to take control of their immediate environment. They had "surveillance opportunities" to exert "territorial influence" over their small patches of green space.[64] Moreover, these little plots collectively formed the courtyards, which faced the public streets, where the open flow of pedestrians and vehicles also acted as a deterrent to crime.

Like Bookchin, Newman blamed Le Corbusier and the legions of followers mesmerized by his iconic high-rise towers in a park. By imposing this urban vision of the Organic City on the poor, he charged, "society may have contributed to the victimization of project residents by setting off their dwellings, stigmatizing them with ugliness, and saying with every status symbol available in the architectural language of our culture that living here is falling short of the human state." Newman provided design guidelines to empower individual householders to take responsibility for protecting their patch of space.[65]

The roadmaps to the future provided by these four proponents of an Eco-City of citizens all reflected common characteristics of a postmodern point of view. As Barry Commoner observed, Earth Day changed the focus of the transnational discourse on the urban environment to problem solving. Their works contributed to this debate by showing the grass roots new ways of planning and building cities from the bottom up.

Planning the Hybrid City of Urban Nature

A few notable planners searched for a top-down "third way" to bridge the diverging paths of the New Right and the New Left.[66] Each of these designers of a hybrid space of urban nature attracted "light green" environmentalists; they were Pied Pipers leading an entranced flock onto the freeway of the modernization race.[67] The most seductive of these mixed approaches appealed to not only environmental reformers of all ages but private developers as well.

One of its leading visionaries was the landscape architect Ian McHarg. In 1969, his hypnotic mantra "Design with nature" combined elements of the Garden City of Ebenezer Howard and the regional survey of his mentor and fellow countryman Patrick Geddes. The expatriate had been trained at Harvard and installed at the University of Pennsylvania, where he became friends with Lewis Mumford. In 1971, the self-proclaimed "steward of the biosphere" was hired by Texas oil baron and land developer George Mitchell to plant a new town in partnership with the federal government. That town, the Woodlands, is located on 17,000 acres (6,900 hectares) of piney forestland thirty miles outside Houston.[68]

For McHarg, nature-based design meant "the place of nature in man's world, my search for a way of looking and a way of doing—a simple plan for man in nature." For example, he turned the site's biggest environmental disadvantages—flash flooding from tropical storms and poor drainage—into highly desirable recreational amenities. Rather than install an expensive network of underground sewers, he exploited the natural topography of bayous to create a greenbelt of meandering streams, golf courses, bike trails, and walking paths. These open spaces cover about one-quarter of the site. They link enclaves of suburban homes, villages of mixed housing and shops, and industrial parks nestled in the pines. The staged development of the Woodlands to almost fifty thousand people in 2000 is perhaps the best measure of the response to McHarg's call to arms for the preservation of the environment.[69]

Yet the limits of human efforts to redesign nature are painfully evident in what has become a widely praised and copied model of smart growth. From the perspective of the street, the Woodlands is a city growing inside a forest. From the perspective of a satellite, however, McHarg's well-intentioned plan has caused irreparable damage to the ecosystem. Making ingenious use of Landsat images, Diane C. Bates shows that a tipping point in this unforeseen direction was reached when just 15 percent of the watershed was paved over. "At the regional level," she finds, "master-planned communities [like the Woodlands] allow a more privileged fraction of the region's residents to enjoy an aesthetically pleasing environment, while the region as a whole suffers from the systematic degradation of the area's forests."[70]

On a metropolitan scale, Curitiba, Brazil, has been held up by the advocates of systems planning as the global exemplar of a growth machine of sustainable development. The chief designer of this neoliberal version of the Organic City, Jaime Lerner, was an urban planner. In 1971, the military regime gave him dictatorial power over the city and its 250,000 inhabitants. He rejected the commercial-civic elite's demand for a Radiant City plan of L.A.-style freeways and a central cluster of skyscrapers.

Instead, Lerner forced them into a government-business partnership, while luring the grass roots of ordinary residents to participate in his *Plano Diretor* (master plan). Envisioning a light-green cybernetic metropolis, Lerner turned the downtown into a pedestrian mall that showcases the beautiful Art Nouvelle facades of its turn-of-the-century buildings. Restricting auto access in the center, he installed an innovative system of long, articulated buses that operate like fixed-rail streetcars. Running in the middle of arterial roads, they lead from downtown to the periphery. Zoning and building codes channeled new housing construction along these routes.[71]

To enlist the disfranchised masses in his top-down plan, Lerner offered incentives such as free bus tickets, subsidized housing, and educational programs on public health and neighborhood conservation. In preexisting favelas, where streets are too narrow for refuse trucks, residents earned bus passes and food packages when they took their bags of garbage to a collection center.

In this case of turning theory into shapes on the ground, top-down planning came up against social and political limits rather than ecological ones. The mobilization of working-class neighborhoods resulting from officially orchestrated activism was more media hype than community empowerment. The social stratification of a military-technocratic dictatorship remained embedded in the production of urban space. Curitiba too would build gated communities such as Alphaville Graciosa and other fortified enclaves of security, privilege, and prestige.[72]

Programming the Cyborg City of Flows

In an increasing number of cities around the world, systems planners and policy makers became symbiotic partners in giving computer-generated models of a Cyborg City of flows a value-free mantle of objectivity. By the 1960s, their number-crunching software became sophisticated enough to add a new source of seemingly independent scientific authority in urban planning. The reports generated by computers played a significant role in the formation of public policy. After the uprisings of the sixties, those proposing to solve real urban problems with algorithms of virtual cities gained the ascendency over the advocates of other approaches. Like their partners in the business world, the wave of New Right political leaders being swept into office throughout the West integrated systems planning in the decision-making processes of government.

Beginning in the mid-1950s, the highway engineers had led the way in designing mathematical programs to predict the future. Under the financial sponsorship of the U.S. government in 1956, they had been given a head start in writing computer software that could simulate urban functions and alternative scenarios of future trends of development. Under the patronage of Chicago's new mayor, Richard J. Daley (1955–1976), they had gotten the political support to build the first, "rational planning model" of a real city. Over the next seven years, the Chicago Area Transportation Study became a seedbed of innovation in systems planning.[73]

As soon as the roadbuilding plans were announced, however, the civil engineers and their political sponsors confronted resistance from the grass roots. They had anticipated it because protests against new highways predate the assimilation of computer models into the formation of public policy. Coming out of World War II, the nation's planners had encouraged local officials to route the inner-city segments of the interstate system through red-zoned slum districts. Their demolition projects produced an immediate blowback against "Negro Removal."[74] Protest campaigns against the planners by neighborhoods facing the urban renewal bulldozer became one of the taproots of the civil rights movement.

Environmentalists also began expressing concerns about the limits of the city in the public sphere by contesting plans to carve it up with expressways. By the mid-1960s, their visions of the future would be producing alternative hybrid plans of urban aesthesis and social justice, landscape architecture and neighborhood design, global ecology and community empowerment. These still-amorphous concepts of an Eco-City of citizens would have to compete against the increasing precision of the computer's simulations of a Cyborg City of flows.[75]

By the turning point of the urban crisis, the highway planners felt stripped bare of their political shields and under siege in the public sphere as the creators of "concrete monsters."[76] "Perhaps a majority," the historians Mark Rose and Bruce Seely report, "developed a sense of betrayal and resentment that produced intransigence, resistance to change, and a reaffirmation of the traditional values of traffic service and narrowly technical criteria."[77] Consider, for instance, the Civil Rights Act of 1964, which threw up a roadblock of racial and environmental justice against the urban renewal bulldozer. Five years later, the National Environmental Policy Act added an impact statement and a review process as prerequisites for all federal funding. And in 1972, the creation of the Department of Transportation displaced the highwaymen from their comfort zone in the progrowth Commerce Department and put them under a new regime of politically sensitive nonengineers.[78]

Even before the uprisings of 1968, then, the highway planners had already entered a postmodern, political topography of complexity, contradiction, and contested authority. The politicians had not only recaptured the power to set policy from the technocrats; they also rechanneled the decision making "processes of urban struggle" into an institutional minefield of public hearings, administrative reviews, and court rulings. During the crossroads of transnational urbanism, revolts against the road builders in American cities evolved from not-in-my-backyard (NIMBY) campaigns into much broader coalition movements to demand a voice in planning city growth. They illuminate how the economic, political, and ideological forces of urban social movements combined into something novel: postmodernist visions of the Organic City.

These technocrats were also among the first of their class to be thrust onto the new cultural battlefield of expert versus expert. "In common with physicists and physicians," Rose and Seely surmise, "highway engineers had to fortify their presentations to legislators with new methodologies and advanced statistics, all part of efforts to build unassailable arguments that could advance their interests in the formal political arena."[79]

The highway revolts in American cities also shed light on how systems planners and policy makers used computer programs as political shields to blunt the constant counterattacks of urban social movements. There was a symbiotic blending of roles; the experts and politicians took on characteristics of the other in confronting resistance from the grass roots. The role reversal became complete when computers seemed to become an independent voice of scientific authority in policy debates. Like organic metaphors of the city as a natural system, these human-made machines were given characteristics of autonomous living things. The systems planners used the computer to turn their visions of a Cyborg City of flows into both self-serving and self-fulfilling prophecies.

Three short stories of contestation over building the urban environment illustrate the ascendency of systems planning during the decade following the uprisings of 1968. San Francisco presents an early example of a postmodern kind of translocal if not transnational urban social movement of the grass roots, which contested the design and pace of the city's economic development. If its successful freeway revolt was representative of the new, contested terrain of urban planning, the outcome of the taxpayers' revolt in Atlanta in favor of its unlimited growth alliance of local real estate developers and state highway planners was more typical of the American experience. A third story about New York shows what could go terribly wrong when policy makers substituted the computer simulations of the planners' imaginations for the concrete reality of city streets.

San Francisco's vigilant defenders of nature began protesting soon after the war, when the state highway department unveiled its bold plan to superimpose twenty-five miles of "skyways" on the central area in addition to erecting two new bridges parallel to the existing ones. The city's long-standing "green political culture" meant that environmental advocacy within the community had already achieved a public voice through the election of local officials.[80]

To be sure, the Bay Area had its fair share of progrowth boosters. One of its most influential industrialists, Edgar F. Kaiser, became the public face and directing spirit of the Bay Area Council, a group of top business, civic, and labor executives. Represented by local politicians such as Marin County's John F. "Jack" McCarthy, this lobby in favor of maximizing the pace of the growth machine became a powerful ally of the state's transportation planners.[81]

Nonetheless, they still had to confront a formidable opposition of antihighway protesters marching under a green Save the Environment banner and the quality of everyday life in the metropolitan area. The municipal charter, moreover, gave the city's elected board of supervisors veto power over the state's plans. Local streets could not be closed without their approval, and constructing expressways-in-the-sky through the inner city, of course, would require many permits.

From the beginning of the postwar era, a second struggle raged over transportation policy. Party officeholders and civil servants at every level of the federal system fought among themselves over the question of who rules. Fighting over the throttle of the Bay Area's growth machine on this crowded battlefield were the city, county, state, and national governments in addition to a multicounty independent special district, the Golden Gate Bridge and Highway District.[82]

Hoisting a red-white-and-blue banner for "HOME RULE," the Bay Area's professional politicians marched with the green protesters. They recast their movements to protect the urban environment into a much broader democratic appeal for local self-government. In the Bay Area, a numerous, if scattered, array of private groups and public officials revolted in protest as soon as the state highway engineers attempted to move ahead with their postwar plans to relieve traffic congestion.

With the backing of such a broad constituency at the grass roots, a city supervisor, William C. Blake, became its official spokesman. As chair of the Streets Committee, he helped channel their scattergun protests into a concerted opposition. He kept the highway planners in a deadlock while marshaling his supporters into a lobby with clout in the state and national capitals.

After almost two decades of struggle among the grass roots, planners, and policy makers, the antihighway, save-the-environment movement claimed victory. In March 1966, the board of supervisors rejected the state's scaled-down plan for a single interstate through the city's west side. After this decisive defeat, the political fortunes of the Bay Area's most outspoken booster, Jack McCarthy, quickly went from bad to worse. In becoming a visionary of a planning agency on a metropolitan scale, he had lost sight of the elected official's most basic rule of survival: all politics are local.[83]

McCarthy's growth machine of developers had been transformed into a growth-control majority of insurgent citizens. "For the first time," the historian Louise Nelson Dyble concludes, "opposition to a major transportation project represented the *entire* spectrum of interest groups and localities in the county. . . . Under tremendous public pressure, mayors and city council members had abandoned the growth machine, and soon county-level politics would be transformed, as well."[84] While the success of the freeway revolt in the Bay Area was exceptional, its urban social movements were representative of the translocal nature of the politics of planning in cities across the country.[85]

The story of the Atlanta Regional Commission (ARC) illuminates how the systems planners learned to navigate the urban crisis to advance their personal and professional goals. Computer programs like EMPIRIC became their new protective shields of scientific authority. "Regional planners," the historian Carlton Basmajian underscores, "learned to depend on the sophistication of their analytic tools for validation of the existence of the planning process itself."[86]

In this Southern city, regional planners also became expert at channeling the racial antipathies and the environmental concerns of its white majority to their political advantage. In the decade following the 1954 ruling in the *Brown v. Board of Education* case, the federal courts ordered Atlanta to desegregate its parks, recreational facilities, schools, and buses. Its biracial, commercial-civic elite kept the social peace to project a global image of a progressive New South. This approach to integration, however, triggered white flight from the city in addition to class warfare within it.[87]

Atlanta's Old South political culture of white privilege makes its policy debate over the urban environment an early example of the nationwide rise of a taxpayers' revolt of citizen-homeowners. As the historian Kevin Kruse underscores, "The desegregation of urban public spaces brought about not actual racial integration but instead a new division in which the public world was abandoned to blacks and a new private one was created for whites."[88] Outnumbering African Americans two to one, the white working classes felt not only robbed by them but "abandoned" as well by upper-class whites.[89]

The wealthy had already withdrawn behind the racially restrictive walls of private schools and country clubs in expensive suburban subdivisions. Less affluent whites boycotted en masse what had previously been their virtually exclusive rights to the city. "As whites fled from these public spaces," Kruse writes, "they fought to take their finances with them. And so, they staged an early, though often overlooked, tax revolt, rebelling against the use of their taxes to support municipal spaces and services that they no longer used."[90]

By the early 1960s, Atlanta's whites who could afford to get out of the city wanted to move to all-white suburbs. The technocrats at the ARC used their computer programs to package this racism into a progressive vision of urban growth and equal opportunity for unlimited individual achievement: the American way. By now adept at the politics of urban planning, the highway experts presented their reports in ways that obscured the model's built-in assumptions and shortcuts. They shrank reality to fit a computer screen.

Their reports were designed, moreover, to deflect the anticipated opposition to their regional development plans by antigrowth and other stop-the-freeway protesters. "The visualizations of numeric projections that the EMPIRIC model produced," Basmajian notes, "provided perhaps the most dramatic example of how the model and policies worked together. Projected changes in employment and development were presented as maps and graphs and drawings of possible future development."[91]

In Atlanta, the computer model successfully defined the terms of the public debate. The experts' technical jargon made their plan appear to be the result of pure science. In 1975, the regional development plan was adopted as official policy by the area's local governments. But, Basmajian objects, "how ARC used the projection model to create Atlanta's 1975 [regional development plan] challenges the idea that the roots of sprawling urban regions emerge out of absent or fragmented regional planning. Rather, through the process of writing the [regional development plan], ARC developed a level of expertise and regional influence that helped engender what could only be a self-fulfilling prophecy."[92]

In spite of their complete triumph in Atlanta and at least partial victories in most other cities, American highway planners believed that narrow-minded NIMBY politics had defeated their grand visions of a Cybernetic City of flows. Still locked within the bitter, first afterlife of the uprisings of 1968, they could not see that economic rather than political shortcomings were the primary reasons roadbuilding slowed to a snail's pace.

Most important, the oil embargo of 1973–1974 sharply raised the price of gas and reduced the flow of revenue into their gas-tax funds. The shock of the energy crisis, moreover, gave fuel-efficient cars traction in the marketplace for the first time. The period of stagflation that followed also led to an increase in construction and maintenance costs. But policy makers balked at an offsetting hike in the gas tax because of the hardship it would cause during the recession. The highwaymen used the downturn in work on the job to perfect their rational systems models of simulated utopias. There, politicians were banished and the planners became Wizards of Flow hidden behind a computer screen with their hands on the throttle of the city's growth machines.[93]

What is most striking about the two case studies is how both of these policy debates over planning the city of tomorrow ended up embedding the privileges of race and class in the production of urban space. In McCarthy's Marin County, a local majority of wealthy homeowners threw the postwar planners' growth machine into reverse to keep the peninsula's extraordinary environmental amenities to themselves. By slowing the flow of traffic, they effectively restricted access to its public spaces and facilities to an elite, who were rich enough to buy into their suburban enclave.

In Atlanta, a regional alliance between its biracial commercial-civic leadership and the state's highway engineers harnessed white working-class resistance against desegregation into a progrowth, antitax majority. Although after 1962 it would begin voting down local bond issues for public works improvements, it would also support the ARC's plans for building better highway access between the center and the periphery with extralocal gas-tax funds.

For the upper classes, the privatization of urban space became a substitute for civic engagement on racial integration. Affluent blacks as well as whites could afford to live in a segregated-by-choice suburb. For a majority of citizens, ARC's alluring color-blind projections of upward social mobility proved to be a convincing argument in favor of unbridled sprawl, unrestrained markets, and unlimited individualism.[94]

In New York, the employment of systems planners to manage the fire department further illustrates how computer programs acted as a quasi-autonomous voice if not decisive source of authority in the formation of public policy. It is a story of how the ambitions of a fire chief, city mayor, think tank of computer geeks, and the federal judiciary combined to create a tragedy of good intentions. Closing firehouses in the wrong places, the computer program resulted in several neighborhoods burning down. "It's a warning," Joe Flood shows in his account of this planning disaster, "about the tendency of modelers to become so wrapped up in the complicated process of building a model that they can forget that the model isn't necessarily a perfect stand-in for reality."[95] It's also a cautionary tale of the heavy costs paid when the grass roots is excluded from the policy-making process.

To save money, city leaders came to depend on computer printouts as a shield of value-free science behind which to hide heavily laden, political decisions on where to close firehouses. The "war years" is what the men of the department called the period of fighting fires between 1965 and 1978.[96] In Chief John T. O'Hagan, the incoming administration of Mayor John Lindsay found its ideal champion, a department head devoted to professionalism, modernization, and political correctness.

In the midst of the urban crisis, moreover, the new mayor of the world's First City seemed to personify the hybrid politicians of the postmodern period. In 1965, Lindsay was a clean-government Republican with a New Left style and message of civil rights and multiculturalism. Under his mandate to cut waste, O'Hagan turned to the Rand Institute of New York City to rationalize stationhouse locations.

Its systems planners proposed studying the response times between companies receiving alarms and their arrival at the scene of the fire. Closing stations was the easiest way for the chief to slash the budget without having to touch his self-serving pet projects. He wanted to become a national leader in upgrading fire departments with the latest technologies. For the computer geeks at the Rand Institute, the challenge of optimizing emergency vehicle response times with a minimum of firefighters and equipment presented a logical progression of their work from modeling traffic flow on highways.[97]

But Chief O'Hagan was also politically savvy enough to know that city hall would never approve plans to close the least used stations, which were located in the best-served neighborhoods of the rich and the powerful. Instead, the books were cooked, so to speak, by the software designers to make the computer spit out reports that recommended putting backup companies in the most fire-prone districts at the top of the hit list. For example, the speed of fire trucks was assumed to be always the same, in contravention of the fact that one inching its way through a Midtown gridlock at rush hour traveled far slower than one roaring through the empty residential streets of Queens at midnight.

This fudge factor helped the chief close stationhouses in some of the greatest battlefields of the "War Years" of fighting fires, neighborhoods such as the South Bronx, East Harlem, and Brooklyn. Flood, in The Fires, points out that it was not a coincidence that most of the affected companies were also on the chief's personal hit list of firehouses filled with union troublemakers. These companies were located in the very areas already devastated by the wrecker's ball of another larger-than-life planner, Robert Moses. His highways had torn the community fabric of these working-class districts asunder.

In return for the cooperation of the Rand Institute systems planners, Chief O'Hagan turned a blind eye on obvious false assumptions in the software that made them look like geniuses. After the Rand Institute study became official policy in 1972, its programmers won awards from professional associations of mathematicians, insurance actuaries, and operations researchers in addition to the NATO Systems Science Prize. The federal courts too looked to the report's recommendations as their way out of the quagmire of having become the policy makers of last resort on civil rights. Supreme Court rulings left local district judges in the uncomfortable position of serving as the chief administrators of city departments ranging from the schools to parks, police, and fire. They used the Rand Institute report to throw out the firefighter union's suit against the city for racial and ethnic discrimination.

A computer could not discriminate, the court ruled. A machine could not target stations disproportionately in the poorest African American and Latino communities, which were also the most fire prone. "And so," Flood found, "everyone involved was willing to look the other way as plans to close busy fire stations went into effect while the neighborhoods around them burned to the ground."[98]

The three stories of contestation over the urban environment demonstrate that the 1970s represented a crossroads in the transnational conversation about the future of the city. These struggles resulted in a broad range of outcomes, from successful revolts against the planners to planning triumphs by progrowth coalitions and planning disasters by computer smokescreens of political power and privilege.

The San Francisco Bay Area proved to be the exception to the general trend toward the use of urban planning to build physical spaces of social distance and private access. In this unique place, a green political culture combined with an equally venerable identity as a national center of avant-garde culture production to foster a planning regime of urban conservation. The city of San Francisco did not want to become a dense concentration of high-rise apartment towers like New York or São Paulo. Land-use and zoning regulations preserved its premodernist housing stock, while strict rent control laws protected its poets and artists from eviction by gentrification. Growing out of its revolt against the highway, its board of supervisors started turning dreams of an Eco-City of citizens into an institutional mechanism of advocacy planning and community empowerment.[99]

Nonetheless, the larger Bay Area fits the general pattern of spatial segregation and social fragmentation emerging out the urban crisis of the sixties.

Oakland in the East Bay, for example, had many of the same problems as Watts–South Gate in Los Angeles. Reflecting these trends, California in 1978 would pass Proposition Thirteen, the People's Initiative to Limit Property Taxation. "Thus, the tax revolt," Robert O. Self contends, "was one manifestation of a return in suburban California to a classic growth machine politics that postwar liberalism had temporarily displaced."[100]

In a postmodern world of urban social movements with neither ideological consensus nor political patronage to protect them, the planning profession took refuge behind their computer models of a Cybernetic City of flows. Their input-output models and graphic simulations of the future became the roadmaps of the way forward to break out of the stranglehold of stagflation on economic development. Their veneer of mathematical science gave academics and practitioners alike a new shield of apolitical expertise to defend themselves in the highly contested terrain of the public sphere.

During such uncertain times of social unrest and economic restructuring, business and government leaders came to rely on the computer programs of the planners. It was in just such a setting of extreme fiscal stringency that New York City adopted the Rand Institute's planning model of firehouse closures. Holding most of city hall's unsustainable burden of bonded indebtedness, Wall Street insisted on the privatization of its service functions wherever possible and cutbacks in the others, including the fire department. In this tragic case of the ascendency of systems planning, whole neighborhoods of the city became fourth worlds of burned-out buildings, mean streets, and poor people written off by a computer printout.

Yet these devastated communities became spaces of resistance, seedbeds of a transnational popular culture that resonated from the inner city to the peripheral shantytowns. The South Bronx became the birthplace of ghetto rap, break dancing, graffiti tagging, and underground DJ parties. "Rap music," the historian Tricia Rose points out, "more than any other contemporary form of black cultural expression, articulates the chasm between black urban lived experience and dominant, 'legitimate' (e.g., neo-liberal) ideologies regarding equal opportunity and racial inequality."[101]

7

Case Studies, 1968–1980

The history of building the urban environment in our seven cities reveals hotly contested struggles over physical space and its social meaning. Although all of them became more tightly woven into worldwide webs of interdependence, their national governments and local conditions shaped outcomes that were more different than alike. Events in each city also gave voice to the struggle between the reascendency of modernist visions of the Organic City and the resistance to the authority of its advocates from the grass roots.

The result of this struggle was new hybrid shapes on the ground and spheres of daily life. Each city became more complicated and multilayered in the process as its metropolitan region was simultaneously interconnecting and fragmenting, expanding and contracting, transcending localism and subverting globalism. Some districts in the cities became walled in and plugged in to the future of an electronic "space of flows."[1] Other "spaces of place"[2] were either devolving into discarded "ghettos of exclusion"[3] or springing up into illegal shantytowns of noncitizenship.

This chapter explores these processes and their impact on the built environment as well as the struggles of the city's inhabitants against such victimization. Since emphasis here focuses on interactions between the global and the local, insurgent planning histories can be narrowed to one representative case from each continent. São Paulo illustrates the globalization of fear and the construction of the "Carceral City."[4] But it also highlights the evolution of grassroots organizations into new forms of empowerment over the quality of life in the neighborhoods. Rotterdam demonstrates the possibilities of planning from the bottom up in the Multicultural City. It also exposes the limits of democracy, when the globalization of migration remakes everyone into a minority. Chicago is emblematic of the emerging topography of the Global City as a crazy quilt of ever-expanding and overlapping centers, peripheries, and hybrid spaces. At the same time, this production of new urban space reproduced old social patterns of racial/ethnic and class segregation, only now on a regional scale. Taken together, these three stories of transnational urbanism show how the global and the local influenced each other in redirecting the path of city building during the crises-wracked seventies.

São Paulo, Brazil: Planning Centers in the Periphery

The logical starting point is the gated community of Alphaville in the suburbs of São Paulo, Brazil. Its groundbreaking in 1974 happened at the same time as the global energy crisis and subsequent recession.[5] This was also the nadir of the country's oppression and suffering under the brutal regime of the military dictatorship. Equally dependent on foreign oil supplies and the loans to pay for them, Brazil's national economy began a transition from ten years of "economic miracle" to a "lost decade" of stagnation during the eighties.[6] The oil embargo not only deepened social inequality between the poor and the rich but also made Brazil the most indebted nation of the third world to the first world.[7]

Perhaps the ultimate expression of the ascendancy of technocratic, neoliberal approaches to urban planning, Alphaville is void of public space. It is a fortress city with layer upon layer of security and walls within walls of exclusive access to its various residential enclaves, commercial offices, and recreational venues. In 2011, its police force had over a thousand armed men, who guarded the walls containing over 2,300 businesses and 35,000 residents in fourteen separate villages. Many residents in addition to 150,000 commuters from the "outlands" work here. They have to pass through a series of checkpoints on limited-access toll roads into the citadel.[8]

Yet this whole scenario takes place within a physical space surrounded by a twenty-foot (six-meter) security fence and a psychological environment permeated with fear. "Everything is conditioned by the possibility of violence," the scholar Christopher Lindner reminds us by retelling how "the narrator of Teixeira Coelho's brilliant comic novella *Niemeyer, Um Romance* (2001) has a neurotic dread of the city he inhabits, returning time and again to his 'belief that he will be killed at any minute.'"[9]

Equally pivotal in the planning history of São Paulo is that Alphaville represents a historic break in the city center's path of growth in a southwestern direction. From the coming of the electric trolley at the turn of the century to the mid-1970s, the expansion of a dense core of commercial and residential tower blocks defined a line in time and space that divided the high-security center from the lawless *periferia* (periphery). This moving line also divided the desirable west side from the east side, which became a neglected area of factories, warehouses, and remnants of working-class *corticos* (tenements).

Alphaville's design as a self-contained minicity with American-style suburban housing represented a symbolic as well as a physical break from a half century of rapid growth. "The general character of the city," the historian Christopher Lindner remarks, "is wealthy, white, [and] middle-class, and in physical appearance it is closely related to small cities in North America."[10] Building it began a process of metropolitan deconcentration that erected high-security zones of first world urban space within the periphery's badlands. This fortified enclave was built on farmland in the municipality of Barueri, which is fourteen miles (twenty-three kilometers) northwest of the 1900s *Centro Novo* (New Center). The developers coordinated their plans with the opening of a superhighway nearby. They had to ensure their elite clientele a convenient and secure passageway through the outlands to the relative safety of downtown.[11]

The periphery became more complicated. It was turning into a crazy quilt of disconnected, layered, and overlapping places linked more or less into larger flows of information, power, and money (see Map 11). The interconnectivity of modern technologies on both intraurban and extralocal levels made these new hybrid patterns of economic development and residential settlement possible. The official planners' expansion of the "networked city" of modern infrastructure from the central zone into the illegal favelas also made pivotal changes in the quality of everyday life for their residents, especially with respect to water and sewer hookups. While the builders of these do-it-yourself homes (*construçãos*) could see solid gains being made in their health and environment, others were being forced to construct shelters in remote areas, where conditions of deprivation and misery were worse than ever.[12]

The prime engine driving the transformation of São Paulo into a sprawling megacity without limits was an exploding population. During the 1970s alone, the metropolitan region grew by 4.5 million people to a total of 12.5 million. The city absorbed 2.5 million of this upsurge within enlarged borders, which subdivided 656 square miles (700 square kilometers) into ninety-six districts, or wards. Yet the suburbs were gaining new inhabitants at twice the rate. Spilling over into thirty-nine surrounding municipalities and beyond, the metropolitan region covered 3,000 square miles (8,000 square kilometers) of land. This demographic tidal wave swept over an area of land that was 900 percent larger in 1990 than thirty years earlier.[13]

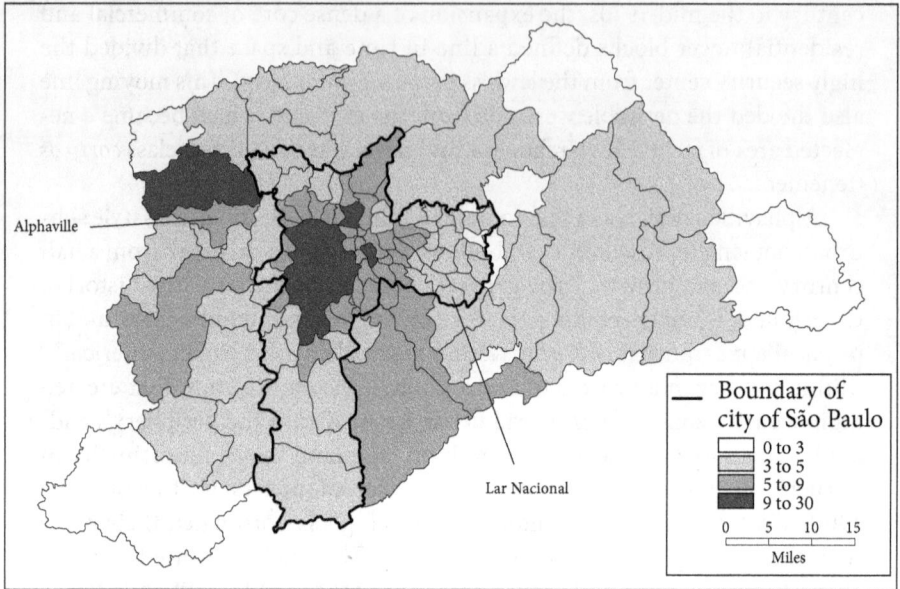

Map 11 São Paulo: Average Income of Heads of Households (in minimum salaries), 1991 (Republished with permission of Teresa Pires do Rio Caldeira, *City of Walls: Crime, Segregation, and Citizenship in São Paulo* [Berkeley: University of California Press, 2000], map 2, p. 242)

Bursting political and environmental boundaries, São Paulo's swelling numbers simultaneously added to congestion in the central zone. Gridlock in the streets, overcrowding on the sidewalks, crime and fear of crime everywhere soared to unbearable levels of claustrophobia. It rivaled New York and Hong Kong in sheer density of population. "But there is something more impressive—or terrifying—about São Paulo for the first-time visitor," Lindner notes, "because unlike those other high-rise cities, this one appears to have no end. . . . [T]here is barely space to breathe."[14]

From a postmodernist point of view, this exploding city can be seen as a "no place," an urban space without an identity. "Unlike Mexico City and other Latin American cities," according to Justin A. Read, "São Paulo is not marked by history, but by a fundamental modernity erasing the past. . . . Indeed one's ground-level perspective in São Paulo is largely marked by a *lack of vision*, left amidst a seemingly endless sea of 20- to 30-story concrete buildings that block out both sunrise and sunset."[15]

Ever since the trolley line began traversing the Anhangabaú Valley from the old center to the *Centro Novo* in the early 1900s, the city had been growing too fast to gain an identity of place. Like downtown development's moving line, São Paulo's other districts also underwent constant change in land uses and residential patterns by a succession of different social groups. Portuguese Brazilians, African Brazilians, Italians, Japanese, and mixed-race groups had created their own communities in distinct neighborhoods.

But the swelling and migrating high-security zone of the upper classes in the city center had expelled the lower classes to the lawless outskirts of town. There, they changed from being apartment renters to homeowners. In such a fragmented and impermanent landscape of kaleidoscope-like change, its inhabitants experienced the city in so many different ways as to preclude the crystallization of a single, fixed image of the place where they were living.[16]

On the contrary, the city and its meaning remain in a perpetual state of contestation. Casting the seventies within a much longer historical context of Latin American colonization puts Read in Immanuel Wallerstein's camp of continuity in the development of globalization. Read disagrees with Manuel Castell's observation that the global restructuring of capitalism after 1974 gave birth to a process of "simultaneous economic development and underdevelopment, social inclusion and social exclusion."[17] Rather than describing the emergence of a new type of Global City, Read argues that these conditions have been present in São Paulo ever since the early twentieth century, when it became an exploding city.[18]

From his point of view, the cities of the first world such as New York, London, and Paris are simply catching up with the São Paulos of the third world. Calling this process "obverse colonization," Read posits that it "has not resulted from a recent structural shift in the global political-economic order, even if the shift to globalization has exacerbated the Latin American city's problems. Rather . . . structural disequilibrium is the historical constant of São Paulo's urban growth. In essence, São Paulo has been generating its own 'Fourth World' for most of its modern history, long before the structural alterations of globalization. What has changed is that the 'First World' global city has merely lagged behind São Paulo in terms of poverty growth and concentration."[19]

Alphaville is a perfect expression of these post-1968 reversals of the center with the periphery, the local and the global. São Paulo's first fortified suburban enclave represents the postsixties trend of everyday life toward social fragmentation into disconnected private worlds. This minicity of walls within walls reflects the postmodern condition of polycentric enclaves of metropolitan space and segregated geographies of social inequality. Pulling out the lens on the Brazilian megalopolis, Lúcia Sá observes, "Perhaps this provisional portrait, made up of incomplete parts, mirrored, incommunicable and multiplying each other to infinity, in the end might be the only viable realism for the São Paulo of our time."[20]

The commodification of residential space into private neighborhoods like Alphaville also illustrates how the postsixties crosscurrents of the global and the local became new hybrid forms of urban space and culture. The marketing of gated communities, or common-interest developments, worldwide reveals the production of a full line of consumer packages, which were tailored to fit national fashions and laws. While some were advertised by playing on fears of the "other," many were sold in positive terms. They appealed to individual desires for social prestige, improved amenities, better administration, and the good life within a retirement, golf, or arts community.

Rather than a privatization or secession of urban space, common-interest developments are the kind of public-private partnerships that came to epitomize the restructuring of the economy of cities, especially after the 1973–1974 oil embargo. Local governments collected property taxes but were relieved from infrastructure costs and service provision in exchange for putting control of public space in private hands. In addition to residential developments, other more or less privatized security zones included enclosed shopping malls and fortified office towers.[21]

An emerging postmodern world of free market capitalism blurred the dividing line between both the physical spaces and the social spheres of public and private life. In Mexico City, for example, turning residential neighborhoods into gated security zones and forming homeowner associations to fund them is illegal. Yet older elite districts like Los Lomas took control of the streets into their own hands with the passive approval of local authorities.

The erection of barriers of defense was not limited to the rich and famous. The fragmentation of the city into fortified patches of disconnected groups extended down the class ladder to the bottom rungs of society. In Chicago, on the one hand, grassroots organizations of working-class homeowners on the West Side had through streets barricaded as a planning strategy to keep crime from getting into their neighborhoods. In Los Angeles, on the other hand, the police sealed off poor communities in the South Central area, making them Narcotics Enforcement Areas, as a way of keeping suspected gangsters from getting out of their hoods. And in the foothills of Mexico City, illegal squatters in the shantytown of Ajusco organized to stand their ground with sticks and stones against the repeated assaults of the "*desalojo* [eviction] machines" of the police.[22]

Perhaps the spread of ghetto rap and graffiti, a new form of urban popular culture, was equal to Alphaville in giving expression to these postmodern hybrid landscapes of the local and the global. They are both deeply rooted in local identities of place, and their creation takes place within a self-conscious framework of an international youth culture. "Hence," Lúcia Sá declares, "the street functions for the rappers [and the spray painters] as a space of resistance, which they can create and change through their art."[23]

Sá, a São Paulo native, interviewed members of the city's most prominent rap group, the Racionais Mc's (Rationals). Its leader, Mano Brown, traces his influences to the American radical Malcolm X by way of the Long Island, New York, group Public Enemy. "The US rap groups that influenced Racionais with the idea of a socially committed rap," Sá discovered, "also inspired them with a conception of race relations that is at the centre of their idea of neighbourhood."[24]

Whether culture production in the ghettos or master-planned common-interest developments in the suburbs, the urban crisis of the sixties set into motion a different set of forces. They would give shape to urban space and society for the next quarter century. Economists give emphasis to the global restructuring and integration of markets in redirecting the path of city building. In Los Angeles, for example, factories closed in the inner rings, while new plants making high-tech products were opening at a safe distance in the outer suburbs. At the same time, its downtown and other areas were enjoying a building boom as the American commercial headquarters of the Pacific Rim.[25]

São Paulo again serves as a leading example of the impacts of this global economic restructuring on local settlement patterns and social relationships. Under the technocratic regime of the military dictatorship, international capital flowed into Brazil after it imposed major wage cuts on its workforce. The resulting boost of economic development enriched an enlarging middle class in São Paulo. However, it came at a cost, which was paid by the impoverishment of much, much larger number of the city's factory and service workers. The growing gap in incomes was expressed spatially in the widening distances and conditions of daily life between the center and the periphery. Crime rates, for instance, were much higher in the lawless outlands than in the high-security zone of the center.

Nevertheless, gnawing fear of crime became pervasive throughout society as the metropolis underwent explosive population growth from newcomers in search of jobs. The creation of Alphaville after a decade of economic restructuring reflected the willingness of the elite to pay a high price for security in terms of money and altered suburban lives behind the walls. Its residents also collectively bought an array of environmental amenities, including a waterworks and sanitation services.

In analogous ways, the Racionais Mc's and the graffiti artists of the favelas also transformed the built environment, turning public places such as transit stations and highway overpasses into civic spaces of resistance. Moreover, the creation of liberation theology's ecclesiastical base communities on a neighborhood form of organization represented yet another response to the new regime of oppression in the workplace. As fear of the "other" permeated São Paulo, its diverse class, racial, ethnic, and migrant-origin groups fractured into residential enclaves of self-defense.[26]

Perhaps the prototype of the long-term evolution of the capitalist city toward extremes in social and physical divisions, São Paulo is also a leading exemplar of the ascendency of systems planning during the seventies. In 1964, the generals put the technocrats in charge of reviving the flow of foreign investment into economic development. By squeezing rural incomes even more than urban wages, the nation's economic planners sustained the resulting migration from the farms to factory and service jobs in the industrial centers.

The local planners put in charge of coping with this upsurge in population—four and a half million people—responded with a massive public works program. They drew master plans to expand the network of modern infrastructure to cover the entire metropolitan area in the future. Besides adding roads, pipes, and wires, the official planners were given the responsibility of tackling the housing shortage on a Fordist scale of mass production.

Unlike the artificial boundaries drawn up by the security forces between *centro* and *periferia*, the city's engineers were trained to uphold professional standards of scientific integrity and political nonpartisanship. Yet they could not escape the larger context of their political culture in drawing plans and making decisions. Brazil had always divided society between a landowning elite of legal citizens and an undocumented mass of illiterate, unfree workers.

The influence of globalization on building São Paulo was filtered through this national, Janus-faced lens of class relations. A statistical analysis of the location of spending on public works exposes the deep-seated biases of the engineers that drew a sharp dividing line between *centro* and *periferia*. Consequently, the neighborhoods of the rich always got a disproportionate share of the budget. Nonetheless, districts of the poor in the illegal outlands consistently received significant upgrades in their physical surroundings.[27]

Lacking a democratic tradition, Brazil's professional class used city building to reinforce the great social divide between the elite and the masses. After 1968, the planners no longer had to face resistance from urban social movements or even elected officials. A study of infrastructure spending found a pattern of "hierarchical selectivity of policies. . . . According to this selectivity idea, the priorities of the state should follow the social structure, supplying services (and better quality services) first to the social groups that are richer and better educated."[28]

The investigators created a social geography, which shows a clear internal borderline drawn by the movement of the high-security central zone. The upper and middle classes clustered on the southwest side. The northeast side was more fragmented into lower-middle class neighborhoods, "consolidated" hybrids, and built-up shantytowns of the poor. The periphery contained the majority of areas currently undergoing settlement by people in even more dire circumstances.[29]

Under the new regime of stronger public-private partnerships, systems approaches to urban planning gained the ascendency in the formation of public policy. Both the city's public works department and the foreign-owned utility companies came to rely on computers to generate models of environmental improvement. Yet their software seemed stuck in the postwar era of the first world's urban renewal and reconstruction. São Paulo's growth machine of the 1970s closely resembled Boss Daley's Chicago of the 1960s.

Facing no freeway revolt, for example, the city bulldozed superhighways through the periphery with impunity, displacing homeowners by the thousands. In the overjammed center, the highway engineers adopted Robert Moses's plan of double-decker skyways thirty to forty feet (ten to twelve meters) above the 1920s boulevards. They quickly gained the derisive label of *minhocãos*, or the giant monster worms of Amazon folklore. In the early 1970s, moreover, the planners routed the construction of the first underground transit line of the Metro by digging trenches through poor inner-city neighborhoods.[30]

Brazil's dictators also initiated a social housing program for its exploding cities that seemed like a time warp to the pre-1968 approaches of the United States and Europe. In 1964, they created the National Housing Bank, which took about four years to ratchet up the construction industry to assembly-line methods of production. In São Paulo, the housing authority built its own versions of Paris's Sarcelles. In the early 1970s, the housing authority put 30,000 families in the tower block apartments of the Itaquera (District) Project, which was located twelve miles (eighteen kilometers) east of the center on 14,300 acres (5,800 hectares) of green space. The district's population had ballooned twelvefold, to 444,000 residents, by the end of the decade.

But unlike the poor people warehoused in the *grands ensembles* of the first world, this minicity was earmarked for the technocracy of white-collar civil servants. The government-owned monopoly built privately owned condominiums. "It is only with the creation of a federal housing system," Gil Shidlo contends, "that the co-optation of the middle sectors by the government became institutionalized."[31] Adhering to a political culture of "hierarchical selectivity," São Paulo's policy makers restricted the vast majority of condominium buyers to families earning middle-class incomes.

Officials corrupted the selection process to create their own form of plantation politics. They established a regime of middle-class client-patron relationships that excluded blue-collar applicants, except for a token number. They were required to have all their official documents in order as well as written records from their local employers testifying they had been working faithfully on the job for at least two years. Given the tremendous shortage of decent housing and the oversupply of violent crime, the waiting list numbered in the hundreds of thousands.[32]

The oil embargo proved pivotal in the history of São Paulo. The economic crisis abroad triggered multiple crises at home, forcing major changes in the direction of urban planning and social reform. Although its planners made physically Herculean, albeit socially skewed, efforts to improve the urban environment, they were simply overrun and overwhelmed by the tsunami of newcomers. A decade of economic development brought a declining standard of living for the working classes. Society's single best indicator of its people's general health and well-being, infant mortality rates, went into reverse. By 1975, death rates had returned to 1945 levels, wiping out two generations of progress earned through the work of health-care providers and sanitation engineers.

The global shockwaves of economic hardship also amplified the local rate of crime, especially property-related offenses such as burglary, robbery, and car theft. But most alarming to the affluent classes was the transformation of kidnapping for ransom into a major business enterprise. An urban proverb of the working class expressed the sense of a Robin Hood folk justice being carried out: "When the rich steal from the poor, the poor steal the rich."[33]

In addition, the blurring of the city's two-faced space into a more complicated topography of more or less "networked" and "consolidated" neighborhoods amplified the crisis of fear set off by the crime wave. According to Teresa Pires do Rio Caldeira, improvements in environmental conditions in the favelas had the perverse effect of undermining the middle classes' sense of social status. "A context of uncertainty, in which people feel threatened socially and see transformations occurring," she reports, "seems to stimulate the policing of social boundaries. . . . In other words, proximity leads to the refinement of separations in order to sustain a perception of difference."[34] Alphaville offered the elite not only a relatively safe haven from crime but also a new status symbol of difference.

Raising paranoia and claustrophobia to epidemic levels in the city center, the same pressures of population and impoverishment also created an ecological crisis related to sprawl. The most desperate inhabitants were pushing over the tops of the river valleys and down into the watersheds of the three big reservoirs and power dams: Guarapiranga, Billings, and Cantareira. To stop the deforestation, erosion, and human contamination of the water supply, the state government in 1975–1976 enacted the Watershed Protection Acts. They forbade any settlement in an outer ring, including over half the land in seventeen of its thirty-nine suburbs and the critical wooded areas around the reservoirs. The planners' computer programs had drawn an ideal model of environmental preservation.[35]

But this grand plan of urban containment had unintended consequences that offer a classic case of the perverse effects of the rational systems approach. The acts prohibited the issuance of building permits within the ecozone, leading legitimate businesses to build their factories, stores, and subdivisions elsewhere. By keeping these private developers out, the watersheds became a safe haven for illegal *construçãos*. Both families being displaced by gentrification in the center and newcomers arriving with only their dreams sought shelter in the most protected spaces available.

For them, the favelas arising along the riverbeds and around the reservoirs became safety zones of "no-place" because of an absence of law enforcement. Their self-built homes were relatively secure from both police raids and thugs (*capangas*) hired by landowners and swindlers (*grileiros*) to burn them out. During the 1970s and 1980s, these land invaders joined the two out of three inhabitants of São Paulo who lived in illegal dwellings without property titles or building permits.[36]

Producing just the opposite of watershed protection, the technocrats' systems approach to the urbanization of the land represents a case study of "perverse" planning, according to James Holston. In the 1970s, he studied illegal settlements in districts at the edge of the city. Their insurgent planning histories of resistance shed light on how the planners' models of physical space exacerbated the problems of social instability, violent crime, and moral disorder.[37]

Like Justin Read, Holston takes a long view of Brazil's economic development and the continuities between past and present. He concurs that "spatial segregation and citizenship differentiation were concurrent processes in a project of national modernization." Since the sixteenth century, the planter elites had been building a land system of institutional chaos to keep their families' illegal appropriations tangled in a Gordian knot of official red tape. As the folk saying went, "Those who do not register, do not own."[38]

In the postwar era, São Paulo perpetuated and further complicated this already indecipherable system into a "misrule of law."[39] The planners used it to draw a sharp line in their land-use maps between the center, defined as urban, and the periphery, which was zoned as rural. Yet the official division of urban space into two zones had perverse effects. Left outside the gaze of the official plan, the shantytowns became seedbeds of democracy.

The battle over who owned the land in the subdivision of Lar Nacional shows how this process of community self-defense fed into larger political mobilizations for full rights to the city. In 1967, the developer began subdividing a property into five hundred lots in the municipal district of Sapopemba for a market niche of skilled factory workers, salesmen, and self-employed small businessmen. He built two hundred starter houses in this Levittown-like subdivision. The developer sold the houses on installment contracts, with most of the down payment rolled into the monthly payments. Over the next five years, families moved into these new homes. They believed that they were the legal landowners (*loteamentos*) and that they were on their way toward the achievement of the exulted status of *casa propria* (property owner).[40]

In 1972, however, their dreams were smashed when an official suddenly appeared with court-ordered eviction notices. The homebuyers were victims of a swindler, who had disappeared with their money and the property sales records. But to further muddy the legal waters, the judicial decree for eviction failed to account for improvements on the rural land, which persuaded the official not to enforce the evictions. After enduring a second wave of crooked lawyers, hired guns, and other criminal predators descending on the neighborhood, the remaining families organized a chapter of the Societies of Friends of the Neighborhoods (Sociedades Amigos de Bairro; SABs). Dating back to the late 1940s, these organizations delivered blocks of votes in return for patronage from the district representative. One representative, Janio Quatros, was a populist champion of the SABs and rose from mayor to governor to, in 1960, the presidency, when SABs numbered in the hundreds. After 1968, hundreds more formed in the periphery.[41]

On the basis of the idea of citizen rights to the city, the Lar Nacional SAB turned for help to the law school at the University of São Paulo. One of the students, Antonio Benedito Margarido, took on their case. He was brilliant in defending his clients, disproving the claims of the new landowner to have all required documentation. The lawyer kept the landowner in check by pursing the legal status of a virtually endless trail of land records riddled with technical errors, irregularities, and outright fraud.

While the Lar Nacional's lawyer turned the "misrule of law" to the advantage of the homebuyers, their SAB became a school of citizenship. The first thing they learned was the complexity of land law. To save their dreams, the members of the SAB became insurgent planners. They demanded full rights as citizens through a process of attending public hearings and court proceedings, creating a land records archive, and presenting petitions to officeholders and bringing them to their neighborhood on fact-finding missions.

In their struggle, the homebuyers of Lar Nacional gained new identities of place as both individuals and members of a place-based community. This process of insurgent citizenship is reflected in the ways they contrasted themselves against the *ocupaçõs* (land invaders). For members of the SAB, their self-image was as hard-working *casa proprias* who lived in substantial brick homes. The "others" living "down there" were portrayed as bums (*vagabundos*) who were too lazy to build anything other than rudimentary shacks (*barracos*).

In the process of demanding the legal rights of homeownership, the meetings of the SAB became a hothouse for the growth of new collective and gender relationships. In 1982, women were elected to the organization's top three positions. "These women transformed the SAB," Holston observes, "from an association that focused almost exclusively on the land crisis to one that organized educational, recreational, and revindicatory activities. Under their leadership, the SAB became the neighborhood center."[42]

The SAB functioned as an incubator of insurgent citizenship. Under the military regime of terror, labor and student activists took refuge in local place-based groups. They served as training grounds for a core of grassroots leaders who began to enter the political arena during the eighties. In the meantime, Lar Nacional underwent significant environmental improvement and community formation based on a new sense of rights to the city in a democratic society.[43]

Rotterdam, Netherlands:
Creating Participatory Planning

Rotterdam, a community of blue-collar workers, was particularly hard hit by the oil embargo of 1973–1974. The aftershocks of crisis marked a decisive turning point in the physical and social landscapes of Rotterdam. The global restructuring of capitalism produced a parallel revolution in transportation technology. Europe's largest port, the city had to modernize its docks to accommodate giant container ships and oil tankers. Rotterdam suffered triple blows of a sharp drop in shipping during the ensuing recession, the downsizing of its shipyards, and the closure of its second-most-important industry, petrochemical refineries (see Map 12).

Many unskilled jobs were permanently lost to technological modernization. For instance, hundreds of manual workers on the docks were replaced by a handful of crane operators moving truck-sized containers on and off ships. During this period of economic restructuring of global markets, many inner-city neighborhoods suffered rapid physical deterioration and social disorder. Rotterdam would lose one quarter of its population from a peak in 1965 of 731,000 inhabitants to 555,000 twenty years later.[44]

In 1974, the local and the national governments initiated bold new departures in physical planning. Rejecting environmental determinism, the reformers designed a new planning machine. In Rotterdam, this meant the end of the functionalist approach of the postwar Van Traa plan, which had divided land use and privileged the commercial zone. The Urban Renewal Areas Act gave priority instead to the regeneration of declining residential districts. It institutionalized a social constructionist approach to the production of urban space. Practitioners took up the challenge of changing roles from technical experts of environmental design to social facilitators of "advocacy and pluralism in planning."[45]

Marking a turning point, new arenas of civic discourse emerged from this process of making plans for the conservation and rehabilitation of the

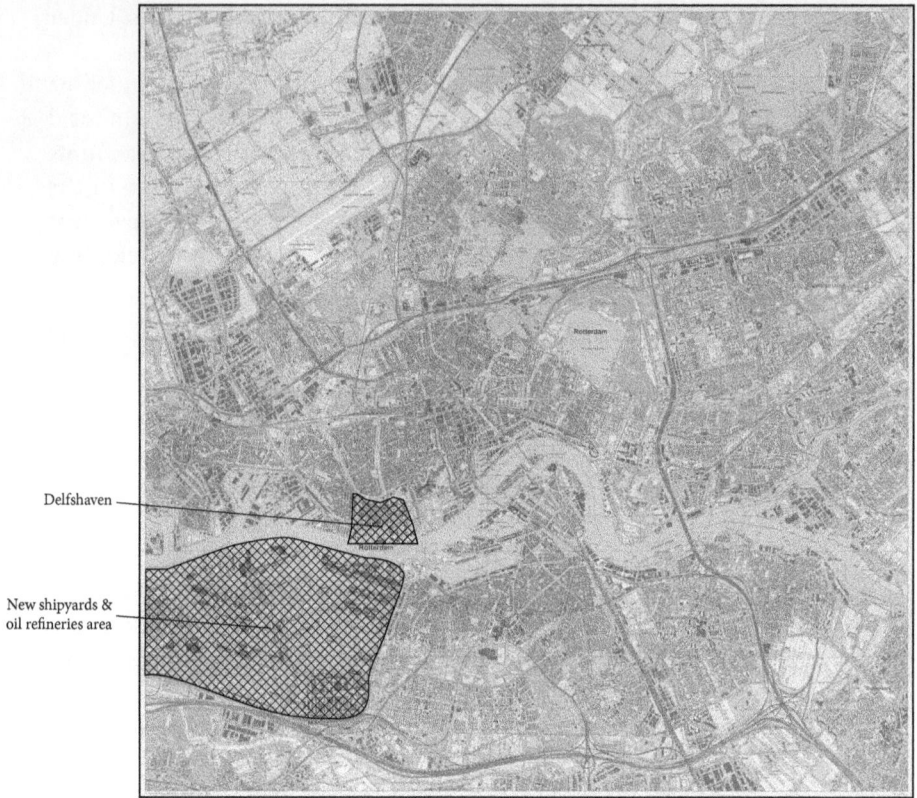

Map 12 Rotterdam: Rotterdam Metropolitan Area (Wikipedia, http://commons.wiki media.org/wiki/File:Rotterdam-plaats-OpenTopo.jpg, Rotterdam-plaats-OpenTopo CC BY-SA 3.0 Janwillemvanaalst)

neighborhoods. The history of one of them, Delfshaven, illuminates the success of participatory planning in restoring consensus democracy in the public sphere. But this is also a story of the limits of a bottom-up approach to the formation of public policy in a neighborhood undergoing a disruptive demographic transition. Its population was changing from native white, blue-collar workers to ethnic/religious immigrants on welfare.

The urban revolts of the sixties in the Netherlands had begun the process of structural reform of city government. The reverberations of the "crisis of civil disorder" within its cities triggered a related "crisis of legitimacy" within its planning profession.[46] Like the American Robert Goodman, some of its insiders began to question its authority to act as social engineer, regardless of good intentions. A national commission was established to study this question. It recommended devolving power to the grass roots. Lip service to community participation was replaced with a significant shift in decision-making power from centralized bureaucracies to neighborhood councils.

In 1969, the issue that galvanized the citizens of Rotterdam into a grassroots movement of opposition was the official plan to expand the central business district beyond the original limits of the war-bombed area. Their successful revolt against the planners illustrates how an insurgent citizenship changed the direction of public policy on building the urban environment. In this case, the port city's Advisory Community Councils set up after the war underwent reform from appointed to elected positions.

From the city planners' point of view, the logical direction for the growth of the city center was to the west. They proposed extending it from the anchor of the new Central Train Station along the west side of one of the city's oldest landscaped canals, the Westersingel. Their report proposed an urban renewal project of clean-sweep demolition to make room for commercial development. It would displace thirty thousand households in the Oude Westen (Old Western) neighborhood. In this case, "old" meant a relatively new residential area built up in the 1890s–1910s along a community main street, Nieuwe Binnenweg Straat. To be sure, many buildings needed rehabilitation, and some were beyond repair. Yet these eyesores were more than offset by the neighborhood's many charming features and historic architecture. In addition, its residents enjoyed easy pedestrian access to the central business district as well as the park-filled museum district to the south.[47]

For many different reasons, they organized a Save the Neighborhood campaign to reject the official plan. Their resistance movement gained momentum as other communities on the edges of the business district organized to stop the urban renewal bulldozers from demolishing their homes. Local activists learned how to influence public policy in the Advisory Community Councils and took them over in 1972, when their officials became chosen by election. Two years later, the protesters ousted the incumbent mayor and took charge of the city council.

With the Urban Renewal Areas Acts, the insurgents instructed the planners to change direction toward conserving the neighborhoods bordering the central business district. "In fact," historian John McCarthy states, "a major shift in spatial planning in Rotterdam arose in the mid-1970s, with a move away from a 'functionalist' approach emphasizing business uses in the central area to a 'participatory' approach stressing the need for mixed uses in the inner city."[48]

With its political culture of consensus democracy and trade union activism, the port city became a leader in giving new meaning to old ideas about collaborative planning between top-down technocracies and grassroots organizations. This challenge raised the practical political question of whose stories of the city had legitimacy when making plans. What steps should local government take to ensure that these stories represented the voice of the grass roots? Even more problematic, should city hall take on the additional responsibility of actively encouraging the formation of place-based organizations? Or should it limit its support to preexisting groups, which could establish claims as stakeholders in the planning process?

Delfshaven became the test grounds of the new politics of planning because it was Rotterdam's most notorious battleground of drugs and crime. It was compared to Chicago's South Side and Los Angeles's Watts. "While it is problematic to talk of ghettos in the Dutch context, and at the same time questionable to equate diverse ethnicity with poverty," the social scientists Justin Beaumont and Maarten Loopmans explain, "a clear process of urban socio-spatial segregation in terms of standard of living and quality of life is evident across the city."[49] The widening gap was no more evident than the stark contrast between the decline of Delfshaven and the upgrading taking place in suburbs with single-family homes.[50]

Originally a separate port for Rotterdam's nearby rival, Delft, the riverfront district had become an old, "decent neighbourhood for members of the higher-paid segments of the Rotterdam working class," according to another team of researchers.[51] Typical of these residential districts, about 80 percent of its dwellings were rental units owned by various public institutions.

At the center of Delfshaven was a Progressive Era housing project, the Spangen. Located about three miles (five kilometers) southwest of the central station, its long streets of row house apartments formed a star-shaped design with a soccer stadium at the top for a city team, the Spartans. As in many other inner-city neighborhoods during the sixties, the residents had formed a group to represent their interests, the Wijk Organisatie Spangen (WOS; Neighborhood Organization Spangen).[52]

To implement its renewal act of 1974, the regime of the social constructionists at city hall funded an independent organization, the Rotterdam Institute for Community Support. Its job was to set up neighborhood project groups, organize advocacy forums of discussion, and facilitate communication among a full range of technical experts, civic leaders, special-interest stakeholders, and community groups like the WOS. Over the course of the next decade, the old-time residents in control of the WOS worked with the institute to achieve consensus. In return, they received "generous subsidies" for their cooperation.[53]

Beneath the surface of this seemingly successful civic experiment in participatory planning, however, the residential base of Delfshaven was in the midst of a turbulent turnover. With a demographic aging from the loss of young families to the suburbs, it suffered the full brunt of the oil embargo and loss of jobs on the docks. In 1976, the national government passed a so-called Disabilities Act to take care of these displaced workers. In Delfshaven, they became the left behinds of a growing exodus to the suburbs by those who could afford to relocate there.[54]

Filling the vacant apartments in the Spangen were recent immigrants, who came from countries without traditions of democracy. The newcomers were Surinamese, Antilleans, Turks, and Moroccans. Most of them came with less education and technical skills than their native Dutch counterparts. In 1977, these immigrants occupied 19 percent of the housing project, a proportion rising steadily to a majority over the next two decades. Opening storefront shops and small businesses, some would prosper in Rotterdam, but many others would join the recession-swelled welfare rolls of the unemployed. In a Dutch context, then, poverty did not mean insufferable material deprivation but a loss of social status and the freedom to choose where to live.[55]

In Delfshaven, the refusal of its growing immigrant population to participate in the public sphere undermined the city's social constructionist approach to planning. Unfortunately, their stories of passive resistance remain unrecorded. But what the record does show is a neighborhood that was downgraded in the citywide competition for urban conservation funds. The upgrading of other districts widened the gap in rental rates, making the Spangen a refuge for those at the economic bottom of society.

Crackdowns on crime in gentrified districts pushed the drug trade and other illegal activities into communities that were too disorganized to defend themselves. Delfshaven was one of them. It showed more and more classic signs of urban decline: derelict buildings, dirty streets, and dangerous people hanging around night and day. It was becoming a Dutch version of an "emerging ghetto," a fourth world of physical segregation and social exclusion.[56]

On a metropolitan scale, Rotterdam showed clear trends toward dividing into a social geography of center and periphery. In 1971, the most prestigious residential zones formed a second ring around the inner-city neighborhoods on both sides of the river, which encircled the business district. During the decade, a suburban exodus upgraded the socioeconomic status of the periphery and downgraded the center.

This second residential ring of what had been the city's most desirable places to live suffered noticeable decline. In five out of six of these districts, the average income of its residents went down. Although too early to halt this rising tide of out-migration, the renewal act began to sort out winners and losers among the five inner-city districts. While revitalization projects and community activism started pushing up rental values in some neighborhoods, several others like Delfshaven began a downward slide in their ability to fill their lengthening lists of vacancies.[57]

Here, switching maps from class to ethnicity and religion projections exposes in sharp relief a second, related pattern of residential movement within the city. It was dividing into native and immigrant zones. Three of these "spaces of place" began emerging. They would continue to consolidate into ethnic and religious enclaves, where immigrants constituted more than twice their average proportion in the Rotterdam census. Additional maps of redlining of residential mortgages confirm that lower-class and minority status worked together to make immigrant neighborhoods into fourth world ghettos of exclusion. They were shortchanged in receiving their fair share of the benefits from the city's new consensus in favor of urban regeneration.

By the 1990s, the neighborhoods that did succeed in upgrading further complicated settlement patterns. They became gentrified urban zones for a hip generation of single-person households. By then, some of the outer suburbs were in decline, creating a more mixed social geography of hybrid spaces on a metropolitan scale. The extent to which the renewal acts of 1974 helped slow the exodus to the suburbs and beyond has not yet been determined.[58]

In 1974, the national government also instituted a new planning regime to stop the encroachment on the *Groene Hart* of the *Randstad* by the flow of people out of city centers to the periphery. The national government's *Third Report on Physical Planning* sought to reduce the expansion of the suburbs by giving priority to the regeneration of older inner-city neighborhoods and newer growth centers.[59] Besides making adjustments for the geographic mobility of the population, the regional planners had to take into account a marked decline in birth rates during the hard times of the seventies. The inhabitants of the *Randstad* were draining away to the south and east, creating a new class of Dutch society, the long-distance commuter.

In effect, the *Third Report* expanded a regional into a national plan. It incorporated the green spaces on the outside periphery of the Rim City within its two prime directives of concentrated deconcentration and environmental protection of the Green Heart. As with Rotterdam's plan, it is hard to measure the extent to which national planning helped retard suburban sprawl.

Painfully evident, nevertheless, were the tight limits of conscious, formal planning in a country that put a high premium on not only technical expertise but also individual freedom of choice. From the sixties into the nineties, the Dutch preferred to move out of their city centers to single-family homes in the surrounding countryside. In the hands of the grass roots, participatory planning became a double-edged tool. On the one hand, the Dutch used it for the environmental protection of public spaces and the revitalization of city neighborhoods. On the other, they turned it into an instrument of social engineering to safeguard their private rights as consumers in the marketplace.[60]

Chicago, United States:
Deconstructing the City of Neighborhoods

In March 1975, Nelson Algren moved out of Chicago. The famous author of *The Man with the Golden Arm* (1949) had long been treated like a leper in his hometown, but he had stuck it out. In retaliation for his caustic portraits of the city's power elite in *Chicago: City on the Make* (1951), Algren had been banned from the public libraries, blacklisted by private foundations, and belittled in the mass media. Forced to auction off his possessions to pay moving expenses, his bitterness spilled out in response to a reporter's questions: "Until now the city never did a thing for me, you know, there are all these organizations full of rich patrons—the Friends of this and the Friends of that—but hell; no one was ever my friend. I never got a nickel from any of them. I don't owe this city a thing."[61]

Declaring the death of the "city of neighborhoods," Algren sensed that Chicago had reached a historic point of no return. Unlike his fellow Depression-era chroniclers of the dispossessed, James T. Farrell and Richard Wright, he had not left Chicago. The sixty-five-year-old bachelor was still living in the same poor, Polish-Catholic neighborhood of Polonia on the near northwest side. "Once you've come to be part of this particular patch," he admitted, "you'll never love another. Like living with a woman with a broken nose, you may well find lovelier lovelies. But never a lovely so real."[62] So, the reporter asked, after enduring so many years of economic hardship and artistic emptiness, why was he giving up and leaving town in the winter of 1975?[63]

Algren lamented that Chicago had changed in fundamental ways; he now felt like a stranger. "I guess I lost touch with the city," he reflected. "I don't know anyone anymore. . . . I don't even know my downstairs neighbor other than to say '*buenos dias*' when we meet in the hallway."[64]

Indeed, Polonia was in the midst of racial/ethnic succession. It was changing hands during the white flight of its old immigrant families toward the far northwest side and suburbs and their newcomer replacements from Latin America. To be sure, some characteristics of the neighborhood streets looked the same during the daytime. There was still a predominance of blue-collar workers and their children in parochial school uniforms. But Algren knew that his world of the midnight hours had been swept away. "I used to know the cops, the pols, the junkies, the thieves, the addicts," he reminisced, "but then that whole crowd passed on. I don't know anyone in the new crowd" (see Map 13).[65]

By the time Algren moved away, the long-term impacts of the economic restructuring of global capitalism had knocked the wheels off the city's

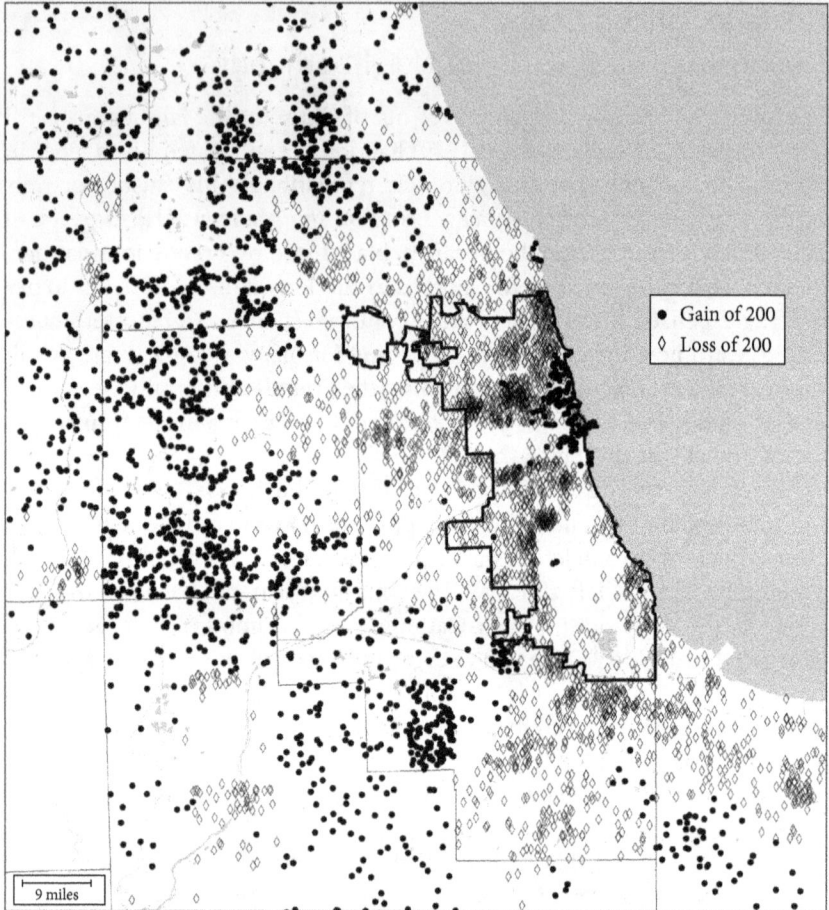

Map 13 Chicago: White Population Change in the Chicago Metropolitan Region, 1980–1990 (Christopher Winters, Department of Geography, University of Chicago, http://www.lib.uchicago.edu/e/collections/maps/c89popr.gif)

growth machine and left it in ruins. It would take twenty years to rebuild after 1968, when it crashed into a wall of civic trauma following the violent insurrection of the West Side and the "police riot" at the national Democratic convention.[66] City hall's long-standing policy of racial containment had broken down, trampled underfoot by a stampede of white residents and businesses getting away from the city center.

Five years later, the slingshot effects from this racial backlash of the urban crisis were bolstered by two heavy outside blows on the local economy: the oil embargo and the end of the Vietnam War. The rapid acceleration of the loss of factory jobs and white people from Chicago forms the structural context of change in the metropolitan region's spatial form and social geography during the crossroads of transnational urbanism. Consider that twice as many people left the city during the seventies as during the previous decade. Over these twenty years, Chicago's net decline in population of 550,000 was equal to the 1985 census of people living in Rotterdam.[67]

For the first time, moreover, the inner ring of suburbs within Chicago's Cook County lost population, almost a quarter million people. In contrast, green spaces on the outer periphery showed increasing signs of urbanization. And inner-city zones were being redeveloped into suburban shopping malls on public streets as well as inside privately owned skyscrapers.[68]

At the same time, local and national politics played an equally significant supportive role in the spatial fragmentation and social deconstruction of the metropolis. After the uprisings of 1968, Mayor Richard J. Daley scorned systems approaches to planning in favor of the naked exercise of power, what he called the "pure deal." The local politician had been thrown on the defensive in the national media, portrayed as an "American Pharaoh."[69]

Challenges to Mayor Daley's authority as the supreme powerbroker came from above by the federal government and also below. Striking back in February 1971 to regain control, he dissolved the Office of Zoning Review and threw the "zoning game" of his Democratic Party's clientele regime wide open to developers large and small. For the big "pure deals," Daley continued to rely on his partnership with insiders on the Central Area Committee. For the little ones, the ward bosses reaped the tribute within their respective fiefdoms from their absolute control over the zoning variances needed by virtually every business start-up and construction project.[70]

Chicago, then, represents an exception to the ascendency of systems planning during the first afterlife of 1968. Although politics had always trumped planning under Daley, his respect for expertise had given these professionals considerable influence in the formation of public policy, including transportation, public housing, and urban design. But the double-barreled blasts of 1968 shocked him into closing ranks within a tight circle of loyalists. As the attacks mounted on his administration, he adopted a bunker mentality and began rewarding friends and punishing enemies. Turning the city's land-use system into a "zoning game" was emblematic of the complete politicization of planning during the final phase of Boss Daley's authoritarian regime.

Combined with economic restructuring, the result of the mayor's abandonment of systems approaches to planning was spatial fragmentation on a regional scale and social conflict on a neighborhood level of contestation over control of the streets. At the end of World War II, Chicago was the Pentagon's top contractor. But the dismantling of manufacturing, the main engine of the city's growth machine, began immediately in the wake of the war.[71]

Again, a combination of global economic restructuring and decisions by local businessmen accounts for a steady decline in the number of these industries. Between 1972 and 1985, this eroding sector of the local economy collapsed into a sinkhole of depression following the oil embargo. The state of Illinois lost one out of four manufacturing jobs, or 160,000 positions. Affecting an estimated 640,000 people, industrial decline goes a long way in accounting for the exodus of Nelson Algren's old neighbors and his sense of alienation in his own backyard.[72]

The success story of the Motorola Company helps illustrate in a paradoxical way the negative impacts of deindustrialization on inner-city neighborhoods. As the manufacturing firm grew bigger, it kept moving farther away from the city. Unlike the Zenith radio, Hotpoint refrigerator, Schwinn bicycle, and Ford automobile factories that closed their doors in Chicago, the Motorola Company could not keep up with demand for its expanding array of high-tech products.

In 1928, Paul and Joseph Gavin had set up a company just west of the central business district to make battery eliminators, or black boxes that allowed radios to be connected to an electric socket. A few years later, they started selling car radios (motor-olas), and in 1937, they had to build a much larger production plant. It was about five miles (eight kilometers) outside the city center on the West Side, just north of the West Garfield Park neighborhood. They choose this spacious site, covering several blocks, because it allowed room for future expansion, bordered railroad tracks, and was surrounded by communities full of working-class families. On the eve of World War II, the Gavins invented a portable telephone-radio, the walkie-talkie, that helped the Allies to victory.

Continuing to grow and innovate after the war, they moved again in 1953 to suburban Franklin Park, about ten miles (sixteen kilometers) from the Loop. While workers from the old plant were within commuting distance of the new one, more and more of the new jobs generated by the Gavins' ingenuity were located outside the metropolitan region. The year before, the Motorola Company had become a multinational when it opened a subsidiary in Toronto, Canada. A much more damaging blow to the local economy came in 1955, when the Gavins chose Phoenix, Arizona, for developing their new product, semiconductors, as the place with the most promising signs of future growth. Barry Goldwater's mecca of "Sunbelt Capitalism" sold itself as the anti-Chicago: no smoke, no slums, no unions, and no racial strife.[73]

The dismantling of the company's operations in Chicago's central business district took another step in 1967, when its thriving communications division moved twenty-five miles (forty kilometers) away, to Schaumburg, a suburb of Chicago that bordered a new superhighway. The booming company drew not only its own production workers out of the city; it also spurred office and retail developments, turning this suburb into one of the largest business centers in the Midwest. Not to be left behind in the exodus from the Loop to the crabgrass frontier, retailers in 1971 opened the world's largest enclosed shopping center, the Woodfield Mall.

Chicago continued to suffer losses when Motorola sold its TV division to a Japanese company in 1974 and relocated its world headquarters to Schaumburg two years later. In less than a quarter century, an open prairie had been turned into a downtown that exceeded the economic importance of other Rustbelt central business districts, including Rockford, Illinois; Milwaukee, Wisconsin; and St. Paul, Minnesota. Schaumburg was just one of the suburbs with manufacturing, office, and retail centers bordering an interstate highway, according to the historian Robert Bruegmann, that account for the "recentering of the metropolitan area."[74] By 1980, there would be over 350 industrial parks in the periphery, which now collectively had more workers than the city.[75]

Jeff Fort was a mastermind of organized crime who imposed a reign of terror over the entire South Side. The success of his street gang is a story about the rise of a major, criminal business and the creation of alternative spaces of transnational urbanism in the neighborhoods of those left behind in the inner city. Fort was commander in chief of an army of armed foot soldiers that numbered in the thousands. He had a mesmerizing public persona and was a grassroots organizer of young people and an outspoken champion of the political empowerment and self-determination of the community.[76]

During the sixties, Fort's new-style supergangs of African Americans and Latinos replaced Nelson Algren's familiar crowd of disreputable characters. These criminal organizations not only took over all illegal activities in the old territories of the white-run outfits; they also broke the rules of Daley's clientele regime. "The Black P. Stone Nation [Fort's gang] is resistance, is 3,000 black young men saying a giant hell-no to America," its chief defender, Rev. John R. Fry, proclaimed.[77] Fort stopped paying the customary kickback Daley's cronies had long come to expect from this most lucrative sector of the informal economy. In 1968, in fact, Fort would call a press conference to issue a declaration of war on Mayor Daley and his police department.[78]

Supergangs like the Black P. Stone Nation, whose name changed to El Rukns after Fort's conversion to Islam, contributed significantly to the disintegration of community in Chicago's inner-city neighborhoods. They caused a dramatic rise in violent death and mayhem. Crime and fear of crime fueled an exodus from the city by whites and the black middle class.

Exacerbating the city's economic losses from global restructuring, the national government's antipoverty programs to revitalize the urban economy had perverse, unintended consequences. They contributed to the loss of Jane Jacobs's neighborhood persisters, the crucial "continuity of people" needed to sustain community identities of place.[79] "It is ironic," Daley scholar Roger Biles notes, "Chicago's ghettos became poorer as a result of federal policy—a condition that seemed to be repeated throughout urban America."[80]

If Jeff Fort personified violent resistance to the Daley regime, Dorothy Gautreaux became the human face of suffering under his policy of racial containment. This poor African American woman would turn a federal courtroom into a theater of resistance to Daley's authority from the bottom up. Her story, like Algren's and Fort's, tells tales of the "obverse colonization" of inner-city neighborhoods in the first world to fourth world status. Taken together, they reveal a matrix of mechanisms that dismantled the city's growth machine in the decade following its civic trauma of violent disorder.

In 1953, Gautreaux and her husband had applied for public housing to move their four children from a one-bedroom apartment to a bigger space. At her interview, the Chicago Housing Authority clerk had informed her that if she chose one of the projects in the Black Belt, her application would receive prompt attention. If she listed housing authority sites in white neighborhoods, in contrast, she could expect a very long wait before escaping her overcrowded dwelling. Left with no practical options, Gautreaux had chosen the Dearborn Homes on the near South Side, but she was assigned to the Altgeld Garden project on the outskirts of town. It had been built for African American war workers in the midst of a toxic industrial zone.

In 1966, Dorothy Gautreaux filed a class action suit on behalf of the tenants of the housing authority for maintaining a systematic policy of racial segregation. The courtroom where her case was heard was the scene of a personal duel between the federal judge hearing her case and the mayor. It became one in a series of legal proceedings under the Civil Rights Act of 1964 that eventually took control of all the city's major institutions away from the mayor, including the schools, parks, and the police, fire, and public works departments. Under the so-called Shackman decree, moreover, Daley's political powers as patronage boss of the local Democratic Party came under the ongoing scrutiny of the federal courts.[81]

Gautreaux's case put the Chicago Housing Authority and the federal Department of Housing and Urban Development (HUD) on trial for racial discrimination. They had placed 99.4 percent of public housing units built between 1955 and 1968 in the first ghetto of African American neighborhoods. In February 1969, U.S. District Judge Richard Austin agreed with Gautreaux's dedicated lawyer, Alexander Polikoff, holding that racial discrimination was the only way to explain the housing authority's site selections, to say nothing of the fact that 99 percent of the tenants in the second ghetto were now African Americans.

He approved the civil rights activists' plan to turn the housing authority from a bastion of segregation into an instrument of racial and class integration. Under the scattered-site plan, it would build seven hundred low-density units in census tracts that were at least 70 percent white. New construction would be sited in a three-to-one ratio between white and black neighborhoods.

But Mayor Daley stonewalled Judge Austin. With the 1971 local elections approaching, Daley appealed to his shrinking base of support in the Bungalow Belt of mostly white homeowners. He pledged that the city would not put any public housing where it was not wanted, only where it was needed. He made one excuse after another to explain why the housing authority's construction program had come to a virtual halt.

Frustrated, Polikoff pursued Gautreaux's case against HUD to expand the integration plan beyond the city borders to the suburbs. Finally, in April 1976, the U.S. Supreme Court ruled in Gautreaux's favor.[82] The court agreed with a lower court that HUD had played a "pervasive" role and "willingly acquiesced" in the discriminatory selection of public housing sites throughout the metropolitan region.[83]

While the decision upheld the ideals of equal justice under law in theory, the national government was taking deliberate steps in just the opposite direction to uphold the segregation of the suburbs in practice. While Gautreaux's case had been on appeal in 1974, the Republicans passed a housing act that turned local housing authorities into administrators instead of builders. They were put in charge of overseeing grants of Section 8 vouchers, subsidies for low-income households, for HUD-qualified apartments in the private sector.

As Judge Austin discovered, holders of the vouchers were excluded by low availability and high rents from most white neighborhoods within the city and virtually all the surrounding suburbs. Over the next two decades, about 350 households a year on the Chicago Housing Authority's eligible list of 40,000 were relocated. A right to open housing proved an empty promise without a substantive policy to dismantle segregation.[84]

The following year, the same Supreme Court that was breaking down the color line within the city built a new racial barrier between the center and the periphery. In an analogous case involving a Chicago suburb, all seven of the recent Republican appointees on the nine-person bench pretended to be color blind. In the 1970s, Arlington Heights had 27 African Americans living in a community of 64,000. Civil rights activists formed a development corporation to integrate the suburb by building an apartment complex, in which 40 percent of the units would be set aside for low-income households. After local officials denied the project a building permit under the village's zoning laws, the activists sued, charging racial discrimination under the 1968 Fair Housing Act.[85]

As with the Gautreaux case, what other reason could explain the rejection of a well-designed subdivision? But the court ruled that showing the policy effects of segregation was not enough; an evil intent to discriminate had to be proved as well. As a housing expert concluded, "The [Warren] Burger Court transformed the vision of low-income suburban housing into a pipe dream in *Arlington Heights*."[86]

Taken together, this anthology of Chicago stories from the 1970s reads like a tragedy of urban decline. A complex matrix of economic restructuring and political decision making gutted its center in a great escape of white flight to the periphery. Disaggregating the demographics of the net loss of 550,000 inhabitants from the city between 1960 and 1980 exposes a much more profound change in its racial/ethnic composition. The number of whites fell by 1,250,000, reducing a white majority of three out of every four residents to slightly less than half the city's population.

In contrast, the population of blacks went up by 385,000, almost doubling their representation to 40 percent of the people. Even more revealing, other ethnic groups swelled to 10 percent, including 425,000 persons of Hispanic origin. During the 1980s, these trends toward making everyone a minority continued as the stream of immigrants from a multiethnic array of countries replaced the whites moving out of the city.[87]

Even this level of demographic analysis masks the impacts of deindustrialization and suburbanization on the neighborhoods of the inner city. Algren's West Town community area was typical. It moved from 98 percent white to 62 percent Hispanic. It lost about 40 percent of its population; about nine out of every ten residents leaving were white. Algren was one of them, moving to Patterson, New Jersey. Hollowed out and speaking a different, foreign language, Polonia had indeed become an alien space for the writer of the horrors of urban poverty and discrimination.[88]

The deconstruction of Chicago's growth machine not only left its neighborhoods in a shambles but also threw its government into disarray at the time of Mayor Daley's death. Its jobs had gone to the suburbs, Phoenix, and São Paulo. Its more affluent inhabitants had left in fear-driven panic, leaving behind an increasingly disproportionate share of the poor living in the metropolitan region.

Daley had hidden city hall's shrinking tax base and mounting debts behind a mask of false reassurance. In 1979, the funding of the public schools would enter a decade-long receivership of half rations. It turned out that the mayor had been paying for "the city that works" with unsustainable sweetheart deals with the almost all-white public sector unions (e.g., public school teachers, fire fighters, police) and trade unions.[89]

And like other autocrats, Daley had made sure there were no likely candidates waiting in the wings to succeed him. His sudden death in 1976, just a year into his sixth four-year term, plunged local Democrats into a decade of political cannibalism. Unfortunately, this interregnum of public default of planning to the marketplace could not have come at a worse time of global economic restructuring. What the city needed most after the trauma of 1968 was strong civic leadership. It needed a new plan to rebuild a postindustrial growth machine and restore the sense of community that had once made Chicago Nelson Algren's beloved city of neighborhoods.

Conclusions: Milton Keynes, United Kingdom—Building American Suburbs

The Milton Keynes housing project tells another story of the production of hybrid space as an unintended result of the rationalist systems approach to planning. The development of this new town was typical of the British way of "muddling through" the seventies, without decisive leadership to steer their sputtering ship of state either left or right.[90] This project was intended to showcase a second generation of the planners' ideal model of the Garden City. About forty-eight miles (seventy-five kilometers) from London on the M1 motorway, the satellite suburb was designed for a quarter million people, much larger than that the first generation of new towns, to overcome their major failings (see Map 14).[91]

Mark Clapson, a historian of this ambitious project, underscores once again the importance of the point of view of the storyteller. In what might be called the many afterlives of Milton Keynes, its development generated several official accounts and at least two alternative storylines by its would-be residents. They refused to move there until they were offered vernacular-style houses in traditional-looking neighborhoods of similar-priced properties. Planned as an antidote to sprawl in 1967, Milton Keynes became a part of it over the next twenty years. By then, its history had been rewritten in official accounts to celebrate its developers' vision of a "grand suburban design."[92]

Clapson calls the new town a "gentle paradox . . . of urban intentions and suburban outcomes."[93] He and other scholars have reconstructed how the planners of the new town kept changing its history to maintain their self-cast roles as the heroic creators of a utopian Organic City. Unpacking their version of history, Ruth Finnegan reveals that their original intention followed in the footsteps of Ebenezer Howard.[94] The planners wanted to give birth to an organic process of urban growth that would flower into the British ideal of his Garden City.

While subsequent retellings of their story paid lip service to the Milton Keynes Master Plan of 1970 as being an autonomous process, they really gave homage to it as a finished product, a "fulfillment of its pre-ordered destiny." The planners' tales were told by the Milton Keynes Development Corporation (MKDC), which was in charge of drawing a blueprint for the

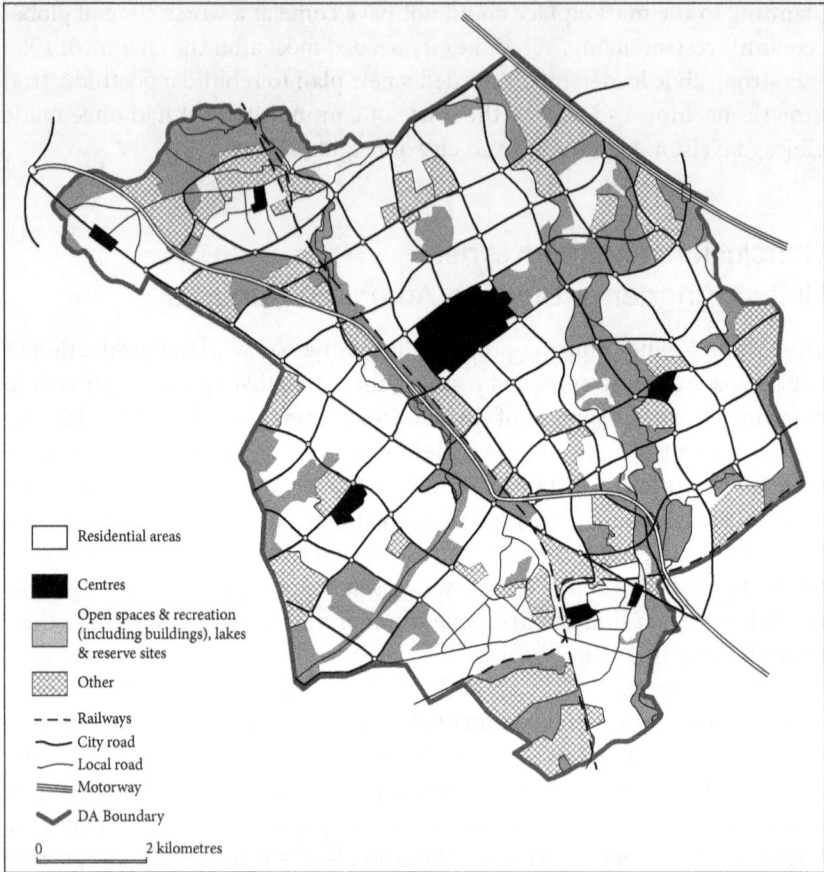

Map 14 London: Milton Keynes Master Plan, 1970 (Milton Keynes Development Corporation, http://www.rudi.net/files/34C883261E9D499EA3241201F5A612E7.pdf)
Note: The Milton Keyes Development Corporation dissolved in 1992.

twenty-two-thousand-acre (nine-thousand-hectare) site. The MKDC continued to manage the project until 1989, when it sold off its last major asset, the city's shopping center, to Japanese investors.[95]

The first story of Milton Keynes, the planners' heroic and visionary achievement of a "grand suburban design," indeed comes from the pen of the science-fiction world of George Orwell's Big Brother. In his satire of Cold War totalitarianism, *1984*, the historical record is constantly revised to support the current positions of an infallible dictator. One of the MKDC master planners, Derek Walker, designed England's first American-style enclosed shopping mall to occupy the central place in the new town. Walker leaves little doubt that this Organic City was envisioned as an urban place. In a memoir, he proclaims that the new town would foster "a feeling of intensity of use and of people gathering together; a range of social, recreational, cultural and economic possibilities made possible by urban densities and scale; a positive contrast with the countryside; an enjoyment and a celebration of urbanity."[96]

The ultimate goal of the planners was to build a perpetual-motion growth machine that would inevitably mature into a Garden City. In the master plan, the first chairman of the MKDC, Lord Campbell, declared, "Our intention is that the Plan shall lay the foundation upon which an organic process of development will grow and become a living reality. . . . Our purpose is . . . in the end, to build a good city."[97] But this empowerment of potential settlers with "freedom of choice" backfired.[98] Homebuyers refused during the seventies to move to the modernist city that the planners were busy erecting in a distant rural area. Nothing could better illustrate the disconnect between these disciples of the International Style and the citizens they were supposed to be serving than the architecture of the rental units being constructed by the MKDC. While they were winning awards from their fellow professionals for their aluminum facades and other design innovations, almost everyone else hated them.

A second storyline, the counternarrative to the planners' prophesies of an organic Garden City, was the joint composition of these frustrated homebuyers and unhappy tenants forced to live in "tin boxes." As one newcomer remembered thinking on seeing her family's new home for the first time, "'My God, what has this man brought me to!' It was horrendous. I thought 'I'm not living in a biscuit tin.' . . . However, I didn't have any choice at that time."[99] Families like hers provided the MKDC a captive market of tenants who had been displaced by the wrecking ball of inner-city urban renewal. Like other recipients of social housing, she moved into one of the row house apartments in spite of its repulsive appearance.

Covering the second half of the seventies, this was the period when "Milton Keynes was like the worst horrors of science fiction," according to Finnegan's analysis of residents' oral histories.[100] The planners were portrayed as "deranged" masterminds responsible for superimposing an alien landscape of modernism on the English countryside. In fact, the mass media made six concrete cows—an artist's gift to the garden city—the enduring icon of the suburb in the popular imagination. For the local community and the national media, they became a symbol of the loss of nature to the hubris of an overurbanized society of runaway technology.[101]

The third story, the creation of a historical Milton Keynes, grew out of the residents' need to reconcile the inherent contradictions embedded in not only this piece of public art but, more importantly, the oxymoron of the planners' imagination: a Garden City. To offset the brutalist architecture and gridiron design of the MKDC, resident activists formed groups to give human agency to the process of community building. Adding to the colorful personalities, places, and events of the past, local history was brought up to contemporary times by including tales of Milton Keynes initial settlers.[102] They recast the planners' "thing from outer space" in colonial tropes of heroic pioneers and their determination to overcome the faceless forces of nature.[103]

To a great extent, this third storyline was constructed after 1979, when both the national government and the local MKDC changed hands. Led by Prime Minister Thatcher, Parliament passed a housing act and other legislation that decisively shifted planning authority from the public to the private sector. People finally got what they wanted: single-family houses in a suburban setting filled with neighbors of equal status and income. During the eighties, the resulting influx of homebuyers brought the population of Milton Keynes to almost 180,000 inhabitants. In search of the suburban dream, they accounted for the vast majority of the 56,000 newcomers, an equal number to those who had arrived during the seventies.[104]

To answer her question, "Whose stories of the city?" Finnegan gives emphasis to this updated postmodernist version of the Anglo-American suburban ethos. The longing of the residents to live in a utopian Garden City motivated them to override their deeply ingrained binary conflict between the town and the country. They replaced it with a new myth, "one in which urban life is a natural setting for creative human lives, no more artificial or alien than that of the countryside."[105]

In the end, this is a tale of hybrid space, a "suburban outcome" that was the result of the unintended consequences of the planners' "urban intentions." The new town's skyline of Los Angles–like sprawl did little to revise the planners' trope of triumphalism. They continue to make prophetic claims of a "grand suburban design." In the foreword to Clapson's 2003 book on the new town, the U.K. minister of state for Regeneration and Regional Development declared that "the fact that Milton Keynes is now embarking with confidence on a new phase of growth . . . is clear evidence that successful integrated development can produce an appetite for change and a belief that growth, properly managed, can produce real benefits for local communities." In creating the many afterlives of Milton Keynes, contestation over its skyline and its identity has become the new normal of the postmodern condition.[106]

Conclusions

City of Flows—City of Citizens

Webs of Transnational Urbanism

In the postseventies era of transnational urbanism, the reverberation of ideas, goods, and people was amplified, giving birth to a hybrid "cosmopolis" of "mongrel cities" and "global suburbs." While its growth machine sputtered back to life in the United States and Western Europe, the communist regimes to the east collapsed. Announcing the end of the Cold War in 1991, U.S. president George H. W. Bush proclaimed the founding of a "new world order." Echoing the Club of Rome, he promised that global capitalism would replace the social disorder and economic distress of the recent past with a golden age of free markets. Their self-regulating systems of rational resource allocation would fairly reward individuals according to their adherence to the neoliberal tenets of the enterprise culture.[1]

But less than a year later, contestation among planners, policy makers, and the grass roots entered a new era of local geographies of global insecurity. The terrifying eruption of mob violence by poor people in Los Angeles declared the arrival of "complexity and contradiction" in the building of the urban environment. The riots exposed all the distinguishing features that made Los Angeles the world's first "Heteropolis," according to Charles Jencks. The uprising taught the prolific theorist of postmodernism that Los Angeles had become a place where everyone was a minority. "And for this reason," he proposed, "it may well characterize the global megalopolis of the future."[2]

On April 29, 1992, a jury in the edge city of Simi Valley acquitted several white L.A. police officers of using excessive force while arresting an African American, Rodney King. He was beaten bloody after a high-speed pursuit for a traffic violation. This local case of police brutality was distinguished, however, by its taking place in the postmodern, high-tech era of global inter-connectivity. The ten-minute beating of King taking blow after blow while he lay defenseless on the ground was videotaped by a citizen and broadcast around the world by the mass media. The international spotlight shining on this appalling incident led to the removal of the trial of the policemen to the relative safety of Simi Valley, a fortified enclave of research parks and gated communities.

Outraged by the miscarriage of justice, angry people took to streets and set off six days of the worst civil disorder in the United States since the 1863 antidraft riots in New York City. Fifty-three people died, two thousand were injured, and seventeen thousand were arrested. Radiating out from the South Central area, the rioters looted thousands of stores and set them on fire, destroying almost a billion dollars' worth of property. The national me-dia portrayed the riots in the racial terms of the sixties. Calling in the army and the marines, President Bush addressed the nation on television. The social unrest, he stated, "[is] not a message of protest. It's been the brutality of a mob, pure and simple. And let me assure you: I will use whatever force is necessary to restore order."[3]

What also set this urban uprising apart from the past was its polyglot, multidimensional layers of racial/ethnic conflict. Heteropolis became a civil war of multiculturalism. Battles took place between every combination of African American versus Anglo-American versus Latino American versus Asian American versus newly arrived immigrant from anywhere. Attacks on Korean shopkeepers were especially egregious. In the final tally of arrests, people with Spanish surnames were the single largest group on the police blotter, while blacks were second at about 40 percent, and white offenders at one in ten.[4]

In the days following the military occupation of the streets, local policy makers promised to launch a $50 million project called Rebuild Los An-geles. It never got off the ground. On the contrary, burned-out shops did not reopen, and other businesses and people moved away in droves. The city, moreover, lost ground in the global competition for trade, while fear of violent crime rose to São Paulo levels of imminent, personal danger. On a national level, the aftermath of the L.A. riots proved no better for President Bush, who failed to win reelection. While he claimed credit for helping end the Cold War abroad, his opponent, Bill Clinton, defeated him with a cam-paign strategy focused on social malaise at home: "It's the economy, stupid."[5]

From an international perspective, Clinton's victory signaled a changing of the guard in the first world countries to a new generation of policy makers, New Left conservatives. Along with France's Jacques Chirac and Great Britain's Tony Blair, the incoming president of the United States projected a youthful spirit of individual success and an uplifting message of social reform. The fall of the New Right paralleled the depressing slide of the global economy during the late eighties back into recession. For the United States and Western Europe, this downturn proved to be only a temporary dip in a long-term recovery lasing another twenty years.

But for countries like Mexico and Brazil, the slowdown of global markets was enough to make their domestic economies ever more dependent on foreign loans. In 1994, after a decade of heavy borrowing, Mexico plunged into a peso crisis of devaluation. The U.S. Treasury would have to bail it out with a $20 billion line of credit. Despite the return to civilian rule in 1985, Brazil too was thrown into a state of crisis. Between 1989 and 1994, its economy collapsed under the weight of hyperinflation. Its political system also broke down, leading to the impeachment of the president.

Since then, grassroots movements in Brazil and throughout the world have been demanding full citizenship rights to the city. This insurgent democracy from the bottom up has been mobilizing around place-based issues of social and environmental reform. In the postmodern era, contestation among planners, policy makers, and the grass roots has become institutionalized in the production of urban space.[6]

Taking the Cold War's end and the L.A. riots as the endpoint of an era, we can draw final conclusions about the rise and fall of high modernism and assess the successes and the failures of the postwar consensus behind its vision of the Organic City. This endpoint can also serve as a vantage point to reflect on that vision's impacts on the course of city building over the next twenty years. To sketch out the direction of these trends, we can collapse our seven case studies down to one, Los Angeles. In Heteropolis, all the social and spatial forces of transnational urbanism were occurring simultaneously in one place.[7]

Geographies of Global Insecurity

In addition to multiculturalism, Jencks realized, the constant fluctuation of the city's centers and peripheries made Los Angeles the prototype of the "global megalopolis of the future." Developers planned Alphaville-like Simi Valleys as centers at the periphery, while young Latinos deported for criminal offenses re-created patches of L.A. ganglands in several foreign capitals. The city's social, economic, and cultural influences resonated between the local and the transnational to create a new heterogeneity in the production of urban space.

At the same time, this land of sunshine became the national capital of homelessness. During the post-1973 recession, hard times saw a 90 percent increase in overcrowding, especially in the immigrant neighborhoods surrounding the central business district. Approximately two hundred thousand people had to move into garages, which were illegally converted into homes. On any given night, another thirty-five thousand to seventy thousand even more destitute people were left to roam the streets in search of shelter.

The city became a patchwork geography of global insecurity. The presence of the homeless on the streets added to a pervasive fear of the racial/ethnic "other." A crescendo of violent crime from the international drug trade reached a peak during the period leading up to the 1992 riots.[8]

In the weeks following the restoration of law and order, the urban critic Mike Davis interviewed Salvadorian immigrants in the MacArthur Park–Pico-Union area and African American gang members in Watts and Compton. Their common ground was poverty. The uprising, he reported, "was as much about empty bellies and broken hearts as it was about police batons and Rodney King." Although the acquittal of the policemen triggered expression of community grievances, long-term unemployment furnished the explosive force of its rage. "As even the *Los Angeles Times*, main cheerleader for 'World City L.A.,' now editorially acknowledges," Davis railed, "the 'globalization of Los Angeles' has produced 'devastating poverty for those weak in skills and resources.'"[9]

For Los Angeles and other urban centers around the world, the end of the arms race raised the stakes in the race of technological modernization. Steady advances in communications and transportation threw nations and their cities into a new round of fierce competition with each other. The new world order reestablished the legitimacy of planning experts as major players in building the urban environment. It boosted them and their systems approaches to the global stage of economic development, especially as urbanization itself became a prime engine of production. The planners now promised investors and policy makers that they could make cities into central processing nodes of the ever more liquid currents of information, money, and jobs flowing around world.

After 1973, the lowering of trade barriers had spurred the proliferation of multinational corporations, transforming William H. Whyte's "organization man [and woman]" into globetrotters.[10] Helping usher in the age of information, they were outsourced to the countries offering their employers the most favorable terms of trade. However, the worldwide recession following the oil embargo undermined the ability of local governments to provide a safe environment for these elite visitors, let alone their own citizens. Economic restructuring forced deep cuts in town hall budgets, including police departments and public space maintenance. Long-term settlement patterns of suburbanization, often accelerated by the urban crisis of the sixties, further reduced their capacities to fulfill the most basic duty of the social contract between the government and its people. To survive, more and more desperate people were moving simultaneously into the informal economy, including the underworld of crime.

The ensuing drug wars of the 1980s fueled a dramatic rise in gun violence, heightening demand for defensible space. The growing gap of inequality between the rich and the poor became reflected in the fragmentation of society into radical new forms of gated urban space. The breakdown of civic society in urban centers around the world into fortified enclaves is what gives Mike Davis reason to call them "Carceral Cities."[11]

The enclaves ranged from private islands of white-collar elites living in places like Simi Valley in Ventura County to the public housing projects of the lowest-income families like Jordan Downs in Watts. In between, homeowners closed off streets into their neighborhoods to keep criminals out. In Los Angeles, moreover, the police developed strategies to lock in racial/ethnic groups suspected of criminal activity, setting up roadblocks around the Pico-Union area and other Latino barrios.[12]

In addition to new levels of crime and fear of crime, two other new conditions of urban life added momentum to the psychological panic of residents and businesses in search of defensible space. The developers of gated communities used scare tactics in their marketing campaigns to stampede potential homebuyers to their properties. Furthermore, the example of the cosmopolitan "organization man" acted as a social magnet of prestige and exclusivity for local elites and the upwardly mobile middle class. In the United Kingdom, for example, a 2001 census listed one thousand gated communities in spite of very low violent crime rates.[13]

In both the advertising campaigns of gated developments and the buyers' responses to opinion surveys, security was listed as the top priority in the decision of where to live. Yet paradoxically, locking themselves behind the gates heightened their anxiety of becoming a victim of violent crime. "[For] some . . . residents . . . the apparent safety afforded by gated development did not necessarily translate into a reduction in the fear of crime. In some ways [investigators] saw an increased sensitivity to problems, or at least their changing relativity."[14] Living inside a high-security zone magnified inhabitants' paranoia of the unknown, the demons lurking on the other side. Even more frightening for these residents, this fear bred thoughts that security inside the perimeter could not keep them out.[15]

In part, the global nomadic lifestyles of their residents explains the disconnect between the perception of an imminent threat of personal assault and the reality of low crime rates in the neighborhoods surrounding their islands of defense. The investigators, Rowland Atkinson and John Flint, are worth quoting at length because they expand the local neighborhood concept of the gated community into a transnational "time-space trajectory of segregation."[16]

What they mean is that white-collar globetrotters flow within high-security corridors in private vehicles from one urban "non-place[]" to another, such as airports, hotels, business centers, and brand-name shopping malls. "An emphasis on work, long hours and regular relocation," they report, "provided a recurring theme as detailed by residents and those outside the [gated communities] who regarded this as a barrier to social interaction, both within and beyond the [gated community]. This was attributed to the 'international' lifestyle of residents, many of whom worked for multinational companies, and were foreign nationals."[17]

For both the insiders and the outsiders, the physical barrier of spatial segregation stimulated a socially corrosive mentality of "us and them." Insiders moved within insular time-space tunnels of work, family, and friends separated from contact with outsiders by bodyguards, armored cars, VIP lounges, and first-class preboarding airline passes. For them, security was a consumer commodity, which they put a premium on owning. For neighbors and shopkeepers outside the gates, these fortified enclaves were seen as iconic symbols of social exclusion.[18]

From the international perspective, geographies of insecurity after 1973 can be pictured in postmodern terms as centers and peripheries that keep reversing position. The ancient dichotomy between metropolis and colony has become more complicated by obverse processes of the production of urban space in the first world by influences coming out of the third world. The global restructuring of capitalism following the oil embargo widened the gap of inequality, raised fear of urban crime, and triggered a search for defensible space by rich and poor alike.

Whether at home or moving through the space-time corridors of non-places, security has become a commodity. On the one hand, Whyte's corporate managers could afford to live in gated communities of safety. On the other hand, underworld nomads in the criminal cartels had to struggle to survive in urban ganglands of violent death.

A counternarrative to the multinational corporation is the criminal syndicate operating between Los Angeles and San Salvador, El Salvador. Salvadorians belonging to street gangs became what Elana Zilberg calls "the embodiment of a forced transnationality. Youth deported from Los Angeles walking the streets of San Salvador calling themselves 'homies' are the shock effects of globalization as it clashes with nationalism."[19]

Since the 1992 riots, an estimated sixty thousand of these no-where men have been deported from Southern California. Belonging to two rival gangs, the Mara Salvatrucha (MS-13) and the Barrio 18, they have been fighting an endless civil war on the streets of San Salvador. They have turned it into a murder capital of Latin America, with a death rate fifteen times higher than that of Los Angeles's. Simi Valley has even lower crime rates than Los Angeles, making it one of the ten safest cities in the nation.[20]

True to his word, President Bush had sent in not only an army of occupation but also a swarm of secret agents to infiltrate the gangs. "Now, one week [after the riot]," Mike Davis reported, "MacArthur Park is in a state of siege." Hundreds in police custody were being turned over to federal immigration officers for deportation. This crackdown on undocumented young Latinos became the start of an anti-immigrant crusade. It would percolate up the federal system from the backlash to the riots in Los Angeles to become national policy four years later.[21]

Creating a "politics of simultaneity," Los Angeles and San Salvador have become centers and peripheries of a criminal underworld at the same time. One story recorded by Zilberg is about a deported homie who had identified with his local hood, rather than his international ethnicity. His membership in the Mexican American Barrio 18th Street gang proved fatal. He was murdered in San Salvador by exiles from his gang's archrival, the MS-13. In another narrative, membership in the Westside Los Crazies saved the life of a dislocated youth from the Pico Park neighborhood. Since the Salvadoran gangs could not locate this barrio, they could not identify him as a friend or an enemy to be added to the death lists.[22]

Coming full circle to link the fourth world's ghettos of exclusion to the third world and back again to the first world, the incarcerated exiles morphed into a business organization engaged in illegal enterprises in Los Angeles and other cities throughout the Americas. Repressive national policies in the United States and El Salvador backfired; the prisons became incubators of these criminal organizations. During the 1980s, an insatiable consumer appetite for cocaine worldwide transformed the drug trade into a multibillion-dollar operation that funded subsidiary ventures in weapons and human trafficking. The economic restructuring of the MS-13 and other local street gangs into multinational business cartels completed the causal links between the ultimate ghettos of exclusion, overcrowded prisons, and the fortress enclaves of exclusivity in places like Simi Valley.

Ecologies of Urban Nature

Los Angeles furnished not only the original Heteropolis of the coming twenty-first century; it had already established its historic place as the global prototype of a city built by water imperialism. The downfall of this vast transregional empire of urban nature at the hands of a grassroots movement at the edges of its periphery provides a complement of environmental reform to the transnational urbanism of its multicultural society. As the city's population grew, so did its demand for water.

By the early 1960s, however, the very success of this empire of water began to produce more and more conflicts among the various urban, agricultural, energy, and recreational users of this limited natural resource. Los Angeles responded in typical fashion by building a second aqueduct to Mono Lake. After it opened in 1970, the city's stepped-up withdrawals began to cause irreversible damage to the lake's fragile ecology. In a classic David-and-Goliath battle, an unlikely band of eco-tourists, science nerds, and community activists took on the mighty "water buffalos" of Los Angeles.[23]

In 1978, concerned citizens formed the Mono Lake Committee to stop the destruction of this unique place. They were determined to turn off the tap of this source of fuel for the growth machine of Los Angeles before Mono Lake suffered the same fate as Owens Lake. They were equally set on stopping Los Angeles from destroying some other community to replace Mono Lake's water. This political strategy would allow them to broaden their appeal from a not-in-my-backyard (NIMBY) complaint to a broader campaign for environmental justice. A year later, the committee began what became a protracted fifteen-year battle in the courts of civil law and public opinion to restore the lake to prediversion levels.

In 1983, the California Supreme Court gave new meaning to an ancient code of environmental ethics. Rereading the Roman emperor Justinian's public trust doctrine, the ruling reversed the course of a century of state water law. In *National Audubon Society v. Los Angeles Department of Water and Power*, the court ordered the city to redirect the flow of water from its aqueducts back to the countryside's streams and riverbeds. The judiciary took a proactive stewardship role in the restoration of nature to a condition of ecological health. In this and related cases in the defense of Mono Lake, the court's answer to who owns the rain was the people of the state.[24]

The court's interpretation and subsequent enforcement of the public trust doctrine contributed to a contemporary ethics of the environment in a number of ways. Its rulings illuminate the intersections of social values, ecological science, and public policy. Justinian's declaration that "by the law of nature these things are common to mankind: the air, running water, the sea and consequently the shores of the sea" is a taproot of legal systems throughout the Western world. And like ancient Rome, Los Angeles was built on imperial ambitions. In each case, treasure from distant colonies fueled powerful urban growth machines but at a cost of sucking these hinterlands dry of their natural and human resources.[25]

Moreover, the city's network of pipes and pumps maps a geography of social and environmental inequalities. This often-hidden infrastructure nonetheless makes visible the ethical links between town and country, sub-urbia and farmland, place and energy, and ultimately, humans and the rest of the biosphere. As *Chinatown*, Roman Polanski's noir film of Los Angeles's first aqueduct, portrays, water is power. Over the next half century, this pipe-line was expanded into a far-flung network of hydroelectric dams, pumping stations, and artificial rivers that turned a sunbaked landscape into a Garden of Eden, a gigantic water-theme park.[26]

The case of Los Angeles represents an iconic illustration of the environ-mental inequities of water imperialism. Like the ships of old filled with gold, spices, or silk, the pipelines of the modern metropolis transport a precious commodity from periphery to center. Unlike other types of imperialism, exploitation of this unique resource robs the hinterlands of not only their natural wealth but also their peoples' livelihoods. Rather than being put to work in mines, fields, and forests, they are forced to abandon their parched land. Nevertheless, Los Angeles's model of the growth machine and the "technological sublime" of the Hoover Dam continue to inspire wannabe megacities around the world to similar imperial ambitions.[27]

Although Los Angeles fought back with an aggressive defense for almost a decade after the landmark ruling of 1983, it eventually surrendered. In the media, its public image became indelibly cast as a modern, true-life version of *Chinatown* and the rape of Mother Earth. In February 1990, an angry California Supreme Court Judge Terrence Finney grew tired of its delaying tactics. He personally supervised the allocation of water to its various com-peting users. The court ordered Los Angeles to restore lake levels, cooperate with the eco-protesters, and reduce its reliance on natural resources coming under the protection of the state's never-ending responsibility to preserve them for future generations. The crucial concession by the city to the lake's defenders was its agreement to reduce its demand by the amount lost rather than replace it by taking someone else's water.

The practical application of the public trust doctrine in California has been furnishing the megacities of the world with a new model of environ-mental restoration on the cutting edge of ecological science and engineer-ing. Judge Finney ordered Los Angeles to not only return Mono Lake to prediversion levels but make the waters flow, the plants grow, and the fish swim again in the lake's feeder streams as well. Teams of experts in partner-ship with community-based organizations began working to bring a human-made desert back to a semblance of its former natural habitat. Coming in the midst of six years of drought, the decision forced Los Angeles to declare its first emergency shortage of water in the summer of 1990.

The court's adoption of a stewardship role allowed it to apply a balancing test to allocate limited "public trust resources" among competing users.[28] Most important, the doctrine's conservation mandate forced all users to apply best management practices, which has resulted in major reforms at both ends of the pipeline. On one side, the city has discarded its imperial image as a water park and now projects an asceticism of environmental preservation. Its "water buffalos" have morphed into desert camels.

On the other side, the rising price of water to market rates in the Central Valley of California caused a shift to less thirsty crops and animals. In between, users have formed new partnerships to upgrade the quality of the entire transregional watershed.

At both ends, the courts have empowered community-based organizations and their experts by giving them a place at the table in the political negotiations leading to policy formation. The Mono Lake case, then, helps illuminate important dimensions of our current crisis of water, equity, and place. Moreover, it provides an ongoing, work-in-progress example of the devolution of power to give democratic meaning to the public side of the public trust doctrine.[29]

No doubt, any single case has inherent limitations as an ideal model or global prototype. In spite of the universal justice of the public trust doctrine, its general principles have to filter through the lens of each nation's political institutions. American law framed this conflict over the environment within a particular federal system of civil litigation and judicial finality. In addition, the unique configuration of events that brought together political movements, weather patterns, and legal trends in a successful defense of the environment can never again be duplicated. The special hydrologic conditions of center and periphery in this case further constrain whatever lessons can be learned from their ongoing joint experiments in nature restoration and urban conservation.[30]

Nonetheless, the legacy of the environmental reforms resulting from this grassroots movement shows the postmodern processes of urban policy formation. The institutionalization of contestation among competing stakeholders has empowered an insurgent citizenship. Environmental defense litigation could not have overcome the obstruction of the policy makers without the persistent activism of the eco-protesters and their political strategy.

This microhistory teaches the basic lesson that legal theories in the abstract have little meaning until they are put into practice. Rejecting a NIMBY posture of defense, the Mono Lake Committee framed its cause in inclusive terms of an overarching stewardship of nature. It reached out from its community-based movement to embrace the court's balancing test of equity among all the stakeholders and the places inadvertently linked by the pipes and pumps of the city's empire of water.

Over the course of the protracted litigation of the Mono Lake case from 1979 to 1994, the environmental movement gained political strength throughout California and the nation, especially in the wake of the transregional drought of the early nineties. The eco-protesters won their improbable David-and-Goliath victory because they insisted that the restoration of Mono Lake had to be met by reduction not replacement of the city's water supply. Even in a litigious society like the United States, getting control of a runaway technology required a coordinated campaign of legal and political activism.

This public trust case also demonstrates how science and technology can act as a mediator in the settlement of disputes within inadvertent heterogeneous communities of water users competing for overappropriated supplies. The doctrine's directive to make the most beneficial uses of scarce natural resources has been translated into ecological knowledge and best management practices. A good example is the agreement reached between town and country, factory and farm, to enlarge storage capacity as a safeguard against droughts and other natural catastrophes like earthquakes. In this agreement, the Eastside Reservoir Project will double Southern California's capacity, providing a six-month supply if the city is cut off from more distant imported water.[31]

Another lesson to be learned from the Mono Lake case is the importance of community-based participation and empowerment in the formation of public policy. While outside experts helped build a legal defense of nature, the local knowledge of its fishermen and naturalists proved to be the critical information that tipped the scales of justice in favor of restoring the lake to prediversion levels. Local historians also contributed to the restoration process by helping reconstruct what the wildlife and landscape was like in the days before Los Angeles's first aqueduct from the Owens Valley.

In analogous ways, a century of local experience accumulated by the "drainage doctors" of Los Angeles has been a crucial part of moving its environmental policy forward from conservationism to the frontiers of the restoration of urban nature.[32] Much of its sewage previously befouling the coastal ecosystem and public beaches is now being treated and injected underground as a barrier against saltwater infiltration of the freshwater aquifers flowing below the metropolitan region. Working with community-based organizations, the city's hydraulic engineers have even been taking steps to reclaim pieces of the Los Angeles River for recreational use.[33]

The importance of local knowledge in the city's water planning process brings this case study full circle to its starting point in place-based politics. It reinforces the conclusion that planning theory and practice remains a contested terrain of "complexity and contradiction."[34] This fractured condition is both the cause and the effect of the fragmented metropolitan regions of physical walls and social barriers the planners helped build. Although their systems approaches regained the ascendency among policy makers in the new world order, the diverging paths of their shattered vision of the Organic City keep radiating in all directions.

In other countries, for example, the instrumental use of the law to give practical meaning to the public trust doctrine takes other forms of political expression. In the postdictatorship era in Brazil, Luiz Inácio Lula da Silva's Workers' Party spearheaded constitutional reforms to institutionalize community participation in watershed governance. Mexico too has devolved power over water planning from central technocratic control to regional councils. In both cases, women have been taking a more assertive role in the empowerment of an insurgent citizenship. The opening of civil society in these countries has encouraged local participation in giving practical meaning to the social ethic of the public trust doctrine.[35]

In different ways, then, nations have begun to translate ideals of an equitable balance in the use of natural resources not only among humans but also between them and the rest of the living world into public policy. In Los Angeles, the implementation of its water plans has produced a cultural shift in the private behavior of its inhabitants from profligate consumers to conscientious savers. A package of public incentives and penalties has combined with grassroots activism to make green aesthetics fashionable among all classes of the population. Ghetto-gardens in the center, rain barrels in the suburbs, and high-tech eco-houses in the edge cities like Simi Valley are all signs of new social values and hybrid spaces of urban nature.

Revisions of the Organic City

In 1945, after almost a half century of consensus building behind a vision of the Organic City, the planners were finally put in charge by war-weary societies. The subsequent escalation of Cold War tensions reinforced the profession's influence among national policy makers as the world became engaged in a bipolar race of technological modernization. "Seeing like a state" blinded Le Corbusier and his legions of followers to the human, social, and environmental costs of their clean-sweep, finished blueprints of the city of tomorrow. Insulated from public criticism, they went about changing the skyline to conform to a monolithic, International Style of architecture and urban design.[36]

But beginning with the ghetto uprisings of the midsixties, the planners' fall from grace splintered their postwar consensus into divergent ways of seeing and knowing. For the conservators of modernism, the pursuit of ecosystems theory is leading to a conviction that their computer simulations of "Spaceship Earth" are more real than the natural world.[37] Their models of physical space envision a Cyborg City of flows.

For the prophets of postmodernism, the search for spontaneous experience—"the DNA of urbanism"—means looking to community-based organizations for inspiration. Their plans of social space foresee an Eco-city of citizens. Not surprisingly, the fractured state of planning mirrors the current status of our fragmented cities of walls and ghettos of exclusion.[38]

Equally emblematic of the post-1973 devolution of the city into islands of defensible space was the inescapable dependence of public planning bureaucracies, private development groups, and community-based organizations on each other to turn visions of the future into shapes on the ground. Under this regime of public-private-community partnerships, a remarkable diversity of planning outcomes was produced for various patches of space within the metropolitan region. All the planners in the age of ecology were painting their models in a shade of green that depended on their point of view—from Mount Olympus to the street corner.

Despite a wide range of new theories of planning, they all shared an underlying metaphorical concept of the city as an organic system. Moreover, they all retained an unstated assumption of environmental determinism: physical design could influence social behavior. Traditional analogies between the metabolism and morphology of the human body were freely intermixed with more dynamic models of open ecosystems. Refracted through a lens of technology acting as a mediator between society and nature, the result has been a new spectrum of multifaceted visions of the Organic City.

During the 1980s, neomodernist planners welcomed the revival of the urban growth machines in the United States and Europe. They were finally given a chance to put their systems theories of rational self-interest into practice. Input-output computer programs could now keep account of more and more real-time changes in the flows of urban life. More feedback mechanisms became available to measure them, including shopping patterns, traffic bottlenecks, land-use trends, crime geographies, and air and water quality.

For the postmodernists in these first world countries as well, the devolution of power during the seventies was seen as an opportunity to put advocacy planning into practice. Perfecting the techniques of community organizing, activists mobilized neighborhoods into vehicles of political empowerment and self-determination. In the eighties, the "suburban warriors" of the New Right kept their antistatist battalions on the battlefields of civic engagement.[39] The street corner guardians of the New Left remained equally committed to the cause of "guerrilla architecture"[40] and "Buddhist economics."[41] Neighborhood conservation began turning into gentrification, reversing the postwar exodus of the middle class and reclaiming the city block by block.[42]

Urban social movements not only became ubiquitous in the wake of the uprisings of the sixties; they evolved in novel ways by the turn of the century into transnational communities, virtual and real. Local activists ranged from little old ladies from Pasadena, California, fighting NIMBY crusades to mothers from São Paulo favelas demanding rights to the city. On the Internet, local groups formed global networks of shared planning experience and cultural cross-fertilization of expression such as hip-hop music and graffiti art.

Transnational urbanism extended from the ethereal matrix of digital bits to the underworld of criminal cartels. These ethnic-based, hybrid gangs of native-born, immigrant, refugee, and deportee members gave birth to a new type of globetrotting "organization man," the trafficker in illegal drugs, guns, and slaves. And like their legitimate counterparts, these multinational enterprises had major impacts on urban life worldwide, raising both the rates and the fear of violent crime to new levels. A first world of privilege was building futuristic internets of computers and satellites at the same time that a fourth world of exclusion was rebuilding age-old networks of smugglers and human traffickers.[43]

In hindsight, it is difficult to come to any conclusion about the postwar modernists' vision of the Organic City other than that it failed to achieve its goals in their own terms. The International Style school's leaders taught a philosophy of science that seemed to uncouple their clean-sweep drawings of physical space from their social engineering aspirations to create healthy, inspiring, and inviting places to live. Policy makers throughout the West brushed aside countertraditions of nature-based plans of urban conservation and affordable housing for poor people. They rejected the pleas of experienced experts to adapt low-rise construction methods that were proven successes in private and public housing projects for families with a large number of children.

Le Corbusier personifies the fatal disconnect between theory and practice. He consistently stated that "the home of man" was the starting point of architecture and urbanism. Translating this "machine for living" into organic metaphors in the Athens Charter, he explained, "The initial nucleus of urbanism is a cell for living."[44] And like its biological needs, he declared, "sun, vegetation, and space are the three raw materials of urbanism." From these "postulates," the modernists derived their prime directive: "Man, the human scale, and their indissoluble relationships with the environment are the measuring-rod, the rule that leads to harmony. That rule is the law of the sun and a respect for the conditions of nature."[45]

In these terms alone, we can see a large shortfall in reaching this goal during the post-1945 period of the Cold War. Beginning in the midsixties, the uprisings against the planners shocked the academic stars of the profession, who had come to share Le Corbusier's belief that "architecture is the key to everything."[46] Design-based methods of practice that produced massive clean-sweep urban renewal plans and gigantic housing projects like the Taylor Homes in Chicago and the St. Denis ghetto in Paris failed the test of human scale.

In the United States alone, the Housing Act of 1949 led to the displacement of over a million people from the demolition of four hundred thousand housing units, composing 2,500 neighborhoods in one thousand cities. While poor people occupied almost all these districts, African American communities bore a disproportionate, at 64 percent, share of the bulldozing. Human dislocation on such a large scale comes at great cost to society, according to the psychiatrist and public health expert Mindy Fullilove.

The consequences, she finds, are "root shock." It is "a traumatic stress reaction to the destruction of all or part of one's emotional ecosystem." On a collective scale, Fullilove speculates, root shock helps account for the upsurge of violent crime rates and the eruption of urban riots like the 1992 civil war of multiculturalism in Los Angeles.[47]

These psychological kinds of human costs need to be weighed against the benefits from improving the physical conditions of millions of city people who were living in substandard dwellings after the war. Hindsight should not gloss over the horrendous conditions in Europe and the Americas. Something had to be done to relieve the shortages, especially for low-income families, who had chronically been locked out of the marketplace of decent housing. Residents of public housing in cities across the West offer compelling testimony of general satisfaction and pride in their new units, at least during the early years. And in many cases, tower block apartment complexes continue to serve the needs of some groups such as senior citizens, singles, and households without children.

Yet there are probably just as many counternarratives, of life in hell and in the gangs. The globalization of modernism in the postwar period helps account for the rapid cross-fertilization of a hip-hop culture of ghetto protest against the loss of an identity of place. These oral histories, the urban revolts, and the ultimate demolition of a large share of the high-rise projects in the United States and Europe have tipped the scales of judgment against high modernism. In the final balance, their end-point models resulted in making the cities better physical spaces but at too great a cost of turning them into worse places to live, work, and play.

On a larger scale of planning metropolitan regions, the modernists also failed to achieve their goal of speed. Cold War politics contributed to the race for technological modernization by screening out alternatives other than the car and the highway to empty the city of its working classes and belching factories. Eliel Saarinen's "organic decentralization" plan of urban containment perfectly reflects the utopian illusions of both the Garden City and the Radiant City ideas.[48] Indeed, the private housing industry accounted for the bulk of the new towns built during the thirty golden years of postwar economic recovery and expansion.

At the same time, the policy makers underwrote and encouraged these community builders with subsidized freeways and home mortgages in addition to implementing advantageous land-use regulations. In places as different as London and Los Angeles, however, plans of urban containment produced the same results: sprawl, congestion, and pollution. The widening gap between suburban ideals and realities also generated a conservative backlash of homeowners against both the planners and the public welfare recipients living in the projects. In the United States, for instance, these suburban warriors put Ronald Reagan in the governor's mansion of California in 1967 and in the White House thirteen years later.

By then, the dethronement of the regime of high modernism from the centers of political power had produced a backlash of its own among the planners. The collapse of design-based theory allowed a badly needed infusion of fresh ideas and practices within the profession. Environmental perspectives played a key part in shifting its point of view from the Olympian heights of utopia to more earthbound systems of space, place, and nature. Its practitioners refocused attention on neighborhood design.

Calling for a new urbanism, the European Council of Town Planners issued a fitting proclamation of their rebellion in 1998, the "Towards the New Charter of Athens: From the Organic City to the City of the Citizens." The insurgents took a vantage point of the "urban village," in which Jane Jacobs's eulogy to the anarchistic activities of the street corner becomes a postmodernist mantra of diversity and mixed-use everything. In place of the old technological fix of the city as machine, the new model has a biological analogue as ecosystem.[49]

Yet environmental perspectives on the revolt against the reign of the academic elite of the systems planners expose two unresolved contradictions of the New Urbanism. In the realm of theory, nature-based models of "sustainable cities" are as conceptually flabby as Ebenezer Howard's Garden City idea.[50] The term has already become virtually meaningless. It has been interpreted in so many ways from so many different points of view, each with conflicting claims to have the roadmap to the Emerald City. As Michael Sorkin incisively comments, "The 'new urbanists,' for example, romanticise the small town in a Disneyesque reverie of artificial halcyon, celebrating the captive nature of the front lawn, that perfect lane of green, *minima naturalia*." But this is just one of a seemingly endless range of possible scenarios of the "sustainable city."[51]

In the realm of practice, environmental perspectives also shed light on the paradox of using the science of biology to construct a systems approach that portrays the urban process as a simulated virtual reality. In the 1970s and 1980s, the effort of planners to construct these "sim-cities" was one response to critics who contested planners' authority as founded on irrational, normative values, not empirical data. But this morphing of planning practice from art to science was a charade disguising the same old modernists' objectification of nature and society behind a flashing computer screen.

The systems planners' holistic "city of bits" appeared to offer new promise of achieving the dream of a comprehensive model of the Cyborg City of flows.[52] Yet it seemed to blind them to seeing that their quantifiable data was limited to the material world and left out the world of living things. Like Le Corbusier's faith in the moral order of Euclidian geometry, Nigel Taylor writes, "so too was the belief that, with a proper scientific understanding of the environment as a 'system,' coupled with the application of a rational method of decision-making and action, cities and the environment generally could be planned to improve—even 'maximise'—human well-being."[53]

A final reflection on the building of the urban environment since 1945 highlights the problematic nature of using organic metaphors to describe the city. This kind of imagery tended to obscure rather than enlighten public discourse on the causal forces of human agency involved in the production of urban space. The use of organic metaphors calls into question our notions of historical causation and the ways storytelling influences how people think about their power to shape the future of their neighborhoods and cities.

Planners, of course, were not the only ones describing the city as a natural system in the language of morphology and metabolism. To put Christopher Alexander's 1965 famous protest against the planners to new use, "the city is not a tree." It is not an autonomous living thing but a hybrid place of society and nature, an artificial environment built up over time by countless individual and collective decisions. Charles Jencks helps us reenvision the city as a multilayered place of simultaneity. He reminds us not to lose sight of the street corner, seeing the city one block at a time.[54]

Notes

INTRODUCTION

1. Teddy Cruz, *Border Postcards: Chronicles from the Edge*, James Stirling Memorial Lectures on the City, Canadian Centre for Architecture, Montreal, October 28, 2004, audio file, 48:28, available at http://www.cca.qc.ca/en/education-events/259 -teddy-cruz-border-postcards-chronicles-from-the-edge.

2. Robert Goodman, *After the Planners* (New York: Simon and Schuster, 1972), 187.

3. Cruz, *Border Postcards*. Also see Nicolai Ouroussoff, "Shantytowns as a New Suburban Ideal," *New York Times*, March 12, 2006, available at http://www.nytimes .com/2006/03/12/arts/design/12ouro.html?pagewanted=all; and Pilar Viladas, "The Nifty 50: Teddy Cruz, Architect," *New York Times*, January 21, 2010, available at http:// tmagazine.blogs.nytimes.com/2010/01/21/the-nifty-50-teddy-cruz-architect/.

4. Alison Ravetz, *Remaking Cities: Contradictions of the Recent Urban Environment* (London: Croom Helm, 1980), 14. Also see Mary Corbin Sies and Christopher Silver, "The History of Planning History," in *Planning the Twentieth-Century City*, ed. Mary Corbin Sies and Christopher Silver (Baltimore: Johns Hopkins University Press, 1996), 1–36; Mel Scott, *American City Planning since 1890* (Berkeley: University of California Press, 1969); Anthony Sutcliffe, *Towards the Planned City: Germany, Britain, the United States and France, 1780–1914* (New York: St. Martin's, 1981); and Robert Fishman, *Urban Utopias in the Twentieth Century: Ebenezer Howard, Frank Lloyd Wright, Le Corbusier* (New York: Basic Books, 1977).

5. James C. Scott, *Seeing like a State: How Certain Schemes to Improve the Human Condition Have Failed* (New Haven, Conn.: Yale University Press, 1998). Also see Henri Lefebvre, *The Production of Space* (Oxford: Blackwell, 1991); Raymond Williams, *The Country and the City* (New York: Oxford University Press, 1973); and Theodor G. Wyeld

and Allan Andrew, "The Virtual City: Perspectives on the Dystrophic Cybercity," *Journal of Architecture* 11, no. 5 (2006): 613–620.

6. Marshall Berman, *All That Is Solid Melts into Air: The Experience of Modernity* (New York: Simon and Schuster, 1982), 5. Also see Modris Eksteins, *Rites of Spring: The Great War and the Birth of the Modern Age* (New York: Anchor, 1990); Lawrence W. Levine, *Highbrow/Lowbrow: The Emergence of Cultural Hierarchy in America* (Cambridge, Mass.: Harvard University Press, 1988); and T. J. Jackson Lears, *No Place of Grace: Antimodernism and the Transformation of American Culture, 1880–1920* (Chicago: University of Chicago Press, 1994).

7. Berman, *All That Is Solid Melts into Air*, 5.

8. Serhii Chrucky, "Edgewater Golf Club," available at http://forgottenchicago .com/features/edgewater-golf-club/ (accessed November 9, 2013).

9. "Northerly Island: Creating an Ecological Urban Habitat," available at http:// www.studiogang.net/work/2007/northerly-island (accessed January 5, 2013). On Jeanne Gang, see "Inside Studio Gang," an exhibit at the Art Institute of Chicago (Chicago: 2011–2012); and Whet Moser, "Jeanne Gang and Robert Cassidy: Two Generations of Urban Planners on the Chicago River," *Chicago Magazine*, December 7, 2011, available at http://www.chicagomag.com/Chicago-Magazine/The-312/December-2011/Jeanne -Gang-and-Robert-Cassidy-Two-Generations-of-Urban-Planners-on-the-Chicago -River/. Also see Williams, *The Country and the City*; Morton White and Lucia White, *The Intellectual versus the City: From Thomas Jefferson to Frank Lloyd Wright* (Cambridge, Mass.: Harvard University Press, 1962); Barbara Novak, *Nature and Culture: American Landscape and Painting, 1825–1875* (New York: Oxford University Press, 1980); and Christopher C. Sellers, *Crabgrass Crucible: Suburban Nature and the Rise of Environmentalism in Twentieth-Century America* (Chapel Hill: University of North Carolina Press, 2012).

10. Cruz, *Border Postcards*.

11. Ibid. Also see Ouroussoff, "Shantytowns"; Eran Ben-Joseph, "Commentary: Designing Codes: Trends in Cities, Planning and Development," *Urban Studies* 46, no. 12 (November 2009): 2691–2702; Peter Marcuse, "Depoliticizing Globalization: From Neo-Marxist to Network Society of Manuel Castells," in *Understanding the City: Contemporary and Future Perspectives*, ed. John Eade and Christopher Mele (Oxford: Blackwell, 2002), 131–158; and David Harvey, "The Right to the City," in *The Emancipatory City: Paradoxes and Possibilities*, ed. Loretta Lees (London: Sage, 2004), 236–239.

12. See William Sites, "Global City, American City: Theories of Globalization and Approaches to Urban History," *Journal of Urban History* 29 (March 2003): 222–246; and Paul S. Sutter, "The World with Us: The State of American Environmental History," *Journal of American History* 100 (June 2013): 94–119.

13. Mike Davis, *Magical Urbanism: Latinos Reinvent the U.S. City* (New York: Verso, 2000), 53.

14. Ibid.; Guatemala Human Rights Commission/USA, *Gangs in Guatemala*, 2013, available at http://www.ghrc-usa.org/wp-content/uploads/2011/12/GangFactSheet.pdf (accessed July 8, 2013); and Eric Popkin, "Transnational Migration and Development in Postwar Peripheral States: An Examination of Guatemalan and Salvadoran State Linkages with Their Migrant Populations in Los Angeles," *Current Sociology* 51, no. 3–4 (2003): 347–374. Also see Elana Zilberg, "Fools Banished from the Kingdom:

Remapping Geographies of Gang Violence between the Americas (Los Angeles and San Salvador)," *American Quarterly* 56 (2004): 759–779; Oliver Jutersonke, Robert Muggah, and Dennis Rodgers, "Gangs, Urban Violence, and Security Interventions in Central America," *Security Dialogue* 40, no. 4–5 (2009): 373–397; and Alma Guillermoprieto, "In the New Gangland of El Salvador," *New York Review of Books*, November 10, 2011, 45–48.

15. Zilberg, "Fools Banished from the Kingdom," 774.

16. Ravetz, *Remaking Cities*.

17. See Joshua Dunsby, "Localizing Smog: Transgressions in the Therapeutic Landscape," in *Smoke and Mirrors: The Politics and Culture of Air Pollution*, ed. E. Melanie DuPuis (New York: New York University Press, 2004), 170–200. For Latin America, see Suzana Pasternak, "Squatter Settlements and Slums in Brazil: Twenty Years of Research and Policy," in *Housing the Urban Poor: Policy and Practice in Developing Countries*, ed. Brian C. Aldrich and R. S. Sandhu (London: Zed Books, 1995), 185–223. Also see James Holston, *Insurgent Citizenship: Disjunctions of Democracy and Modernity in Brazil* (Princeton, N.J.: Princeton University Press, 2008); and Mike Douglass and John Friedmann, eds., *Cities for Citizens: Planning and the Rise of Civil Society in a Global Age* (Chichester, U.K.: Wiley, 1998). Who owns the city, "not in the sense of direct individual control of an asset, but in the collective sense of each group's ability to access employment and culture, to live in a decent home and suitable living environment, to obtain a satisfying education, to maintain personal security, and to participate in urban governance," is defined by Susan S. Fainstein, in "Planning Theory and the City," *Journal of Planning Education and Research* 25 (2005): 126.

18. Leonie Sandercock, *Cosmopolis II: Mongrel Cities of the 21st Century* (New York: Continuum, 2003), 56.

19. See Jane Jacobs, *Cities and the Wealth of Nations: Principles of Economic Life* (New York: Random House, 1984); and J. Donald Hughes, *Pan's Travail: Environmental Problems of the Ancient Greeks and Romans* (Baltimore: Johns Hopkins University Press, 1994).

20. See Mike Davis, *Planet of Slums* (New York: Verso, 2006).

21. See Ian Tod and Michael Wheeler, *Utopia* (London: Orbis, 1978); and David Harvey, *The Urbanization of Capital: Studies in the History and Theory of Capitalist Urbanization* (Baltimore: Johns Hopkins University Press, 1985).

22. Ravetz, *Remaking Cities*, 23, passim.

23. See James C. Scott, "Authoritarian High Modernism," in *Readings in Planning Theory*, ed. Scott Campbell and Susan S. Fainstein, 2nd ed. (Malden, Mass.: Blackwell, 2003), 125–141.

24. Clara H. Greed, *Women and Planning: Creating Gendered Realities* (London: Routledge, 1994); Susan S. Fainstein and Lisa J. Servon, eds., *Gender and Planning: A Reader* (New Brunswick, N.J.: Rutgers University Press, 2005); Maureen Flanagan, "Private Needs, Public Space: Public Toilets Provision in the Anglo-Atlantic Patriarchal City—London, Dublin, Toronto and Chicago," *Urban History* 41, no. 2 (May 2014): 265–290; Alison Isenberg, *Downtown America: A History of the Place and the People Who Made It* (Chicago: University of Chicago Press, 2004); and Michele Nickerson, *Mothers of Conservatism: Women and the Postwar Right* (Princeton, N.J.: Princeton University Press, 2012).

25. Janet L. Abu-Lughod, *New York, Chicago, Los Angeles: America's Global Cities* (Minneapolis: University of Minnesota Press, 1999); and Justin A. Read, "Obverse Colonization: São Paulo, Global Urbanization, and the Poetics of the Latin American City," *Journal of Latin American Cultural Studies* 15 (December 2006): 281–300.

26. Shelly Hornstein, "Curating Place: Maps, Starchitecture and Museums-without-Borders," in *Time Refigured: Myths, Foundation Texts and Imagined Communities*, ed. Martin Prochazka and Onrej Pliny (Prague: Literraria Pragensia, 2005), 190–206.

27. Ravetz, *Remaking Cities*, 185. Also see Kristin Ross, *Fast Cars, Clean Bodies: Decolonization and the Reordering of French Culture* (Cambridge, Mass.: MIT Press, 1995); and Alvin Toffler, *Future Shock* (New York: Random House, 1970).

28. Ouroussoff, "Shantytowns."

29. Ibid. Also see "Learning from Tijuana: Hudson, N.Y., Considers Different Housing Model," *New York Times*, February 18, 2008, available at http://www.nytimes .com/2008/02/19/arts/design/19hous.html (accessed April 20, 2015).

CHAPTER 1

1. See Frank Lloyd Wright, *The Natural House* (New York: Horizon, 1954), which reprinted seminal essays from the 1930s. Also see Robert Fishman, *Urban Utopias in the Twentieth Century: Ebenezer Howard, Frank Lloyd Wright, Le Corbusier* (New York: Basic Books, 1977), 91–162; Peder Anker, "The Bauhaus of Nature," *Modernism/ Modernity* 12, no. 2 (2005): 229–251; Judi Loach, "Le Corbusier and the Creative Use of Mathematics," *British Journal of the History of Science* 31 (1998): 185–215; Vittoria Di Palma, "Architecture and the Organic Metaphor," *Journal of Architecture* 11, no. 4 (2006): 385–390; and the articles that follow in this special issue on the subject.

2. Frank Lloyd Wright, *Ausgeführte Bauten und Entwürfe*, 2 vols. (Berlin: Wasmuth, 1910) ("Wasmuth Portfolio," available at http://en.wikipedia.org/wiki/Wasmuth _Portfolio [accessed August 3, 2006]). Also see Ludwig Mies van der Rohe, "Frank Lloyd Wright," in *Mies van der Rohe*, ed. Philip Johnson, 3rd ed. (New York: Museum of Modern Art, 1978), 200–201; and Detlef Mertins, "Living in a Jungle: Mies, Organic Architecture, and the Art of City Building," in *Mies in America*, ed. Phyllis Lambert (New York: Abrams, 2001), 590–641.

3. Wright, *Natural House*, 16–17 (emphasis in original). This statement was originally published in 1936 in *Architect's Journal of London*.

4. Ibid., 21 (emphasis added). Also originally published in 1936 in *Architect's Journal of London*.

5. Ibid., 46. This statement was first published in his 1943 *Autobiography*. In the Wasmuth Portfolio, Wright says of organic architecture, "By knowledge of nature in this sense alone are . . . guiding principles to be established. Ideals gained within these limitations are never lost, and an artist may defy 'education.' If he is really for nature in this sense, he may be a 'rebel against his time and its laws but never lawless'" (Wright, *Ausgeführte Bauten und Entwürfe*, 1:5, available at http://content.lib.utah.edu/cdm4/ browse.php?CISOROOT=/FLWright-jp2 [accessed August 5, 2006]).

6. Paul Boyer, *Urban Masses and Moral Order in America, 1820–1920* (Cambridge, Mass.: Harvard University Press, 1978). Also see Daniel T. Rodgers, *Atlantic Crossings: Social Politics in the Progressive Age* (Cambridge, Mass.: Harvard University Press,

1998); and John W. Cole and Eric R. Wolf, *The Hidden Frontier: Ecology and Ethnicity in an Alpine Valley* (New York: Academic, 1974).

7. Christoph Bernhardt and Geneviève Massard-Guilbaud, eds., *The Modern Demon: Pollution in Urban and Industrial European Societies* (Clermont-Ferrand, France: Presses Universitaires Blaise Pascal, 2002); Dieter Schott, Bill Luckin, and Geneviève Massard-Guilbaud, eds., *Resources of the City: Contributions to an Environmental History of Modern Europe* (Aldershot, U.K.: Ashgate, 2005); Raymond Williams, *The Country and the City* (New York: Oxford University Press, 1973), 215–307; Rodgers, *Atlantic Crossings*; Anthony Sutcliffe, *Towards the Planned City: Germany, Britain, the United States and France, 1780–1914* (New York: St. Martin's, 1981); and Paul Emmons, "Embodying Networks: Bubble Diagrams and the Image of Modern Organicism," *Journal of Architecture* 11, no. 4 (2006): 441–461.

8. Thomas S. Hines, *Burnham of Chicago: Architect and Planner* (Chicago: University of Chicago Press, 1978); Fishman, *Urban Utopias*, 23–90; Stephen V. Ward, ed., *The Garden City: Past, Present and Future* (London: Spon, 1992); Murray Bookchin, *The Limits of the City* (New York: Harper and Row, 1974); and Stanley Buder, *Visionaries and Planners: The Garden City Movement and the Modern Community* (New York: Oxford University Press, 1990).

9. See Tom Wolfe, *From Bauhaus to Our House* (New York: Farrar, Straus and Giroux, 1981), 10–20.

10. Mervyn Miller, *Raymond Unwin: Garden Cities and Town Planning* (London: Leicester University Press, 1992), 139.

11. Ibid., 139–160.

12. Alison Ravetz, *Remaking Cities: Contradictions of the Recent Urban Environment* (London: Croom Helm, 1980), 23, passim, for the concept of the "clean sweep." Also see James C. Scott, "Authoritarian High Modernism," in *Readings in Planning Theory*, ed. Scott Campbell and Susan S. Fainstein, 2nd ed. (Malden, Mass.: Blackwell, 2003), 125–141.

13. Di Palma, "Architecture," 386. Also see Mari Hvattum, "'Unfolding from Within': Modern Architecture and the Dream of Organic Totality," *Journal of Architecture* 11, no. 4 (2006): 497–509; and Matthew Gandy, "Cyborg Urbanization: Complexity and Monstrosity in the Contemporary City," *International Journal of Urban and Regional Research* 29 (2005): 26–49.

14. For the United States, Los Angeles is a good example. Essential reading are Marc A. Weiss, *The Rise of the Community Builders: The American Real Estate Industry and Urban Land Planning* (New York: Columbia University Press, 1987); Greg Hise, *Magnetic Los Angeles: Planning the Twentieth-Century Metropolis* (Baltimore: Johns Hopkins University Press, 1997); and Mike Davis, *The City of Quartz* (New York: Vintage, 1990).

15. Le Corbusier, *Precisions: On the Present State of Architecture and City Planning*, trans. Edith Schreiber Aujame (Cambridge, Mass.: MIT Press, 1991 [1929–1930]), 103. Also see Peter Hall, *Cities of Tomorrow: An Intellectual History of Urban Planning and Design in the Twentieth Century*, rev. ed. (Cambridge, Mass.: Blackwell, 1996); and Helen Elizabeth Meller, *Towns, Plans and Society in Modern Britain* (Cambridge: Cambridge University Press, 1997).

16. Le Corbusier, *The City of To-morrow and Its Planning* (London: John Rodher, 1929), xxv. Also see Camillo Sitte, *City Planning According to Artistic Principles*,

trans. George R. Collins and Christiane Crasemann Collins (London: Phaidon, 1889); Sigfried Giedion, *Space, Time and Architecture: The Growth of a New Tradition* (Cambridge, Mass.: Harvard University Press, 1941); Richard Guy Wilson, Dianne H. Pilgrim, Dickran Tashjian, and Brooklyn Museum, eds., *The Machine Age in America, 1918–1941* (New York: Brooklyn Museum / Abrams, 1986); and Clay McShane, *Down the Asphalt Path: The Automobile and the American City* (New York: Columbia University Press, 1994).

17. See Weiss, *Rise of the Community Builders*.

18. Sharon E. Kingsland, *Modeling Nature: Episodes in the History of Population Ecology: Science and Its Conceptual Foundations*, 2nd ed. (Chicago: University of Chicago Press, 1995), 5. Also see Joel Bartholemew Hagen, *An Entangled Bank: The Origins of Ecosystem Ecology* (New Brunswick, N.J.: Rutgers University Press, 1992), 78–99. Hagen attributes the first use of the term "ecosystem" in the 1930s to British plant ecologist Arthur Tansley. Also see Robert Lilienfeld, *The Rise of Systems Theory: An Ideological Analysis* (New York: Wiley, 1978).

19. Quoted in Mertins, "Living in a Jungle," 605. Also see William Jordy, "The Aftermath of the Bauhaus in America: Gropius, Mies, and Breuer," in *The Intellectual Migration: Europe and America, 1930–1960*, ed. Donald Fleming and Bernard Bailyn (Cambridge, Mass.: Harvard University Press, 1969), 485–543; and Emmons, "Embodying Networks."

20. Michael Sorkin, "Foreword," in *The Modern City Revisited*, ed. Thomas Deckker (London: Spon, 2000), ix–xii. Also see Williams, *The Country and the City*; Morton White and Lucia White, *The Intellectual versus the City: From Thomas Jefferson to Frank Lloyd Wright* (Cambridge, Mass.: Harvard University Press, 1962); Carl Sussman, ed., *Planning the Fourth Migration: The Neglected Vision of the Regional Planning Association of America* (Cambridge, Mass.: MIT Press, 1976); Robert Wojtowicz, *Lewis Mumford and American Modernism: Eutopian Theories for Architecture and Urban Planning* (Cambridge: Cambridge University Press, 1996); and Jane Jacobs, *Cities and the Wealth of Nations: Principles of Economic Life* (New York: Random House, 1984).

21. See Clarence Arthur Perry, *Housing for the Machine Age* (New York: Russell Sage Foundation, 1939), 23. Also see his original formulation, Clarence Arthur Perry, "A Neighborhood Unit," in *Regional Plan of New York and Its Environs*, vol. 7, *Neighborhood and Community Planning* (New York: Committee for the Regional Survey of New York and Its Environs, 1929), 30–35; Dirk Schubert, "The Neighbourhood Paradigm: From Garden Cities to Gated Communities," in *Urban Planning in a Changing World: The Twentieth Century Experience*, ed. Robert Freestone (London: Spon, 2000), 118–138; Howard J. Gillette Jr., "The Evolution of Neighborhood Planning: From the Progressive Era to the 1949 Housing Act," *Journal of Urban History* 9 (August 1983): 421–444; and Robert Fishman, "The Metropolitan Tradition in American Planning," in *The American Planning Tradition: Culture and Policy* (Washington, D.C.: Woodrow Wilson Center Press, 2000), 65–88.

22. Perry, *Housing for the Machine Age*, 23. Also see Gillette, "Evolution of Neighborhood Planning"; Reginald R. Isaacs, "The 'Neighborhood Unit' Is an Instrument for Segregation," *Journal of Housing* 5 (August 1948): 215–218; and Schubert, "Neighbourhood Paradigm."

23. Esther McCoy, *Richard Neutra* (New York: Braziller, 1960), 8. Also see Richard Joseph Neutra, *Building with Nature* (New York: Universe, 1971); and Richard Joseph Neutra, *Survival through Design* (New York: Oxford University Press, 1954).

24. Sorkin, "Foreword," x.

25. CIAM, "CIAM: The La Sarraz Declaration," in *Programs and Manifestoes on 20th-Century Architecture*, ed. Ulrich Conrads (Cambridge, Mass.: MIT Press, 1970 [1928]), 109–114.

26. Le Corbusier, *The Athens Charter* (New York: Grossman, 1973), available at http://www.planering.org/images/artikelbilder/pdf/ffs_syd_CIAM_4_The_Athens _Charter.pdf.

27. Ibid. Also see Jordy, "Aftermath of the Bauhaus"; Sokratis Georgiadis, *Sigfried Giedion: An Intellectual Biography* (Edinburgh: Edinburgh University Press, 1993); Wolf Tegethoff, "From Obscurity to Maturity: Mies van der Rohe's Breakthrough to Modernism," in *Mies van der Rohe: Critical Essays*, ed. Franz Schulze (New York: Museum of Modern Art, 1989), 28–94; and Eric Paul Mumford, *The CIAM Discourse on Urbanism, 1928–1960* (Cambridge, Mass.: MIT Press, 2000).

28. Le Corbusier, *The Radiant City* (London: Faber and Faber, 1933), 117. Also see Le Corbusier, *Precisions*, 133.

29. Quoted in Fishman, *Urban Utopias*, 191. Also see Anker, "Bauhaus of Nature"; and Mertins, "Living in a Jungle."

30. Johnson, *Mies van der Rohe*; Tegethoff, "From Obscurity to Maturity"; Wolfe, *From Bauhaus to Our House*, 45–65; and Jordy, "Aftermath of the Bauhaus."

31. Eliel Saarinen, *The City: Its Growth, Its Decay, Its Future* (Cambridge, Mass.: MIT Press, 1943), 151, 149.

32. Ibid., 200–266.

33. Ibid., 216.

34. F. M. Dieleman and Sako Musterd, eds., *The Randstad: A Research and Policy Laboratory* (Dordrecht: Kluwer, 1992); and Pim Kooij and Paul van de Laar, "The Randstad Conurbation: A Floating Metropolis in the Dutch Delta," in *The European Metropolis, 1920–2000*, ed. Henk van Dijk (Berlin: European Social Foundation, 2003), 1–20.

35. Marco Bontje, "A 'Planner's Paradise' Lost? Past, Present and Future of Dutch National Urbanization Policy," *European Urban and Regional Studies* 10, no. 2 (2003): 135–151.

36. Giedion, *Space, Time and Architecture*, 793–813.

37. Dieter Schott, "London and Its 'New Towns' and Randstad Holland: Metropolitan Planning on Both Sides of the Channel after 1945," in *Die europäische Stadt im 20. Jahrhundert*, ed. Friedrich Lenger and Klaus Tenfelde (Cologne: Böhlau, 2005), 283–306.

38. Cordula Rooijendijk, "Urban Ideal Images in Post-war Rotterdam," *Planning Perspectives* 20 (April 2005): 179.

39. Ibid., 177–209.

40. Ibid. Also see Percy Edwin Alan Johnson-Marshall, *Rebuilding Cities* (Chicago: Aldine, 1966), 318–348; and Jeffry M. Diefendorf, *In the Wake of War: The Reconstruction of German Cities after World War II* (Oxford: Oxford University Press, 1993).

41. Johnson-Marshall, *Rebuilding Cities*, 318–348; W.A.J. Vanstiphout, *J. H. van den Broek*, summary of Ph.D. diss., 2005, available at dissertations.ub.rug.nl/FILES/faculties/arts/2005/w.a.j.vanstiphout/summary.pdf; and Wikipedia NL, *W. G. Witteveen*, available at http://sbp.arch.rwth-aachen.de/downloads/14_Witteveen%20bis%201940.pps, PowerPoint file (accessed November 3, 2007).

42. Raymond Unwin, *Nothing Gained by Overcrowding! How the Garden City Type of Development May Benefit Both Owner and Occupier* (London: P. S. King and Son, 1912).

43. Meller, *Towns, Plans and Society*, 51, and see chap. 4.

44. Miller, *Raymond Unwin*, 138.

45. Marco Amati and Makoto Yokohari, "The Establishment of the London Greenbelt: Reaching Consensus over Purchasing Land," *Journal of Planning History* 6 (November 2007): 311–337.

46. Ibid. Also see J. A. Yelling, "Land, Property and Planning," in *The Cambridge Urban History of Britain*, ed. Martin Daunton (Cambridge: Cambridge University Press, 2000), 467–494; and Meller, *Towns, Plans and Society*, 58–61.

47. Nigel Taylor, *Urban Planning Theory since 1945* (London: Sage, 1998), 41 (emphasis in original); and Meller, *Towns, Plans and Society*, 61. Also see Miller, *Raymond Unwin*, 161–188; Lord Woolton, *Ancoats: A Study of a Clearance Area: Report of a Survey Made in 1937–38* (Manchester, U.K.: Manchester University Settlement, 1945); and Marc Fried, "Grieving for a Lost Home: Psychological Costs of Relocation," in *Urban Renewal: The Record and the Controversy*, ed. James Q. Wilson (Cambridge, Mass.: MIT Press, 1966), 359–379.

48. Anthony Sutcliffe, *The Autumn of Central Paris: The Defeat of Town Planning, 1850–1970* (London: Edward Arnold, 1970), 219; and Colin Jones, *Paris: Biography of a City* (New York: Viking, 2005), 385. Also see David S. Barnes, *The Making of a Social Disease: Tuberculosis in Nineteenth-Century France* (Berkeley: University of California Press, 1995).

49. Jones, *Paris*, 359, 385–425.

50. Kenneth T. Jackson, *Crabgrass Frontier: The Suburbanization of the United States* (New York: Oxford University Press, 1985).

51. Quoted in ibid. Also see Robert Fishman, "Re-imagining Los Angeles," in *Rethinking Los Angeles*, ed. Michael J. Dear, H. Eric Schockman, and Greg Hise (Thousand Oaks, Calif.: Sage, 1996), 151–152. Also see William H. Wilson, *The City Beautiful Movement* (Baltimore: Johns Hopkins University Press, 1989); Robert G. Barrows, "Beyond the Tenement—Patterns of American Urban Housing, 1870–1930," *Journal of Urban History* 9 (1983): 395–420; and Mel Scott, *American City Planning since 1890* (Berkeley: University of California Press, 1969).

52. Los Angeles Almanac, available at http://www.laalmanac.com/population/po02.htm and http://www.laalmanac.com/population/po26.htm (accessed March 9, 2015). Also see Fishman, "Re-imagining Los Angeles," 251–262; Hise, *Magnetic Los Angeles*, chap. 1; and Robert M. Fogleson, *The Fragmented Metropolis: Los Angeles, 1850–1930* (Cambridge, Mass.: Harvard University Press, 1967).

53. Quoted in William B. Fulton, *The Reluctant Metropolis: The Politics of Urban Growth in Los Angeles* (Baltimore: Johns Hopkins University Press, 2001), 108.

54. Marc Reisner, *Cadillac Desert: The American West and Its Disappearing Water*, rev. and updated ed. (New York: Penguin, 1993), 55. Also see Blake Gumprecht, *The Los Angeles River: Its Life, Death, and Possible Rebirth* (Baltimore: Johns Hopkins University Press, 1999); and Jared Orsi, *Hazardous Metropolis: Flooding and Urban Ecology in Los Angeles* (Berkeley: University of California Press, 2004).

55. L.A. Department of Water and Power, available at https://www.ladwp.com/ladwp/faces/wcnav_externalId/a-w-fact-hist?_adf.ctrl-state=1c47qszbrg_21&_afr Loop=200601535211935 (accessed March 9, 2015). Also see Reisner, *Cadillac Desert*; William L. Kahrl, *Water and Power: The Conflict over Los Angeles' Water Supply in the Owens Valley* (Berkeley: University of California Press, 1982); Norris Hundley, *The Great Thirst: Californians and Water, 1770s–1990s* (Berkeley: University of California Press, 1992); and Davis, *City of Quartz*.

56. See Adam Rome, *The Bulldozer in the Countryside: Suburban Sprawl and the Rise of American Environmentalism* (New York: Cambridge University Press, 2001); Mike Davis, *Ecology of Fear: Los Angeles and the Imagination of Disaster* (New York: Metropolitan, 1998); Reisner, *Cadillac Desert*, 54–108; and Hundley, *Great Thirst*, 119–201.

57. Donald Worster, *Rivers of Empire: Water, Aridity, and the Growth of the American West* (New York: Pantheon, 1985); and Hundley, *Great Thirst*, 201–232.

58. David E. Nye, *American Technological Sublime* (Cambridge, Mass.: MIT Press, 1994).

59. Reisner, *Cadillac Desert*, 85–86, 125–150. Also see Robert Gottlieb and Margaret FitzSimmons, *Thirst for Growth: Water Agencies as Hidden Government in California* (Tucson: University of Arizona Press, 1991); Steven P. Erie and Harold David Brackman, *Beyond Chinatown: The Metropolitan Water District, Growth, and the Environment in Southern California* (Stanford, Calif.: Stanford University Press, 2006); Richard C. Wade, *The Urban Frontier: The Rise of Western Cities, 1790–1830* (Cambridge, Mass.: Harvard University Press, 1959); Donald Worster, *Nature's Economy: A History of Ecological Ideas*, 2nd ed. (Cambridge: Cambridge University Press, 1994); Blaine A. Brownell, "The Commercial-Civic Elite and City Planning in Atlanta, Memphis, and New Orleans in the 1920s," *Journal of Southern History* 41 (1975): 339–368; Samuel P. Hays, *Conservation and the Gospel of Efficiency: The Progressive Conservation Movement, 1890–1920* (Cambridge, Mass.: Harvard University Press, 1959); Donald C. Swain, *Federal Conservation Policy, 1921–1933* (Berkeley: University of California Press, 1963); Thomas K. McCraw, *TVA and the Power Fight, 1933–1939* (Philadelphia: Lippincott, 1971); and Walter T. K. Nugent, *Habits of Empire: A History of American Expansion* (New York: Knopf, 2008).

60. Scott, *American City Planning*, 199, 199–210. Also see Mike Davis, "How Eden Lost Its Garden: A Political History of the Los Angeles Landscape," in *The City: Los Angeles and Urban Theory at the End of the Twentieth Century*, ed. Allen John Scott and Edward W. Soja (Berkeley: University of California Press, 1996), 160–185.

61. See Fishman, "Re-imagining Los Angeles"; Scott, *American City Planning*, 199–210; Tom Sitton, "Private Sector Planning for the Environment," in *Land of Sunshine: An Environmental History of Metropolitan Los Angeles*, ed. William Francis Deverell and Greg Hise (Pittsburgh: University of Pittsburgh Press, 2005), 152–166; and Hise, *Magnetic Los Angeles*, chap. 2.

62. Margaret Garb, *City of American Dreams: A History of Home Ownership and Housing Reform in Chicago, 1871–1919* (Chicago: University of Chicago Press, 2005), 2–10. Also see Jackson, *Crabgrass Frontier*; Gail Radford, *Modern Housing for America* (Chicago: University of Chicago Press, 1995); Paul K. Conkin, *Tomorrow a New World: The New Deal Community Program* (Ithaca, N.Y.: Cornell University Press, 1959); Joseph L. Arnold, *The New Deal in the Suburbs: A History of the Greenbelt Town Program, 1935–1954* (Columbus: Ohio State University Press, 1971); Buder, *Visionaries and Planners*; and David M. Freund, *Colored Property: State Policy and White Racial Politics in Suburban America* (Chicago: University of Chicago Press, 2007).

63. James R. Grossman, *Land of Hope: Chicago, Black Southerners, and the Great Migration* (Chicago: University of Chicago Press, 1989), chap. 6; St. Clair Drake and Horace E. Cayton, *Black Metropolis: A Study of Negro Life in a Northern City* (New York: Harcourt, 1945); Allan H. Spear, *Black Chicago: The Making of a Negro Ghetto, 1890–1920* (Chicago: University of Chicago Press, 1967); Margaret Garb, "Drawing the 'Color Line': Race and Real Estate in Early Twentieth-Century Chicago," *Journal of Urban History* 32 (2006): 773–778; and Margaret Garb, *City of American Dreams*. Also see John T. McGreevy, *Parish Boundaries: The Catholic Encounter with Race in the Twentieth-Century Urban North* (Chicago: University of Chicago Press, 1996); Eileen McMahon, *Which Parish Are You From? A Chicago Irish Community and Race Relations* (Lexington: University Press of Kentucky, 1995); William M. Tuttle, *Race Riot: Chicago in the Red Summer of 1919* (New York: Atheneum, 1970); and Janet L. Abu-Lughod, *Race, Space, and Riots in Chicago, New York, and Los Angeles* (Oxford: Oxford University Press, 2007), 43–78.

64. McGreevy, *Parish Boundaries*; McMahon, *Which Parish Are You From?*; Abu-Lughod, *Race, Space, and Riots*, 64–67; John M. Allswang, *A House for All Peoples: Ethnic Politics in Chicago, 1890–1936* (Lexington: University Press of Kentucky, 1971); Douglas Bukowski, *Big Bill Thompson, Chicago, and the Politics of Image* (Urbana: University of Illinois Press, 1998); Roger Biles, *Big City Boss in Depression and War: Mayor Edward J. Kelly of Chicago* (DeKalb: Northern Illinois University Press, 1984); Harold L. Platt, *Shock Cities: The Environmental Transformation and Reform of Manchester and Chicago* (Chicago: University of Chicago Press, 2005); Thomas Lee Philpott, *The Slum and the Ghetto: Neighborhood Deterioration and Middle-Class Reform, Chicago, 1880–1930* (New York: Oxford University Press, 1978); and Lizabeth Cohen, *Making a New Deal: Industrial Workers in Chicago, 1919–1939* (Cambridge: Cambridge University Press, 1990).

65. Wendy Plotkin, "Deeds of Mistrust: Race, Housing and Restrictive Covenants in Chicago, 1900–1953" (Ph.D. diss., University of Illinois at Chicago, 1999), 2, 1–42.

66. Quoted in ibid., 37–38. Also see Christopher Silver, "The Racial Origins of Zoning in American Cities," in *Urban Planning and the African American Community: In the Shadows*, ed. June Manning Thomas and Marsha Ritzdorf (Thousand Oaks, Calif.: Sage, 1997), 23–42; and Joseph P. Schwieterman, Dana M. Caspall, and Jane Heron, *The Politics of Place: A History of Zoning in Chicago* (Chicago: Lake Claremont Press, 2003).

67. Richard Wright, *Native Son* (New York: Harper and Brothers, 1940). Wright's novel is based on a true story. See Richard Cahan, "Another Native Son," *Chicago Magazine*, June 2001, 89–91, 124–130. Also see Devereux Bowly, *The Poorhouse: Subsidized*

Housing in Chicago, 1895–1976 (Carbondale: Southern Illinois University Press, 1978); and Philpott, *The Slum and the Ghetto*.

68. Otis Dudley Duncan and Beverly Duncan, *The Negro Population of Chicago: A Study of Residential Succession* (Chicago: University of Chicago Press, 1957), 142–156; and Philpott, *The Slum and the Ghetto*. Also see Biles, *Big City Boss*; Drake and Cayton, *Black Metropolis*; Arvarh E. Strickland, *History of the Chicago Urban League* (Urbana: University of Illinois Press, 1966); and Jesse Thomas Moore, *A Search for Equality: The National Urban League, 1910–1961* (University Park: Pennsylvania State University Press, 1981).

69. See Garb, *City of American Dreams*; Allswang, *House for All Peoples*; Cohen, *Making a New Deal*; David R. Roediger, *The Wages of Whiteness: Race and the Making of the American Working Class* (London: Verso, 1991); and Thomas J. Sugrue, "Revisiting the Second Ghetto," *Journal of Urban History* 29 (March 2003): 281–290. Also see Charles Shanabruch, *Chicago's Catholics: The Evolution of an American Identity* (Notre Dame, Ind.: University of Notre Dame Press, 1981); and Robert A. Slayton, *Back of the Yards: The Making of a Local Democracy* (Chicago: University of Chicago Press, 1986).

70. Duncan and Duncan, *Negro Population*, 145. Also see Gwendolyn Brooks, *A Street in Bronzeville* (New York: Harper and Brothers, 1945).

71. Bowly, *Poorhouse*, 17–54; and D. Bradford Hunt, *Blueprint for Disaster: The Unraveling of Chicago Public Housing* (Chicago: University of Chicago Press, 2009).

72. Roberto P. Guimaraes, *The Ecopolitics of Development in the Third World: Politics and Environment in Brazil* (Boulder, Colo.: Lynne Rienner, 1991), 78. Also see Luis Roniger, *Hierarchy and Trust in Modern Mexico and Brazil* (New York: Praeger, 1990); Gil Shidlo, *Social Policy in a Non-Democratic Regime: The Case of Public Housing in Brazil* (Boulder, Colo.: Westview, 1990); and Barbara Weinstein, "Presidential Address: Developing Inequality," *American Historical Review* 113 (February 2008): 1–18.

73. Raquel Rolnik, "São Paulo in the Early Days of Industrialization: Space and Politics," in *Social Struggles and the City: The Case of São Paulo*, ed. Lúcio Kowarick (New York: Monthly Review Press, 1994), 77–93; Robert M. Levine, *The History of Brazil* (Westport, Conn.: Greenwood, 1999), 98–120; and Marie Huchzermeyer, "Informal Settlements: Production and Intervention in Twentieth-Century Brazil and South Africa," *Latin American Perspectives* 29 (January 2002): 83–105.

74. Christopher Armstrong, *Southern Exposure: Canadian Promoters in Latin America and the Caribbean, 1896–1930* (Toronto: University of Toronto Press, 1988), 43–61. Also see Peter B. Evans, *Dependent Development: The Alliance of Multinational, State, and Local Capital in Brazil* (Princeton, N.J.: Princeton University Press, 1979).

75. Miller, *Raymond Unwin*, 140–160; and Barry Parker, "Two Years in Brazil," *Garden Cities and Town Planning* 9, no. 8 (1919): 143–151. Also see Rolnik, "São Paulo in the Early Days"; Fabiano Lemes de Oliveira, "Planning a Green City versus Private Land-Partition: Park Systems and Urban Development in São Paulo in the First Decades of the 20th Century," in *Proceedings of the 13th Biennial Meeting of the International Planning History Society* (Chicago: International Planning History Society, 2008), 295–309; and Teresa Pires do Rio Caldeira, *City of Walls: Crime, Segregation, and Citizenship in São Paulo* (Berkeley: University of California Press, 2000), 213–255. For the environmental statistics, see "São Paulo," available at http://en.wikipedia.org/wiki/São_Paulo (accessed March 5, 2009).

76. See Martha Huggins and Phillip D. Snow, *Water Resources of Sao Paulo, Brazil 1998*, available at http://ghaly.union.edu/~ghalya/civil-history/Brazil/Brazil98/Info.htm (accessed March 17, 2009); and Caldeira, *City of Walls*, 213–255. Also see Lemes de Oliveira, "Planning a Green City."

77. Lúcio Kowarick and Nabil G. Bonduki, "Urban Space and Political Space: From Populism to Redemocratization," in *Social Struggles and the City: The Case of São Paulo*, ed. Lúcio Kowarick (New York: Monthly Review Press, 1994), 127, 121–147. Also see Nabil G. Bonduki, "The Housing Crisis in the Postwar Years," in ibid., 94–120.

78. Levine, *History of Brazil*, 98–120.

79. Peter M. Ward, *Mexico City*, 2nd ed. (New York: Wiley, 1998); Diane E. Davis, "Whither the Public Sphere: Local, National, and International Influences on the Planning of Downtown Mexico City, 1910–1950," *Space and Culture* 7 (May 2004): 193–222; Diane E. Davis, *Urban Leviathan: Mexico City in the Twentieth Century* (Philadelphia: Temple University Press, 1994); John Lear, *Workers, Neighbors, and Citizens: The Revolution in Mexico City* (Lincoln: University of Nebraska Press, 2001); and Roniger, *Hierarchy and Trust*.

80. See Fernando Romero, "ZMVM: Zona Metropolitana del Valle de México," in *ZMVM: Zona Metropolitana del Valle de México*, ed. Fernando Romero and Laboratorio de la Ciudad de México (San Angel: Laboratorio de la Ciudad de México, 2000); and Martha Schteingart, "The Environmental Problems Associated with Urban Development in Mexico City," *Environment and Urbanization* 1 (April 1989): 40–50. Also see Gustavo G. Garza Merodio, "Technological Innovation and the Expansion of Mexico City, 1870–1920," *Journal of Latin American Geography* 5, no. 2 (2006): 109–126; Emily Wakild, "Naturalizing Modernity: Urban Parks, Public Gardens and Drainage Projects in Porfirian Mexico City," *Mexican Studies / Estudios Mexicanos* 23 (Winter 2007): 101–123; and Araceli Garcia Parra, "The Beginning of Mexico City's Growth: The Reconstruction of an Urban Process" (paper presented at the 13th Biennial Meeting of the International Planning History Society, Chicago, July 2008).

81. Cf. Oscar Lewis, *Five Families: Mexican Case Studies in the Culture of Poverty* (New York: Basic Books, 1959); and Lúcia Sá, *Life in the Megalopolis: Mexico City and São Paulo* (Milton Park, U.K.: Routledge, 2007). Also see Elena Poniatowska, *Nothing, Nobody: The Voices of the Mexico City Earthquake*, trans. Aurora Camacho de Schmidt and Arthur Schmidt (Philadelphia: Temple University Press, 1995); Diane E. Davis, "The Social Construction of Mexico City: Political Conflict and Urban Development, 1950–1966," *Journal of Urban History* 24 (1998): 364–415; and Susan Eckstein, "Poor People versus the State and Capital: Anatomy of a Successful Community Mobilization for Housing in Mexico City," *International Journal of Urban and Regional Research* 14, no. 2 (1990): 274–296.

82. Parra, "Beginning of Mexico City's Growth"; Garza Merodio, "Technological Innovation"; and David J. Fox, "Man-Water Relationships in Metropolitan Mexico," *Geographical Review* 55 (1965): 523–545.

83. Wakild, "Naturalizing Modernity," 119. Also see Davis, "Whither the Public Sphere"; and Rebecca E. Biron, "Mexico City: The Sewer and the Metro," *Delaware Review of Latin American Studies* 6 (2005): 1–3.

84. Fox, "Man-Water Relationships"; and Davis, "Whither the Public Sphere."

85. Wakild, "Naturalizing Modernity," 121. Also see Alan Zarembo, "The Canal from Hell," *Newsweek*, May 21, 2001, available at http://www.newsweek.com/id/79441; and Biron, "Mexico City."

86. Germán E. Figueroa Vega, "Case History No. 9.8., Mexico., D.F., Mexico," in *Guidebook to Studies of Land Subsidence due to Ground-Water Withdrawal*, ed. Joseph F. Poland (Paris: United Nations Educational, Scientific and Cultural Organization, 1984), 217–232; and Romero, "ZMVM," 101–121. Also see Elinor G. K. Melville, *A Plague of Sheep: Environmental Consequences of the Conquest of Mexico* (Cambridge: Cambridge University Press, 1994); Joel Simon, *Endangered Mexico: An Environment on the Edge* (San Francisco: Sierra Club Books, 1997); and Alfred W. Crosby, *The Columbian Exchange: Biological and Cultural Consequences of 1492* (Westport, Conn.: Greenwood, 1972).

87. Davis, *Urban Leviathan*, app. B.

88. Sá, *Life in the Megalopolis*, 79–106; and John C. Cross, *Informal Politics: Street Vendors and the State in Mexico City* (Stanford, Calif.: Stanford University Press, 1998).

89. Davis, "Whither the Public Sphere," 208.

90. Parra, "Beginning of Mexico City's Growth."

91. Davis, "Whither the Public Sphere," 209.

92. Sutcliffe, *Towards the Planned City*, chap. 6; and Janet L. Abu-Lughod, *New York, Chicago, Los Angeles: America's Global Cities* (Minneapolis: University of Minnesota Press, 1999).

93. Scott, "Authoritarian High Modernism," 127.

94. Frank Lloyd Wright, *When Democracy Builds* (Chicago: University of Chicago Press, 1945), 48; see 129–131 for information on the origins of the book.

95. Ibid., 36.

96. Ibid., 28.

97. Ibid., 31.

CHAPTER 2

1. Helen A. Harrison and Joseph P. Cusker, *Dawn of a New Day: The New York World's Fair, 1939/40* (New York: Queens Museum / New York University Press, 1980); Hugh Ferriss, *The Metropolis of Tomorrow* (New York: Washburn, 1929); and John King, "The Draftsman [Hugh Ferriss]," *Dwell* 8 (September 2008): 118–124. Also see Lizabeth Cohen, *A Consumers' Republic: The Politics of Mass Consumption in Postwar America* (New York: Knopf, 2003).

2. Le Corbusier, *The City of To-morrow and Its Planning* (London: John Rodher, 1929), 179; and see the Le Corbusier–inspired manifesto of the International Congresses of Modern Architecture (Congrès Internationaux d'Architecture Moderne, or CIAM), Le Corbusier, *The Athens Charter* (New York: Grossman, 1973), available at http://www.planering.org/images/artikelbilder/pdf/ffs_syd_CIAM_4_The_Athens_Charter.pdf. Also see Robert Fishman, *Urban Utopias in the Twentieth Century: Ebenezer Howard, Frank Lloyd Wright, Le Corbusier* (New York: Basic Books, 1977), 163–264; Jane Jacobs, *The Death and Life of Great American Cities* (New York: Random House, 1961); Nicolai Ouroussoff, "A Triumph That's Almost Le Corbusier's," *New York Times*, July 30, 2006; Steven V. Ward, "Re-examining the International Diffusion of Planning,"

in *Urban Planning in a Changing World: The Twentieth Century Experience*, ed. Robert Freestone (London: Spon, 2000), 40–60.

3. Jeffry M. Diefendorf, "Skyscrapers and Healthy Cities: Walter Gropius and Martin Wagner between Germany and America," in *From Manhattan to Mainhattan: Architecture and Style as Transatlantic Dialogue, 1920–1970, Bulletin of the German Historical Institute*, suppl. 2, ed. Cordula Grewe (Washington, D.C.: German Historical Institute, 2005), 29–50; and Christoph Bernhardt, "Planning Urbanization and Urban Growth in the Socialist Period: The Case of East German New Towns, 1945–1989," *Journal of Urban History* 32 (2005): 104–119.

4. Michelle Nickerson, "Domestic Threats: Women, Gender, and Conservatism in Cold War Los Angeles, 1945–1966" (Ph.D. diss., Yale University, 2003).

5. Betty Friedan, *The Feminine Mystique* (New York: Norton, 1963).

6. Nickerson, "Domestic Threats, 166.

7. Ibid., 133; and Elaine Tyler May, *Homeward Bound: American Families in the Cold War Era* (New York: Basic Books, 1988). Also see Michele Nickerson, *Mothers of Conservatism: Women and the Postwar Right* (Princeton, N.J.: Princeton University Press, 2012); Jack Schneider, "Escape from Los Angeles: White Flight from Los Angeles and Its Schools, 1960–1980," *Journal of Urban History* 34 (September 2008): 995–1012; and Laura Pulido, "Rethinking Environmental Racism: White Privilege and Urban Development in Southern California," *Annals of the Association of American Geographers* 90 (March 2000): 12–40.

8. See Diefendorf, "Skyscrapers and Healthy Cities"; and Bernhardt, "Planning Urbanization."

9. John P. Rasmussen, ed., *The New American Revolution: The Dawning of the Technetronic Era* (New York: Wiley, 1972); James C. Scott, *Seeing like a State: How Certain Schemes to Improve the Human Condition Have Failed* (New Haven, Conn.: Yale University Press, 1998); Robert Lilienfeld, *The Rise of Systems Theory: An Ideological Analysis* (New York: Wiley, 1978); David F. Noble, *Forces of Production: A Social History of Industrial Automation* (New York: Oxford University Press, 1986); Neil Postman, *Technopoly: The Surrender of Culture to Technology* (New York: Vintage, 1992); and Donald Worster, *Nature's Economy: A History of Ecological Ideas*, 2nd ed. (Cambridge: Cambridge University Press, 1994), chap. 16.

10. Scott, *Seeing like a State*.

11. Alexander Sedlmaier, "Berlin's Europa-Center (1963–1965)," in *From Manhattan to Mainhattan: Architecture and Style as Transatlantic Dialogue, 1920–1970, Bulletin of the German Historical Institute*, suppl. 2, ed. Cordula Grewe (Washington, D.C.: German Historical Institute, 2005), 65–86; Oscar Niemeyer, *Oscar Niemeyer* (Milan: Mondadori, 1975); and Thomas Deckker, "Brasília: City versus Landscape," in *The Modern City Revisited*, ed. Thomas Deckker (London: Spon, 2000), 167–194.

12. June Manning Thomas, "Educating Planners: Unified Diversity for Social Action," in *Readings in Planning Theory*, ed. James C. Scott and Susan S. Fainstein, 2nd ed. (Malden, Mass.: Blackwell, 2003), 363, 356–375. Also see Chunglin Kwa, "Representations of Nature Mediating between Ecology and Science Policy: The Case of the International Biological Programme," *Social Studies of Science* 17 (1987): 413–442; Herbert Marcuse, *One-Dimensional Man: Studies in the Ideology of Advanced Industrial Society* (Boston: Beacon, 1964); William Hollingsworth Whyte Jr., ed., *The Exploding*

Metropolis, 2nd ed. (Berkeley: University of California Press, 1993); and Jacobs, *Death and Life of Great American Cities*.

13. See William Jordy, "The Aftermath of the Bauhaus in America: Gropius, Mies, and Breuer," in *The Intellectual Migration: Europe and America, 1930–1960*, ed. Donald Fleming and Bernard Bailyn (Cambridge, Mass.: Harvard University Press, 1969), 485–543; and Wolfgang Thöner, "From an 'Alien, Hostile Phenomenon' to the 'Poetry of the Future': On the Bauhaus Reception in East Germany, 1945–1970," in *From Manhattan to Mainhattan: Architecture and Style as Transatlantic Dialogue, 1920–1970, Bulletin of the German Historical Institute*, suppl. 2, ed. Cordula Grewe (Washington, D.C.: German Historical Institute, 2005), 115–137. Also see Edward R. Burian, ed., *Modernity and the Architecture of Mexico* (Austin: University of Texas Press, 1997); Niemeyer, *Niemeyer*; and David G. Epstein, *Brasília, Plan and Reality: A Study of Planned and Spontaneous Urban Development* (Berkeley: University of California Press, 1973).

14. Le Corbusier, *Concerning Town Planning* (London: Architectural Press, 1948). Also see Fishman, *Urban Utopias*, 243–254; and Thomas McQuillan, "Edouard among the Machines: A Discussion of Le Corbusier's Technological Agenda" (Ph.D. diss., Oslo School of Architecture and Design, 2006).

15. Le Corbusier, *Concerning Town Planning*, 13; and Patrick Geddes, *Cities in Evolution: An Introduction to the Town Planning Movement and to the Study of Civics* (London: Williams and Norgate, 1915).

16. Le Corbusier, *Concerning Town Planning*, 11. Also see Harold L. Platt, "World War I and the Birth of American Regionalism," *Journal of Policy History* 5, no. 1 (1993): 128–152.

17. Quoted in Norma Evenson, *Le Corbusier: The Machine and the Grand Design, Planning and Cities* (London: Studio Vista, 1969), 110.

18. Daniel H. Burnham and Edward H. Bennett, *Plan of Chicago* (Chicago: Commercial Club, 1909).

19. Daniel T. Rodgers, *Atlantic Crossings: Social Politics in the Progressive Age* (Cambridge, Mass.: Harvard University Press, 1998).

20. Evenson, *Le Corbusier*, 108.

21. Percival Goodman and Paul Goodman, *Communitas: Means of Livelihood and Ways of Life* (1947; repr., Chicago: University of Chicago Press, 1960), 46.

22. Gijs Mom, *The Electric Vehicle: Technology and Expectations in the Automobile Age* (Baltimore: Johns Hopkins University Press, 2003), 33.

23. Maria Kaika, *City of Flows: Modernity, Nature, and the City* (New York: Routledge, 2005).

24. Michael Dear, "In the City, Time Becomes Visible: Intentionality and Urbanism in Los Angeles, 1781–1991," in *The City: Los Angeles and Urban Theory at the End of the Twentieth Century*, ed. Allen John Scott and Edward W. Soja (Berkeley: University of California Press, 1996), 81. Also see Kaika, *City of Flows*.

25. Phyllis Lambert, ed., *Mies in America* (New York: Abrams, 2001); Franz Schulze, ed., *Mies van der Rohe: Critical Essays* (New York: Museum of Modern Art, 1989); and Werner Blaser, *Mies Van Der Rohe* (New York: Praeger, 1972). Also see Roberta Moudry, ed., *The American Skyscraper: Cultural Histories* (New York: Cambridge University Press, 2005).

26. Jordy, "Aftermath of the Bauhaus," 514.

27. Detlef Mertins, "Living in a Jungle: Mies, Organic Architecture, and the Art of City Building," in *Mies in America*, ed. Phyllis Lambert (New York: Abrams, 2001), 609.

28. Kenneth Frampton, *Le Corbusier* (London: Thames and Hudson, 2001), 88–101; and Frank Lloyd Wright, *When Democracy Builds* (Chicago: University of Chicago Press, 1945).

29. Le Corbusier, *Concerning Town Planning*, 85.

30. Le Corbusier, *Precisions: On the Present State of Architecture and City Planning*, trans. Edith Schreiber Aujame (Cambridge, Mass.: MIT Press, 1991), 85.

31. Le Corbusier, *Athens Charter*; and Evenson, *Le Corbusier*, 21–32.

32. Evenson, *Le Corbusier*, 97–106; and Fishman, *Urban Utopias*, 253–263.

33. Marshall Berman, *All That Is Solid Melts into Air: The Experience of Modernity* (New York: Simon and Schuster, 1982), 167. Also see Dear, "In the City"; and Clay McShane, *Down the Asphalt Path: The Automobile and the American City* (New York: Columbia University Press, 1994).

34. Francis Bello, "The City and the Car," in *The Exploding Metropolis*, ed. William Hollingsworth Whyte Jr., 2nd ed. (Berkeley: University of California Press, 1993), 53–80.

35. Mom, *Electric Vehicle*, 33. Also see Evenson, *Le Corbusier*; and James J. Flink, *The Car Culture* (Cambridge, Mass.: MIT Press, 1975).

36. Diefendorf, "Skyscrapers and Healthy Cities"; and Ward, "Re-examining the International Diffusion of Planning."

37. Arnold R. Hirsch, *Making the Second Ghetto: Race and Housing in Chicago, 1940–1960* (New York: Cambridge University Press, 1983), 170, 273–274. Also see E. Michael Jones, *The Slaughter of Cities: Urban Renewal as Ethnic Cleansing* (South Bend, Ind.: St. Augustine's, 2004); Kenneth T. Jackson, *Crabgrass Frontier: The Suburbanization of the United States* (New York: Oxford University Press, 1985); and Mark S. Foster, *From Streetcar to Superhighway: American City Planners and Urban Transportation, 1900–1940* (Philadelphia: Temple University Press, 1981).

38. Tom Wolfe, *From Bauhaus to Our House* (New York: Farrar, Straus and Giroux, 1981); and Serge Guilbaut, *How New York Stole the Idea of Modern Art: Abstract Expressionism, Freedom, and the Cold War* (Chicago: University of Chicago Press, 1983).

39. Fairfield Osborn, *Our Plundered Planet* (Boston: Little, Brown, 1948).

40. See Alison Ravetz, *Remaking Cities: Contradictions of the Recent Urban Environment* (London: Croom Helm, 1980), 185.

41. According to Wikipedia, Max Horkheimer first used the term in a 1937 essay, "Traditional and Critical Theory," available at http://en.wikipedia.org/wiki/Critical_ theory (accessed March 9, 2015).

42. Max Horkheimer and Theodor W. Adorno, *Dialectic of Enlightenment*, trans. John Cumming (1944; repr., New York: Continuum, 1972).

43. Ibid. Also see Jacques Ellul, *The Technological Society* (New York: Knopf, 1964); and Stephen Edelston Toulmin, *Cosmopolis: The Hidden Agenda of Modernity* (New York: Free Press, 1990).

44. Horkheimer and Adorno, *Dialectic*, 4.

45. Ibid., 6.

46. Ibid., 9. Also see Thomas S. Kuhn, *The Structure of Scientific Revolutions* (Chicago: University of Chicago Press, 1962).

47. Toulmin, *Cosmopolis*, 194.

48. Osborn, *Our Plundered Planet*, 48.

49. Ibid., ix. Also see Julian Huxley, "World Population," *Scientific American* 194 (1956): 64–76.

50. Aldo Leopold, *A Sand County Almanac, and Sketches Here and There* (1949; repr., New York: Oxford University Press, 2001), 171. Also see Worster, *Nature's Economy*.

51. Goodman and Goodman, *Communitas*, 6–7.

52. Ibid., 17.

53. Horkheimer and Adorno, *Dialectic*, 29.

54. Jane Jacobs, "Downtown Is for People," in *The Exploding Metropolis*, ed. William Hollingsworth Whyte Jr. (Berkeley: University of California Press, 1993), 157–184.

55. William Hollingsworth Whyte Jr., "Introduction," in *Exploding Metropolis*, 23.

56. Ibid., 11.

57. Ibid., 52.

58. Jacobs, "Downtown Is for People," 157.

59. Ibid., 159.

60. Ibid., 173.

61. Ibid., 179.

62. "Corbu," *Time*, May 5, 1961, cover image. Also see May, *Homeward Bound*.

63. Lilienfeld, *Rise of Systems Theory*.

64. Marshall McLuhan, *Understanding Media: The Extensions of Man* (New York: McGraw-Hill, 1964). Also see Rob Bartram and Sarah Shobrook, "Body Beautiful: Medical Aesthetics and the Reconstruction of Urban Britain in the 1940s," *Landscape Research* 26, no. 2 (2001): 119–135.

65. Kaika, *City of Flows*, 49.

66. Andrew Ross, *The Chicago Gangster Theory of Life: Nature's Debt to Society* (London: Verso, 1994), 121.

67. Manuel Castells, *The Informational City: Information Technology, Economic Restructuring and the Urban-Regional Process* (Oxford: Blackwell, 1989); and Bill McKibben, *The Age of Missing Information* (New York: Random House, 1992).

68. Norbert Wiener, *Cybernetics* (New York: Wiley, 1948), 11.

69. Ibid., 1–29. For a brief biographical sketch, see J. J. O'Connor and E. F. Robertson, eds., "Norbert Wiener," available at http://www-history.mcs.st-andrews .ac.uk/Biographies/Wiener_Norbert.html (accessed September 28, 2008).

70. Wiener, *Cybernetics*, 26.

71. Ibid., 28. Also see Noble, *Forces of Production*, 71–76; and Harry Braverman, *Labor and Monopoly Capital: The Degradation of Work in the Twentieth Century* (New York: Monthly Review Press, 1975).

72. Sharon E. Kingsland, *Modeling Nature: Episodes in the History of Population Ecology*, 2nd ed. (Chicago: University of Chicago Press, 1995), 3–4; and Kwa, "Representations of Nature," 413.

73. Edward O. Wilson and Evelyn G. Hutchinson, "Robert Helmer MacArthur," *National Academy of Sciences Biographical Memoirs* 58 (1989): 322, available at http:// books.nap.edu/openbook.php?record_id=1645&page=318 (accessed September 30, 2008).

74. Worster, *Nature's Economy*, 374. Also see Robert H. MacArthur, "On the Relative Abundance of Bird Species," *Proceedings of the National Academy of Science* 43 (1957): 293–295; and Stephen D. Fretwell, "The Impact of Robert Macarthur on Ecology," *Annual Review of Ecology and Systematics* 6 (1975): 319–327.

75. Worster, *Nature's Economy*, 375.

76. Ibid.; Fretwell, "Impact of Robert MacArthur"; and Kingsland, *Modeling Nature*, 215–216.

77. Jennifer S. Light, "Nationality and Neighborhood Risk at the Origins of FHA Underwriting," *Journal of Urban History* 20 (June 2010): 1–38. Also see Jennifer S. Light, *The Nature of Cities: Ecological Visions and the American Urban Professions, 1920–1960* (Baltimore: Johns Hopkins University Press, 2009); John T. Metzger, "Planned Abandonment: The Neighborhood Life-Cycle Theory and National Urban Policy," *Housing Policy Debate* 11, no. 1 (2000): 7–40; Raymond A. Mohl, "The Second Ghetto and the 'Infiltration Theory' in Urban Real Estate, 1940–1960," in *Urban Planning and the African American Community: In the Shadows*, ed. June Manning Thomas and Marsha Ritzdorf (Thousand Oaks, Calif.: Sage, 1997), 58–74; Robert A. Beauregard, "More Than Sector Theory: Homer Hoyt's Contributions to Planning Knowledge," *Journal of Planning History* 6 (August 2007): 248–271; LaDale Winling, "Students and the Second Ghetto: The University of Chicago and Postwar Urban Development" (paper presented at the meeting of the Urban History Society, Houston, 2008). For Hoyt's works, see Homer Hoyt, *One Hundred Years of Land Values in Chicago: The Relationship of the Growth of Chicago to the Rise in Its Land Values, 1830–1933* (Chicago: University of Chicago Press, 1933); Homer Hoyt, *The Structure and Growth of Residential Neighborhoods in American Cities* (Washington, D.C.: Federal Housing Administration, 1939); and Homer Hoyt, *According to Hoyt: Fifty-Three Years of Homer Hoyt: Articles on Law, Real Estate Cycle, Economic Base, Sector Theory, Shopping Centers, Urban Growth, 1916–1969* (Washington, D.C.: Homer Hoyt Institute, 1970).

78. Calvin Bradford, "Financing Home Ownership: The Federal Role in Neighborhood Decline," *Urban Affairs Review* 14 (March 1979): 321. Also see Beauregard, "More Than Sector Theory"; and Hoyt, "Preface," *According to Hoyt*, n.p.

79. Sam Bass Warner Jr., *Streetcar Suburbs: The Progress of Growth in Boston, 1870–1900* (Cambridge, Mass.: Harvard University Press, 1962), 67.

80. Adna Ferrin Weber, *The Growth of Cities in the Nineteenth Century* (New York: Macmillan for Columbia University, 1899).

81. Kevin Lynch, *The Image of the City* (Cambridge, Mass.: MIT Press, 1960); and Alexander von Hoffman, *Local Attachments: The Making of an American Urban Neighborhood, 1850 to 1920* (Baltimore: Johns Hopkins University Press, 1994). Also see Rodgers, *Atlantic Crossings*; Harold L. Platt, "Burnham's Transatlantic Crossings and the Birth of Modern Planning" (paper presented at the Chicago Architecture Foundation / DePaul University Symposium on "Burnham, Chicago, and Beyond: Politics, Planning, and the Progressive Era City," Chicago, June 2009); and Michael Keith, "Street Sensibility? Negotiating the Political by Articulating the Spatial," in *The Urbanization of Injustice*, ed. Andy Merrifield and Erik Swyngedouw (New York: New York University Press, 1997), 137–160.

82. Light, "Nationality and Neighborhood Risk."

83. Hoyt, *One Hundred Years*, 316.

84. Ernest Burgess, "Residential Segregation in American Cities," *Annals of the American Academy of Political and Social Science* 140 (1928): 112; and Paul Boyer, *Urban Masses and Moral Order in America, 1820–1920* (Cambridge, Mass.: Harvard University Press, 1978). Also see Hoyt, *One Hundred Years*, 311.

85. Hoyt, *One Hundred Years*, 314.

86. Hoyt, *Structure and Growth of Residential Neighborhoods*, 121.

87. Ibid., 54.

88. Ibid.

89. Richard Wright, *Native Son* (New York: Harper and Brothers, 1940); and Lorraine Hansberry, *A Raisin in the Sun* (New York: Random House, 1958). Also see St. Clair Drake and Horace E. Cayton, *Black Metropolis: A Study of Negro Life in a Northern City* (New York: Harcourt, 1945); Otis Dudley Duncan and Beverly Duncan, *The Negro Population of Chicago: A Study of Residential Succession* (Chicago: University of Chicago Press, 1957); Harold L. Platt, "Exploding Cities: Housing the Masses in Paris, Chicago, and Mexico City, 1850–2000," *Journal of Urban History* 36 (September 2010): 575–593; and Daniel Bluestone, "Chicago's Mecca Flat Blues," *Journal of the Society of Architectural Historians* 57 (1998): 382–403.

90. Light, "Nationality and Neighborhood Risk," 14.

91. Jackson, *Crabgrass Frontier*; and Homer Hoyt, "General Session: Changing Patterns of Land Values," in Hoyt, *According to Hoyt*, 487.

92. "World Population," available at http://en.wikipedia.org/wiki/World_Population (accessed October 13, 2008); Mike Davis, *Planet of Slums* (New York: Verso, 2006); and Tom Angotti, "Apocalyptic Anti-urbanism: Mike Davis and His Planet of Slums," *International Journal of Urban and Regional Research* 30 (2006): 961–967.

93. Davis, *Planet of Slums*, 1–19; and Angotti, "Apocalyptic Anti-urbanism."

94. Oscar Lewis, *Five Families: Mexican Case Studies in the Culture of Poverty* (New York: Basic Books, 1959). Also see Janice E. Perlman, *The Myth of Marginality: Urban Poverty and Politics in Rio de Janeiro* (Berkeley: University of California Press, 1976), 1–17.

95. Perlman, *Myth of Marginality*; Lúcia Sá, *Life in the Megalopolis: Mexico City and São Paulo* (Milton Park, U.K.: Routledge, 2007); and Teresa Pires do Rio Caldeira, *City of Walls: Crime, Segregation, and Citizenship in São Paulo* (Berkeley: University of California Press, 2000). For the classic depiction of the slums in Latin America, see Lewis, *Five Families*; and Oscar Lewis, *The Children of Sánchez: Autobiography of a Mexican Family* (New York: Random House, 1961).

96. Goetz Frank Ottmann, *Lost for Words? Brazilian Liberationism in the 1990s* (Pittsburgh: University of Pittsburgh Press, 2002); and Loretta Lees, ed., *Emancipatory City? Paradoxes and Possibilities* (London: Sage, 2004).

CHAPTER 3

1. Peter Hall, *Urban and Regional Planning*, 3rd ed. (London: Routledge, 1992), 63.

2. Dennis Hardy, *From Garden Cities to New Towns: Campaigning for Town and Country Planning, 1899–1946* (London: Spon, 1991); Mark Clapson, *Suburban Century: Social Change and Urban Growth in England and the United States* (Oxford: Berg, 2003);

and Rob Bartram and Sarah Shobrook, "Body Beautiful: Medical Aesthetics and the Reconstruction of Urban Britain in the 1940s," *Landscape Research* 26, no. 2 (2001): 119–135.

3. Gordon Emanuel Cherry, *Town Planning in Britain since 1900: The Rise and Fall of the Planning Ideal* (Oxford: Blackwell, 1996), 122. Also see Hall, *Urban and Regional Planning*, 63–89; Alison Ravetz, *Remaking Cities: Contradictions of the Recent Urban Environment* (London: Croom Helm, 1980), 19–42; Lionel Esher, *A Broken Wave: The Rebuilding of England, 1940–1980* (London: Allen Lane, 1981); and Nick Tiratsoo, "The Reconstruction of Blitzed British Cities, 1945–55: Myths and Reality," *Contemporary British History* 14 (Spring 2000): 27–44.

4. Cherry, *Town Planning*, 158.

5. Helen Elizabeth Meller, *Towns, Plans and Society in Modern Britain* (Cambridge: Cambridge University Press, 1997), 82. Also see note 2; and Patrick Dunleavy, *The Politics of Mass Housing in Britain, 1945–1975: A Study of Corporate Power and Professional Influence in the Welfare State* (Oxford: Clarendon, 1981).

6. Clapson, *Suburban Century*.

7. Patrick Abercrombie, Standing Conference on London Regional Planning, and Ministry of Housing and Local Government Great Britain, *Greater London Plan 1944* (London: His Majesty's Stationery Office, 1945).

8. Meller, *Towns, Plans and Society*, 67–84. Also see Carol Corden, *Planned Cities: New Towns in Britain and America* (Beverly Hills, Calif.: Sage, 1977).

9. Cherry, *Town Planning*, 157–168.

10. J. A. Yelling, "Expensive Land, Subsidies, and Mixed Development in London, 1943–56," *Planning Perspectives* 9 (1994): 142, 139–152; and Nicholas Bullock, "Ideas, Priorities and Harsh Realities: Reconstruction and the LCC, 1945–51," *Planning Perspectives* 9 (1994): 87–101.

11. Christopher Booker, *The Neophiliacs: A Study of the Revolution in English Life in the Fifties and Sixties* (London: Collins, 1969).

12. Bronwen Edwards and David Gilbert, "'Piazzadilly!' The Re-imagining of Piccadilly Circus (1952–1972)," *Planning Perspectives* 23 (October 2008): 455–502; and Ravetz, *Remaking Cities*, 98–121.

13. Ravetz, *Remaking Cities*, 122–157; and Dunleavy, *Politics of Mass Housing*.

14. Hall, *Urban and Regional Planning*, 118.

15. Keith Jacobs and Tony Manzi, "Urban Renewal and the Culture of Conservatism: Changing Perceptions of the Tower Block and Implications for Contemporary Renewal Initiatives," *Critical Social Policy* 18, no. 2 (1998): 162; Hall, *Urban and Regional Planning*, 92–114; Cherry, *Town Planning*, 157–168; and Michael James Miller, *The Representation of Place: Urban Planning and Protest in France and Great Britain, 1950–1980* (Aldershot, U.K.: Ashgate, 2003), 64–76.

16. Dunleavy, *Politics of Mass Housing*; and Corden, *Planned Cities*.

17. Dunleavy, *Politics of Mass Housing*, 80–103, which shows that up to 60 percent of the dwellings demolished in the name of urban renewal were classified as in fair or good condition by an independent study of the practices of London's housing authorities.

18. Clare Melhuish, "Towards a Phenomenology of the Concrete Megastructure: Space and Perception at the Brunswick Centre, London," *Journal of Material Culture* 10, no. 1 (2005): 13; and Meller, *Towns, Plans and Society*, 78. Also see Ravetz, *Remaking*

Cities, 165–194; Dunleavy, *Politics of Mass Housing*, 34–52; and Miles Glendinning and Stefan Muthesius, *Tower Block: Modern Public Housing in England, Scotland, Wales, and Northern Ireland* (New Haven, Conn.: Yale University Press for the Paul Mellon Centre for Studies in British Art, 1994).

19. Cherry, *Town Planning*, 130.

20. Peter Geoffrey Hall, *The Containment of Urban England*, vol. 2 (London: Allen and Unwin for PEP Sage Publications, 1973); and Corden, *Planned Cities*, 86–88.

21. Dunleavy, *Politics of Mass Housing in Britain*, 80.

22. Alvin Toffler, *Future Shock* (New York: Random House, 1970).

23. Kristin Ross, *Fast Cars, Clean Bodies: Decolonization and the Reordering of French Culture* (Cambridge, Mass.: MIT Press, 1995), 5. Also see Michael Bess, *The Light-Green Society: Ecology and Technological Modernity in France, 1960–2000* (Chicago: University of Chicago Press, 2003).

24. Hall, *Urban and Regional Planning*, 167–179; Miller, *Representation of Place*; James M. Rubenstein, *The French New Towns* (Baltimore: Johns Hopkins University Press, 1978); and Nicholas Bullock, "Developing Prototypes for France's Mass Housing Programme, 1949–53," *Planning Perspectives* 22 (January 2007): 5–28.

25. Ross, *Fast Cars, Clean Bodies*, 39, 15–70; and Stephen Meyer III, *The Five Dollar Day: Labor Management and Social Control in the Ford Motor Company, 1908–1921* (Albany: State University of New York Press, 1981).

26. Cathie Lloyd and Hazel Waters, "France: One Culture, One People?," *Race and Class* 32, no. 3 (1991): 49–65; and Godula Castles and Stephen Castles, "Immigrant Workers and Class Structure in France," *Race and Class* 12, no. 3 (1971): 303–315.

27. Norma Evenson, *Paris: A Century of Change, 1878–1978* (New Haven, Conn.: Yale University Press, 1977), 232–278; Anthony Sutcliffe, *The Autumn of Central Paris: The Defeat of Town Planning, 1850–1970* (London: Edward Arnold, 1970); Miller, *Representation of Place*, 39–74; and Bullock, "Developing Prototypes."

28. Manuel Castells, *City, Class, and Power* (London: Macmillan, 1978), 24; and Bullock, "Developing Prototypes."

29. Bullock, "Developing Prototypes"; and W. Brian Newsome, "The Rise of the *Grands Ensembles*: Government, Business, and Housing in Postwar France," *The Historian* 66 (Winter 2004): 793–816.

30. Hall, *Urban and Regional Planning*, 90–114, 167; Jean-François Gravier, *Paris et le désert français: Décentralisation, équipement, population* (Paris: Portulan, 1947); and Sara B. Pritchard, "'Paris et le desert francais': Urban and Rural Environments in Post–World War II France," in *The Nature of Cities*, ed. Andrew C. Isenberg (Rochester, N.Y.: University of Rochester Press, 2006), 175–192.

31. Evenson, *Paris*, 238. Also see Daniel Noin and Paul White, *Paris* (Chichester, U.K.: Wiley, 1997), 55–82; Miller, *Representation of Place*, 39–74; and Ross, *Fast Cars, Clean Bodies*, 1–13.

32. Noin and White, *Paris*, 79. Also see David Harvey, *Consciousness and the Urban Experience: Studies in the History and Theory of Capitalist Urbanization* (Baltimore: Johns Hopkins University Press, 1985); Ann-Louise Shapiro, *Housing the Poor of Paris, 1850–1902* (Madison: University of Wisconsin Press, 1985); David H. Pinkney, "Migration to Paris during the Second Empire," *Journal of Modern History* 25 (March 1953): 1–12; Colin Jones, *Paris: Biography of a City* (New York: Viking, 2005),

96–166; and Harold L. Platt, "Exploding Cities: Housing the Masses in Paris, Chicago, and Mexico City, 1750–2000," *Journal of Urban History* 36 (September 2010): 575–593.

33. Evenson, *Paris*, 279.

34. Castells, *City, Class, and Power*; and David Pinder, *Visions of the City: Utopianism, Power, and Politics in Twentieth-Century Urbanism* (New York: Routledge, 2005).

35. Ross, *Fast Cars, Clean Bodies*, chap. 2.

36. Newsome, "Rise of the *Grands Ensembles*."

37. Lloyd and Waters, "France: One Culture, One People?"; and Rubenstein, *French New Towns*.

38. Rubenstein, *French New Towns*.

39. John McCarthy, "The Redevelopment of Rotterdam since 1945," *Planning Perspectives* 14 (1999): 292.

40. Ibid.

41. Ibid., 291–309; Cordula Rooijendijk, "Urban Ideal Images in Post-War Rotterdam," *Planning Perspectives* 20 (April 2005): 177–209; and Dieter Schott, "London and Its 'New Towns' and Randstad Holland: Metropolitan Planning on Both Sides of the Channel after 1945," in *Die Europaische Stadt im 20. Jahrhundert*, ed. Friedrich Lenger and Klaus Tenfelde (Cologne: Böhlau, 2005), 283–306.

42. Percy Edwin Alan Johnson-Marshall, *Rebuilding Cities* (Chicago: Aldine, 1966), 318–348; and "Emptiness," in *Crimson Architectural Historians 1994–2002: Too Blessed to Be Depressed* (Rotterdam: 010, 2002), 33–51.

43. Johnson-Marshall, *Rebuilding Cities*, 323. Also see McCarthy, "Redevelopment"; and Michael Dear, "In the City, Time Becomes Visible: Intentionality and Urbanism in Los Angeles, 1781–1991," in *The City: Los Angeles and Urban Theory at the End of the Twentieth Century*, ed. Allen John Scott and Edward W. Soja (Berkeley: University of California Press, 1996), 76–105.

44. Justin Beaumont and Maarten Loopmans, "Towards Radicalized Communicative Rationality: Resident Involvement and Urban Democracy in Rotterdam and Antwerp," *International Journal of Urban and Regional Research* 32 (March 2008): 101.

45. Ibid., 95–113.

46. Johnson-Marshall, *Rebuilding Cities*, 321.

47. Paul Groenendijk and Piet Vollaard, *Architectuurgids Rotterdam* [Architectural guide to Rotterdam] (Rotterdam: Uitgeverij 010, 2004); and my observation of the mall.

48. McCarthy, "Redevelopment," 295.

49. Groenendijk and Vollaard, *Architectuurgids Rotterdam*.

50. Schott, "London and Its 'New Towns.'"

51. Peter M. Ward, *Mexico City*, 2nd ed. (New York: Wiley, 1998), 1–86. Also see Fernando Romero, "ZMVM: Zona Metropolitana del Valle de México," in *ZMVM: Zona Metropolitana del Valle de México*, ed. Fernando Romero and Laboratorio de la Ciudad de México (San Angel: Laboratorio de la Ciudad de México, 2000).

52. Susan Eckstein, "Poor People versus the State and Capital: Anatomy of a Successful Community Mobilization for Housing in Mexico City," *International Journal of Urban and Regional Research* 14, no. 2 (1990): 281. Also see Elena Poniatowska, *Nothing, Nobody: The Voices of the Mexico City Earthquake*, trans. Aurora Camacho

de Schmidt and Arthur Schmidt (Philadelphia: Temple University Press, 1995), x; Diane E. Davis, "The Social Construction of Mexico City: Political Conflict and Urban Development, 1950–1966," *Journal of Urban History* 24 (1998): 364–415; and Mercedes González de la Rocha, "From the Resources of Poverty to the Poverty of Resources? The Erosion of a Survival Model," *Latin American Perspectives* 28 (July 2001): 72–100.

53. John C. Cross, *Informal Politics: Street Vendors and the State in Mexico City* (Stanford, Calif.: Stanford University Press, 1998), chaps. 1–3; and Diane E. Davis, "Whither the Public Sphere: Local, National, and International Influences on the Planning of Downtown Mexico City, 1910–1950," *Space and Culture* 7 (May 2004), 209, 193–222. Also see Davis, "Social Construction of Mexico City"; and Emily Wakild, "Naturalizing Modernity: Urban Parks, Public Gardens and Drainage Projects in Porfirian Mexico City," *Mexican Studies / Estudios Mexicanos* 23 (Winter 2007): 101–123.

54. Quoted in Mauro F. Guillen, "Modernism without Modernity: The Rise of Modernist Architecture in Mexico, Brazil, and Argentina, 1890–1940," *Latin American Research Review* 39 (2004): 6. Also see Valerie Fraser, *Building the New World: Studies in the Modern Architecture of Latin America, 1930–1960* (London: Verso, 2000), chap. 1; and Alfonso Perez-Mendez, "Advertising Suburbanization in Mexico City" (paper presented at the 13th Biennial Meeting of the International Planning History Society, Chicago, July 2008).

55. Edward R. Burian, "The Architecture of Juan O'Gorman: Dichotomy and Drift," in *Modernity and the Architecture of Mexico*, ed. Edward R. Burian (Austin: University of Texas Press, 1997), 127–150; Celia Ester Arredondo Zambrano, "Modernity in Mexico: The Case of the Ciudad Universitaria," in ibid., 91–106; Keith Eggener, "Postwar Modernism in Mexico: Luis Barragán's Jardines del Pedregal and the International Discourse on Architecture and Place," *Journal of the Society of Architectural Historians* 58 (1999): 122–145; and Guillen, "Modernism without Modernity."

56. Miguel Díaz-Barriga, "Urban Politics in the Valley of Mexico: A Case Study of Urban Movements in the Ajusco Region of Mexico City, 1970–1987" (Ph.D. diss., Stanford University, 1991), 43–89.

57. Eggener, "Postwar Modernism in Mexico"; and Perez-Mendez, "Advertising Suburbanization in Mexico City."

58. Noe Carlos Botello, quoted in Eggener, "Postwar Modernism in Mexico," 129.

59. Perez-Mendez, "Advertising Suburbanization in Mexico City."

60. Louise Noelle Merles, "The Architecture and Urbanism of Mario Pani: Creativity and Compromise," in *Modernity and the Architecture of Mexico*, ed. Edward R. Burian (Austin: University of Texas Press, 1997), 177–190; and Zambrano, "Modernity in Mexico."

61. Burian, "Architecture of Juan O'Gorman," 141. Also see Guillen, "Modernism without Modernity."

62. Alberto Kalach, "Architecture and Place: The Stadium of the University City," in *Modernity and the Architecture of Mexico*, ed. Edward R. Burian (Austin: University of Texas Press, 1997), 110.

63. Carlos Fuentes, *Where the Air Is Clear* (New York: Obolensky, 1960).

64. Quoted in David G. Epstein, *Brasília, Plan and Reality: A Study of Planned and Spontaneous Urban Development* (Berkeley: University of California Press, 1973),

51. Also see James Holston, *The Modernist City: An Anthropological Critique of Brasília* (Chicago: University of Chicago Press, 1989); Thomas Deckker, "Brasília: City versus Landscape," in *The Modern City Revisited*, ed. Thomas Deckker (London: Spon, 2000), 167–194; and Richard J. Williams, "Modernist Civic Space and the Case of Brasília," *Journal of Urban History* 32 (November 2005), 120–137.

65. Mauri Garcia and Timothy Harding, "Interview with Luis Inácio da Silva ('Lula'), President of the Sindicato dos Metalúrgicos de São Bernardo do Campo," *Latin American Perspectives* 6, no. 4 (1979): 90–100; John D. French, *The Brazilian Workers' ABC: Class Conflict and Alliances in Modern São Paulo* (Chapel Hill: University of North Carolina Press, 1992); and Silvio Bava, "Neighborhood Movements and the Trade Unions: The São Bernardo Experience," in *Social Struggles and the City: The Case of São Paulo*, ed. Lúcio Kowarick (New York: Monthly Review Press, 1994), 202–224. In addition to São Bernardo do Campo, the other three municipalities making up the ABCD Region are Santo André, São Caetano do Sul, and Diadema.

66. Pedro R. Jacobi, "The Challenges of Multi-stakeholder Management in the Watersheds of São Paulo," *Environment and Urbanization* 16 (October 2004): 199–211. Also see Raquel Rolnik, "São Paulo in the Early Days of Industrialization: Space and Politics," in *Social Struggles and the City: The Case of São Paulo*, ed. Lúcio Kowarick (New York: Monthly Review Press, 1994), 77–93; George Reid Andrews, *Blacks and Whites in São Paulo, Brazil, 1888–1988* (Madison: University of Wisconsin Press, 1991); Teresa Pires do Rio Caldeira, *City of Walls: Crime, Segregation, and Citizenship in São Paulo* (Berkeley: University of California Press, 2000); and Ney dos Santos Oliveira, "Favelas and Ghettos: Race and Class in Rio de Janeiro and New York City," *Latin American Perspectives* 23 (Autumn 1996): 71–89.

67. Peter B. Evans, *Dependent Development: The Alliance of Multinational, State, and Local Capital in Brazil* (Princeton, N.J.: Princeton University Press, 1979); John D. Wirth, Edson de Oliveira Nunes, and Thomas E. Bogenschild, eds., *State and Society in Brazil: Continuity and Change* (Boulder, Colo.: Westview, 1987); Roberto P. Guimaraes, *The Ecopolitics of Development in the Third World: Politics and Environment in Brazil* (Boulder, Colo.: Lynne Rienner, 1991); and Robert M. Levine, *The History of Brazil* (Westport, Conn.: Greenwood, 1999).

68. Lúcio Kowarick and Nabil G. Bonduki, "Urban Space and Political Space: From Populism to Redemocratization," in *Social Struggles and the City: The Case of São Paulo*, ed. Lúcio Kowarick (New York: Monthly Review Press, 1994), 127, 121–147; Suzana Pasternak, "Squatter Settlements as a Kind of Perverse Outcome: History of Popular Housing Policies in São Paulo," in *Proceedings of the 13th Biennial Meeting of the International Planning History Society* (Chicago: International Planning History Society, 2008), 1182–1201; and Richard Batley, "Urban Renewal and Expulsion in São Paulo," in *Urbanization in Contemporary Latin America: Critical Approaches to the Analysis of Urban Issues*, ed. Alan Gilbert, Jorge Enrique Hardoy, and Ronaldo Ramírez (Chichester, U.K.: Wiley, 1982), 231–262.

69. Maria Cristina da Silva Leme, "The Role of Foreign Experts—Robert Moses and the International Basic Economic Corporation—in Transforming the Latin American Modern City [São Paulo]," in *Proceedings of the 13th Biennial Meeting of the International Planning History Society* (Chicago: International Planning History Society, 2008), 389.

70. Ibid., 378–393; and Robert A. Caro, *The Power Broker: Robert Moses and the Fall of New York* (New York: Knopf, 1974).

71. Kowarick and Bonduki, "Urban Space and Political Space"; Leme, "Role of Foreign Experts"; and Lúcio Kowarick and Clara Ant, "One Hundred Years of Overcrowding: Slum Tenements in the City," in *Social Struggles and the City: The Case of São Paulo*, ed. Lúcio Kowarick (New York: Monthly Review Press, 1994), 69–71.

72. *Correio Paulistano* (Mexico City), August 11, 1946, quoted in Kowarick and Bonduki, "Urban Space and Political Space," 124.

73. Quoted in Maureen Dowd, "Blue Eyed Greed?," *New York Times*, March 29, 2009.

74. Caldeira, *City of Walls*, 105–213.

75. Kowarick and Bonduki, "Urban Space and Political Space, 127.

76. Ibid., 138; and see "Security in Brazil: Bullet-proof in Alphaville," *The Economist*, August 16, 2001.

77. Kowarick and Bonduki, "Urban Space and Political Space."

78. Ibid.; Vera da Silva Telles, "The 1970s: Political Experiences, Practices, and Spaces," in *Social Struggles and the City The Case of São Paulo*, ed. Lúcio Kowarick (New York: Monthly Review Press, 1994), 174–201; and Goetz Frank Ottmann, *Lost for Words? Brazilian Liberationism in the 1990s* (Pittsburgh: University of Pittsburgh Press, 2002).

79. Lúcia Sá, *Life in the Megalopolis: Mexico City and São Paulo* (Milton Park, U.K.: Routledge, 2007); George Yudice, "The Funkification of Rio," in *Microphone Fiends: Youth Music and Youth Culture*, ed. Andrew Ross and Tricia Rose (New York: Routledge, 1994), 193–220; and Norma Evenson, *Chandigarh* (Berkeley: University of California Press, 1966).

80. Quoted in Deckker, "Brasília," 174.

81. Epstein, *Brasília, Plan and Reality*, 26–60.

82. James C. Scott, *Seeing like a State: How Certain Schemes to Improve the Human Condition Have Failed* (New Haven, Conn.: Yale University Press, 1998).

CHAPTER 4

1. Robert M. Fogelson, "White on Black: A Critique of the McCone Commission Report on the Los Angeles Riots," *Political Science Quarterly* 82 (September 1967): 337–367; Lynell George, *No Crystal Stair: African-Americans in the City of Angels* (New York: Verso, 1992); Gerald Horne, *Fire This Time: The Watts Uprising and the 1960s* (Charlottesville: University of Virginia Press, 1995); Mike Davis, *The City of Quartz* (New York: Vintage, 1990); Raphael Sonenshein, *Politics in Black and White: Race and Power in Los Angeles* (Princeton, N.J.: Princeton University Press, 1993); Josh Sides, *L.A. City Limits: African American Los Angeles from the Great Depression to the Present* (Berkeley: University of California Press, 2003); and Janet L. Abu-Lughod, *Race, Space, and Riots in Chicago, New York, and Los Angeles* (Oxford: Oxford University Press, 2007). Also see Eric Avila, *Popular Culture in the Age of White Flight: Fear and Fantasy in Suburban Los Angeles* (Berkeley: University of California Press, 2004); George J. Sanchez, "'What's Good for Boyle Heights Is Good for the Jews': Creating Multiracialism on the Eastside during the 1950s," *American Quarterly* 56 (2004): 633–661; and note 3.

2. Kristin Ross, *May '68 and Its Afterlives* (Chicago: University of Chicago Press, 2002); Martin Klimke and Joachim Scharloth, eds., *1968 in Europe: A History of Protest and Activism, 1956–1977* (New York: Palgrave Macmillan, 2008); and Alison Ravetz, *Remaking Cities: Contradictions of the Recent Urban Environment* (London: Croom Helm, 1980), chaps. 5–6. Also see Langdon Winner, *Autonomous Technology: Technics-out-of-Control as a Theme in Political Thought* (Cambridge, Mass.: MIT Press, 1977); Manuel Castells, *The City and the Grassroots: A Cross-Cultural Theory of Urban Social Movements* (Berkeley: University of California Press, 1983); W. Brian Newsome, "The Rise of the *Grands Ensembles*: Government, Business, and Housing in Postwar France," *The Historian* 66 (Winter 2004): 793–816; Larry Busbea, *Topologies: The Urban Utopia in France, 1960–1970* (Cambridge, Mass.: MIT Press, 2007); and note 4.

3. For the United States, see Malcolm X, with Alex Haley, *The Autobiography of Malcolm X* (New York: Grove, 1965); Kenneth Bancroft Clark, *Dark Ghetto: Dilemmas of Social Power* (New York: Harper and Row, 1965); Stokely Carmichael and Charles V. Hamilton, *Black Power: The Politics of Liberation in America* (New York: Random House, 1967); Stokely Carmichael, *Stokely Speaks: Black Power Back to Pan-Africanism* (New York: Random House, 1971); Eldridge Cleaver, "Domestic Law and International Order," in *Policing America*, ed. Anthony M. Platt and Lynn Cooper (Englewood Cliffs, N.J.: Prentice Hall, 1974), 24–30; Michael T. Klare, "Policing the Empire," in ibid., 56–65; Manning Marable, *Race, Reform and Rebellion: The Second Reconstruction in Black America, 1945–1982* (Jackson: University Press of Mississippi, 1984); Francis Njubi Nesbitt, *Race for Sanctions: African Americans against Apartheid, 1946–1994* (Bloomington: Indiana University Press, 2004); Cedric Johnson, *Revolutionaries to Race Leaders: Black Power and the Making of African American Politics* (Minneapolis: University of Minnesota Press, 2007); and Devin Fergus, *Liberalism, Black Power, and the Making of American Politics, 1965–1980* (Athens: University of Georgia Press, 2009). For Latin America and Europe, see George Reid Andrews, *Blacks and Whites in São Paulo, Brazil, 1888–1988* (Madison: University of Wisconsin Press, 1991); Kristin Ross, *Fast Cars, Clean Bodies: Decolonization and the Reordering of French Culture* (Cambridge, Mass.: MIT Press, 1995); Godula Castles and Stephen Castles, "Immigrant Workers and Class Structure in France," *Race and Class* 12, no. 3 (1971): 303–315; Cathie Lloyd and Hazel Waters, "France: One Culture, One People?," *Race and Class* 32, no. 3 (1991): 49–65; and Cathy Lisa Schneider, "Police Power and Race Riots in Paris," *Politics and Society* 35 (December 2007): 523–549.

4. Jeffrey L. Gould, "Solidarity under Siege: The Latin American Left, 1968," *American Historical Review* 114 (April 2009): 348–375; Arturo Escobar and Sonia E. Alvarez, eds., *The Making of Social Movements in Latin America: Identity, Strategy, and Democracy* (Boulder, Colo.: Westview, 1992); Thomas Angotti, "Latin American Urbanization and Planning: Inequality and Unsustainability in North and South," *Latin American Perspectives* 23 (1996): 12–34; and Susan Eckstein and Manuel A. Garretón Merino, *Power and Popular Protest: Latin American Social Movements* (Berkeley: University of California Press, 2001). Also see Eric Zolov, "Showcasing the 'Land of Tomorrow': Mexico and the 1968 Olympics," *The Americas* 61 (October 2004): 159–188; Elena Poniatowska, *Massacre in Mexico* (New York: Viking, 1975); Juan Manuel Ramírez Saiz, *El Movimiento Urbano Popular en México* (Mexico City: Siglo Veintiuno, 1986); Joe Foweraker and Ann L. Craig, eds., *Popular Movements and*

Political Change in Mexico (Boulder, Colo.: Lynne Rienner, 1990); Elaine Carey, *Plaza of Sacrifices: Gender, Power, and Terror in 1968 Mexico* (Albuquerque: University of New Mexico Press, 2005); Michael Soldatenko, "México '68: Power to the Imagination!," *Latin American Perspectives* 32 (July 2005): 111–132; John D. Wirth, Edson de Oliveira Nunes, and Thomas E. Bogenschild, eds., *State and Society in Brazil: Continuity and Change* (Boulder, Colo.: Westview, 1987); Lúcio Kowarick, ed., *Social Struggles and the City: The Case of São Paulo* (New York: Monthly Review Press, 1994); Barbara Weinstein, *For Social Peace in Brazil: Industrialists and the Remaking of the Working Class in São Paulo, 1920–1964* (Chapel Hill: University of North Carolina Press, 1996); and João Roberto Martins Filho and John Collins, "Students and Politics in Brazil, 1962–1992," *Latin American Perspectives* 25 (January 1998): 156–169.

5. Kristin Ross, "Establishing Consensus: May '68 in France as Seen from the 1980s," *Critical Inquiry* 28 (Spring 2002): 650–676; Philipp Gassert and Martin Klimke, "Introduction," in *1968—Memories and Legacies of a Global Revolt, Bulletin of the German Historical Institute*, suppl. 9, ed. Philipp Gassert and Martin Klimke (Washington, D.C.: German Historical Institute, 2009), 5–24; Robert M. Collins, "The Economic Crisis of 1968 and the Waning of the 'American Century,'" *American Historical Review* 101 (April 1996): 396–422; Jeremi Suri, "The Rise and Fall of an International Counterculture, 1960–1975," *American Historical Review* 114 (February 2009): 45–68; Michael W. Flamm, *Law and Order: Street Crime, Civil Unrest, and the Crisis of Liberalism in the 1960s* (New York: Columbia University Press, 2005); Karen Ferguson, "Organizing the Ghetto: The Ford Foundation, CORE, and White Power in the Black Power Era, 1967–69," *Journal of Urban History* 24 (November 2007): 67–100; Theodore Roszak, *The Making of a Counter Culture: Reflections on the Technocratic Society and Its Youthful Opposition* (Garden City, N.Y.: Doubleday, 1969); David R. Farber, *Chicago '68* (Chicago: University of Chicago Press, 1988); Klimke and Scharloth, *1968 in Europe*; Gould, "Solidarity under Siege"; and Soldatenko, "México '68."

6. Devra Davis, *When Smoke Ran like Water* (New York: Basic Books, 2002). Also see Geneviève Massard-Guilbaud, Harold L. Platt, and Dieter Schott, eds., *Cities and Catastrophes: Coping with Emergency in European History—Villes et catastrophes: Réactions face à l'urgence dans l'histoire européenne* (New York: Lang, 2002); Peter Thorsheim, *Inventing Pollution: Coal, Smoke, and Culture in Britain since 1800* (Athens: Ohio University Press, 2006); and B. W. Clapp, *An Environmental History of Britain since the Industrial Revolution* (London: Longman, 1994).

7. John Robert McNeill, *Something New under the Sun: An Environmental History of the Twentieth-Century World* (New York: Norton, 2000); and Peter A. Coates, *Nature: Western Attitudes since Ancient Times* (Berkeley: University of California Press, 1998). Also see Robert Gottlieb, *Forcing the Spring: The Transformation of the American Environmental Movement* (Washington, D.C.: Island, 1993); Raymond H. Dominick, *The Environmental Movement in Germany: Prophets and Pioneers, 1871– 1971* (Bloomington: Indiana University Press, 1992); Elim Papadakis, *The Green Movement in West Germany* (London: Croom Helm, 1984); and Michael Bess, *The Light-Green Society: Ecology and Technological Modernity in France, 1960–2000* (Chicago: University of Chicago Press, 2003).

8. My interpretation of planning history draws heavily on Nigel Taylor, *Urban Planning Theory since 1945* (London: Sage, 1998). Also see Henri Lefebvre, *The Urban*

Revolution (Minneapolis: University of Minnesota Press, 2003); Henri Lefebvre, *The Production of Space* (Oxford: Blackwell, 1991); Erik Swyngedouw, "The City as Hybrid: On Nature, Society and Cyborg Urbanization," *Capitalism, Nature, Socialism* 7 (June 1996): 65–80; Matthew Gandy, "Cyborg Urbanization: Complexity and Monstrosity in the Contemporary City," *International Journal of Urban and Regional Research* 29 (2005): 26–49; and Maria Kaika, *City of Flows: Modernity, Nature, and the City* (New York: Routledge, 2005).

9. Ross, *May '68*.

10. Ross, "Establishing Consensus," 650; and Christopher Lasch, *The Culture of Narcissism: American Life in an Age of Diminishing Expectations* (New York: Norton, 1978).

11. Lessie Jo Frazier and Deborah Cohen, "Defining the Space of Mexico '68: Heroic Masculinity in the Prison and 'Women' in the Streets," *Hispanic American Historical Review* 83 (November 2003): 617–650. Also see Jeffrey L. Gould, "Solidarity under Siege," *American Historical Review* 114 (April 2009): 348–375; Sara M. Evans, "Sons, Daughters, and Patriarchy: Gender and the 1968 Generation," *American Historical Review* 114 (April 2009): 331–347; and Eric Zolov, *Refried Elvis: The Rise of the Mexican Counterculture* (Berkeley: University of California Press, 1999).

12. One often-repeated example can be called the one-dimensional man myth. Many textbooks make the author of the book with this title, Herbert Marcuse, the political guru who inspired the postwar generation of protestors. In fact, most activists remember learning about his subversive critique of the modernization race long after 1968, when they were informed that they should have read it before they started marching. Herbert Marcuse, *One-Dimensional Man: Studies in the Ideology of Advanced Industrial Society* (Boston: Beacon, 1964).

13. Jane Jacobs, *The Death and Life of Great American Cities* (New York: Random House, 1961).

14. Ibid., 13.

15. Ibid., 4. Also see Jane Jacobs, "Downtown Is for People," in *The Exploding Metropolis*, ed. William Hollingsworth Whyte Jr. (Berkeley: University of California Press, 1993), 157–184. "Indeed," Nigel Taylor states, "her book remains arguably the most important planning theory text published since the end of the Second World War." Taylor, *Urban Planning Theory*, 46. Also see Charles E. Lindblom, "The Science of 'Muddling Through,'" *Public Administration Review* 19 (Spring 1959): 79–88.

16. Patrick Geddes, *Cities in Evolution: An Introduction to the Town Planning Movement and to the Study of Civics* (London: Williams and Norgate, 1915).

17. Homer Hoyt, *The Structure and Growth of Residential Neighborhoods in American Cities* (Washington, D.C.: Federal Housing Administration, 1939), 81; and Homer Hoyt, "Savings and Homeownership," *First Federal Savings and Loan of Chicago Newsletter*, March 1951.

18. Homer Hoyt, *One Hundred Years of Land Values in Chicago: The Relationship of the Growth of Chicago to the Rise in Its Land Values, 1830–1933* (Chicago: University of Chicago Press, 1933), 312.

19. Jacobs, *Death and Life of Great American Cities*, 5. Also see Geddes, *Cities in Evolution*; Robert Ezra Park, Ernest Watson Burgess, Roderick Duncan McKenzie, and Louis Wirth, *The City* (Chicago: University of Chicago Press, 1925); Donald Worster,

Nature's Economy: A History of Ecological Ideas, 2nd ed. (Cambridge: Cambridge University Press, 1994); Sharon E. Kingsland, *The Evolution of American Ecology, 1890–2000* (Baltimore: Johns Hopkins University Press, 2005); Jennifer S. Light, "The City as National Resource: New Deal Conservation and the Quest for Urban Improvement," *Journal of Urban History* 35 (May 2009): 531–560; and Jennifer S. Light, *The Nature of Cities: Ecological Visions and the American Urban Professions, 1920–1960* (Baltimore: Johns Hopkins University Press, 2009).

20. Jacobs, *Death and Life of Great American Cities*, 6.

21. Ibid., 8.

22. Ibid., 277.

23. Ibid., 271; and Teddy Cruz, *Border Postcards: Chronicles from the Edge*, James Stirling Memorial Lectures on the City, Canadian Centre for Architecture, Montreal, October 28, 2004, audio file, 48:28, available at http://www.cca.qc.ca/en/education -events/259-teddy-cruz-border-postcards-chronicles-from-the-edge. Also see Mike Davis, *Planet of Slums* (New York: Verso, 2006); Nicholas Bullock, "Developing Prototypes for France's Mass Housing Programme, 1949–53," *Planning Perspectives* 22 (January 2007): 5–28; Lloyd and Waters, "France"; and Castles and Castles, "Immigrant Workers and Class Structure in France."

24. Jacobs, *Death and Life of Great American Cities*, 271.

25. Ibid., 310.

26. Ibid., 301.

27. Ibid., 283.

28. Ibid., 21–90. Also see Light, "City as National Resource."

29. Rachel Carson, *Silent Spring* (Boston: Houghton Mifflin, 1962).

30. Ibid. Also see Linda J. Lear, *Rachel Carson: Witness for Nature* (New York: Holt, 1997); and Samuel P. Hays, *Beauty, Health, and Permanence: Environmental Politics in the United States, 1955–1985* (New York: Cambridge University Press, 1987).

31. Gottlieb, *Forcing the Spring*; Adam Rome, *The Bulldozer in the Countryside: Suburban Sprawl and the Rise of American Environmentalism* (New York: Cambridge University Press, 2001); Stephan J. Schmidt, "The Evolving Relationships between Open Space Preservation and Local Planning Practice," *Journal of Planning History* 7 (May 2008): 91–112; Andrew Hurley, *Environmental Inequalities: Class, Race, and Industrial Pollution in Gary, Indiana, 1945–1980* (Chapel Hill: University of North Carolina Press, 1995); Becky M. Nicolaides, *My Blue Heaven: Life and Politics in the Working-Class Suburbs of Los Angeles, 1920–1965* (Chicago: University of Chicago Press, 2002); Lisa McGirr, *Suburban Warriors: The Origins of the New American Right* (Princeton, N.J.: Princeton University Press, 2001); Michelle Nickerson, "Domestic Threats: Women, Gender, and Conservatism in Cold War Los Angeles, 1945–1966" (Ph.D. diss., Yale University, 2003); Elizabeth D. Blum, *Love Canal Revisited: Race, Class, and Gender in Environmental Activism* (Lawrence: University Press of Kansas, 2008); and Steven Conn, "Back to the Garden: Communes, the Environment, and Anti-urban Pastoralism at the End of the Sixties," *Journal of Urban History* 36, no. 6 (2010): 831–848.

32. Lewis Heber [Murray Bookchin], *Our Synthetic Environment* (New York: Knopf, 1962). Bookchin wrote under a pseudonym because he was blacklisted as a communist.

33. Ibid., 69.

34. Maurice Robert Stein, *The Eclipse of Community: An Interpretation of American Studies* (Princeton, N.J.: Princeton University Press, 1960); and David Riesman, *The Lonely Crowd: A Study of the Changing American Character* (New Haven, Conn.: Yale University Press, 1950).

35. Jacques Ellul, *The Technological Society* (New York: Knopf, 1964).

36. Ibid., 6. Also see C. Wright Mills, *White Collar: The American Middle Classes* (New York: Oxford University Press, 1951); Roszak, *Making of a Counter Culture*; Harry Braverman, *Labor and Monopoly Capital: The Degradation of Work in the Twentieth Century* (New York: Monthly Review Press, 1975); and Olivier Zunz, *Making America Corporate, 1870–1920* (Chicago: University of Chicago Press, 1990).

37. Marshall McLuhan, *Understanding Media: The Extensions of Man* (New York: McGraw-Hill, 1964), vii. Also see Marshall McLuhan and Quentin Fiore, *War and Peace in the Global Village: An Inventory of Some of the Current Spastic Situations That Could Be Eliminated by More Feedforward* (New York: McGraw-Hill, 1968); and William Kuhns, *The Post-industrial Prophets: Interpretations of Technology* (New York: Harper and Row, 1971).

38. Marcuse, *One-Dimensional Man*, 12 (emphasis in original).

39. Ibid., 12, 10.

40. Fogelson, "White on Black"; and Anthony M. Platt, ed., *The Politics of Riot Commissions, 1917–1970: A Collection of Official Reports and Critical Essays* (New York: Macmillan, 1971).

41. Oscar Lewis, *Five Families: Mexican Case Studies in the Culture of Poverty* (New York: Basic Books, 1959).

42. Fogelson, "White on Black," 342; and Platt, *Politics of Riot Commissions*.

43. Edward J. Escobar, "Zoot-Suiters and Cops: Chicano Youth and the Los Angeles Police Department during World War II," in *The War in American Culture: Society and Consciousness during World War II*, ed. Lewis A. Erenberg and Susan E. Hirsch (Chicago: University of Chicago Press, 1996), 284–312.

44. See note 1.

45. Nigel Taylor, "Anglo-American Town Planning Theory since 1945: Three Significant Developments but No Paradigm Shifts," *Planning Perspectives* 14, no. 4 (1999): 334.

46. Ravetz, *Remaking Cities*, 266. Also see Gordon Emanuel Cherry, *Town Planning in Britain since 1900: The Rise and Fall of the Planning Ideal* (Oxford: Blackwell, 1996); Mel Scott, *American City Planning since 1890* (Berkeley: University of California Press, 1969); and Anthony Sutcliffe, *The Autumn of Central Paris: The Defeat of Town Planning, 1850–1970* (London: Edward Arnold, 1970).

47. Quoted in Gwen Bell and Jaqueline Tywhitt, eds., *Human Identity in the Urban Environment* (New York: Penguin, 1972), 421.

48. Ibid., 428.

49. Quoted in H.W.E. Davies, "Brian McLoughlin and the Systems Approach to Planning," *European Planning Studies* 5 (December 1997): 722. Also see J. Brian McLoughlin, *Urban and Regional Planning: A Systems Approach* (New York: Praeger, 1969); Taylor, "Anglo-American Town Planning Theory"; Patsy Healey, "Brian McLoughlin [Obituary]," *Town Planning Review* 65, no. 4 (October 1994): 341–347; and

George F. Chadwick, *A Systems View of Planning: Towards a Theory of the Urban and Regional Planning Process* (Oxford: Pergamon, 1971).

50. Quoted in Davies, "Brian McLoughlin," 725.

51. Yona Friedman, *L'architecture mobile* (Paris: printed by author, 1958). Also see Busbea, *Topologies*.

52. Andreas Faludi, *A Reader in Planning Theory* (Oxford: Pergamon, 1973); and Andreas Faludi, *Planning Theory* (Oxford: Pergamon, 1973).

53. Busbea, *Topologies*, 6.

54. Robert Venturi, *Complexity and Contradiction in Architecture* (New York: Museum of Modern Art, 1966).

55. Vincent Scully, "Introduction," in ibid., 11–16.

56. Ibid., 15.

57. Ibid., 11.

58. Robert Goodman, *After the Planners* (New York: Simon and Schuster, 1972).

59. Taylor, "Anglo-American Town Planning Theory."

60. Goodman, *After the Planners*, 12.

61. Ibid., 114, also see 92–170.

62. Ibid., 187.

63. Ibid., 109.

64. Davies, "Brian McLoughlin," 28; and see Healey, "Brian McLoughlin."

65. Healey, "Brian McLoughlin," 342.

66. Quoted in Davies, "Brian McLoughlin," 29. Also see Richard E. Klosterman, "Evolving Views of Computer-Aided Planning," *Journal of Planning Education and Research* 6 (1992): 249–260; John Friedmann, "Teaching Planning History," *Journal of Planning Education and Research* 14 (1995): 156–162; and Howell S. Baum, "Why the Rational Paradigm Persists: Tales from the Field," *Journal of Planning Education and Research* 15 (1996): 127–135.

67. Philip Cooke and Gareth Rees, "Faludi's 'Sociology in Planning Education': A Critical Comment," *Urban Studies* 14 (1977): 215–218; and Andreas Faludi, "'Sociology in Planning Education': A Rejoinder," *Urban Studies* 14 (1977): 223–224. Also see David Frost, "Faludi's 'Sociology in Planning Education': A Comment," *Urban Studies* 14 (1977): 219–222; and Linda C. Dalton, "Why the Rational Paradigm Persists: The Resistance of Professional Education and Practice to Alternative Forms of Planning," *Journal of Planning Education and Research* 5 (1986): 147–153.

68. James C. Scott, "Authoritarian High Modernism," in *Readings in Planning Theory*, ed. Campbell Scott and Susan S. Fainstein, 2nd ed. (Malden, Mass.: Blackwell, 2003), 125–141; Leonie Sandercock, *Cosmopolis II: Mongrel Cities of the 21st Century* (New York: Continuum, 2003); Taylor, *Urban Planning Theory*, 60; Cherry, *Town Planning in Britain*, 145; Robert Bailey, *Radicals in Urban Politics: The Alinsky Approach* (Chicago: University of Chicago Press, 1974); Robert A. Slayton, *Back of the Yards: The Making of a Local Democracy* (Chicago: University of Chicago Press, 1986); and Sanford D. Horwitt, *Let Them Call Me Rebel: Saul Alinsky—His Life and Legacy* (New York: Knopf, 1989).

69. Cherry, *Town Planning in Britain*, 133–168.

70. Ibid.

71. Ibid.

72. Ravetz, *Remaking Cities*, 274.

73. Faludi, "Sociology in Planning Education," 223.

74. Stephen Edelston Toulmin, *Cosmopolis: The Hidden Agenda of Modernity* (New York: Free Press, 1990), ix. Also see Thomas L. Harper and Stanley M. Stein, "Out of the Postmodern Abyss: Reserving the Rationale for Liberal Planning," *Journal of Planning Education and Research* 14 (1995): 233–244.

75. Quoted in Mike Marqusee, "Sport and Stereotype: From Role Model to Muhammad Ali," *Race and Class* 36, no. 4 (1995): 21.

76. Ibid., 1–29; and Tommie Smith and David Steele, *Silent Gesture: Autobiography of Tommie Smith* (Philadelphia: Temple University Press, 2007). Also see Douglas Hartmann, *Race, Culture, and the Revolt of the Black Athlete: The 1968 Olympic Protests and Their Aftermath* (Chicago: University of Chicago Press, 2003); Zolov, "Showcasing the 'Land of Tomorrow'"; Winston A. Van Horne, "The Concept of Black Power: Its Continuing Relevance," *Journal of Black Studies* 37 (January 2007): 365–389; and Richard Hoffer, *Something in the Air: American Passion and Defiance in the 1968 Mexico City Olympics* (New York: Knopf, 2009).

77. Sandercock, *Cosmopolis II*, 76. Also see Gregory McLauchlan and Gregory Hooks, "Last of the Dinosaurs? Big Weapons, Big Science, and the American State from Hiroshima to the End of the Cold War," *Sociological Quarterly* 36 (Autumn 1995): 749–776; Andrew D. Grossman, "The Early Cold War and American Political Development: Reflections on Recent Research," *International Journal of Politics, Culture, and Society* 15 (Spring 2002): 471–483; and Wendy Wall, *Inventing the "American Way": The Politics of Consensus from the New Deal to the Civil Rights Movement* (Oxford: Oxford University Press, 2008).

78. Soldatenko, "México '68," 113. Also see ibid., 111–132; Leonie Sandercock, "Introduction: Framing Insurgent Historiographies for Planning," in *Making the Invisible World Visible: A Multicultural Planning History*, ed. Leonie Sandercock (Berkeley: University of California Press, 1998), 1–36; and James Holston, "Spaces of Insurgent Citizenship," in ibid., 37–56.

79. Peniel E. Joseph, "The Black Power Movement: A State of the Field," *Journal of American History* 96 (December 2009): 752.

80. Ibid., 751–776. Also see Peniel E. Joseph, *Waiting 'Til the Midnight Hour: A Narrative History of Black Power in America* (New York: Henry Holt, 2006); and Ferguson, "Organizing the Ghetto."

81. See note 76; and Lewis A. Erenberg, *The Greatest Fight of Our Generation: Louis vs. Schmeling* (New York: Oxford University Press, 2006).

82. Rubem A. Alves, *A Theology of Human Hope* (Washington, D.C.: Corpus, 1969).

83. Gustavo Gutiérrez, *A Theology of Liberation: History, Politics, and Salvation* (Maryknoll, N.Y.: Orbis, 1973); Gould, "Solidarity under Siege"; Manzar Foroohar, "Liberation Theology: The Response of Latin American Catholics to Socioeconomic Problems," *Latin American Perspectives* 13 (Summer 1986): 37–58; Marvin G. Dunn, "Liberation Theology and Class Analysis: A Reassessment of Religion and Class," *Latin American Perspectives* 13 (Summer 1986): 59–60; Edward J. Martin, "Liberation Theology, Sustainable Development, and Postmodern Public Administration," *Latin*

American Perspectives 30 (July 2003): 69–91; and Goetz Frank Ottmann, *Lost for Words? Brazilian Liberationism in the 1990s* (Pittsburgh: University of Pittsburgh Press, 2002).

84. Constantinos A. Doxiadis, *Between Dystopia and Utopia* (Hartford, Conn.: Trinity College Press, 1966); and Constantinos A. Doxiadis, *Ekistics: An Introduction to the Science of Human Settlements* (New York: Oxford University Press, 1968). For extensive historical and archival information, see the websites of the World Society for Ekistics at http://www.ekistics.org; and for the man, http://www.doxiadis.org (accessed February 16, 2011).

85. See note 84.

86. Doxiadis, *Between Dystopia and Utopia*, 1.

87. Ibid., 11. Also see Doxiadis, *Ekistics*.

88. Doxiadis, *Between Dystopia and Utopia*, 59.

89. Ibid., 75.

90. Donella H. Meadows, Dennis L. Meadows, Jørgen Randers, and William W. Behrens III, *The Limits to Growth: A Report for the Club of Rome's Project on the Predicament of Mankind* (New York: Universe, 1972), available at http://www .donellameadows.org/wp-content/userfiles/Limits-to-Growth-digital-scan-version .pdf (accessed March 15, 2015); and Donella Meadows, Jørgen Randers, and Dennis L. Meadows, *The Limits to Growth: The 30-Year Update* (White River Junction, Vt.: Chelsea Green, 2004). Also see Francis Sandbach, "The Rise and Fall of the Limits of Growth Debate," *Social Studies of Science* 8 (1978): 495–520; and H.S.D. Cole, Christopher Freeman, Marie Jahoda, and K.L.R. Pavitt, eds., *Models of Doom: A Critique of* The Limits to Growth (New York: Universe, 1973).

91. Italo Calvino, *Invisible Cities* (New York: Harcourt Brace Jovanovich, 1974).

CHAPTER 5

1. Leonie Sandercock, *Cosmopolis II: Mongrel Cities of the 21st Century* (New York: Continuum, 2003), 38.

2. Jeremi Suri, "The Rise and Fall of an International Counterculture, 1960–1975," *American Historical Review* 114 (February 2009): 48, 45–68; Sara M. Evans, "Sons, Daughters, and Patriarchy: Gender and the 1968 Generation," *American Historical Review* 114 (April 2009): 331–347; Sandercock, *Cosmopolis II*, 47, chap. 2; and Michele Nickerson, *Mothers of Conservatism: Women and the Postwar Right* (Princeton, N.J.: Princeton University Press, 2012). Also see James Holston, "Spaces of Insurgent Citizenship," in *Making the Invisible World Visible: A Multicultural Planning History*, ed. Leonie Sandercock (Berkeley: University of California Press, 1998), 37–56; Janet L. Abu-Lughod, *Race, Space, and Riots in Chicago, New York, and Los Angeles* (Oxford: Oxford University Press, 2007); and George Lipsitz, "The Possessive Investment in Whiteness: Racialized Social Democracy and the 'White' Problem," *American Quarterly* 47 (September 1995): 369–387.

3. Mike Davis, *The City of Quartz* (New York: Vintage, 1990), 160.

4. Becky M. Nicolaides, *My Blue Heaven: Life and Politics in the Working-Class Suburbs of Los Angeles, 1920–1965* (Chicago: University of Chicago Press, 2002).

5. See Lisa McGirr, *Suburban Warriors: The Origins of the New American Right* (Princeton, N.J.: Princeton University Press, 2001); Raphael Sonenshein, *Politics in*

Black and White: Race and Power in Los Angeles (Princeton, N.J.: Princeton University Press, 1993); Nickerson, *Mothers of Conservatism*; Josh Sides, *L.A. City Limits: African-American Los Angeles from the Great Depression to the Present* (Berkeley: University of California Press, 2003), chaps. 1–3; Edward W. Soja, "Los Angeles, 1965–1992: From Crisis-Generated Restructuring to Restructuring-Generated Crisis," in *The City: Los Angeles and Urban Theory at the End of the Twentieth Century*, ed. Allen John Scott and Edward W. Soja (Berkeley: University of California Press, 1996), 426–462; and Allen J. Scott, "High-Technology Industrial Development in the San Fernando Valley and Ventura County: Observations on Economic Growth and the Evolution of Urban Form," in ibid., 276–311.

6. Gerald Horne, *Fire This Time: The Watts Uprising and the 1960s* (Charlottesville: University of Virginia Press, 1995), 249.

7. Nicolaides, *My Blue Heaven*, 27.

8. Ibid. Also see Sides, *L.A. City Limits*, chap. 6. For an anthology of eyewitness accounts of life in Watts leading up to the revolt of 1965, see Robert E. Conot, *Rivers of Blood, Years of Darkness* (Toronto: Bantam, 1967).

9. Nicolaides, *My Blue Heaven*, 276.

10. Ibid., 275; see ibid., chap. 7; and Lipsitz, "Possessive Investment in Whiteness."

11. Michael N. Danielson, *The Politics of Exclusion* (New York: Columbia University Press, 1976); William Sharpe and Leonard Wallock, "Bold New City or Built-up 'Burb? Redefining Contemporary Suburbia," *American Quarterly* 46 (March 1994): 1–30; and Jack Schneider, "Escape from Los Angeles: White Flight from Los Angeles and Its Schools, 1960–1980," *Journal of Urban History* 34 (September 2008): 997, 995–1012. Also see Setha M. Low, *Behind the Gates: Life, Security, and the Pursuit of Happiness in Fortress America* (New York: Routledge, 2003); Kevin Michael Kruse, *White Flight and the Making of Modern Conservatism* (Princeton, N.J.: Princeton University Press, 2005); and Edward James Blakely and Mary Gail Snyder, *Fortress America: Gated Communities in the United States* (Washington, D.C.: Brookings Institution Press, 1997).

12. Schneider, "Escape from Los Angeles."

13. Sonenshein, *Politics in Black and White*, 67.

14. Horne, *Fire This Time*, 67; Nicolaides, *My Blue Heaven*, chap. 7; and Robert Bauman, "The Black Power and Chicano Movements in the Poverty Wars in Los Angeles," *Journal of Urban History* 33 (2007): 277–296.

15. Nicolaides, *My Blue Heaven*, 275.

16. Ibid., chap. 7.

17. McGirr, *Suburban Warriors*, chap. 4.

18. Quoted in ibid., 214.

19. Homer Hoyt, *According to Hoyt: Fifty-Three Years of Homer Hoyt: Articles on Law, Real Estate Cycle, Economic Base, Sector Theory, Shopping Centers, Urban Growth, 1916–1969* (Washington, D.C.: Homer Hoyt Institute, 1970).

20. McGirr, *Suburban Warriors*, 199; and see Lipsitz, "Possessive Investment in Whiteness."

21. Nicolaides, *My Blue Heaven*, 312.

22. Ibid., 308–315.

23. Michael W. Flamm, *Law and Order: Street Crime, Civil Unrest, and the Crisis of Liberalism in the 1960s* (New York: Columbia University Press, 2005), 67.

24. Nicolaides, *My Blue Heaven*, chap. 7; McGirr, *Suburban Warriors*, chap. 5; and Abu-Lughod, *Race, Space, and Riots*, chap. 6.

25. Nicolaides, *My Blue Heaven*, 326.

26. Ibid., 275.

27. Kruse, *White Flight*, 164. Also see Thomas Byrne Edsall and Mary D. Edsall, *Chain Reaction: The Impact of Race, Rights, and Taxes on American Politics* (New York: Norton, 1991); Peter Trubowitz, *Defining the National Interest: Conflict and Change in American Foreign Policy* (Chicago: University of Chicago Press, 1998); Wendell E. Pritchett, "Which Urban Crisis? Regionalism, Race, and Urban Policy, 1960–1974," *Journal of Urban History* 34 (January 2008): 266–286; Wendy Wall, *Inventing the "American Way": The Politics of Consensus from the New Deal to the Civil Rights Movement* (Oxford: Oxford University Press, 2008); Joseph E. Lowndes, *From the New Deal to the New Right: Race and the Southern Origins of Modern Conservatism* (New Haven, Conn.: Yale University Press, 2008); and Devin Fergus, *Liberalism, Black Power, and the Making of American Politics, 1965–1980* (Athens: University of Georgia Press, 2009).

28. Abu-Lughod, *Race, Space, and Riots*, 26.

29. Ibid., chap. 1.

30. Ibid., chap. 6. Also see Amanda I. Seligman, "'But Burn—No': The Rest of the Crowd in Three Civil Disorders in 1960s Chicago," *Journal of Urban History* 37, no. 2 (2011): 230–255.

31. Governor's Commission on the Los Angeles Riots [McCone Commission], *Violence in the City: An End or a Beginning?* (Los Angeles: State of California, 1965), available at http://www.usc.edu/libraries/archives/cityinstress/mccone/contents.html (accessed March 18, 2015).

32. Robert M. Fogelson, "White on Black: A Critique of the McCone Commission Report on the Los Angeles Riots," *Political Science Quarterly* 82 (September 1967): 337–367; and Flamm, *Law and Order*, chap. 3.

33. Governor's Commission on the Los Angeles Riots, *Violence in the City*, passim.

34. Ibid.

35. Ibid.

36. Ibid.

37. Schneider, "Escape from Los Angeles."

38. Mike Davis, "Fortress Los Angeles: The Militarization of Urban Space," in *Variations on a Theme Park: The New American City and the End of Public Space*, ed. Michael Sorkin (New York: Noonday, 1992), 154–180.

39. Richard Slotkin, *Gunfighter Nation: The Myth of the Frontier in Twentieth-Century America* (New York: Atheneum / Maxwell Macmillan International, 1992). Also see Low, *Behind the Gates*; Kevin Fox Gotham, "Review Essay: Racialized Uneven Development—Race, Class, and Segregation in the Postwar Era," *Journal of Urban History* 33 (January 2007): 332–341; and Elaine Tyler May, "Presidential Address: Security against Democracy—The Legacy of the Cold War at Home," *Journal of American History* 97 (March 2011): 937–957.

40. Nicolaides, *My Blue Heaven*, 327, table 7.3.

41. Flamm, *Law and Order*, 67. Also see McGirr, *Suburban Warriors*; and Abu-Lughod, *Race, Space, and Riots*.

42. Robert A. Beauregard, "More Than Sector Theory: Homer Hoyt's Contributions to Planning Knowledge," *Journal of Planning History* 6 (August 2007): 248–271; Roger Biles, *Richard J. Daley: Politics, Race and the Governing of Chicago* (DeKalb: Northern Illinois University Press, 1995); D. Bradford Hunt and Jon B. DeVries, *Planning Chicago* (Chicago: Planners Press, 2013); and David Alexander Spatz, "Roads to Postwar Urbanism: Expressway Building and the Transformation of Metropolitan Chicago, 1930–1975" (Ph.D. diss., University of Chicago, 2010).

43. Matthew Edel, "Urban Renewal and Land Use Conflicts," *Review of Radical Political Economics* 3 (1971): 76–89; Raymond A. Mohl, "The Second Ghetto and the 'Infiltration Theory' in Urban Real Estate, 1940–1960," in *Urban Planning and the African-American Community: In the Shadows*, ed. June Manning Thomas and Marsha Ritzdorf (Thousand Oaks, Calif.: Sage, 1997), 58–74; Elaine Lewinnek, "Inventing Suburbia: Working-Class Suburbanization in Chicago, 1865–1919" (Ph.D. diss., Yale University, 2005); Robert Bruegmann, *Sprawl: A Compact History* (Chicago: University of Chicago Press, 2005); and Will Cooley, "Moving Up, Moving Out: Race and Social Mobility in Chicago, 1914–1972" (Ph.D. diss., University of Illinois at Urbana, 2008).

44. Charles E. Silberman, "Up from Apathy: The Woodlawn Experiment," in *Urban Planning and Social Policy*, ed. Bernard J. Frieden and Robert Morris (New York: Basic Books, 1968), 183–197; and Dominic A. Pacyga, "Responding to the Second Ghetto: Chicago's Joe Smith and Sin Corner," *Journal of Urban History* 37 (January 2011): 73–89. Also see the firsthand accounts of Arthur M. Brazier, *Black Self-Determination: The Story of the Woodlawn Organization* (Grand Rapids, Mich.: Eerdmans, 1969); John Hall Fish, *Black Power / White Control: The Struggle of the Woodlawn Organization in Chicago* (Princeton, N.J.: Princeton University Press, 1973); Margery Frisbie, *An Alley in Chicago: The Ministry of a City Priest* (Kansas City, Mo.: Sheed and Ward, 1991); Richard T. Sale, *The Blackstone Rangers: A Reporter's Account of Time Spent with the Street Gang on Chicago's South Side* (New York: Random House, 1972); and Jane Jacobs, "Chicago's Woodlawn—Renewal by Whom?," *Architectural Forum* 116 (May 1962): 122–124.

45. Silberman, "Up from Apathy," 196.

46. William W. Ellis, *White Ethics and Black Power: The Emergence of the West Side Organization* (Chicago: Aldine, 1969); and Bernard O. Brown, *Ideology and Community Action: The West Side Organization of Chicago, 1964–67* (Chicago: Center for the Scientific Study of Religion, 1978). Also see Robert A. Slayton, *Back of the Yards: The Making of a Local Democracy* (Chicago: University of Chicago Press, 1986).

47. The best introduction to Chicago history is Biles, *Daley*. Also see St. Clair Drake and Horace E. Cayton, *Black Metropolis: A Study of Negro Life in a Northern City* (New York: Harcourt, 1945); and Barbara Ferman, *Challenging the Growth Machine: Neighborhood Politics in Chicago and Pittsburgh* (Lawrence: University Press of Kansas, 1996). Also see John M. Allswang, "Richard J. Daley—America's Last Boss," in *The Mayors: The Chicago Political Tradition*, ed. Paul M. Green and Melvin G. Holli (Carbondale: Southern Illinois University Press, 1987), 144–164; Arnold R. Hirsch, "Martin H. Kennelly: The Mugwump and the Machine," in ibid., 126–143; Christopher Manning, *William L. Dawson and the Limits of Black Electoral Leadership* (DeKalb: Northern Illinois University

Press, 2009); Andrew J. Diamond, *Mean Streets: Chicago Youths and the Everyday Struggle for Empowerment in the Multiracial City, 1908–1969* (Berkeley: University of California Press, 2009), 253–258; Richard C. Lindberg, *To Serve and Collect: Chicago Politics and Police Corruption from the Lager Beer Riot to the Summerdale Scandal* (New York: Praeger, 1991); and William J. Grimshaw, *Bitter Fruit: Black Politics and the Chicago Machine, 1931–1991* (Chicago: University of Chicago Press, 1992).

48. Adam Cohen and Elizabeth Taylor, *American Pharaoh: Mayor Richard J. Daley: His Battle for Chicago and the Nation* (Boston: Little, Brown, 2000), 593–599.

49. See Richard M. Flanagan, "The Housing Act of 1954: The Sea Change in National Urban Policy," *Urban Affairs Review* 33 (November 1997): 265–286; LaDale Winling, "Students and the Second Ghetto: Federal Legislation, Urban Politics, and Campus Planning at the University of Chicago," *Journal of Planning History* 10, no. 1 (January 2011): 59–86; and Hunt and DeVries, *Planning Chicago.*

50. Joseph P. Schwieterman, Dana M. Caspall, and Jane Heron, *The Politics of Place: A History of Zoning in Chicago* (Chicago: Lake Claremont Press, 2003), chap. 5; Biles, *Daley*, 47, 88–89; and Cohen and Taylor, *American Pharaoh*, 178–179. James Downs's son-in-law, David Stahl, was appointed deputy mayor by Mayor Daley. Downs's son, Anthony, was a member of the National Commission on Urban Problems and a consultant to the Kerner Commission Report. See United States National Advisory Commission on Civil Disorders [Kerner Commission], *Report of the National Advisory Commission on Civil Disorders* (Washington, D.C.: U.S. Government Printing Office, 1968); and John T. Metzger, "Planned Abandonment: The Neighborhood Life-Cycle Theory and National Urban Policy," *Housing Policy Debate* 11, no. 1 (2000): 12–15.

51. Cohen and Taylor, *American Pharaoh*, 177; Ferman, *Challenging the Growth Machine*, 54–99; and Joel Rast, "Creating a Unified Business Elite: The Origins of the Chicago Central Area Committee," *Journal of Urban History* 37, no. 4 (June 2011): 583–605.

52. City of Chicago, Department of City Planning, *Development Plan for the Central Area of Chicago* (Chicago: Department of City Planning, 1958); Schwieterman, Caspall, and Heron, *Politics of Place*, chap. 5; Biles, *Daley*, chap. 2; Ferman, *Challenging the Growth Machine*, 54–99; and Cohen and Taylor, *American Pharaoh*, chap. 6.

53. Ross Miller, "City Hall and the Architecture of Power: The Rise and Fall of the Dearborn Corridor," in *Chicago Architecture and Design, 1923–1993: Reconfiguration of an American Metropolis*, ed. John Zukowsky (Munich: Prestel, 1993), 247–263.

54. Allswang, "Daley"; and Biles, *Daley*, 62–63.

55. Chicago Plan Commission, "A Report on Relocation," in *Population and Housing Report No. 2* (Chicago, December 1956), 15–21. Also see Amanda I. Seligman, *Block by Block: Neighborhoods and Public Policy on Chicago's West Side* (Chicago: University of Chicago Press, 2005), 78.

56. Ferman, *Challenging the Growth Machine*, 21. Also see Grimshaw, *Bitter Fruit*, chaps. 5–6.

57. Seligman, *Block by Block*, chap. 4. Also see Andrew Ross, *The Chicago Gangster Theory of Life: Nature's Debt to Society* (London: Verso, 1994).

58. Seligman, *Block by Block*, chap. 4; George Rosen, *Decision-Making Chicago-Style: The Genesis of a University of Illinois Campus* (Urbana: University of Illinois

Press, 1980); and Carolyn Eastwood, *Near West Side Stories: Struggles for Community in Chicago's Maxwell Street Neighborhood* (Chicago: Lake Claremont Press, 2002).

59. Abu-Lughod, *Race, Space, and Riots*, chap. 3.

60. Beryl Satter, *Family Properties: Race, Real Estate, and the Exploitation of Black Urban America* (New York: Metropolitan, 2009), chap. 6; and Cohen and Taylor, *American Pharaoh*, 221.

61. Seligman, *Block by Block*, 34–35.

62. Grimshaw, *Bitter Fruit*, 115, 125, chap. 6.

63. Ferman, *Challenging the Growth Machine*, 33.

64. See Biles, *Daley*, 80–83; Allswang, "Daley"; Cohen and Taylor, *American Pharaoh*, 296–301; Seligman, *Block by Block*, 86; and Eastwood, *Near West Side Stories*, 182–184.

65. Orlando W. Wilson, quoted in Diamond, *Mean Streets*, 254.

66. Quoted in Abu-Lughod, *Race, Space, and Riots*, 101. Daley said, "Shoot to kill arsonists and to maim and cripple anyone looting the stores."

67. John L. Rury, "Race, Space, and the Politics of Chicago's Public Schools: Benjamin Willis and the Tragedy of Urban Education," *History of Education Quarterly* 39 (1999): 117–142; and Biles, *Daley*, chap. 4.

68. Quoted in Diamond, *Mean Streets*, 241.

69. Quoted in Cohen and Taylor, *American Pharaoh*, 223.

70. Satter, *Family Properties*, chap. 6; Diamond, *Mean Streets*, chap. 6; Seligman, "But Burn—No"; and Abu-Lughod, *Race, Space, and Riots*, chaps. 1, 3.

71. Ferman, *Challenging the Growth Machine*, 75. Also see David J. Garrow, *Chicago 1966: Open Housing Marches, Summit Negotiations, and Operation Breadbasket, Martin Luther King, Jr. and the Civil Rights Movement* (Brooklyn, N.Y.: Carlson, 1989); James R. Ralph, *Northern Protest: Martin Luther King, Jr., Chicago, and the Civil Rights Movement* (Cambridge, Mass.: Harvard University Press, 1993); and David R. Farber, *Chicago '68* (Chicago: University of Chicago Press, 1988).

72. Diamond, *Mean Streets*, chap. 6; Biles, *Daley*, chaps. 5–7; and Satter, *Family Properties*, chap. 6.

73. Diamond, *Mean Streets*, 268.

74. Garrow, *Chicago 1966*; Biles, *Daley*, chap. 6; Cohen and Taylor, *American Pharaoh*, chaps. 9–12; and Seligman, *Block by Block*, 201–221. Also see Dionne Danns, "Black Student Empowerment and Chicago School Reform Efforts in 1968," *Urban Education* 37 (November 2002): 631–655; and Dionne Danns, "Chicago High School Students' Movement for Quality Public Education, 1966–1971," *Journal of African-American History* 88 (Spring 2003): 138–150.

75. Satter, *Family Properties*, chap. 7; and Grimshaw, *Bitter Fruit*, chap. 7. Also see Brian D. Boyer, *Cities Destroyed for Cash: The FHA Scandal at HUD* (Chicago: Follett, 1973); and David Elek Kirchner, "Challenging Private Power: Neighborhood Opposition to Redlining in Three Midwestern Cities" (Ph.D. diss., Washington University, St. Louis, 2001).

76. Jeffrey L. Gould, "Solidarity under Siege: The Latin American Left, 1968," *American Historical Review* 114 (April 2009): 348–375; David Barkin, *Distorted Development: Mexico in the World Economy* (Boulder, Colo.: Westview, 1990); and Kenneth Paul Erickson and Patrick V. Peppe, "Dependent Capitalist Development,

U.S. Foreign Policy, and Repression of the Working Class in Chile and Brazil," *Latin American Perspectives* 3 (Winter 1976): 19–43.

77. See Eric Zolov, *Refried Elvis: The Rise of the Mexican Counterculture* (Berkeley: University of California Press, 1999); Michael Soldatenko, "México '68: Power to the Imagination!," *Latin American Perspectives* 32 (July 2005): 111–132; Evans, "Sons, Daughters, and Patriarchy"; Edward J. McCaughan, "Mexico's Long Crisis: Toward New Regimes of Accumulation and Domination," *Latin American Perspectives* 20 (Summer 1993): 6–31; Diane E. Davis, "The Dialectic of Autonomy: State, Class, and Economic Crisis in Mexico, 1958–1982," *Latin American Perspectives* 20 (Summer 1993): 46–75; Diane E. Davis, "The Social Construction of Mexico City: Political Conflict and Urban Development, 1950–1966," *Journal of Urban History* 24 (1998): 364–415; and Judith Adler Hellman, "Mexican Popular Movements, Clientelism, and the Process of Democratization," *Latin American Perspectives* 21 (Spring 1994): 124–142.

78. Donald Clark Hodges and Ross Gandy, *Mexico under Siege: Popular Resistance to Presidential Despotism* (London: Zed Books, 2002), 58–82.

79. Zolov, *Refried Elvis*, 8, and see chaps. 1–2.

80. Soldatenko, "México '68," 113.

81. Zolov, *Refried Elvis*, chaps. 1–2; and Marshall McLuhan, *Culture Is Our Business* (New York: McGraw-Hill, 1970).

82. Zolov, *Refried Elvis*, chaps. 2–3.

83. Ibid.; and McCaughan, "Mexico's Long Crisis."

84. Zolov, *Refried Elvis*, 114.

85. Elena Poniatowska, *Massacre in Mexico* (New York: Viking, 1975); and Beth E. Jörgensen, "Framing Questions: The Role of the Editor in Elena Poniatowska's *La noche de Tlatelolco*," *Latin American Perspectives* 18 (Summer 1991): 80–90.

86. Quoted in Zolov, *Refried Elvis*, 120.

87. Quoted in Poniatowska, *Massacre in Mexico*, 329.

88. Quoted in ibid., 20. Martinez de las Roca was a representative on the Action Committee of the Faculty of Sciences, UNAM, and later a prisoner in Lecumberri Prison.

89. Soldatenko, "México '68," 118. Also see Lessie Jo Frazier and Deborah Cohen, "Defining the Space of Mexico '68: Heroic Masculinity in the Prison and 'Women' in the Streets," *Hispanic American Historical Review* 83 (November 2003): 617–650.

90. Poniatowska, *Massacre in Mexico*, 55.

91. Quoted in ibid., 58.

92. Quoted in ibid., 88–89; and see ibid., pt. 2; Brian Glanville, "Murder in Mexico," *Index of Censorship* 37, no. 2 (2008): 10–14; Andrea Noble, "Recognizing Historical Injustice through Photography: Mexico 1968," *Theory, Culture, and Society* 27, no. 7–8 (2010): 184–213; and Eric Zolov, "Showcasing the 'Land of Tomorrow': Mexico and the 1968 Olympics," *The Americas* 61 (October 2004): 159–188.

93. Davis, "Dialectic of Autonomy," 51.

94. McCaughan, "Mexico's Long Crisis," 13; and see Davis, "Dialectic of Autonomy."

95. Diane E. Davis, "Failed Democratic Reform in Contemporary Mexico: From Social Movements to the State and Back Again," *Journal of Latin American Studies* 26 (1994): 375–340. Also see Hellman, "Mexican Popular Movements."

96. Colin Jones, *Paris: Biography of a City* (New York: Viking, 2005), 448–456; and Steven L. Goldman, "Images of Technology in Popular Films: Discussion and

Filmography," *Science, Technology, and Human Values* 14 (Summer 1989): 275–301. Also see Matthew Gandy, "Urban Visions," *Journal of Urban History* 26 (March 2000): 368–379; and Theodor G. Wyeld and Andrew Allan, "The Virtual City: Perspectives on the Dystopic Cybercity," *Journal of Architecture* 11, no. 5 (2006): 613–620.

97. Kristin Ross, *Fast Cars, Clean Bodies: Decolonization and the Reordering of French Culture* (Cambridge, Mass.: MIT Press, 1995), 3–4. Also see Kristin Ross, *May '68 and Its Afterlives* (Chicago: University of Chicago Press, 2002); Alvin Toffler, *Future Shock* (New York: Random House, 1970); Ingrid Gilcher-Holtey, "France," in *1968 in Europe: A History of Protest and Activism, 1956–1977,* ed. Martin Klimke and Joachim Scharloth (New York: Palgrave Macmillan, 2008), 111–124; Manuel Castells, "Urban Renewal and Social Conflict in Paris," *Social Science Information* 11, no. 2 (1972): 93–124; Michael Bess, *The Light-Green Society: Ecology and Technological Modernization in France, 1960–2000* (Chicago: University of Chicago Press, 2003); and Larry Busbea, *Topologies: The Urban Utopia in France, 1960–1970* (Cambridge, Mass.: MIT Press, 2007).

98. Jones, *Paris*, 449, and see 448–456.

99. Christiane Rochefort, *Les petits enfants du siècle* (Paris: Grasset, 1961), 124–125, quoted in Daniel Noin and Paul White, *Paris* (Chichester, U.K.: Wiley, 1997), 221. Also see Busbea, *Topologies*, 108–137; and Norma Evenson, *Paris: A Century of Change, 1878–1978* (New Haven, Conn.: Yale University Press, 1977), 232–278.

100. Ross, *Fast Cars, Clean Bodies*, chap. 1.

101. Henri Lefebvre as quoted in ibid., 7; and Henri Lefebvre, *Critique of Everyday Life* (London: Verso, 1991).

102. David Pinder, *Visions of the City: Utopianism, Power, and Politics in Twentieth-Century Urbanism* (New York: Routledge, 2005), 137. Also see Castells, "Urban Renewal"; Ross, *Fast Cars, Clean Bodies*, 1–13; Lefebvre, *Critique of Everyday Life*; Henri Lefebvre, *The Urban Revolution* (Minneapolis: University of Minnesota Press, 2003); and Guy Debord, *The Society of the Spectacle* (Detroit: Black and Red, 1970).

103. Gilcher-Holtey, "France," 117, and see 111–124.

104. Ibid., 120–121.

105. Suri, "Rise and Fall," 48.

106. Ibid.

107. Stephen Edelston Toulmin, *Cosmopolis: The Hidden Agenda of Modernity* (New York: Free Press, 1990), ix, and see 161.

108. Matthew Gandy, "Cyborg Urbanization: Complexity and Monstrosity in the Contemporary City," *International Journal of Urban and Regional Research* 29 (2005): 26–49.

109. Robert Venturi, *Complexity and Contradiction in Architecture* (New York: Museum of Modern Art, 1966).

110. Quoted in Jones, *Paris*, 456.

CHAPTER 6

1. Fred Turner, "R. Buckminster Fuller: A Technocrat for the Counterculture," in *New Views on R. Buckminster Fuller,* ed. Hsiao-yun Chu and Roberto G. Trujillo (Stanford, Calif.: Stanford University Press, 2009), 146, and see 146–159.

2. R. Buckminster Fuller, *Operating Manual for Spaceship Earth* (Carbondale: Southern Illinois University Press, 1969).

3. William Kuhns, *The Post-industrial Prophets: Interpretations of Technology* (New York: Harper and Row, 1971); Anthony Giddens, *The Third Way and Its Critics* (Cambridge: Cambridge University Press, 2000); and Timothy W. Luke, "Ephemeralization as Environmentalism: Rereading R. Buckminster Fuller's *Operating Manual for Spaceship Earth*," *Organization and Environment* 23, no. 3 (2010): 354–356.

4. William I. Robinson, "Globalization and the Sociology of Immanuel Wallerstein: A Critical Appraisal," *International Sociology* 26, no. 6 (October 2011): 723–745. Robinson defines transnationalism as "*qualitatively* different from internationalization processes, involving not merely the geographical extension of economic activity across national boundaries but also the transnational fragmentation of these activities and their *functional integration*" (739; emphasis in original).

5. Gaylord Nelson, *How the First Earth Day Came About*, available at http://www.nelsonearthday.net/earth-day/index.htm (accessed November 25, 2011). Adam Rome, "'Give Earth a Chance': The Environmental Movement and the Sixties," *Journal of American History* 90 (September 2003): 525–554. Also see Samuel P. Hays, *Beauty, Health, and Permanence: Environmental Politics in the United States, 1955–1985* (New York: Cambridge University Press, 1987); Robert Gottlieb, *Forcing the Spring: The Transformation of the American Environmental Movement* (Washington, D.C.: Island, 1993); Hal Rothman, *Saving the Planet: The American Response to the Environment in the Twentieth Century* (Chicago: Ivan R. Dee, 2000), 146–148; Paul Wapner, "Politics beyond the State: Environmental Activism and World Civic Politics," *World Politics* 47 (April 1995): 311–314; and Adam Rome, *The Genius of Earth Day: How a 1970 Teach-in Unexpectedly Made the First Green Generation* (New York: Hill and Wang, 2013).

6. Quoted in Jeffrey C. Ellis, "On the Search for a Root Cause: Essentialist Tendencies in Environmental Discourse," in *Uncommon Ground: Toward Reinventing Nature*, ed. William Cronon (New York: Norton, 1995), 258 (emphasis in original).

7. Barry Commoner, Michael Corr, and Paul J. Stamler, "The Causes of Pollution," *Environment* 13 (April 1971), cited in Ellis, "On the Search for a Root Cause," 256–268. Also see Barry Commoner, *The Closing Circle: Nature, Man, and Technology* (New York: Knopf, 1971); and Adam Rome, *The Bulldozer in the Countryside: Suburban Sprawl and the Rise of American Environmentalism* (New York: Cambridge University Press, 2001).

8. Nigel Taylor, *Urban Planning Theory since 1945* (London: Sage, 1998); Donella H. Meadows, Dennis L. Meadows, Jørgen Randers, and William W. Behrens III, *The Limits to Growth: A Report for the Club of Rome's Project on the Predicament of Mankind* (New York: Universe, 1972); and "The Story of the Club of Rome," available at http://www.clubofrome.org (accessed November 28, 2011).

9. See Greg Lindsay, *A City in the Cloud: Living PlanIT Redefines Cities as Software*, August 23, 2010, available at http://www.fastcompany.com/1684055/city-cloud-living-planit-redefines-cities-software; and Greg Lindsay, "Not-So-Smart Cities," *New York Times*, September 25, 2011; and Eric Woods, *PlanIT Valley: A Blueprint for the Smart City*, March 30, 2011, available at http://www.navigantresearch.com/blog/articles/planit-valley-a-blueprint-for-the-smart-city.

10. Taylor, *Urban Planning Theory*, 139.

11. H.S.D. Cole, Christopher Freeman, Marie Jahoda, and K.L.R. Pavitt, eds., *Models of Doom: A Critique of* The Limits to Growth (New York: Universe, 1973); Andrew Ross, *The Chicago Gangster Theory of Life: Nature's Debt to Society* (London: Verso, 1994); Peter Hall, *Urban and Regional Planning*, 3rd ed. (London: Routledge, 1992), chap. 6; André Gorz, *Ecology as Politics* (Boston: South End, 1980); Michael Bess, *The Light-Green Society: Ecology and Technological Modernization in France, 1960–2000* (Chicago: University of Chicago Press, 2003); and Donella H. Meadows, Jørgen Randers, and Dennis L. Meadows, *The Limits to Growth: The 30-Year Update* (White River Junction, Vt.: Chelsea Green, 2004).

12. Christian Caryl, *Strange Rebels: 1979 and the Birth of the 21st Century* (Philadelphia: Basic Books, 2013).

13. Margaret Thatcher, quoted in Brian D. Jacobs, *Fractured Cities: Capitalism, Community, and Empowerment in Britain, and America* (London: Routledge, 1992), 9.

14. Ayn Rand, *Atlas Shrugged* (New York: Random House, 1957).

15. Also see Jennifer Burns, "Godless Capitalism: Ayn Rand and the Conservative Movement," in *American Capitalism: Social Thought and Political Economy in the Twentieth Century*, ed. Nelson Lichtenstein (Philadelphia: University of Pennsylvania Press, 2006), 271–290; Wendell E. Pritchett, "Which Urban Crisis? Regionalism, Race, and Urban Policy, 1960–1974," *Journal of Urban History* 34 (January 2008): 266–286; and Caryl, *Strange Rebels*.

16. Andy Thornley, *Urban Planning under Thatcherism: The Challenge of the Market* (London: Routledge, 1991); Jacobs, *Fractured Cities*; Hall, *Urban and Regional Planning*; Dennis Hardy, *From New Towns to Green Politics: Campaigning for Town and Country Planning, 1946–1990* (London: Spon, 1991); and Derek Walker, *The Architecture and Planning of Milton Keynes* (London: Architectural Press, 1982).

17. Ravetz, *Remaking Cities*, 197–235.

18. Jacobs, *Fractured Cities*, 15–16 (emphasis in original). Also see Mercedes Gonzalez de la Rocha, "From the Resources of Poverty to the Poverty of Resources? The Erosion of a Survival Model," *Latin American Perspectives* 28 (July 2001): 72–100; Michael James Miller, *The Representation of Place: Urban Planning and Protest in France and Great Britain, 1950–1980* (Aldershot, U.K.: Ashgate, 2003); Thomas Sugrue, *The Origins of the Urban Crisis: Race and Inequality in Postwar Detroit* (Princeton, N.J.: Princeton University Press, 1998); Frank Moulaert, Arantxa Rodríguez, and Erik Swyngedouw, eds., *The Globalized City: Economic Restructuring and Social Polarization in European Cities* (Oxford: Oxford University Press, 2003); and Mike Davis, *Planet of Slums* (New York: Verso, 2006). For globalization in Latin America, see Thomas Angotti, *Metropolis 2000: Planning, Poverty, and Politics* (London: Routledge, 1993); Robert K. Home, "Outside De Soto's Bell Jar: Colonial/Postcolonial Land Law and the Exclusion of the Peri-urban Poor," in *Demystifying the Mystery of Capital: Land Tenure and Poverty in Africa and the Caribbean*, ed. Robert K. Home and Hilary Lim (London: GlassHouse, 2004), 11–30; Diana Alarcon-Gonzalez and Terry Mckinley, "The Adverse Effects of Structural Adjustment on Working Women in Mexico," *Latin American Perspectives* 26 (May 1999): 103–117; Gareth A. Jones and Peter M. Ward, "Privatizing the Commons: Reforming the *Ejido* and Urban Development in Mexico," *International Journal of Urban and Regional Research* 22, no. 1 (1998): 76–93; William Robinson, "Latin America in the Age of Inequality: Confronting the New 'Utopia,'" *International*

Studies Review 1 (Autumn 1999): 41–67; Bryan R. Roberts, "Globalization and Latin American Cities," *International Journal of Urban and Regional Research* 29 (2005): 110–123; Bryan R. Roberts and Alejandro Portes, "Coping with the Free Market Cities: Collective Action in Six Latin American Cities at the End of the Twentieth Century," *Latin American Research Review* 41 (2006): 57–83; and Barbara Weinstein, "Presidential Address: Developing Inequality," *American Historical Review* 113 (February 2008): 1–18.

19. Hall, *Urban and Regional Planning*, chap. 6.

20. June Manning Thomas, "Educating Planners: Unified Diversity for Social Action," in *Readings in Planning Theory*, ed. Scott Campbell and Susan S. Fainstein, 2nd ed. (Malden, Mass.: Blackwell, 2003), 356–375; and Taylor, *Urban Planning Theory*, 58–62. Also see Ravetz, *Remaking Cities*; Gordon Emanuel Cherry, *Town Planning in Britain since 1900: The Rise and Fall of the Planning Ideal, Making Contemporary Britain* (Oxford: Blackwell, 1996); Hall, *Urban and Regional Planning*; Anthony Giddens, *Capitalism and Modern Social Theory: An Analysis of the Writings of Marx, Durkheim and Max Weber* (Cambridge: Cambridge University Press, 1971); Robert Lilienfeld, *The Rise of Systems Theory: An Ideological Analysis* (New York: Wiley, 1978); Jennifer S. Light, *The Nature of Cities: Ecological Visions and the American Urban Professions, 1920–1960* (Baltimore: Johns Hopkins University Press, 2009); and Sharon E. Kingsland, *Modeling Nature: Episodes in the History of Population Ecology*, 2nd ed. (Chicago: University of Chicago Press, 1995).

21. Lewis Mumford, *The Pentagon of Power* (New York: Harcourt Brace Jovanovich, 1974).

22. Meadows, Meadows, Randers, and Behrens, *Limits to Growth*, 10.

23. Manuel Castells, "Changer la ville: A Rejoinder," *International Journal of Urban and Regional Research* 30 (March 2006): 219.

24. Timothy Gilfoyle, "White Cities, Linguistic Turns, and Disneylands: The New Paradigms of Urban History," *Reviews in American History* 26 (1998): 175–204. Also see Alain Touraine, *The Post-industrial Society: Tomorrow's Social History: Classes, Conflicts and Culture in the Programmed Society* (New York: Random House, 1971); and Manuel Castells, *The Power of Identity* (Malden, Mass.: Blackwell, 2004), 1–67.

25. Castells, "Changer la ville."

26. David Harvey, *Social Justice and the City* (London: Edward Arnold, 1973), 302.

27. Ibid., 9–19; and David Harvey, "Revolutionary and Counter-Revolutionary Theory in Geography and the Problem of Ghetto Formation," *Antipode* 4, no. 2 (1972): 1–13.

28. Henri Lefebvre, *The Urban Revolution* (Minneapolis: University of Minnesota Press, 2003), 153.

29. James C. Scott, *Seeing like a State: How Certain Schemes to Improve the Human Condition Have Failed* (New Haven, Conn.: Yale University Press, 1998); and Lefebvre, *Urban Revolution*, 157.

30. Lefebvre, *Urban Revolution*, 157. Also see Harvey, *Social Justice and the City*, 303.

31. Lefebvre, *Urban Revolution*, 15. Also see Robert Neuwirth, *Shadow Cities: A Billion Squatters, a New Urban World* (New York: Routledge, 2005); and Davis, *Planet of Slums*.

32. Harvey, *Social Justice and the City*, 310.

33. Italo Calvino, *Invisible Cities* (New York: Harcourt Brace Jovanovich, 1974).

34. Touraine, *Post-industrial Society*, 5.

35. Ibid., 9.

36. Harvey, *Social Justice and the City*, 193, chap. 5.

37. Constance Perin, *Everything in Its Place: Social Order and Land Use in America* (Princeton, N.J.: Princeton University Press, 1977), 4.

38. Ibid., 3–31.

39. Ibid., 3, 81. Also see Derek Gregory, Ron Martin, and Graham Smith, "Introduction," in *Human Geography: Society, Space, and Social Science*, ed. Derek Gregory, Ron Martin, and Graham Smith (Minneapolis: University of Minnesota Press, 1994), 10.

40. Ibid. Also see Raymond Williams, *The Country and the City* (New York: Oxford University Press, 1973).

41. Charles Jencks, *The Language of Post-modern Architecture* (London: Academy, 1977), 9.

42. Ibid., 10.

43. Ibid., 11–12. Also see "Charles Jencks," available at http://en.wikipedia.org/wiki/Charles_Jencks (accessed October 30, 2011); and Robert Venturi, *Complexity and Contradiction in Architecture* (New York: New York Museum of Modern Art, 1966).

44. Jencks, *Language of Post-modern Architecture*, 12.

45. Ibid., 27.

46. Ibid., 27–37.

47. Ibid., 13. Also see Tom Wolfe, *From Bauhaus to Our House* (New York: Farrar, Straus and Giroux, 1981); John M. Findlay, *Magic Lands: Western Cityscapes and American Culture after 1940* (Berkeley: University of California Press, 1992); and Eric Avila, *Popular Culture in the Age of White Flight: Fear and Fantasy in Suburban Los Angeles* (Berkeley: University of California Press, 2004).

48. Williams, *The Country and the City*, 98. Also see A. L. Beier and Roger Finlay, eds., *London 1500–1700: The Making of the Metropolis* (London: Longman, 1986).

49. Williams, *The Country and the City*, 216–217.

50. Ibid., and Mark Clapson, *Suburban Century: Social Change and Urban Growth in England and the United States* (Oxford: Berg, 2003).

51. Immanuel Maurice Wallerstein, *The Modern World-System: Capitalist Agriculture and the Origins of the European World-Economy in the Sixteenth Century* (New York: Academic, 1976).

52. Ibid. Also see Robinson, "Globalization"; and John Bellamy Foster, Robert W. McChesney, and R. Jamil Jonna, "The Global Reserve Army of Labor and the New Imperialism," *Monthly Review* 63 (November 2011): 1–31.

53. Robinson, "Globalization," 740. Also see Erik Swyngedouw, "Neither Global nor Local: 'Glocalization' and Politics of Scale," in *Spaces of Globalization: Reasserting the Power of the Local*, ed. Kevin R. Cox (New York: Guilford, 1997), 137–166; Mustafa Dikec, "Review Essay: Social Movements and Globalization," *International Journal of Urban and Regional Research* 28 (September 2004): 713–716; William Sites, "Global City, American City: Theories of Globalization and Approaches to Urban History," *Journal of Urban History* 29 (March 2003): 222–246.

54. Harvey, *Social Justice and the City*, 306.

55. E. F. Schumacher, *Small Is Beautiful: A Study of Economics as if People Mattered* (London: Blond and Briggs, 1973).

56. Arne Naess, *Ecology, Community and Lifestyle: Outline of an Ecosophy* (Cambridge: Cambridge University Press, 1972), 29. Also see Mumford, *Pentagon of Power*; Lewis Mumford, *The Myth of the Machine* (New York: Harcourt, 1967); Kuhns, *Post-industrial Prophets*; Ivan Illich, *Energy and Equity* (London: Calder and Boyars, 1974); and Bill Devall and George Sessions, *Deep Ecology: Living as if Nature Mattered* (Salt Lake City, Utah: Gibbs Smith, 1985).

57. Schumacher, *Small Is Beautiful*, 50.

58. Ibid., 54. Also see William Morris, *News from Nowhere* (New York: Penguin, 1890); Frank Lloyd Wright, "The Art and Craft of the Machine," in *Frank Lloyd Wright: Writings and Buildings*, ed. Edgar Kaufmann and Ben Raeburn (New York: Horizon, 1960), 53–73; T. J. Jackson Lears, *No Place for Grace: Antimodernism and the Transformation of American Culture, 1880–1920* (New York: Pantheon, 1981); and Rosalind H. Williams, *Notes on the Underground: An Essay on Technology, Society, and the Imagination* (Cambridge, Mass.: MIT Press, 1990).

59. Murray Bookchin, *The Limits of the City* (New York: Harper and Row, 1974).

60. Ibid., 97.

61. See Lewis Heber [Murray Bookchin], *Our Synthetic Environment* (New York: Knopf, 1962); Murray Bookchin, *Post-scarcity Anarchism* (Berkeley: Ramparts, 1971); and Murray Bookchin, *The Ecology of Freedom: The Emergence and Dissolution of Hierarchy* (Palo Alto, Calif.: Cheshire, 1982).

62. Bookchin, *Limits of the City*. Also see Dan L. Miller, *Lewis Mumford: A Life* (New York: Weidenfeld and Nicolson, 1989).

63. Oscar Newman, *Defensible Space: Crime Prevention through Urban Design* (New York: Macmillan, 1972), 27.

64. Ibid., 50.

65. Ibid., 12, chap. 2.

66. Giddens, *Third Way and Its Critics*.

67. Bess, *Light-Green Society*.

68. Ian L. McHarg, *Design with Nature* (Garden City, N.Y.: Natural History Press for the American Museum of Natural History, 1969); Greg Hise, "Whither the Region? Periods and Periodicity in Planning History," *Journal of Planning History* 8, no. 4 (2009): 295–307; Helen Meller, *Patrick Geddes: Social Evolutionist and City Planner* (London: Routledge, 1990); Roger Biles, "The Rise and Fall of South City: Planning, Politics and Race in Recent America," *Journal of Planning History* 4 (February 2005): 52–57; Nicholas Dagen Bloom, *Suburban Alchemy: 1960s New Towns and the Transformation of the American Dream* (Columbus: Ohio State University Press, 2001); James M. Rubenstein, *The French New Towns* (Baltimore: Johns Hopkins University Press, 1978); and Mark Clapson, *Invincible Green Suburbs, Brave New Towns: Social Change and Urban Dispersal in Post-war England* (Manchester, U.K.: Manchester University Press, 1998).

69. McHarg, *Design with Nature*, 5, 1; George T. Morgan Jr. and John O. King, *The Woodlands: New Community Development, 1964–1983* (College Station: Texas A&M University Press, 1978), 49–50; Ann Forsyth, "Ian McHarg's Woodlands: A Second Look," *Planning* 69 (September 2003), 10–13; and "The Woodlands," available at http://en.wikipedia.org/wiki/The_Woodlands,_Texas (accessed September 7, 2006).

70. Diane C. Bates, "Urban Sprawl and the Piney Woods: Deforestation in the San Jacinto Watershed," in *Energy Metropolis: An Environmental History of Houston and the*

Gulf Coast, ed. Martin V. Melosi and Joel A. Tarr (Pittsburgh: University of Pittsburgh Press, 2007), 183.

71. Clara Elena Irazabal, "Curitiba and Portland: Architecture, City-Making, and Urban Governance in the Era of Globalization" (Ph.D. diss., University of California at Berkeley, 2002), 112–171.

72. Ibid.

73. Alan Black, "The Chicago Area Transportation Study: A Case Study of Rational Planning," *Journal of Planning Education and Research* 10, no. 1 (1990): 27–37; and Peter Geoffrey Hall, *Great Planning Disasters* (London: Weidenfeld and Nicolson, 1980). Also see Bruce Edsall Seely, *Building the American Highway System: Engineers as Policy Makers* (Philadelphia: Temple University Press, 1987); Mark H. Rose and Bruce E. Seely, "Getting the Interstate System Built: Road Engineers and the Implementation of Public Policy, 1955–1985," *Journal of Policy History* 2, no. 1 (1990): 23–52; Alan Altshuler and David Luberoff, *Mega-projects: The Changing Politics of Urban Public Investment* (Washington, D.C.: Brookings Institution Press, 2003); Carlton Basmajian, "Projecting Sprawl? The Atlanta Regional Commission and the 1975 Regional Development Plan of Metropolitan Atlanta," *Journal of Planning History* 9 (May 2010): 95–121; Raymond A. Mohl, "Stop the Road: Freeway Revolts in American Cities," *Journal of Urban History* 30 (July 2004): 674–706; Louise Nelson Dyble, "Revolt against Sprawl: Transportation and the Origins of the Marin County Growth-Control Regime," *Journal of Urban History* 34 (November 2007): 38–66; and Louise Nelson Dyble, *Paying the Toll: Local Power, Regional Politics, and the Golden Gate Bridge* (Philadelphia: University of Pennsylvania Press, 2009).

74. Arnold R. Hirsch, *Making the Second Ghetto: Race and Housing in Chicago, 1940–1960* (New York: Cambridge University Press, 1983), 170, 273–274. Also see E. Michael Jones, *The Slaughter of Cities: Urban Renewal as Ethnic Cleansing* (South Bend, Ind.: St. Augustine's, 2004); and Kenneth T. Jackson, *Crabgrass Frontier: The Suburbanization of the United States* (New York: Oxford University Press, 1985).

75. Reginald R. Isaacs, "The 'Neighborhood Unit' Is an Instrument for Segregation," *Journal of Housing* 5 (August 1948): 215–218; Raymond A. Mohl, "Planned Destruction: The Interstates and Central City Housing," in *From Tenements to the Taylor Homes: In Search of an Urban Housing Policy in Twentieth-Century America*, ed. John F. Bauman, Roger Biles, and Kristin Szylvian (University Park: Pennsylvania State University Press, 2000), 226–245; and Thomas J. Sugrue, *Sweet Land of Liberty: The Forgotten Struggle for Civil Rights in the North* (New York: Random House, 2008). Also see William Issel, "Land Values, Human Values, and the Preservation of the 'City's Treasured Appearance': Environmentalism, Politics, and the San Francisco Freeway Revolt," *Pacific Historical Review* 68 (November 1999): 611–646; Louise Nelson Dyble, "Revolt against Sprawl"; Katherine M. Johnson, "Captain Blake versus the Highwaymen: Or, How San Francisco Won the Freeway Revolt," *Journal of Planning History* 8 (February 2009): 47–74; and Zachary M. Schrag, "The Freeway Fight in Washington, D.C.: The Three Sisters Bridge in Three Administrations," *Journal of Urban History* 30 (July 2004): 648–673.

76. Mohl, "Stop the Road," 674.

77. Rose and Seely, "Getting the Interstate System Built," 39.

78. Castells, *City, Class and Power* (London: Macmillan, 1978), 130, chap. 6. Also see Basmajian, "Projecting Sprawl?"; and Johnson, "Captain Blake versus the Highwaymen," 61.

79. Rose and Seely, "Getting the Interstate System Built," 45. Also see Raymond A. Mohl, "The Expressway Teardown Movement in American Cities: Rethinking Postwar Highway Polity in the Post-interstate Era," *Journal of Planning History* 11, no. 1 (2012): 89–103.

80. Richard Walker, *The Country in the City: The Greening of the San Francisco Bay Area* (Seattle: University of Washington Press, 2007), 13.

81. Louise Nelson Dyble, "The Defeat of the Golden Gate Authority: A Special District, a Council of Governments, and the Fate of Regional Planning in the San Francisco Bay Area," *Journal of Urban History* 34 (January 2008): 287–308.

82. Ibid.; Mohl, "Stop the Road"; Issel, "Land Values, Human Values"; and Johnson, "Captain Blake versus the Highwaymen."

83. Issel, "Land Values, Human Values"; and Johnson, "Captain Blake versus the Highwaymen."

84. Dyble, "Defeat of the Golden Gate Authority," 49.

85. Dyble, "Revolt against Sprawl."

86. Basmajian, "Projecting Sprawl?," 98.

87. David Goldfield, *Cotton Fields and Skyscrapers: Southern City and Region, 1607–1980* (Baton Rouge: Louisiana State University Press, 1982); David R. Goldfield, *Region, Race, and Cities: Interpreting the Urban South* (Baton Rouge: Louisiana State University Press, 1997); and Joseph E. Lowndes, *From the New Deal to the New Right: Race and the Southern Origins of Modern Conservatism* (New Haven, Conn.: Yale University Press, 2008).

88. Kevin Michael Kruse, "The Politics of Race and Public Space: Desegregation, Privatization and the Tax Revolt in Atlanta," *Journal of Urban History* 31 (July 2005): 611.

89. Ibid., 610.

90. Ibid., 613. Also see George Lipsitz, "The Possessive Investment in Whiteness: Racialized Social Democracy and the 'White' Problem," *American Quarterly* 47 (September 1995): 369–387; Laura Pulido, "Rethinking Environmental Racism: White Privilege and Urban Development in Southern California," *Annals of the Association of American Geographers* 90 (March 2000): 12–40; Robert O. Self, "Writing Landscapes of Class, Power, and Racial Division: The Problem of (Sub)urban Space and Place in Postwar America," *Journal of Urban History* 27 (January 2001): 237–250; Charles M. Payne, "'The Whole United States Is Southern!': *Brown v. Board* and the Mystification of Race," *Journal of American History* 91 (June 2004): 83–91; and Pritchett, "Which Urban Crisis?"

91. Basmajian, "Projecting Sprawl?," 106; and see Wendy Wall, *Inventing the "American Way": The Politics of Consensus from the New Deal to the Civil Rights Movement* (Oxford: Oxford University Press, 2008).

92. Basmajian, "Projecting Sprawl?," 106.

93. Rose and Seely, "Getting the Interstate System Built."

94. Andrew Wiese, *Places of Their Own: African American Suburbanization in the Twentieth Century* (Chicago: University of Chicago Press, 2004).

95. Joe Flood, *The Fires: How a Computer Formula Burned Down New York City—and Determined the Future of American Cities* (New York: Riverhead, 2010), 207.

96. New York City Fire Museum, "Post-WWII Era Firefighting: 1945–Present," available at http://www.nycfiremuseum.org/history_post_ww2.cfm (accessed March 22, 2015).

97. Ibid.; also see William Anderson Corrigan, "Travel Time Estimation for Emergency Medical Vehicles with Applications to Location Models" (University of California at Santa Barbara, 2005).

98. Flood, *The Fires*, 213; and Corrigan, "Travel Time Estimation." Also see Robert A. Caro, *The Power Broker: Robert Moses and the Fall of New York* (New York: Knopf, 1974); and Christopher Klemek, *The Transatlantic Collapse of Urban Renewal: Postwar Urbanism from New York to Berlin* (Chicago: University of Chicago Press, 2011), chap. 6.

99. Walker, *Country in the City*; and Dyble, "Revolt against Sprawl."

100. Robert O. Self, "Prelude to the Tax Revolt: The Politics of the 'Tax Dollar' in Postwar California," in *The New Suburban History*, ed. Kevin Michael Kruse and Thomas J. Sugrue (Chicago: University of Chicago Press, 2006), 147. Also see Margaret Pugh O'Mara, "Review: Suburbia Reconsidered: Race, Politics, and Property in the Twentieth Century," *Journal of Social History* 39 (Autumn 2005): 229–243; and Kevin Michael Kruse, *White Flight and the Making of Modern Conservatism* (Princeton, N.J.: Princeton University Press, 2005).

101. Tricia Rose, *Black Noise: Rap Music and Black Culture in Contemporary America* (Hanover, N.H.: University Press of New England, 1994), 102.

CHAPTER 7

1. Manuel Castells, *The Power of Identity* (Malden, Mass.: Blackwell, 2004), 1–67.

2. Ibid.

3. Peter Marcuse, "The Ghetto of Exclusion and the Fortified Enclave: New Patterns in the United States," *American Behavioral Scientist* 41 (November–December 1997): 311–326.

4. Mike Davis, *The City of Quartz* (New York: Vintage, 1990), 253.

5. "Alphaville, São Paulo," Wikipedia, http://en.wikipedia.org/wiki/Alphaville, _S%C3%A3o_Paulo (accessed January 24, 2010); and Christopher Lindner, "Architecture and the Economics of Violence: São Paulo as a Case Study," in *Globalization, Violence, and the Visual Culture of Cities*, ed. Richard J. Williams (London: Routledge, 2010), 17–31.

6. Lúcio Kowarick and Milton A. Campanario, "Industrialized Underdevelopment: From Economic Miracle to Economic Crisis," in *Social Struggles and the City: The Case of São Paulo*, ed. Lúcio Kowarick (New York: Monthly Review Press, 1994), 45–59; and João Roberto Martins Filho and John Collins, "Students and Politics in Brazil, 1962–1992," *Latin American Perspectives* 25 (January 1998): 162.

7. Charles Mueller, "Environmental Problems Inherent to a Development Style: Degradation and Poverty in Brazil," *Environment and Urbanization* 7 (October 1995): 67–84; Lúcio Kowarick and Clara Ant, "One Hundred Years of Overcrowding: Slum Tenements in the City," in *Social Struggles and the City: The Case of São Paulo*, ed. Lúcio Kowarick (New York: Monthly Review Press, 1994), 60–76; Kowarick and Campanario, "Industrialized Underdevelopment"; Peter B. Evans, *Dependent Development: The Alliance of Multinational, State, and Local Capital in Brazil* (Princeton, N.J.: Princeton University Press, 1979); Robert M. Levine, *The History of Brazil* (Westport, Conn.: Greenwood, 1999), chap. 6; Andres Rodriguez-Pose and John Tomaney, "Industrial Crisis in the Centre of the Periphery: Stabilization, Economic Restructuring and Policy

Responses in the São Paulo Metropolitan Region," *Urban Studies* 36, no. 3 (1999): 479–498; Jose F. Graziano da Silva, "Capitalist 'Modernization' and Employment in Brazilian Agriculture, 1960–1975: The Case of the State of São Paulo," *Latin American Perspectives* 11 (Winter 1984): 117–136; Verena Stolcke, *Coffee Planters, Workers, and Wives: Class Conflict and Gender Relations on São Paulo Plantations, 1850–1980* (New York: St. Martin's, 1988); and Teresa Pires do Rio Caldeira, *City of Walls: Crime, Segregation, and Citizenship in São Paulo* (Berkeley: University of California Press, 2000).

8. "Alphaville, São Paulo." Also see Mueller, "Environmental Problems"; and Kowarick and Ant, "One Hundred Years of Overcrowding."

9. Lindner, "Architecture and the Economics of Violence," 18.

10. Ibid., 27.

11. Ibid., 18. Also see Robert Fishman, "Global Suburbs" (paper presented at the First Biennial Conference of the Urban History Association, Pittsburgh, September 2002); Justin A. Read, "Obverse Colonization: São Paulo, Global Urbanization and the Poetics of the Latin American City," *Journal of Latin American Cultural Studies* 15 (December 2006): 281–300; and Caldeira, *City of Walls.*

12. Ricardo Silva Toledo, "The Connectivity of Infrastructure Networks and the Urban Space of São Paulo in the 1990s," *International Journal of Urban and Regional Research* 24 (March 2000): 139–164; and Marques and Bichir, "Public Politics."

13. Caldeira, *City of Walls*, 216. Also see Kowarick and Campanario, "Industrialized Underdevelopment"; and Kowarick and Ant, "One Hundred Years of Overcrowding."

14. Lindner, "Architecture and the Economics of Violence," 120, 122.

15. Read, "Obverse Colonization," 290 (emphasis in original).

16. Lúcia Sá, *Life in the Megalopolis: Mexico City and São Paulo* (Milton Park, U.K.: Routledge, 2007). Also see Simon Romero, "At War with São Paulo's Establishment, Black Paint in Hand," *New York Times*, January 29, 2012, 5.

17. Manuel Castells, *End of Millennium* (Malden, Mass.: Blackwell, 1998), 87.

18. Read, "Obverse Colonization," 297.

19. Ibid.

20. Sá, *Life in the Megalopolis*, 32; and see Derek Parkman Pardue, "Blackness and Periphery: A Retelling of Marginality in Hip-Hop Culture of São Paulo, Brazil" (Ph.D. diss., University of Illinois, 2004); Read, "Obverse Colonization"; Fishman, "Global Suburbs"; and William Sites, "Global City, American City: Theories of Globalization and Approaches to Urban History," *Journal of Urban History* 29 (March 2003): 222–246.

21. Edward James Blakely and Mary Gail Snyder, *Fortress America: Gated Communities in the United States* (Washington, D.C.: Brookings Institution Press, 1997); Fishman, "Global Suburbs"; Georg Glasze, Chris Webster, and Klaus Frantz, *Private Cities: Global and Local Perspectives* (London: Routledge, 2006). Also see Davis, *City of Quartz*; John M. Findlay, *Magiclands: Western Cityscapes and American Culture after 1940* (Berkeley: University of California Press, 1992); and Michael Sorkin, ed., *Variations on a Theme Park: The New American City and the End of Public Space* (New York: Noonday, 1992).

22. Miguel Díaz-Barriga, "Urban Politics in the Valley of Mexico: A Case Study of Urban Movements in the Ajusco Region of Mexico City, 1970–1987" (Ph.D. diss., Stanford University, 1991). Also see Keith Pezzoli, *Human Settlements and Planning for Ecological Sustainability: The Case of Mexico City* (Cambridge, Mass.: MIT Press, 1998);

Amanda I. Seligman, *Block by Block: Neighborhoods and Public Policy on Chicago's West Side* (Chicago: University of Chicago Press, 2005); Setha Low, "Battery Park City: An Ethnographic Field Study of the Community Impact of 9/11," *Urban Affairs Review* 40 (May 2005): 655–682; Setha M. Low, *Behind the Gates: Life, Security, and the Pursuit of Happiness in Fortress America* (New York: Routledge, 2003); and Davis, *City of Quartz*.

23. Sá, *Life in the Megalopolis*, 129.

24. Ibid., 123. Also see Will Hermes, *Love Goes to Buildings on Fire* (New York: Faber and Faber, 2011); David Toop, *Rap Attack 2: African Rap to Global Hip Hop* (London: Serpent's Tail, 1994); George Yudice, "The Funkification of Rio," in *Microphone Fiends: Youth Music and Youth Culture*, ed. Andrew Ross and Tricia Rose (New York: Routledge, 1994), 193–220; Hilbourne A. Watson, "Globalization as Capitalism in the Age of Electronics: Issues of Popular Power, Culture, Revolution, and Globalization from Below," *Latin American Perspectives* 29 (November 2002): 32–43; and Murray Forman and Mark Anthony Neal, eds., *That's the Joint! The Hip-Hop Studies Reader* (New York: Routledge, 2004).

25. Edward W. Soja, "Los Angeles, 1965–1992: From Crisis-Generated Restructuring to Restructuring-Generated Crisis," in *The City: Los Angeles and Urban Theory at the End of the Twentieth Century*, ed. Allen John Scott and Edward W. Soja (Berkeley: University of California Press, 1996), 426–462; and Edward W. Soja, *Thirdspace: Journeys to Los Angeles and Other Real-and-Imagined Places* (Cambridge, Mass.: Blackwell, 1996). Also see Davis, *City of Quartz*; William B. Fulton, *The Reluctant Metropolis: The Politics of Urban Growth in Los Angeles* (Baltimore: Johns Hopkins University Press, 2001); Raphael Sonenshein, *The City at Stake: Secession, Reform, and Battle for Los Angeles* (Princeton, N.J.: Princeton University Press, 2004); William I. Robinson, "Globalization and the Sociology of Immanuel Wallerstein: A Critical Appraisal," *International Sociology* 26, no. 6 (October 2011): 723–745; da Silva, "Capitalist 'Modernization'"; and Stolcke, *Coffee Planters*.

26. Lynn Hollen Lees, "Urban Public Space and Imagined Communities in the 1980s and 1990s," *Journal of Urban History* 20 (August 1994): 443–465.

27. Marques and Bichir, "Public Politics."

28. Ibid., 814.

29. Ibid., 818–819.

30. Lindner, "Architecture and the Economics of Violence."

31. Gil Shidlo, *Social Policy in a Non-Democratic Regime: The Case of Public Housing in Brazil* (Boulder, Colo.: Westview, 1990), 47.

32. Ibid., 37–41, 113–128.

33. Caldeira, *City of Walls*, chap. 2.

34. Ibid., 74.

35. Suzana Pasternak, "Squatter Settlements as a Kind of Perverse Outcome: History of Popular Housing Policies in São Paulo," in *Proceedings of the 13th Biennial Meeting of the International Planning History Society* (Chicago: International Planning History Society, 2008), 1182–1201; Pedro R. Jacobi, "The Challenges of Multi-stakeholder Management in the Watersheds of São Paulo," *Environment and Urbanization* 16 (October 2004): 199–211; and Haroldo Torres, Humberto Alves, and Maria Aparecida de Oliveira, "São Paulo Peri-urban Dynamics: Some Social Causes and Environmental Consequences," *Environment and Urbanization* 19, no. 1 (2007):

207–233. Also see Richard Batley, "Urban Renewal and Expulsion in São Paulo," in *Urbanization in Contemporary Latin America: Critical Approaches to the Analysis of Urban Issues*, ed. Alan Gilbert, Jorge Enrique Hardoy, and Ronaldo Ramírez (Chichester, U.K.: Wiley, 1982), 231–262.

36. Lúcio Kowarick and Nabil G. Bonduki, "Urban Space and Political Space," in *Social Struggles and the City: The Case of São Paulo*, ed. Lúcio Kowarick (New York: Monthly Review Press, 1994), 125, 121–147; Pasternak, "Squatter Settlements"; Caldeira, *City of Walls*, 213–255; and Tilman Evers and Claudia Maria Pompan, "Labor-Force Reproduction and Urban Movements: Illegal Subdivision of Land in São Paulo," *Latin American Perspectives* 14 (Spring 1987): 187–203.

37. James Holston, *Insurgent Citizenship: Disjunctions of Democracy and Modernity in Brazil* (Princeton, N.J.: Princeton University Press, 2008), 147.

38. Ibid., 209.

39. Ibid., 204.

40. Ibid., 238 and chaps. 5–7.

41. Ibid., 223–267.

42. Ibid., 244.

43. Ibid., chap. 7. Also see Caldiera, *City of Walls*.

44. John McCarthy, "The Redevelopment of Rotterdam since 1945," *Planning Perspectives* 14, no. 3 (1999): 291–309; Tineke A. Abma, "Playing with/in Plurality: Revitalizing Realities and Relationships in Rotterdam," *Evaluation* 3, no. 1 (1997): 25–48; Justin Beaumont and Maarten Loopmans, "Towards Radicalized Communicative Rationality: Resident Involvement and Urban Democracy in Rotterdam and Antwerp," *International Journal of Urban and Regional Research* 32 (March 2008): 95–113; and see http://en.wikipedia.org/wiki/Rotterdam#Historical_population (accessed April 16, 2012) for population statistics.

45. Paul Davidoff, "Advocacy and Pluralism in Planning," *Journal of the American Institute of Planning* 31, no. 4 (1965): 331; and see Robert Goodman, *After the Planners* (New York: Simon and Schuster, 1972).

46. Abma, "Playing with/in Plurality," 29.

47. Ibid.

48. McCarthy, "Redevelopment of Rotterdam," 298; and see Beaumont and Loopmans, "Towards Radicalized Communicative Rationality." I also draw, in part, on long walks I took and informal conversations I had along the way with long-time residents during a two-week stay in the neighborhood during the summer of 2007. Their pride of place was clearly evident.

49. Beaumont and Loopmans, "Towards Radicalized Communicative Rationality," 102.

50. Karin Meulenbelt, "Upgrading and Downgrading within the Metropolitan Region of Rotterdam, 1970–1990," *Urban Studies* 31, no. 7 (1994): 1167–1190. Also see Abma, "Playing with/in Plurality"; Jack Burgers and Robert Kloosterman, "Dutch Comfort: Postindustrial Transition and Social Exclusion in Spangen, Rotterdam," *Area* 28 (December 1996): 433–445; and Manuel B. Aalbers, "What Types of Neighbourhoods Are Redlined?," *Journal of Housing and the Built Environment* 22 (July 2007): 177–198.

51. Burgers and Kloosterman, "Dutch Comfort," 433.

52. Beaumont and Loopmans, "Towards Radicalized Communicative Rationality."

53. Ibid., 105.

54. Ibid., 104–106; Burgers and Kloosterman, "Dutch Comfort"; and Meulenbelt, "Upgrading and Downgrading."

55. Burgers and Kloosterman, "Dutch Comfort."

56. Ibid., 440. Also see Read, "Obverse Colonization."

57. Meulenbelt, "Upgrading and Downgrading."

58. Ronald van Kempen and Jan van Weesep, "Ethnic Residential Patterns in Dutch Cities: Backgrounds, Shifts and Consequences," *Urban Studies* 35, no. 10 (1998): 1813–1833; Aalbers, "What Types of Neighbourhoods Are Redlined?"; and Daniel R. Vining Jr. and Thomas Kontuly, "Population Dispersal from Major Metropolitan Regions: An International Comparison," *International Regional Science Review* 3, no. 1 (1978): 49–73.

59. Ministry of Housing, VROM, *Derde nota over de ruimtelijke ordening, Deel 2: Verstedelijkingsnota* [Third Report on Physical Planning, Part 2: Urbanization Report] (The Hague: Ministry of Housing, 1977).

60. Peter Hall, *Urban and Regional Planning*, 3rd ed. (London: Routledge, 1992), 197–202; Marco Bontje, "A 'Planner's Paradise' Lost? Past, Present and Future of Dutch National Urbanization Policy," *European Urban and Regional Studies* 10, no. 2 (2003): 135–151; and Pim Kooij and Paul van de Laar, "The Randstad Conurbation: A Floating Metropolis in the Dutch Delta," in *The European Metropolis, 1920–2000*, ed. Henk van Dijk (Berlin: European Social Foundation, 2003), 1–20.

61. Quoted in Rick Soll, "Nelson Algren Bids Final Farewell," *Chicago Tribune*, March 10, 1975; Paul Gapp, "Algren's Final Chapter in the City on the Make," *Chicago Tribune*, February 10, 1975; Marion Odmark, "Time to Break Out of the Grouch Syndrome," *Chicago Tribune*, February 10, 1975; and Bob Wiedrich, "Algren's Chicago Still Bustles Today," *Chicago Tribune*, February 14, 1975. Also see Nelson Algren, *The Man with the Golden Arm, a Novel* (Garden City, N.Y.: Doubleday, 1949); Nelson Algren, *Chicago, City on the Make* (Garden City, N.Y.: Doubleday, 1951); Bettina Drew, *Nelson Algren: A Life on the Wild Side* (New York: Putnam, 1989); and James Richard Giles, *Confronting the Horror: The Novels of Nelson Algren* (Kent, Ohio: Kent State University Press, 1989).

62. Quoted in Gapp, "Algren's Final Chapter."

63. Studs Terkel interview of Nelson Algren, March 1975, available at http://www.youtube.com/watch?v=C_WzEma1t1U (accessed May 24, 2012). Also see Edward R. Kantowicz, *Polish Politics in Chicago, 1880–1940* (Chicago: University of Chicago Press, 1975); and Dominic A. Pacyga, *Polish Immigrants and Industrial Chicago* (Columbus: Ohio State University Press, 1991).

64. Quoted in Soll, "Nelson Algren Bids Final Farewell."

65. Ibid. Also see Peter C. Baldwin, *In the Watches of the Night: Life in the Nocturnal City, 1820–1930* (Chicago: University of Chicago Press, 2012).

66. Daniel Walker, *Rights in Conflict: The Violent Confrontation of Demonstrators and Police in the Parks and Streets of Chicago during the Week of the Democratic National Convention of 1968* (Chicago: National Commission on the Causes and Prevention of Violence, 1968), 11. Also see Roger Biles, *Richard J. Daley: Politics, Race and the Governing of Chicago* (DeKalb: Northern Illinois University Press, 1995), 139–166. Norman Mailer, *Miami and the Siege of Chicago: An Informal History of the*

Republican and Democratic Conventions of 1968 (New York: World, 1968); David R. Farber, *Chicago '68* (Chicago: University of Chicago Press, 1988); and Janet L. Abu-Lughod, *Race, Space, and Riots in Chicago, New York, and Los Angeles* (Oxford: Oxford University Press, 2007).

67. For Chicago, see Biles, *Daley*, 4–9; and for Rotterdam, see http://en.wikipedia.org/wiki/Rotterdam#Historical_population (accessed April 16, 2012) for population statistics.

68. Joel Rast, *Remaking Chicago: The Political Origins of Urban Industrial Change* (DeKalb: Northern Illinois University Press, 1999); Robert Bruegmann, "Schaumburg, Oak Brook, Rosemont, and the Recentering of the Chicago Metropolitan Area," in *Chicago Architecture and Design, 1923–1993: Reconfiguration of an American Metropolis*, ed. John Zukowsky (Munich: Prestel, 1993), 159–178; and Ann Durkin Keating, "Chicagoland: More Than the Sum of Its Parts," *Journal of Urban History* 30 (2004): 213–230.

69. Adam Cohen and Elizabeth Taylor, *American Pharaoh: Mayor Richard J. Daley: His Battle for Chicago and the Nation* (Boston: Little, Brown, 2000).

70. Richard F. Babcock, *The Zoning Game: Municipal Practices and Policies* (Madison: University of Wisconsin Press, 1966). Also see Biles, *Daley*; William J. Grimshaw, *Bitter Fruit: Black Politics and the Chicago Machine, 1931–1991* (Chicago: University of Chicago Press, 1992); Joseph P. Schwieterman, Dana M. Caspall, and Jane Heron, *The Politics of Place: A History of Zoning in Chicago* (Chicago: Lake Claremont Press, 2003); and D. Bradford Hunt and Jon B. DeVries, *Planning Chicago* (Chicago: Planners Press, 2013).

71. Rast, *Remaking Chicago*; Henry Binford, "Multicentered Chicago," in *The Encyclopedia of Chicago*, ed. James R. Grossman, Ann Durkin Keating, Janice L. Reiff, and Newberry Library (Chicago: University of Chicago Press, 2004), 548–553; and Bruegmann, "Schaumburg."

72. Rast, *Remaking Chicago*.

73. Bruegmann, "Schaumburg"; "Motorola," available at http://en.wikipedia.org/wiki/Motorola (accessed April 26, 2012); Elizabeth Tandy Shermer, "Origins of the Conservative Ascendancy: Barry Goldwater's Early Senate Career and the De-legitimazation of Organized Labor," *Journal of American History* 95 (December 2008): 678–709; and Elizabeth Tandy Shermer, *Sunbelt Capitalism: Phoenix and the Transformation of American Politics* (Philadelphia: University of Pennsylvania Press, 2013).

74. Bruegmann, "Schaumburg."

75. "Motorola," available at http://en.wikipedia.org/wiki/Motorola; and Biles, *Daley*, 225, for the statistics.

76. John R. Fry, *Locked-out Americans: A Memoir* (New York: Harper and Row, 1973).

77. Ibid., 11.

78. Andrew J. Diamond, *Mean Streets: Chicago Youths and the Everyday Struggle for Empowerment in the Multiracial City, 1908–1969* (Berkeley: University of California Press, 2009); and Will Cooley, "'Stones Run It': Taking Back Control of Organized Crime in Chicago, 1940–1975," *Journal of Urban History* 37, no. 6 (2011): 911–932. Also see Fry, *Locked-out Americans*; Richard C. Lindberg, *To Serve and Collect: Chicago Politics and Police Corruption from the Lager Beer Riot to the Summerdale Scandal* (New

York: Praeger, 1991); and Andrew Ross, *The Chicago Gangster Theory of Life: Nature's Debt to Society* (London: Verso, 1994).

79. Jane Jacobs, *The Death and Life of Great American Cities* (New York: Random House, 1961), 277.

80. Biles, *Daley*, 171; and see Diamond, *Mean Streets*.

81. Biles, *Daley*, chap. 8; D. Bradford Hunt, *Blueprint for Disaster: The Unraveling of Chicago Public Housing* (Chicago: University of Chicago Press, 2009); Andrea M. Gill, "Moving to Integration? The Origins of Chicago's Gautreaux Program and the Limits of Voucher-Based Mobility," *Journal of Urban History* 38 (2012): 662–686; and Alexander Polikoff, *Waiting for Gautreaux: A Story of Segregation, Housing, and the Black Ghetto* (Evanston, Ill.: Northwestern University Press, 2005).

82. *Hills v. Gautreaux*, 425 U.S. 284 (1976).

83. Gill, "Moving to Integration." Also see Charles M. Lamb, *Housing Segregation in Suburban America since 1960: Presidential and Judicial Politics* (New York: Cambridge University Press, 2005), chap. 6.

84. Gill, "Moving to Integration," 6, 4.

85. *Metropolitan Housing Development Corporation v. Village of Arlington Heights*, 426 U.S. 229 (1976).

86. Lamb, *Housing Segregation*, 224.

87. Biles, *Daley*, 4–9.

88. Ibid.; and see Studs Terkel interview of Nelson Algren; and Drew, *Nelson Algren*.

89. Biles, *Daley*, chaps. 9–11; and Grimshaw, *Bitter Fruit*, chap. 7.

90. Charles E. Lindblom, "The Science of 'Muddling Through,'" *Public Administration Review* 19 (Spring 1959): 79–88.

91. Gordon Emanuel Cherry, *Town Planning in Britain since 1900: The Rise and Fall of the Planning Ideal* (Oxford: Blackwell, 1996), chap. 8.

92. Mark Clapson, "Suburban Paradox? Planners' Intentions and Residents' Preferences in Two New Towns of the 1960s: Reston, Virginia and Milton Keynes, England," *Planning Perspectives* 17 (2002): 145. Also see Mark Clapson, *A Social History of Milton Keynes: Middle England/Edge City* (Portland, Ore.: Frank Cass, 2004); Ruth H. Finnegan, *Tales of the City: A Study of Narrative and Urban Life* (Cambridge: Cambridge University Press, 1998); Dennis Hardy, *From New Towns to Green Politics: Campaigning for Town and Country Planning, 1946–1990* (London: Spon, 1991); and Richard B. Peiser and Alain C. Chang, "Is It Possible to Build Financially Successful New Towns? The Milton Keynes Experience," *Urban Studies* 36, no. 10 (1999): 1679–1703.

93. Clapson, "Suburban Paradox," 150.

94. Finnegan, *Tales of the City*.

95. Ibid., 32. Also see Clapson, "Suburban Paradox," 145–146.

96. Quoted in Clapson, "Suburban Paradox," 150.

97. Quoted in Finnegan, *Tales of the City*, 25.

98. Ibid., 27.

99. Brenda Dawson, quoted in ibid., 67.

100. Ibid., 47.

101. Clapson, "Suburban Paradox," 157.

102. Finnegan, *Tales of the City*, 41.

103. Dave Rimmer, quoted in ibid., 42.

104. Ibid., chap. 6; and Clapson, *Social History of Milton Keynes*, chaps. 5–6.

105. Finnegan, *Tales of the City*, 164, chaps. 6–7; and Ian L. McHarg, *Design with Nature* (Garden City, N.Y.: Natural History Press for the American Museum of Natural History, 1969).

106. Jeff Rooker, quoted in Clapson, *Social History of Milton Keynes*, xii.

CONCLUSIONS

1. George H. W. Bush, "Towards a New World Order," An Address to a Joint Session of Congress" (September 11, 1991). Also see Lynn Hollen Lees, "Urban Public Space and Imagined Communities in the 1980s and 1990s," *Journal of Urban History* 20 (August 1994): 443–465; Leonie Sandercock, *Cosmopolis II: Mongrel Cities of the 21st Century* (New York: Continuum, 2003); Robert Fishman, "Global Suburbs" (paper presented at the First Biennial Conference of the Urban History Association, Pittsburgh, September 2002); and Erik Swyngedouw, "The City as Hybrid: On Nature, Society and Cyborg Urbanization," *Capitalism, Nature, Socialism* 7 (June 1996): 65–80.

2. Charles Jencks, *Heteropolis: Los Angeles, the Riots and the Strange Beauty of Hetero-architecture* (London: Ernst and Sohn, 1993), 7; and Robert Venturi, *Complexity and Contradiction in Architecture* (New York: New York Museum of Modern Art, 1966). Also see Charles Jencks, *What Is Post-modernism?* (London: Academy, 1986); and Robert Gottlieb, *Reinventing Los Angeles: Nature and Community in the Global City* (Cambridge, Mass.: MIT Press, 2007).

3. George H. W. Bush, "Address to the Nation on the Civil Disturbances in Los Angeles, California" (George Bush Presidential Library, May 1, 1992), available at http://bush41library.tamu.edu/archives/public-papers/4241 (accessed September 25, 2013). Also see Joel Garreau, *Edge City: Life on the Frontier* (New York: Doubleday, 1991).

4. Bush, "Address to the Nation"; "51% of Riot Arrests were Latino . . . ," *Los Angeles Times*, June 18, 1992; Mike Davis, "Urban America Sees Its Future in L.A., Burning All Illusions," *The Nation* (June 1, 1992): 743–746; Janet L. Abu-Lughod, *Race, Space, and Riots in Chicago, New York, and Los Angeles* (Oxford: Oxford University Press, 2007), chap. 7; Edward T. Chang and Russell Leong, eds., *Los Angeles: Struggles toward Multiethnic Community—Asian American, African American and Latino Perspectives* (Seattle: University of Washington Press, 1994); Edward T. Chang and Jeannette Diaz-Veizades, *Ethnic Peace in the American City: Building Community in Los Angeles and Beyond* (New York: New York University Press, 1999); and Nancy Foner and George M. Fredrickson, eds., *Not Just Black and White: Historical and Contemporary Perspectives on Immigration, Race, and Ethnicity in the United States* (New York: Russell Sage Foundation, 2004).

5. Abu-Lughod, *Race, Space, and Riots*, chap. 7; George J. Sanchez, "Reading Reginald Denny: The Politics of Whiteness in the Late Twentieth Century," *American Quarterly* 47 (September 1995): 388–394; Mara A. Marks, Matt A. Barreto, and Nathan D. Woods, "Race and Racial Attitudes a Decade after the 1992 Los Angeles Riots," *Urban Affairs Review* 40, no. 1 (September 2004): 3–18; and Victor A. Matheson and Robert A. Baade, "Race and Riots: A Note on the Economic Impact of the Rodney King Riots," *Urban Studies* 41 (December 2004): 2691–2696.

6. See Raphael Sonenshein, *The City at Stake: Secession, Reform, and Battle for Los Angeles* (Princeton, N.J.: Princeton University Press, 2004); Evelyne Huber and Fred Solt, "Successes and Failures of Neoliberalism," *Latin American Research Review* 39 (October 2004): 150–164; Peter B. Evans, *Dependent Development: The Alliance of Multinational, State, and Local Capital in Brazil* (Princeton, N.J.: Princeton University Press, 1979); and Philipp Terhorst, "'Reclaiming Public Water': Changing Sector Policy through Globalization from Below," *Progress in Development Studies* 8, no. 1 (2008): 103–114.

7. Michael Dear, "In the City, Time Becomes Visible: Intentionality and Urbanism in Los Angeles, 1781–1991," in *The City: Los Angeles and Urban Theory at the End of the Twentieth Century*, ed. Allen John Scott and Edward W. Soja (Berkeley: University of California Press, 1996), 76–105; William B. Fulton, *The Reluctant Metropolis: The Politics of Urban Growth in Los Angeles* (Baltimore: Johns Hopkins University Press, 2001); and Mike Davis, *The City of Quartz* (New York: Vintage, 1990).

8. Jennifer Wolch, "From the Global to the Local: The Rise of Homelessness in Los Angeles during the 1980s," in *The City: Los Angeles and Urban Theory at the End of the Twentieth Century*, ed. Allen John Scott and Edward W. Soja (Berkeley: University of California Press, 1996), 390–425; Dana Cuff, "The Figure of the Neighbor: Los Angeles Past and Future," *American Quarterly* 56 (2004): 559–582; George Lipsitz, "Learning from Los Angeles: Another One Rides the Bus," *American Quarterly* 56 (2004): 511–529; and "Crime Rates in Los Angeles County, 1989–2010," Los Angeles Almanac, available at http://www.laalmanac.com/crime/cr02.htm (accessed September 30, 2013).

9. Davis, "Urban America," 743.

10. William Hollingsworth Whyte Jr., *The Organization Man* (New York: Simon and Schuster, 1956).

11. Davis, *City of Quartz*, 253.

12. Ibid., 279, 253, chap. 3; and Andrew H. Whittemore, "Requiem for a Growth Machine: Homeowner Preeminence in 1980s Los Angeles," *Journal of Planning History* 11, no. 2 (2012): 124–140. Also see United Nations Human Settlements Programme, *Enhancing Urban Safety and Security: Global Report on Human Settlements 2007* (London: Earthscan, 2007); and United Nations Human Settlements Programme, *The Challenge of Slums: Global Report on Human Settlements 2003* (London: Earthscan, 2003).

13. Jon Bannister and Nick Fyfe, "Introduction: Fear and the City," *Urban Studies* 38, no. 5–6 (2001): 807–813; Rowland Atkinson and Sarah Blandy, "Introduction," in *Gated Communities*, ed. Rowland Atkinson and Sarah Blandy (London: Routledge, 2006), vii–xvi; William J. V. Neill, "Marketing the Urban Experience: Reflections on the Place of Fear in Promotional Strategies of Belfast, Detroit, and Berlin," *Urban Studies* 38, no. 5–6 (2001): 815–828; Oscar Newman, *Defensible Space: Crime Prevention through Urban Design* (New York: Macmillan, 1972); Rowland Atkinson and John Flint, "Fortress UK? Gated Communities, the Spatial Revolt of the Elites and Time-Space Trajectories of Segregation," *Housing Studies* 19 (November 2004): 875–892; and Sarah Blandy, "Gated Communities in England: Historical Perspectives and Current Developments," *GeoJournal* 66 (2006): 15–26.

14. Atkinson and Flint, "Fortress UK?," 880.

15. Ibid. Also see Blandy, "Gated Communities in England"; Neill, "Marketing the Urban Experience"; Richard Sparks, Evi Girling, and Ian Loader, "Fear and Everyday Urban Lives," *Urban Studies* 38, no. 5–6 (2001): 885–898; Setha M. Low, *Behind the*

Gates: Life, Security, and the Pursuit of Happiness in Fortress America (New York: Routledge, 2003); Edward James Blakely and Mary Gail Snyder, *Fortress America: Gated Communities in the United States* (Washington, D.C.: Brookings Institution Press, 1997), chaps. 5–6; and Thomas W. Sanchez, Robert E. Lang, and Dawn M. Dhavale, "Security versus Status? A First Look at the Census's Gated Community Data," *Journal of Planning Education and Research* 24, no. 3 (2005): 281–291.

16. Atkinson and Flint, "Fortress UK?," 885.

17. Ibid., 887.

18. Ibid; and Blandy, "Gated Communities."

19. Elana Zilberg, "Fools Banished from the Kingdom: Remapping Geographies of Gang Violence between the Americas (Los Angeles and San Salvador)," *American Quarterly* 56 (2004): 762; Oliver Jutersonke, Robert Muggah, and Dennis Rodgers, "Gangs, Urban Violence, and Security Interventions in Central America," *Security Dialogue* 40, no. 4–5 (2009): 373–397; and Eric Popkin, "Transnational Migration and Development in Postwar Peripheral States: An Examination of Guatemalan and Salvadoran State Linkages with Their Migrant Populations in Los Angeles," *Current Sociology* 51, no. 3–4 (2003): 347–374. Also see Elana Zilberg, *Space of Detention: The Making of a Transnational Gang Crisis between Los Angeles and San Salvador* (Durham, N.C.: Duke University Press, 2011); and Alma Guillermoprieto, "In the New Gangland of El Salvador," *New York Review of Books*, November 10, 2011, 45–48.

20. Oscar Martinez, "Making a Deal with Murderers," *New York Times*, Sunday Review, October 6, 2013, 1, 6; and Leah Goldman, *The 13 Safest Cities in America*, June 6, 2011, available at http://www.businessinsider.com/safest-cities-in-america -2011-6?op=1#ixzz2h2t3S1bf.

21. Davis, "Urban America," 743.

22. Zilberg, "Fools Banished." Also see Michael T. Klare, "Policing the Empire," in *Policing America*, ed. Anthony M. Platt and Lynn Cooper (Englewood Cliffs, N.J.: Prentice Hall, 1974), 56–65; and Jutersonke, Muggah, and Rodgers, "Gangs, Urban Violence, and Security Interventions."

23. Fulton, *Reluctant Metropolis*, 104.

24. *National Audubon Society v. Superior Court . . . Los Angeles Department of Water and Power of the City of Los Angeles*, 33 Cal. 3d 419 (1983). The other two leading cases involved in the Mono Lake controversy are *California Trout, Inc. v. State Water Resources Control Board*, 207 Cal. App. 3d 548 (1989) (*Caltrout I*); and *California Trout, Inc. v. Superior Court*, 218 Cal. App. 3d 187 (1990) (*Caltrout II*). Also see State of California and State Department of Water Resources, *Mono Lake Environmental Impact Report*, May 1993, Appendix R, "Legal History of the Mono Lake Controversy"; and Mono Basin Clearinghouse California, *The Public Trust Doctrine*, 2009, available at http://www.monobasinresearch.org/timelines/publictrust.php (accessed June 12, 2010); Joesph Sax, "The Public Trust Doctrine in Natural Resource Law: Effective Judicial Intervention," *Michigan Law Review* 68 (1970): 471–566; and John Hart, *Storm over Mono: The Mono Lake Battle and the California Water Future* (Berkeley: University of California Press, 1996).

25. *Institutes of Justinian*, 2.1.1.

26. Norris Hundley, *The Great Thirst: Californians and Water, 1770s–1990s* (Berkeley: University of California Press, 1992); Marc Reisner, *Cadillac Desert: The*

American West and Its Disappearing Water, rev. and updated ed. (New York: Penguin, 1993); Blake Gumprecht, *The Los Angeles River: Its Life, Death, and Possible Rebirth* (Baltimore: Johns Hopkins University Press, 1999); and Jared Orsi, *Hazardous Metropolis: Flooding and Urban Ecology in Los Angeles* (Berkeley: University of California Press, 2004).

27. David E. Nye, *American Technological Sublime* (Cambridge, Mass.: MIT Press, 1994); David Harvey, *Social Justice and the City* (London: Edward Arnold, 1973); David Harvey, *Consciousness and the Urban Experience: Studies in the History and Theory of Capitalist Urbanization* (Baltimore: Johns Hopkins University Press, 1985); Matthew Gandy, "Water, Modernity and Emancipatory Urbanism," in *The Emancipatory City? Paradoxes and Possibilities*, ed. Loretta Lees (London: Sage, 2004), 178–191; and Maria Kaika, *City of Flows: Modernity, Nature, and the City* (New York: Routledge, 2005).

28. *National Audubon Society*, 33 Cal. 3d.

29. Hart, *Storm over Mono*; and Hundley, *Great Thirst*, 299–349.

30. Craig Anthony Arnold, "Working Out an Environmental Ethic: Anniversary Lessons from Mono Lake," *Wyoming Law Review* 4 (2004): 1–55. Also see Jedidiah Brewer and Gary D. Libecap, "Property Rights and the Public Trust Doctrine in Environmental Protection and Natural Resource Conservation," *Australian Journal of Agricultural and Resource Economics* 53 (2009): 1–17; David B. Hunter, "An Ecological Perspective on Property: A Call for Judicial Protection of the Public's Interest in Environmentally Critical Resources," *Harvard Environmental Law Review* 12, no. 2 (1988): 311–385; Harrison Dunning, "The Public Trust: A Fundamental Doctrine of American Property Law," *Lewis and Clark Law School Environmental Law* 19 (Spring 1989): 515–525; and Harrison C. Dunning, "Revolution (and Counter-Revolution) in Western Water Law: Reclaiming the Public Character of Water Resources," *Fordham Environmental Law Journal* 8 (1997): 439–458.

31. Arleen A. Arita, Michael P. Forrest, and John R. Fotheringham, "The Dams of the Eastside Reservoir Project," in *Proceedings of Waterpower '99* (Reston, Va.: American Society of Civil Engineers, 1999), sec. 6, chap. 2; and Fulton, *Reluctant Metropolis*, chap. 4. Also see Alan L. Olmstead and Paul W. Rhode, "The Evolution of California Agriculture, 1950–2000," in *California Agriculture: Dimensions and Issues*, ed. Jerry Siebert (Berkeley: University of California Press, 2004), 1–28; and Susan S. Hutson, Nancy L. Barber, Joan F. Kenny, Kristin S. Linsey, Deborah S. Lumia, and Molly A. Maupin, "Estimated Use of Water in the United States in 2000," in *U.S. Geological Survey Circular 1268* (Reston, Va.: U.S. Department of Interior, U.S. Geological Survey, 2004).

32. Orsi, *Hazardous Metropolis*, 118.

33. Gumprecht, *Los Angeles River*, chap. 6; and Hundley, *Great Thirst*, chap. 7. Also see State of California and Metropolitan Water District of Southern California, "The Regional Urban Water Management Plan" (Los Angeles: State of California, 2005); State of California, State Water Resources Control Board California, "The Mono Lake Decision: 'A Work in Progress,'" available at http://www.swrcb.ca.gov/waterrights/water_issues/programs/mono_lake/docs/monolakedecision_presentation.pdf (2002); and City of Los Angeles and Department of Water and Power, "Securing L.A.'s Water Supply," available at http://www.greencitiescalifornia.org/assets/water/LA_Emergency-Water-Conservation-Plan_Water-Supply-Report-2008.pdf (accessed May 2008).

34. Venturi, *Complexity and Contradiction in Architecture*.

35. Basil van Horen, "Developing Community-Based Watershed Management in Greater São Paulo: The Case of Santo Andre," *Environment and Urbanization* 13 (April 2001): 209–222; Rosa Maria Formiga Johnsson and Karin Erika Kemper, "Institutional and Policy Analysis of River Basin Management: The Alto-Tiete River Basin, São Paulo, Brazil," in *World Bank Policy Research Reports: WPS3650* (June 2005); Vivienne Bennett, "Gender, Class, and Water: Women and the Politics of Water Service in Monterrey, Mexico," *Latin American Perspectives* 22 (1995): 76–99; and Nicolas Pineda Pablos, "Urban Water Policy in Mexico: Municipalization and Privatization of Water Services" (Ph.D. diss., University of Texas, 1999). Also see John M. Whiteley, Helen M. Ingram, and Richard Warren Perry, "The Importance of Equity and the Limits of Efficiency in Water Resources," in *Water, Place, and Equity*, ed. John M. Whiteley, Helen M. Ingram, and Richard Warren Perry (Cambridge, Mass.: MIT Press, 2008), 1–36; and Terhorst, "Reclaiming Public Water."

36. James C. Scott, *Seeing like a State: How Certain Schemes to Improve the Human Condition Have Failed* (New Haven, Conn.: Yale University Press, 1998).

37. R. Buckminster Fuller, *Operating Manual for Spaceship Earth* (Carbondale: Southern Illinois University Press, 1969).

38. Eran Ben-Joseph, "Commentary: Designing Codes: Trends in Cities, Planning and Development," *Urban Studies* 46, no. 12 (November 2009): 2691–2702; Peter Marcuse, "Depoliticizing Globalization: From Neo-Marxist to Network Society of Manuel Castells," in *Understanding the City: Contemporary and Future Perspectives*, ed. John Eade and Christopher Mele (Oxford: Blackwell, 2002), 131–158; and David Harvey, "The Right to the City," in *The Emancipatory City? Paradoxes and Possibilities*, ed. Loretta Lees (London: Sage, 2004), 236–239.

39. Lisa McGirr, *Suburban Warriors: The Origins of the New American Right* (Princeton, N.J.: Princeton University Press, 2001).

40. Robert Goodman, *After the Planners* (New York: Simon and Schuster, 1972), 187.

41. E. F. Schumacher, *Small Is Beautiful: A Study of Economics as if People Mattered* (London: Blond and Briggs, 1973), 50.

42. See Alexander von Hoffman, *House by House, Block by Block: The Rebirth of America's Urban Neighborhoods* (New York: Oxford University Press, 2003).

43. Manuel Castells, *The Rise of the Network Society* (Malden, Mass.: Blackwell, 1996); and Manuel Castells, *End of Millennium* (Malden, Mass.: Blackwell, 1998).

44. Le Corbusier, *The Athens Charter* (New York: Grossman, 1973), 25, 101.

45. Ibid., 55, 26.

46. Ibid., 71.

47. Mindy Thompson Fullilove, *Root Shock: How Tearing Up City Neighborhoods Hurts America, and What We Can Do about It* (New York: Ballantine, 2004), 11. Also see Mindy Thompson Fullilove, *Urban Alchemy: Restoring Joy in America's Sorted-out Cities* (New York: New Village, 2013).

48. Eliel Saarinen, *The City: Its Growth, Its Decay, Its Future* (Cambridge, Mass.: MIT Press, 1943), 141.

49. European Council of Town Planners, "Towards the New Charter of Athens: From the Organic City to the City of the Citizens" (Athens: European Council of

Town Planners, 1998). Also see Andres Duany, Elizabeth Plater-Zyberk, and Jeff Speck, *Suburban Nation: The Rise of Sprawl and the Decline of the American Dream* (New York: North Point, 2000); Scott Campbell, "Green Cities, Growing Cities, Just Cities? Urban Planning and the Contradictions of Sustainable Development," in *Readings in Planning Theory*, ed. Scott Campbell and Susan S. Fainstein, 2nd ed. (Malden, Mass.: Blackwell, 2003), 435–458; Judith T. Kenny and Jeffrey Zimmerman, "Constructing the 'Genuine American City': Neo-traditionalism, New Urbanism and Neo-liberalism in the Remaking of Downtown Milwaukee," *Cultural Geography* 11 (2003): 74–98; Georg Leidenberger, "The Search for a Useable Past: Modernist Urban Planning in a Postmodern Age," *Journal of Urban History* 32 (March 2006), 451–465; and Sonia A. Hirt, "Premodern, Modern, Postmodern? Placing New Urbanism into a Historical Perspective," *Journal of Planning History* 8, no. 8 (August 2009): 248–273.

50. Ajay M. Garde, "New Urbanism as Sustainable Growth? A Supply Side Story and Its Implication for Public Policy," *Journal of Planning Education and Research* 24 (2004): 154–170.

51. Michael Sorkin, "Foreword," in *Variations on a Theme Park: The New American City and the End of Public Space*, ed. Michael Sorkin (New York: Noonday, 1992), xi.

52. William J. Mitchell, *City of Bits: Space, Place, and the Infobahn* (Cambridge, Mass.: MIT Press, 1995). Also see William J. Mitchell, *Me++: The Cyborg Self and the Networked City* (Cambridge, Mass.: MIT Press, 2003).

53. Nigel Taylor, *Urban Planning Theory since 1945* (London: Sage, 1998), 74.

54. Christopher Alexander, "The City Is Not a Tree," *Architectural Forum* 122, no. 1 (1965): 58–62; also see Camillo Sitte, *City Planning According to Artistic Principles*, trans. George R. Collins and Christiane Crasemann Collins (London: Phaidon, 1889); and Jencks, *Heteropolis*.

Index

Harold L. Platt is Professor of History Emeritus at Loyola University Chicago. He is the author or editor of several volumes, including *Shock Cities: The Environmental Transformation and Reform of Manchester and Chicago*, which won the Abel Wolman Award.